JONATHAN EDWARDS AND
THE AMERICAN EXPERIENCE

Jonathan Edwards
and the
American Experience

edited by

Nathan O. Hatch
University of Notre Dame

Harry S. Stout
Yale University

OXFORD UNIVERSITY PRESS
New York   Oxford

Oxford University Press

Oxford   New York   Toronto
Delhi   Bombay   Calcutta   Madras   Karachi
Petaling Jaya   Singapore   Hong Kong   Tokyo
Nairobi   Dar es Salaam   Cape Town
Melbourne   Auckland

and associated companies in
Berlin   Ibadan

Library of Congress Cataloging-in-Publication Data

Jonathan Edwards and the American experience.
Includes bibliographies and index.
1. Edwards, Jonathan, 1703–1758.   2. United States—
Church history—Colonial period, ca. 1600–1775.
3. Theology, Doctrinal—United States—History—18th
century.   4. Philosophy, American—18th century.
1. Hatch, Nathan O.   II. Stout, Harry S.
BX7260.E3J65   1988   285.8′092′4   87-11246
ISBN 0-19-505118-1
ISBN 0-19-506077-6 (PBK)

2 4 6 8 10 9 7 5 3 1

For
James M. Hatch and Mittie Orr Hatch
and
H. Stober Stout and Norma W. Stout

Contents

THE LEGACY OF EDWARDS

JONATHAN EDWARDS AND
THE AMERICAN EXPERIENCE

1

Introduction

I

Judged over two centuries, Jonathan Edwards stands forth as one of America's great original minds, one of the very few individuals whose depiction of reality has known enduring attraction. Even in our own day, when the conclusions of "that terrible theologian" seem light years removed from modern sensibilities, the allure of Edwards continues. M. X. Lesser's recent bibliography of Edwards's studies reveals that in the last forty years the number of Ph.D. dissertations on Edwards has doubled every decade.[1]

The reasons for this compelling attraction vary widely over time and individual persuasion: some have approached Edwards for religious inspiration, others to exorcize the ghosts of their Puritan forebears; some have come to appreciate true virtue, others to understand the reality of total evil; some have discovered a great anachronism, others a prophet of modernity. But whatever the attraction or personal point of view, 250 years of ongoing attention confirms Henry F. May's conclusion that "Edwards was somehow a great man, whether we admire him most as artist, psychologist, preacher, theologian, or philosopher."

To account for the recent surge in Edwards studies since World War II, one could point to many factors including postwar realism, the rise of neo-orthodoxy and, most importantly, the creative genius of Perry Miller. For three decades and more, Miller's *Jonathan Edwards* (1949) stood at the epicenter of Edwards research and stimulated two generations of scholars in graduate programs across the nation. Whatever the limitations of the book, and there is no lack of critics to point them out, *Jonathan Edwards* succeeded in bringing Edwards to the forefront of scholarly attention in a variety of disciplines including religion, history, literature, and philosophy.

Miller's central achievement in *Jonathan Edwards*, like his achievements in Puritan studies generally, was to provide a broad framework of inquiry that raised innumerable topics for specialized study. From Miller, students of American culture inherited an image of Edwards as an isolated genius who stood so completely above and beyond his immediate culture that our own time is "barely catching up." Like the epic Western hero, Edwards emerges from Miller's pages as a lonely hero riding into town out of nowhere, exploding on the American scene in a brief but brilliant flurry of prophetic genius, and then riding off into the sunset alone. Miller's Edwards was so abstract and "modern" that it was practically impossible to fix him in any concrete historical or philosophical context. He remained, in Sydney Ahlstrom's apt phrase, a "perpetually misunderstood stranger."[2]

Scholarly works in the last two decades have moved beyond this internal and abstract focus, clarifying many dimensions of Edwards's multifaceted thought. Studies have assessed Edwards's role as pastor, his strategies in constructing sermons, the context of his moral thought, and the contours of his thinking in a number of areas: metaphysics, psychological theory, aesthetics, apocalyptic speculation, even his interest in Indian missions.[3]

Yet for all the quality and depth of these individual studies, they have not begun to add up to an integrated and synthetic understanding of Edwards and his contributions to American culture. No serious biography of Edwards has appeared since Miller's in 1949, and none is likely to appear in the near future for at least two simple reasons. First, contemporary writing about Edwards issues from the channels of several disciplines—historical, literary, theological, philosophical—approaches that ask different questions of the Edwards material and understand him in relation to quite different intellectual traditions. A second and related difficulty is the sheer volume and diversity of the Edwards manuscripts themselves: some fifteen hundred unpublished sermons as well as a staggering range of notes and exegetical writings, for example, over fourteen hundred entries (nine manuscript volumes) in the "Miscellanies"[4] and over ten thousand separate entries in the "Blank Bible."[5] Despite an unprecedented number of scholars plumbing facets of Edwards and volumes of unpublished manuscripts brought to light by the editors of the Yale edition of Edwards's *Works*, Edwards scholarship retains an ellusive and segmented quality.

In the fall of 1984, a conference "Jonathan Edwards and the American

Experience" was convened at Wheaton College in an attempt to pull together some of these disparate strands and to make accessible the best of current thinking about this remarkable individual. This book of essays, like that occasion, addresses the subject of Edwards and the American experience in three broad senses. Three opening essays attempt to explain Edwards's enduring hold on the American imagination—from the homage of disciples who remembered him to the scorn of Americans in the Victorian age to the mixture of curiosity, bemusement, and admiration in our own. Tracing Edwards's always vivid reputation is, in some sense, to measure how firmly the "iron of Calvinism" has gripped America's soul.[6] A second set of essays in this volume attempts to ground the development and elaboration of Edwards's thought in a specific cultural context. This new attention to context removes Edwards from the Olympian heights of lonely genius and focuses instead on contemporary influences, religious and philosophical. Such a perspective is not antithetical to earlier internal analyses of Edwards's thought so much as it completes the picture of Edwards by locating him in a concrete past, present, and future. Several of the essays in this second section are able to draw upon unpublished manuscripts in order to present a fuller intellectual portrait of the man. A third group of essays attempts to trace Edwards's specific legacy and influence in theology, psychological theory, philosophy, and literature. Taken altogether, the essays in this final section provide the most complete account to date of the relationship between Edwards and his immediate and self-conscious heirs, and of the extent to which Americans who came to claim the Edwards mantle did so for their own specific ends.

II

In the volume's opening essay, Henry F. May unveils the intense dialogue that generations of Americans have sustained with the figure of Jonathan Edwards. As one who himself has found Edwards at times interesting, repellent, attractive, and moving, May is able to address a range of issues that would have eluded most Edwards specialists. In his deft hands, the figure of Edwards becomes a superb index of how Americans have come to terms with those strands of stern Calvinism that are a central element in their historical identity. Refusing to patronize either Edwards or later generations who have interacted with him, May is able to explain plausibly and emphatically why Edwards has been taken so seriously by successive generations—from the veneration of the New Divinity, to the disdain of Enlightenment figures such as John Adams, to the anguished rejection of Victorians such as Harriet Beecher Stowe and Samuel Clemens. May assists the reader in understanding why, from the middle of the nineteenth to the middle of the twentieth century, the tradition of "deciding against Edwards" seemed so logical and became so entrenched in American culture, premised as it was upon the Enlightenment and the spirit of democratic progress. Edwards, after all, stood firmly against the essential goodness of the common man, denying that most American of notions that what is popular is right. Only an era of war and holocaust has permitted Americans once again to gaze without flinching upon Edwards and his dark and foreboding portrait of reality. May's essay also gives students of Edwards ample challenge to continue the work of fathoming this elusive figure. He also cautions that despite the fact the Edwards is a major figure in American religion and intellectual history he does not stand as the genuine ancestor of any of the major kinds of nineteenth and twentieth century American religion. In the end, May concludes that Edwards's work seems virtually inexhaustible and impossible to pin down.

For all the controversy that Edwards's work stirred up in his own day and beyond, his reputation has been that of a great man, worthy of study and emulation. This is the point of departure for David Levin's meditation on historical character and reputation, which compares historical perceptions of Edwards with those of Cotton Mather and Benjamin Franklin. In contrast to Cotton Mather, whose reputation *was* permanently sullied by his critics, Edwards's reputation as a brilliant thinker remained relatively untouched by friends and foes alike. Why is this so? It is not, Levin shows, because Edwards did not believe himself to be brilliant or deserving of worldly praise. In this sense the two (together with the other luminary of the age, Benjamin Franklin) had much in common. Nor was it because Edwards avoided the sort of self-pity that characterized much of Mather's diary. In the Northampton Farewell sermon, Edwards displayed the same self-righteousness that characterized Mather's attitudes toward his critics. Rather the difference lies in temperament. Edwards was not prone to display himself or expose his feelings to the same degree as Mather, and so avoided the harsh treatment that Mather received. By laying the characters of Edwards, Mather, and Franklin alongside one another, Levin points out the dangers of stereotyping characters and confusing reputation with character. In the process, he confirms how very much Edwards remained in the eighteenth century among a generation who sought to purify and justify their pride through "doing good."

In his essay on Edwards as a "figure" in American history, Donald Weber traces the enduring hold of Edwards on the American imagination with reference to the filial conscience of Samuel Hopkins; the rhetorical reappropriation of Jonathan Edwards, Jr.; the anguished execration of Oliver Wendell Holmes; and the virtual identification of H. Richard Niebuhr. Especially interesting is Weber's treatment of Jonathan Edwards, Jr., who applied his father's thought on the providential meaning of America to the Revolution. From an examination of Edwards, Jr.'s sermons during the Revolutionary era, he shows how Edwards's followers drew on a "blurring" of republicanism, millennialism, and the New Birth that first appeared in Edwards's proclamations during the wars with France. One reason that Calvinism endured into the nineteenth century was its eager participation on the Revolution and in the creation of the American republic. Edwards's thought, it appears, was not only compatible with the theological needs of the new nation but with its social and political needs as well.

Weber's essay also includes a poignant discussion of H. Richard Niebuhr's appropriation of Jonathan Edwards. Niebuhr recognized in Edwards a spiritual ancestor whose voice resonated with divine sovereignty and the heart-quickening strains of revival. In the 1930s Niebuhr found Edwards's realism the perfect antidote to a social reality of disillusionment and uncertainty on the one hand, and a misplaced confidence in human reason that had characterized Protestant Liberalism on the other. Niebuhr's fullest treatment of Edwards, in a speech in Northampton in 1958, reveals how strikingly Niebuhr continued to identify with Edwards. In assailing the complacency of Americans for not having ears to hear of depravity, corruption, unfreedom, and wrath, Niebuhr's message, "The Anachronism of Jonathan Edwards," became his own twentieth century version of "Sinners in the Hands of an Angry God."

III

In the twentieth century, scholars' treatment of Edwards has alternated between extremes. On the one hand, he has been viewed as a solitary figure. Early in the century, scholars found Edwards to be a brilliant, if flawed, anachronism, "a wreck on the remote sands of time." Perry Miller also championed Edwards as a lonely genius equally out of step with his own times but, in his rendering, a prophet of modernity. Yet at the same time Miller also came to view Edwards as a representative American, a genius whose vision came to embody the very meaning of

America. In Alan Heimert's monumental work *Religion and the American Mind from the Great Awakening to the Revolution* (Cambridge, Mass., 1966), Edwards comes to assume this dominant role throughout. Heimert suggests, for instance, that Edwards's work, *Thoughts on the Revival*, was "in a vital respect an American declaration of independence from Europe," and his *History of Redemption* "a scenario for American social and political history in the last half of the eighteenth century." For Heimert, Edwards is key to understanding the emergence of distinct "American" culture.[7]

The six essays comprising the second section of this book evidence the recent inclination of scholars to ground Edwards more firmly in the culture of which he was a part. Leading the way in this revision is Norman Fiering's widely acclaimed study, *Jonathan Edwards's Moral Thought and Its British Context* (Chapel Hill, 1981). In that work, and the essay included in this collection, Fiering ignores questions of Edwards's modernity or uniqueness, and instead demonstrates how thoroughly Edwards's work was caught up in the traffic of conventional seventeenth and eighteenth century debates on the affections and the meaning of true virtue. Edwards's importance, Fiering argues, was less as an innovator than as a synthesizer; more than any of his American contemporaries, Edwards had the ability to draw from a broad range of reading and bring the insights from these works to bear on a defense of traditional Calvinist orthodoxy. He did not so much move forward in his philosophy (as Miller claimed in the most Kierkegaardian terms) as he moved backward in reattaching sentimentalist ethics to their Christian and biblical starting points. This great reversal placed him less in the company of Locke, Shaftsbury, or Hutcheson (though he studied them closely), than in the systematic achievements of Gottfried von Leibniz, Blaise Pascal, or Nicolas Malebranche fifty years earlier.

The attention to context that Fiering encouraged in his study of Edwards's philosophy has been picked up and applied to other aspects of Edwards's thought in essays by Wilson Kimnach, Stephen Stein, John Wilson, Harry Stout, and James Hoopes. All of these studies underscore Edwards's dependence on his past and confirm the limits of his modernity. In so doing, they rely on categories of evidence largely ignored in earlier Edwards scholarship, namely the unpublished manuscripts housed in the rich collections of Yale's Beinecke Library. Recognition of the importance of unpublished manuscripts for understanding Edwards's thought goes back to the pioneering work of Thomas Schafer on Edwards's "Miscellanies." But only recently have scholars extended Schafer's search to include other areas of Edwards's writing that never appeared in print during his lifetime.

Of all the surviving Edwards manuscripts, the most numerous, and the most revealing of his innermost thought, are the sermons. Over fifteen hundred of these sermons survive in Beinecke Library, and other scattered archives. Many of these sermons are currently being prepared for publication in the Yale edition of Edwards's works under the general direction of Wilson Kimnach. When published, the collection of sermons could extend to as many as fifty volumes of printed text.

Naturally a collection as broad as Edwards's sermons is diffuse and includes enough topics to keep another generation of students active in the field. If there is any overarching theme to these sermons, Kimnach argues, it lies in Edwards's unwavering "pursuit of reality." This phrase, Kimnach explains, refers both to Edwards's method of sermon composition in the conventional Puritan formula of text-doctrine-application and to the central themes of his theology as they found expression in the pulpit. Although the sermon form was inherited, no other colonial minister equaled Edwards's achievement in confronting his listeners with the unseen principles that upheld life and moved history to its foreordained end. In each sermon he examines, Kimnach discovers a relentless obsession to push beyond mundane concerns and "deal with the ultimate reality of the Deity." This obsession helps to account for the "unity of effect" one finds in the Edwards sermons and in his thought generally. Informing Edwards's pursuit of reality at every level was his rooting in biblical texts. Edwards was, Kimnach demonstrates, a "textuary in an age of textuaries," and his pursuit of reality was bounded by the world of scripture narratives. Through thousands of pages of sermon manuscripts one discovers less an attention to theological novelty, than a "terrific intensity" to "re-establish the authority of the Christian vision and to refresh the language of orthodoxy."

In his essay on Jonathan Edwards and scriptural exegesis, Stephen Stein picks up the theme of Edwards's biblicism from the vantage point of his unpublished "Harmonies" of the Old and New Testaments, and the handwritten "Blank Bible" where Edwards jotted his commentaries on Bible passages. To establish Edwards's modernity, Miller tended to ignore the all-consuming hold that scriptural exegesis held on Edwards's thought, and because of this he missed the traditional world that Edwards occupied. Edwards's reliance upon the authority of Scripture placed him "squarely in the precritical camp" of exegesis. He read biblical narratives as literally and historically reliable. Instead of reconciling the

diverse worlds of the Old and New testaments through historical criticism
of literary texts, Edwards resorted to the conventional exegetical tool of
"typology," where both testaments came together in a preordained Chris-
tic unity orchestrated by God from the beginning of time. In contrast to
Miller, who treated only Edwards's interest in natural typology, Stein
emphasizes Edwards's interest in biblical typology and finds that the two
were never of "coequal" importance in Edwards's thought. Biblical typology always enjoyed the last word and served as the point of departure for
Edwards's exploration of natural imagery and metaphor.

An unpublished sermon series, "A History of the Work of Redemption," delivered by Edwards in 1739 and published posthumously, forms
the basis for John Wilson's reexamination of Edwards's eschatology. On
the basis of those sermons, Wilson critiques C. C. Goen's influential
essay, "Jonathan Edwards: A New Departure in Eschatology," published
in 1959. In that article Goen acknowledged the influence of Perry Miller
and argued that Edwards was America's first "post-millennial" theologian, whose views of progress and the millennium anticipated nineteenth
century Protestant millennialism. Such a view, Wilson demonstrates, is
not confirmed by a reading of *History of Redemption*. In the first place,
Edwards's views on the millennium were not new and could be found in
the earlier work of New England Puritans and among Protestant theologians on the continent. Second, nineteenth century theologians were less
influenced by Edwards in their thinking about history and progress than
they were by the post-Edwardsian Enlightenment, which swept American
seminaries after the Revolution. While nineteenth century American
theologians rejected the secularism of the Enlightenment and its optimistic views of humankind, they adopted a propositional style of discourse
that was foreign to Edwards and eighteenth century New England
thought generally. In summarizing Edwards's sense of history and the
millennium, Wilson finds that, like his philosophy and biblicism, he was
a "pre-Enlightenment thinker whose philosophy of history grew out of
the soil tilled so thoroughly in New England."

In "The Puritans and Edwards," Harry Stout focuses on one category
of Edwards's unpublished sermons: the occasional or weekday sermons
delivered on days of fasting and thanksgiving. None of these sermons was
ever published in Edwards's lifetime, but they appear frequently in the
corpus of his manuscript sermons, and supply invaluable guides to his
thinking on the providential meaning of New England. Earlier scholars
relying on printed sermons that made no reference to New England's
corporate identity, argued that Edwards repudiated the "federal theology" of the Puritans that held forth promises of temporal rewards and

punishments to nations as well as individuals. Such a view, however, is more a reflection of biases in the publication of Edwards's sermons than an accurate reflection of his thought on the corporate meaning and mission of New England. When viewed as a whole, Edwards's occasional sermons reveal a preacher who adhered exactly to the old Puritan notions of New England as a "peculiar" people and a "city upon a hill," who would be blessed or cursed according to their keeping of the covenant. Instead of breaking with traditional themes of temporal rewards and corporate covenants, Edwards instinctively drew from them in times of great public trial and calamity. Occasional preaching, like philosophy, eschatology, and exegesis, reveal dimensions of Edwards that were far more Puritan and traditional in outlook than previously scholars ever allowed.

If Edwards's own words reveal him to be a product of his age, so also did the words of his contemporary critics. In "A Flood of Errors: Chauncy and Edwards in the Great Awakening," Amy S. Lang examines Charles Chauncy's famous critique of Edwards in terms of Old Light theories of language and authority. According to that theory, Edwards was far less akin to novel views on theology and the church, than he was a throwback to the "antinomian" views of Anne Hutchinson in the seventeenth century. In Chauncy's view, Edwards and Hutchinson were of a piece. Both erred by severing the connection between "sign and meaning" and, in the process, eroding the basis of authority in the church and the state. Just as Hutchinson spoke out of place and justified it by appeals to the Spirit, so also did Edwards threaten to make the relation between pastor and people a "sound without meaning." Language brought Hutchinson and Edwards together in Chauncy's thought and was so important that it furnished "the subtext of *Seasonable Thoughts* as well as its surface."

IV

If the image of Edwards is being revised in terms of past traditions and contemporary influences, the same is true of questions bearing on his legacy. Were there worthy successors to Edwards in nineteenth century Protestantism? Students of Miller tended to say no, and moved their histories of American thought and culture from the Calvinism of Puritanism and Edwards to transcendentalism and the American Renaissance. But, as the concluding five essays in this volume make clear, this sequence rests on a mistake. In fact, there were many talented, self-proclaimed successors to Edwards, each drawing on the master in different ways for inspiration, and each carrying the Calvinist tradition into nineteenth century America. These successors, moreover, were not the half-witted, pedantic dullards that historians earlier portrayed, but a group of widely followed, engaging intellects who constituted a central, if neglected, tradition in American thought.

Of all Edwards's self-proclaimed successors, none enjoyed a more direct lineage than the "New Divinity" theologian-preachers who dominated western Massachusetts and Connecticut well into the nineteenth-century. Included in this group was his own son, Jonathan Edwards, Jr., and Samuel Hopkins and Joseph Bellamy, both of whom had studied divinity with Edwards in Northampton. In reconsidering the work and influence of the New Divinity preachers, William Breitenbach revises their image as narrow "hyper-Calvinist" who petrified Edwards's creative thought into a dead "moralism" and demonstrates how they applied Edwards's thought to American culture in creative ways. Instead of strangling Edwards's thought in a thicket of metaphysical speculation that left their hearers cold, the New Divinity "remained true to Edwards's principles" in every major category, and injected those principles with a life-sustaining vigor. In comparing New Divinity thought to Edwards's *Treatise on the Affections*, Breitenbach shows how both traditions represented a cautious blending of "piety and moralism," rather than one or the other. By so doing, the New Divinity was able to keep the tradition of revivalism alive, alongside the attention to systematic theology that had characterized American Calvinism since the seventeenth-century.

Of all Perry Miller's claims for Edwards's modernity, none was more far-reaching than his claim that Edwards was America's first modern psychologist. According to Miller, Edwards was so advanced over his contemporaries in explorations of the psyche that "it would have taken him about an hour's reading in William James, and two hours in Freud, to catch up completely." Such a view, James Hoopes argues, badly misses the mark and distorts the distance that separated Edwards from modern psychology. Modern psychology is premised on a disjunctive model of mind that ascribes separate and sometimes contradictory impulses to the conscious and unconscious. Edwards's "unitary" model of mind, on the other hand, allowed "no possibility of unconscious mental phenomena." Hoopes argues that the reason Edwards took such a monolithic view of the mind was his commitment to the seventeenth century "way of ideas" and especially Locke's view that "thought" and "consciousness" were synonymous. But Edwards went far beyond Locke in his commitment to the "way of ideas" by denying that there was anything but ideas. Where Locke accepted the traditional view that the human soul is a substance, albeit a spiritual rather than material substance, Edwards held that the human soul was insubstantial and was constituted of nothing but ideas. This was the heart of his famous idealist metaphysics and also of his defense of Calvinist fundamentalism. But Edwards's self-proclaimed successors as defenders of Calvinism were unaware of his metaphysics and accepted the traditional distinction between soul and body, between spiritual and mental substance. Hoopes shows how they were consequently driven more or less against their will to abandon fundamental Calvinist tenets, thus unwittingly and ironically confirming Edwards's brilliant perception that Calvinism was basically irreconcilable with Locke's distinction between mind and body.

Of all the disciplines incorporating an Edwardsian heritage into their survey, none is more problematic than the history of American literature. Edwards, after all, wrote no fiction or poetry, yet he was, in Miller's terms, an "artist in ideas" whose use of language was novel and arresting. In assessing Edwards's heritage from a literary point of view, David Laurence discovers a Boston or Harvard bias in what Americans have come to accept as literature. If all texts composed in America was in some sense "literary," as Laurence believes they are, then Edwards's place in the American literary tradition is clear: "Edwards is not outside and below American literature . . . as secular students of the novel believed," nor is he "outside and above" American literature as Christian publicists believed. Rather, Laurence argues, "he is, simply, one American writer," whose use of language embodies "a certain literary-historical region" that is as equally and authentically "American" as Emerson, Hawthorne, or Melville. Instead of tracing lines of descent "from Edwards to Emerson," Laurence puts forward a concept of American literature as a series of "intellectual episodes" that share in common the quality of "alterity," of being "non-Europe."

Edwards's distinct mark on American philosophy is easier to chart. In his recent book *Churchmen and Philosophers: From Jonathan Edwards to John Dewey* (New Haven, 1985), Bruce Kuklick shows the continuities linking Edwards to the Congregationalist John Dewey. Such a lineage had been largely ignored by earlier studies that concentrated on Transcendentalism and Unitarianism, rather than Trinitarian Congregationalism. In his essay, "Jonathan Edwards and American Philosophy," Kuklick continues this line of inquiry with a critique of surveys of American thought that all but ignored the formative influence of the New Divinity and the New Haven theology. Particularly grievous in these surveys, Kuklick asserts, is the omission of Yale's Nathaniel Taylor who, unlike Emerson or Channing, was "the most talented systematic thinker in America between Edwards and Dewey." Earlier studies of American philosophy, Kuklick concludes, are less a reflection of the evolution of American thought than they are a reflection of "Harvard's dominance of the academic world in the late nineteenth and twentieth centuries." If there is a coherent philosophical tradition in nineteenth century America, it travels a line that largely bypasses Boston and stops instead at prominent stations in Princeton, New Haven, Hartford, New York, and Chicago.

Whatever strains of Edwardsian though can be traced in American literature and philosophy, one finds the most direct legacy of Edwards among theologians in the century and a half after his death. In his survey "Jonathan Edwards and Nineteenth-century Theology," Mark Noll traces three major lines of Edwardsian descent, including the New Divinity, the "New Haven" theology emanating from Yale College, and the Presbyterian theology at Princeton Seminary. All of these traditions claimed Edwards as their progenitor and fought to retain his name in their theological speculations. In fact, Noll observes, each one of these traditions including important aspects of Edwards's thought, but none of them followed the master exactly. Nor could they. Those who were committed to sustaining Edwards's "spirit" of creative philosophical inquiry and relevance to the age had to adjust his theology to the new spirit of a republican culture. This can be seen most clearly in the New Haven theology. Conversely, those who were committed to retaining the exact content of Edwards's theology sacrificed an element of creativity and spontaneity that made Edwards's thought exciting as well as orthodox. This was especially true of the Princeton theologians. If Edwards did not survive intact in any one of these schools of thought, he did continue through the work of all three, and exerted a formative influence on nineteenth century theology.

Taken as a whole, the essays coming out of the Wheaton Conference reveal how far Edwards studies have travelled from the state Henry May described in his keynote address. By opening up Edwards to a larger American context replete with a formative Puritan past and a legitimate group of heirs, it is now possible to speak of Edwards and the American experience in terms that both recognize his greatness and, at the same time, locate that greatness in a history that moves, as Miller once said, "crablike" throughout the pages of American history from the Puritans to a broad spectrum of modern heirs.

Notes

1. M. X. Lesser, *Jonathan Edwards: A Reference Guide* (Boston, 1981), xli. In all, Lesser lists 1800 books, articles, and dissertations on Edwards from the eighteenth century to 1979.

2. Sydney E. Ahlstrom, *A Religious History of the American People* (New Haven, 1972), 312.

3. Two essays by Donald Weber are excellent introductions to the current state of Edwards scholarship. See his review essay, "The Figure of Jonathan Edwards," *American Quarterly* 16 (1983), 157–60 and his "Perry Miller and the Rediscovery of Jonathan Edwards," the introduction to a new edition of the Miller biography (Amherst, Mass., 1981). Also excellent is Daniel B. Shea, "Jonathan Edwards: The First Two Hundred Years," *Journal of American Studies* 14 (1980), 181–197.

4. Wilson H. Kimnach, "The Literary Techniques of Jonathan Edwards," unpub. Ph.D. dissertation, University of Pennsylvania, 1971, pp. 56–57.

5. See the essay by Stephen J. Stein (Chap. 7 of this volume).

6. See the discussion of Oliver Wendell Holmes in the essay by Henry F. May (chap. 2).

7. See Heimert, pp. 14, 98–99. The index of *Religion and the American Mind* shows that Heimert cited Edwards on at least 400 occasions.

*Edwards and
the American Imagination*

2

Jonathan Edwards and America

HENRY F. MAY

When I told a Berkeley friend that I had been asked to give a keynote speech for a conference on Jonathan Edwards, this friend, ever frank, asked the obvious question: "Why you? You don't know all that much about Edwards." He was of course quite right, I don't, and I realized this rather acutely when I saw the list of formidable Edwards experts who were going to be represented in this symposium. Then I thought, maybe that is *why* I am asked to do this. A keynote speech—a term borrowed from American politics—is not expected to be a profound scholarly inquiry. What is it supposed to do? It is supposed to help create an atmosphere of enthusiasm and unity, and perhaps to gloss over deep differences of opinion. Maybe this can't be done by people profoundly involved in passionate argument and can best be attempted by somebody distinctly on the periphery.

Aside from not knowing too much, I have one other qualification for this job. I have long found Edwards deeply interesting, sometime repellent, often attractive and moving. (And we all know the importance, in relation to real understanding, of lively affections.) When I first read as a graduate student that true virtue consists in the disinterested love of being in general, my immediate response was not "how clever, how well put" but rather "how right, how beautiful." Long years later, after teaching a semester run-through of the history of American religion, I once offered to teach an undergraduate seminar on any topic we had covered. I prepared myself to deal with the churches and Vietnam, or the churches and civil rights. Instead, I got the most requests for a seminar on Edwards. Not very many requests of course—there were eight students. All had their special attitudes toward Edwards. At least three were part of the neo-evangelical movement that was flowering on the campuses in the wake of political movements of the sixties. (Incidentally, these were disappointed as they got to know Edwards better—he was not what they wanted him to be.) Of the others, one, the ablest, had a Catholic education, which meant—at that time—a solid grounding in philosophy and theology. At least one was an intelligent and articulate sceptic. We read most of the Edwards writing that was then generally accessible, and a lot of Edwards criticism from Oliver Wendell Holmes and Leslie Stephen through Parrington to—you guessed it—Perry Miller. We arrived at no consensus, and I think this was perhaps the course that I most enjoyed teaching at Berkeley.

More interesting than the question, "Why me?" is the question "Why you?" Why is it that Edwards has attracted not just a passing glance, but the devotion of years of hard work on the part of so many fine scholars? Is it because you believe him, love him, admire him? Is it because you find him complex and baffling, a perfectly engaging puzzle, a figure eternally subject to profound reinterpretation? Is it because he seems to some of you, as he did to Miller and others, to offer a key to the understanding of American culture? I suspect that all these and other powerful attractions helped to incline your wills in the direction of attending this conference.

It is an intriguing fact that, according to M. X. Lesser's massive Edwards bibliography, the number of dissertations on Edwards has doubled in each decade since 1940.[1] And the quality has gone up, as well as the volume. Yet, as with most interesting subjects, the more we know about Edwards, the harder he becomes to deal with. We have learned, for instance, that he did *not* develop on the far frontier isolated from European thought, that he was *not* suddenly changed in college by reading Locke, indeed that he was not really a Lockeian. If you hear a noise, it is the crackling of burning lecture notes.

Who and what was Edwards *really*? It is impossible to answer that question without the divine and spiritual light to which I claim no access. Since I am trained as a historian, all I can do is try to suggest, in most of the rest of this essay, what Edwards has meant to some kinds of Americans during the two centuries leading up to the present explosion of Edwards scholarship. I want to try to deal with motivation as well as understanding, to discuss the power of attraction and repulsion exerted by Edwards on several kinds of people in several historical periods. But before I do this I want to make it clear that I am not intending to patronize the past. Much as I admire the Edwards scholarship of today, I do not want to imply that in the past people saw Edwards through a mist of prejudice, and now we look at him in the clear light of objectivity. I assume that we all look at Edwards from where we are, and that this will always be so.

Most of us, in our first courses in historiography, heard a lot about the dangers of presentism. I agree that it is a disastrous mistake to push and kick one's subject matter so that it will fit into fashionable categories. This is clearly bad, and Edwards has suffered from it. But another kind of presentism gives most of its vitality to historical study, the kind that after rigorous discipline and close study of the sources asks the questions that arise from the most important concerns of the present. I think that the best Edwards scholarship has always done this. From each of the successive views of Edwards that I want briefly to present there is much to learn, about the preoccupations and assumptions of successive periods in intellectual history, but also about Edwards himself.

The first Edwards, of course, was that of his disciples. According to Samuel Hopkins, perhaps his most devoted follower:

> President Edwards, in the esteem of all the judicious, who were well-acquainted with him, either personally, or by his writings, was one of the *greatest—best* and *most useful* of men, that have lived in this age. . . . And that this distinguished light has not shone in vain, there are a cloud of witnesses. . . . And there is reason to hope, that though now he is dead, he will yet speak for a great while yet to come, to the comfort and advantage of the church of Christ; that his publications will produce a yet greater harvest, as an addition to his joy and crown of rejoicing in the day of the Lord.[2]

How many ardent young men followed Edwards as closely as they could is a question much debated among recent scholars.[3] It seems clear that there were several hundred of these all-out Edwardsians, most of them intelligent, articulate, and poor. By the 1820s or 30s the New Divinity, developed directly from Edwards's theology, was being forced into rural strongholds in New England, where it long survived. Yet even in the centers of modified Calvinism, where Edwards's teachings were more and more modified to fit nineteenth century optimism, Edwards was yet venerated by Congregationalist and Presbyterian divines. Timothy Dwight, one of the first of the long list of modifiers, called Edwards "That moral Newton, and that second Paul."[4] Lyman Beecher, the most powerful spokesman of nineteenth century neo-Calvinism, made in his youth a statement he was never to retract: "I had read Edwards's Sermons. There's nothing comes within a thousand miles of them now."[5]

In a statement made by Edwards Amasa Park in 1839 one can hear the dying gasp of Edwardsian loyalty, struggling with the Genteel Tradition and losing:

> We bow before this father of our New England theology with the profoundest veneration. We read his precious volumes with awe in tears. We are so superstitious, that we almost fear to be called profane for lisping a word against the perfect balancing of his character. And yet we can not help wishing that he had been somewhat more of a brother and somewhat less of a champion. . . .
>
> We need and crave a theology, as sacred and spiritual as his, and moreover one that we can take with us into the flower-garden, and to the top of some goodly hill, and in a sail over a tasteful lake, and into the saloons of music, and to the galleries of the painter and the sculptor, and to the repasts of social joy, and to all those humanizing scenes where virtue holds her sway not merely as that generic and abstract duty of a "love to being in general," but also as the more familiar grace of a love to some beings in particular.[6]

Long before this, while the New Divinity was gaining its triumphs, even while Edwards was still alive, he was being rejected in several different ways by the protagonists of the Enlightenment. In New England from Charles Chauncy on, many took on the formidable task of refuting his arguments, and of showing that these were not only mistaken but immoral. The doctrine of necessity was crippling to the conscience. The idea of double predestination was an insult to the moral and benevolent God who established the law of nature and gave us the ability to know and follow it. To Ezra Stiles and John Witherspoon, practical men like most college presidents, the New Divinity was fanatical and obscurantist. To those who moved beyond liberal Christianity toward Enlightened scepticism, Edwards's whole subject matter was without interest. Nobody expressed this better than John Adams:

> Mr. Adams leaves to Homer and Virgil, to Tacitus and Quintilian, to Mahomet and Calvin, to Edwards and Priestley, or, if you will, to Milton's angels reasoning high in pandemonium, all their acute speculations about fate, destiny, foreknowledge absolute, necessity, and predestination. He thinks it problematical whether there is, or ever will be, more than one Being capable of understanding this vast subject.[7]

Quite different in spirit from this sort of eighteenth century dismissal was the nineteenth century revulsion against Edwards as a cruel monster, dangerous because of his great talents. Oliver Wendell Holmes expressed it well:

> It is impossible that people of ordinary sensibilities should have listened to his torturing discourses without becoming at last sick of hearing of infinite horrors and endless agonies.

Of Edwards's uncompromising insistence on the total depravity of unregenerate children Holmes asks:

> Is it possible that Edwards read the text mothers love so well, Suffer little *vipers* to come unto me, and forbid them not, for of such is the kingdom of God.[8]

Harriet Beecher Stowe described the effect of Edwardsian doctrines this way:

> It is a fact that the true tragedy of New England life, its deep, unutterable pathos, its endurances and its sufferings, all depended upon, and were woven into, this constant wrestling of thought with inifinite problems which could not be avoided, and which saddened the day of almost every one who grew up under it. . . .

> Thus was this system calculated, like a skillful engine of torture, to produce all the mental anguish of the most perfect sense of helplessness with the most torturing sense of responsibility.[9]

Mrs. Stowe's Hartford neighbor Samuel Clemens carried this revulsion much further. After reading *Freedom of the Will* Clemens wrote his minister:

> Continuously until near midnight I wallowed and reeked with Jonathan in his insane debauch; rose immediately refreshed and fine at 10 this morning, but with a strange and haunting sense of having been on a three days' tear with a drunken lunatic . . . All through the book is the glare of a resplendent intellect gone mad—a marvellous spectacle. No, not *all* through the book—the drunk does not come on till the last third, where what I take to be Calvinism and its God begins to show up and shine red and hideous in the glow from the fires of hell, their only right and proper adornment. By God I was ashamed to be in such company.[10]

It is not difficult to sympathize with these outraged Victorians. I agree with Holmes. To modify his statement slightly, if we can read the imprecatory sermons without horror, it is because of a failure of imagination. Consistent Calvinism is admired in recent times chiefly by people to whom it has never occurred that its doctrines might really describe the true state of affairs. If one is seriously to follow Edwards, recent scholarship has made clear, one must accept his doctrine of Hell not as a minor blemish on his intellectual system, but as essential to it.[11] One must accept as true his masterly descriptions of intolerable and interminable suffering. Still more difficult, to be a real Edwardsian one must come to terms with his insistence that God hates sinners and holds them in the utmost contempt. Once a human being has had his chance, and has not been able to accept it, God will never feel the slightest pity for him. If a person is saved, part of his duty will be to love all aspects of God forever, including his vindictive justice. Thus he will have to learn to rejoice in the rightness and beauty of eternal suffering for others. To be a real follower of Edwards, one must moreover come to terms with little Phoebe Bartlett, four years old, sure of her own salvation, sorry for her sisters, predicting their death, weeping over the sin of stealing plums but blaming her sister for talking her into it, and expressing plummy love for her minister, Mr. Edwards.

For many nineteenth-century Americans, especially in New England, it was not possible to pick and choose. They had been brought up to believe that Edwards's doctrines or something like them were saving truth. After this, to reject them meant a major emotional struggle, which left its marks. The life of Mrs. Stowe's family had been tragically affected by the preaching of a major Edwardsian. Homes, writing to Mrs. Stowe about Calvinism, describes his upbringing in an image of almost Edwardsian power:

> I have found myself like a nursery-tree, growing up with labels of this and that article of faith wired to my limbs. The labels have dropped off, but the wires are only buried in my flesh, which has grown over them. . . . I do not believe you or I can ever get the iron of Calvinism out of our souls.[12]

Clemens, not being a New Englander, had not had quite this sort of exposure to intellectual Calvinism. Yet many of his works, and still more clearly his marginal comments and letters, bear witness to his prolonged early exposure to the grim aspects of evangelical Protestantism, his fervent revulsion from it, and the fact that its ghost continued to haunt him. The Victorians who hated Calvinism took it and Edwards seriously, and we should take seriously their anguished rejection.

In the early twentieth century, instead of rebelling against Edwards, it became possible to patronize him. Countless writers portrayed him as a talented but tragic figure, who could have been a great poet, a great philosopher, or a great scientist if he hadn't got mired in outworn theology. V. L. Parrington's account, more balanced than one might expect, contains several pages of eloquent appreciation but ends in lament:

> The intellectual powers were his, the inspiration was lacking; like Cotton Mather before him, he was the unconscious victim of a decadent ideal and a petty environment. Cut off from fruitful intercourse with other thinkers, drawn away from the stimulating field of philosophy into the arid realm of theology, it was his fate to devote his noble gifts to the thankless task of re-imprisoning the mind of New England within a system from which his nature and his powers summoned him to unshackle it. He was called to be a transcendental emancipator, but he remained a Calvinist.[13]

Rather similarly, Henry Bamford Parkes lamented in 1930 that Edwards had abandoned his promising early pantheism for Calvinism.

> To have experienced those realities of human nature which are the foundation of Christianity, and yet to reject Calvinism, would have required, in a Connecticut schoolboy, in 1721, a wisdom, almost superhuman; but because Edwards lacked that wisdom, his career is, in its hidden implications, the most tragic in American history. . . . The dark stream of Calvinism is but a tributary to the flood of American culture; Edwards merely carried to its extreme a tendency brought from Europe; in spite of his patriotism he was not really an American.[14]

It is harder for us to admire the progressive patronizers than to respect the forthright rejecters of Victorian times. Patronizing Edwards, they remind us of Edwards's own description of his own liberal contemporaries patronizing the great reformers of the sixteenth century:

> Indeed some of these new writers, at the same time that they have represented the doctrines of these ancient and eminent divines as in the highest degree ridiculous, and contrary to common sense, in an ostentation of a very generous charity, have allowed that they were honest, well-meaning men; yea, it may be, some of them, as though it were in great condescension

and compassion for them, have allowed that they did pretty well for the day in which they lived . . . living in the gloomy caves of superstition [they] fondly embraced, and demurely and zealously taught the most absurd, silly, and monstrous opinions, worthy of the greatest contempt of gentlemen possessed of that noble and generous freedom of thought, which happily prevail in this age of light and inquiry.[15]

This remains a sufficient putdown of liberal presentism. Yet I think one should remember how hard it was in the early twentieth century to approve any ideas that seemed to reject democratic progress. In a sense Parkes was right: there was no place for Edwards in the rise of American civilization. More recently Norman Fiering has warned us in a truly eloquent passage that Edwards was almost alone in the eighteenth century in rejecting the idea of the universal moral sense and the essential goodness of the common man. If we follow him in this we must realize that we are rejecting the most valuable heritage of the Enlightenment: "Only the two great wars of the twentieth century and the Holocaust have been able to shake into ruins, at least temporarily, the psychological optimism of the Shaftesbury-Hutcheson gospel of the innate goodness of man."[16]

It is out of the era of war and holocaust that the most powerful and interesting recent interpretation of Edwards has come: Edwards as a modern or postmodern intellectual. In 1949 Perry Miller presented him as one of the long and honorable line of American intellectuals who indicted utilitarian liberalism, complacency, and the profit motive, in a word (not Miller's), Babbittry. Edwards attacked the philistines, moreover, not in the name of transcendence but in behalf of "what seems rather a glorified naturalism."[17]

Miller has been well and thoroughly jumped on, by consistent naturalists, consistent theologians, and worst of all, by historians who convict him of either misreading or not reading some of the evidence. It is quite clear that Edwards was not any kind of naturalist.

Yet I think something is left of Edwards's modernity (asserted by others besides Miller) if only in terms of analogy. Edwards certainly was an enemy of complacency, and so are most important American writers, including of course Perry Miller. He is one of a long succession of American Jeremiahs, brooding over the grievous faults of their strange Israel. And there is something in Edwards's doctrine of moral necessity highly compatible with much modern thought. We are prevented from doing what we should do, even what we want to do, by our upbringing, our culture, our psychological formation—in short, our diseased will. It is understandable that Miller's *Edwards*, for all its many mistakes, sparked the revival of Edwards scholarship. It remains an interesting book, primarily because it was written by an interesting man.

In 1966 Alan Heimert, who might possibly be described as Miller's Samuel Hopkins, published his *Religion and the American Mind*.[18] With much learning and many exaggerations, Heimert associated Edwards and his followers with the American radical tradition from the Revolution on. One might say that where Miller had made Edwards an intellectual of the 1920s, his younger disciple made Edwards an intellectual of the 1930s. Heimert's book, partly because of a few unfortunate statements, called forth an extraordinary barrage of heavy artillery. And yet I don't think that Heimert was blown clear out of the water.

Edwards himself was not a social radical, not indeed directly interested in issues of social welfare, though Hopkins reports he was personally charitable to the poor. He was no precursor of Jeffersonian, still less of Jacksonian, democracy. He had nothing in common with the generally populist content of later American radicalism. He was in fact one of the greatest opponents of the theory that what is popular is right.

Yet it remains quite true that he offered no comfort to the wealthy and well-placed in their complacency, and that his closest followers were overwhelmingly among the radical supporters of the American Revolution. Heimert, even more clearly than other historians, shows us the reasons for this, the association of virtue, frugality, and sound doctrine with America—of decadence, luxury, and lukewarm religion with England.

There is even a useful analogy between the attraction of the New Divinity in the late eighteenth century and that of Marxism in the 1930s. Both attracted the young, the poor, and the intelligent. Both demanded total surrender and therefore appealed to those who wanted to give themselves completely to a cause. Both asserted that there was only one good force in the world, that from this only came all legitimacy, and that half-measures were evil. Survivors of the thirties find something familiar in the curse of Meroz invoked effectively against liberals.

One more major view of Edwards, related to that of Perry Miller but yet quite different, arose out of the successive revivals of religion in America, beginning with the neo-orthodox movement of the 30s, 40s, and 50s. Miller himself was friendly to this movement but outside it; he and others like him have been called "atheists for Niebuhr." The *theists* for Niebuhr saw a different Edwards, not a precursor of modern existentialism but a serious theologian in the tradition of Augustine and Calvin.

It should be noted that Reinhold Niebuhr himself made very little use of Edwards and at one point disapproved his absolutist ethic as crippling to social responsibility.[19] His brother H. Richard Niebuhr, more interested than Reinhold in the study of the American religious past, listed Edwards's *Nature of True Virtue*, along with works by Pascal, Barth, Calvin, and others, among those books that had most influenced his own philosophy of life.[20]

As early as 1932, Joseph Haroutunian treated the history of New England theology as a long, tragic decline from Edwards's profundity, and announced in his preface that today's world could, *in its own way*, appreciate Calvinism better than it could the recent past:

> Whereas the language of Calvinism is in disrepute, the elements of good sense in Calvinism must always remain wherever there is good sense. . . . The optimism and the humanism of the nineteenth century have already lost their rational quality.

> It is probable that a revival of the "tragic sense of life," together with the wisdom and sobriety which grow out of it, should be forthcoming. It is necessary that men rediscover the truths once signified by the doctrines of divine sovereignty and divine grace, of predestination and election, of depravity and regeneration. . . .

> If the humanitarianism of Channing is modern, a post-modern mind is already in the making. Its spirit is as yet skeptical and "naturalistic." It believes itself to be in an alien world. In order to become religious, it must become reconciled with God.[21]

By 1966, when Conrad Cherry wrote his analysis of the theology of Edwards, the neo-orthodox movement had come and gone, leaving an important residue, at least in the study of the American past. This residue is quite apparent in Cherry's introduction:

> Whatever quarrel one may have with the specific features of the theologies of such thinkers as Karl Barth and Reinhold Niebuhr, they have, in diverse ways, reclaimed Augustinian and Calvinist categories in order to prick the contemporary conscience, wean man away from religious sentimentality, and throw him up against the hard reality of a God who judges as well as forgives. . . . the once deplorable doctrine of predestination symbolizes man's precarious situation in the presence of a God whose will cannot be reduced to our purposes.[22]

Writing from this perspective, Cherry totally rejects Miller's existentialist Edwards. Edwards did not reject either the Puritan past or covenant theology; he remained "first and last a Calvinist theologian," not neo-orthodox but essentially orthodox.

The mass revival of religion of the 1950s, often heartily disapproved of by neo-orthodox and other intellectuals, led to a reemphasis on Edwards as a critical revivalist. In 1959 John E. Smith, introducing Edwards's *Religious Affections* said that "our present religious situation enables us to understand him as perhaps never before. For we are falling or have fallen into some of the very pitfalls he sought to avoid; we are in a better position than any age since Edwards to understand the profundity of his contribution to theological thinking. . . . He has given us a means of exposing the pseudo religions of moralism, sentimentality, and social conformity." While legitimizing revival and "heart religion," Edwards, Smith points out "failed to fall in with revivalism at two crucial points: he denied that the urgency of believing provides any criterion for the truth of religion or the sincerity of the believer, and he was unwilling to follow the pattern of most revivalists and set the religious spirit over against learning and intellect. For Edwards the Word must come in truth as well as in power."[23]

In the current revival of evangelical Protestantism, still another Edwards has been powerfully put before us—Edwards the serious and devoted student of the millennium. A long series of historians, clearly influenced by the new apocalyptic possibilities of the nuclear era, writing from both secular and religious points of view, have brought back to the surface a major part of Christian history long understated and explained away—the study of prophecy and the prediction of the last days. Starting with important hints from H. Richard Niebuhr, Edwards's millennial and apocalyptic thought has been thoroughly explored by a series of careful and insightful scholars including C. C. Goen and Stephen J. Stein.[24] Always eagerly searching the signs of the times for evidence of God's intentions, Edwards in his most optimistic moment in 1743 believed that he saw the millennium dawning in America.

In my opinion, the Edwards that emerges from scholars affected by recent religious movements, the Edwards who is primarily Calvinist, revivalist, and millenarian, is closer to the truth than Edwards the modern existentialist, so daringly and unforgettably presented by Perry Miller. It is valuable to have Edwards seen once more as a major figure in American religious as well as intellectual history. Yet a word of caution is necessary. The best theological students of Edwards know well, but some semipopular writers have forgotten, that Edwards is not really ancestral to any of the major kinds of nineteenth or twentieth century American religion. His millennial predictions about America have nothing in common with the foolish chauvinism of many nineteenth century preachers. Destiny, to Edwards, was never really Manifest. He clearly disapproved the humanist and liberal tendency that has issued in the nearly secular humanitarianism of the mainline churches today. Populistic and uncritical revivalists, who have flourished in all periods, surely cannot claim as their ally the author of *Religious Affections*. Fundamentalists can have little commerce with a man who never feared that the discoveries of contemporary science could be in contradiction to religious truth. Dispensationalists are a long way from a man who thought that the worst trials promised by revelation were over and that the new day might already have dawned. What are most churchgoers to do with a man who, according to the best recent analysis, "explicitly denied the efficacy of petitionary prayer to bring about external change in the world"?[25]

Conclusion

I have tried so far to suggest a few of the main interpretations of Edwards—there are of course many others—that have succeeded each other in the past. It is time to ask where we are left. After this keynote, can the convention agree on a platform? On a few planks, I think.

First, I think we can agree that Edwards was somehow a great man, whether we admire him most as artist, psychologist, preacher, theologian, or philosopher. Second, I think we can probably agree on what was the starting point and motive of all his work: "To one cardinal principle Edwards was faithful—the conception of the majesty and sufficiency of God; and this polar idea provides the clue to both his philosophical and theological systems."[26] This was said not by Haroutunian or Cherry, not by any of the editors of the Yale edition, not by Norman Fiering, but by Vernon Louis Parrington, and it seems to me undeniable. Third, I think we can agree that Edwards, like all thinkers much worth studying, was fully of his own time and yet transcended it. He has had a great deal to say to people who loved and admired him, people who were horrified and haunted by him, people of many kinds of the eighteenth, nineteenth and twentieth centuries. He seems both inexhausible and impossible to pin down.

There are some other things on which I think we cannot and will not agree. First, is his work a massive, successful structure, or a majestic, instructive, and brilliant failure? There are many ways to ask this question. Can we understand the preacher who in one sermon tells his listeners to seek Christ: "You need not hesitate one moment, but may run to him and cast yourself upon him; you will certainly be graciously and meekly received by him,"[27] and in others makes it clear that nothing will avail unless one has been totally changed by the uncontrollable power of the Spirit? Probably there is no real inconsistency of doctrine here, but is there not an inconsistency in homiletic effect?

As for his theology, I am certainly not qualified to criticize it, but hope the theologians will tell me whether there is or is not a contradiction between believing, on the one hand, in a God that is both wholly other and wholly transcendent, and on the other hand, analyzing in detail his nature and intentions. Regarding Edwards's philosophy, Fiering, who regards him as a great and profound thinker, leaves the question of validity wide open: "A difficult question, and one we need not debate here, is whether Edwards's primary, objective, ontological foundation for virtue is philosophically or even theologically tenable." Regarding his effort to reconcile responsibility and predestination Fiering says, "It would be absurd to say that Edwards succeeded in dissolving this theological mystery (all of his solutions seem to be sophistical). . . ."[28]

Finally I come to what is for me the most difficult and interesting question of all. This is the question raised by James Hoopes: "Many modern scholars," says Hoopes, "have no idea what it feels like to perceive holiness [this seems to me a massive understatement], and those who do can no more describe the sensation to the rest of us than one can tell a man blind since birth what it feels like to see."[29] To bring together the affections, the understanding, and the will, Edwards has to rely on the sixth spiritual sense, "a Spiritual and Divine Light, immediately imparted to the soul by God, of a different nature from any that is obtained by natural means."[30] This supreme and crucial faculty is necessarily for unregenerate people, both indefinable and unverifiable. Perhaps Edwards's greatest achievement as a writer is that he comes close through his poetic powers to achieving the impossible. He almost manages to prove to the unilluminated the logical necessity of this supernatural illumination, and even to tell us what it is like.

This can be put in simpler terms arising out of the history of Edwards studies. Is it possible to have a fruitful discussion of a great religious thinker with the frank participation of believers, rejecters, and agnostics? This seems to me a question which a conference on this topic, in this place, needs to be faced head-on.

Notes

1. M. X. Lesser, *Jonathan Edwards: A Reference Guide* (Boston, 1981), xli. This volume has assisted me greatly in preparing the essay, reprinted in this volume.

2. Samuel Hopkins, *The Life and Character of the Late Reverend Mr. Jonathan Edwards* (1765), reprinted in David Levin, ed., *Jonathan Edwards, a Profile* (New York, 1969), 1–2.

3. The latest, and one of the best, contributions to this long debate is Joseph Conforti, *Samuel Hopkins and the New Divinity* (Grand Rapids, 1981). See especially 175–90.

4. Timothy Dwight, *The Triumph of Infidelity*, quoted by Lesser, *Edwards*, p. 46.

5. *The Autobiography of Lyman Beecher*, ed. Barbara M. Cross, 2 vols. (Cambridge, 1961), I, 46.

6. E. A. Park, "The Duties of a Theologian," *American Biblical Repository* II, 4 (1840), 374.

7. John Adams to John Taylor, 1814, reprinted in Adrienne Koch, ed., *The American Enlightenment* (New York, 1965), 222.

8. Oliver Wendell Holmes, "Jonathan Edwards," in *Pages from an Old Volume of Life* (Boston, 1892), 393.

9. Harriet Beecher Stowe, *Oldtown Folks*, ed., Henry F. May (Cambridge, Mass., 1966), 401.

10. Clemens to the Reverend J. H. Twichell, February 1902, in A. B. Paine, *Mark Twain's Letters*, 2 vols. (New York, 1917), II, 719–20.

11. See Norman Fiering, *Jonathan Edwards's Moral Thought and Its British Context* (Chapel Hill, 1981), 200–260.

12. Holmes to Stowe, May 29, 1867, quoted in H. May, Introduction to *Oldtown Folks*, 29.

13. V. L. Parrington, *Main Currents of American Thought*, 3 vols. (New York, 1927, 1930), I, 162–63.

14. Henry Bamford Parkes, *Jonathan Edwards, The Fiery Puritan* (New York, 1930), 254.

15. Jonathan Edwards, "Freedom of the Will," ed., Paul Ramsey (New Haven, 1967), 437.

16. Fiering, *Edwards's Moral Thought*, 148.

17. Perry Miller, *Jonathan Edwards* (New York, 1949), 276.

18. Cambridge, 1966.

19. Reinhold Niebuhr, *Moral Man and Immoral Society* (New York, 1960, 1st ed., 1932), 67.

20. H. R. Niebuhr, "Ex Libris," *The Christian Century*, June 13, 1962, p. 754.

21. Joseph Haroutunian, *Piety versus Moralism* (New York, 1932, paperback ed., New York, 1970), xxxii–xxxiii.

22. Conrad Cherry, *The Theology of Jonathan Edwards* (New York, 1966), 6.

23. John E. Smith, introduction to Edwards, *Religious Affections*, reprinted in Levin, ed., *Jonathan Edwards*, 211, 217.

24. C. C. Goen, "Jonathan Edwards: A New Departure in Eschatology," *Church History* XXXVIII (1959), 25–40; Stephen J. Stein, introduction to Jonathan Edwards, *Apocalyptic Writings* (New Haven, 1977).

25. Fiering, *Edwards's Moral Thought*, 97.

26. Parrington, *Main Currents*, I, 152.

27. Edwards, "The Excellency of Christ," in C. H. Faust and Thomas H. Johnson, *Jonathan Edwards, Representative Selections* (New York, 1925, paperback ed., 1962), 125.

28. Fiering, *Edwards's Moral Thought*, 361, 292.

29. James Hoopes, "Jonathan Edwards's Religious Psychology," *Journal of American History* LXIX (1982–83), 861.

30. Edwards, "A Divine and Supernatural Light," in Faust and Johnson, eds., *Edwards*, 102.

3

Edwards, Franklin, and Cotton Mather: A Meditation on Character and Reputation

DAVID LEVIN

Several scholars have written perceptively about Edwards's character.[1] I have learned, for example, from Richard Bushman's Eriksonian study, from Elizabeth Dodds's book on Sarah and Jonathan Edwards, and from Patricia Tracy's fine narrative of Edwards's career as a pastor. Perhaps we may understand Edwards and ourselves a little better if we reconsider some of the ways in which he resembles and differs from two other men who were celebrated—and maligned—in his day and who have become legendary in our own. I choose Benjamin Franklin and Cotton Mather not only because my courses in American literature often require me to discuss the writings of the three men, but also because Mather and Franklin live in our national myth and in our scholarship as memorable *personalities*.

Edwards and Franklin have often been compared as two geniuses of the American Enlightenment who represent divergent tendencies in Puritanism and in American culture.[2] Edwards represents aspiration toward union with the divine and toward establishing a firm metaphysical structure to support his Calvinist faith; Franklin embodies the Yankee's shrewd combination of self-knowledge and humor, applying his ingenuity to many kinds of social, ethical, and scientific problems to show how character, personal wealth, and the commonwealth can all be improved. Franklin and Cotton Mather, too, have been instructively compared.[3] But Mather and Edwards have rarely been discussed together, even though it has been customary to regard Mather as a man in whose mind the Enlightenment and Puritan orthodoxy struggled in ways that made him even more uncomfortable than his character makes some of us. I shall therefore highlight resemblances among the three men, but of course I do not claim that they were all alike, that we should pronounce the same judgment on them all, or that the differences among them are always less important than the similarities. I hope that the comparisons may help us to appreciate the nature of Edwards's individuality by explicitly recognizing some of our assumptions about how character should be defined and judged.

In these brief reflections on character and reputation, I shall probably seem to be spending more time on reputation than on the actual historical character; for, without poaching on Donald Weber's subject, the recovery of Jonathan Edwards, I hope to persuade some of you that current and traditional preferences have overemphasized peculiarities of personality, and that we have thus overlooked important qualities that all three characters share.

Of course I should warn you that my own attitude is conditioned by years of sometimes embattled exposure to Cotton Mather, and that the best we can hope for in studying the past is to move closer to a just understanding. I do believe that individual character is not a mere figment or fictitious invention, and that our own historical circumstances—and comparisons of modern interpretations with the surviving seventeenth- and eighteenth-century evidence—can help us to restore to the individual portrait actual features that have been neglected or overlooked.

Edwards, Franklin, and Mather, although active and effective in some kinds of social affairs, are all known to us primarily through their writings. We read the character of each man in his prose style, and especially in the way he writes about himself in his diaries or autobiographical narratives. I suspect that one major reason why Edwards has enjoyed a much better press in modern scholarship than either Franklin or Mather is the directness, the relentlessly straightforward quality of his prose. Even when writing about his most intense spiritual experience, moreover, Edwards manages to seem detached if not impartial, describing phenomena in his soul or psyche without calling great attention to his personality.

Mather and Franklin, on the other hand, appear in their respective ways to be writing self-consciously, cannily, perhaps insincerely. I cannot agree with Edmund Morgan that Mather expresses "a false modesty about everything that he does."[4] Mather even introduces the most successful of all his books by refusing to say, "'Sorry 'tis no better.' Instead of *that*," he insists, "I freely tell my readers: I have written what is not unworthy of their perusal. If I did not think so, truly, I would not publish it."[5] Yet when Mather reports in his diary a vision promising that in imminent European revolutions against anti-Christian tyrants "sinful I shall be given a prominent assignment" and that "vast regions of *America*" will be introduced to knowledge of Christ by "poor, vile sinful me,"[6] not even the most sympathetic reader can miss the posing. Mather's awkward efforts to stifle or at least conceal his pride are defeated by his irrepressible delight. When Franklin opens his autobiography by admitting that one of his motives for writing is to gratify his vanity, and that he thanks heaven for vanity, along with "the other comforts of life,"[7] many readers resist his effort to disarm them even as they perceive his joke. Franklin's humor, then, can be read as one more device of a manipulative personality, working his way with us while shutting us out from intimate knowledge of his true self.

Not even his famous rationalization of his pride can placate suspicious readers. When he tells his parable of the speckled axe, he is clearly ridiculing his own tendency to rationalize; his self-mocking irony is evident in the story of the man who decided that he "liked a speckled axe best," rather than an entirely shiny axehead, after the axe grinder agreed to polish the entire head if the customer himself would do the work of turning the grindstone (p. 156). But every year several of my students who have no trouble perceiving Franklin's humor when he says that achieving true humility would amount to "a kind of foppery in morals"— a condition in which he might have been proud of his humility (pp. 160, 156)—every year some of my ablest students protest that here again Franklin is trying to manipulate the reader. Against this effort some of them, and some older scholars, rearm themselves with a moral severity that one would have been more likely to expect from a Puritan than from a liberated modern scholar.

My purpose here is not to explain why that severity is visited on the head of Franklin, nor why so distinguished a scholar as Samuel Eliot Morison would say gratuitously that undergraduate life at Harvard must have returned to normal in 1674, "if that insufferable prig Cotton Mather"—then only 11 years old—"was being kicked about, as he so richly deserved."[8] Mather's latest biographer explains his own contemptuous judgment of Mather as an objection to insincerity when he coins the term "Matherese" to signify an ambiguous, self-deceptive language that professes friendship while revealing "a vengeful egotist nakedly transparent."[9] "This impossibly provocative fusion of the conciliator and the trouble-maker, of his goodwill and his rage," Kenneth Silverman writes, is what has "always made [Mather] seem at once splendid and contemptible" (p. 256). And Edmund Morgan, in two essay-reviews in the last six years, has made it plain that what nauseates him is Mather's egomania, his trivializing of the divine, a gross confusion in which self-glorification is mistaken for, or misrepresented as, the glorification of God. When Mather professes—or at least tries—to "feel a secret Joy" in one of the most bitter disappointments of his life, "because I am thus conformed unto Him who was despised and rejected of Men," Morgan acknowledges the appropriateness of Mather's disappointment, that he "*was* the most eminent minister in New England" and therefore "an obvious candidate" for the presidency of Harvard. "But Jesus Christ he was not," Morgan says—as if Mather had seen no difference between being "conformed unto" Christ and being identified with Him—"and failure to become president of Harvard was not crucifixion."[10] I doubt if Morgan's judgment here would be modified if he had remembered that Cotton Mather, at the age of seven or eight, failed to understand why his father "seemed glad" to hear that young Cotton had been beaten for rebuking his playmates' "wicked words and ways," but that afterwards Cotton Mather came to appreciate the "Heavenly Principle" behind his father's reaction.[11]

This mixture of condescension and sarcasm might need more explanation if other scholars, from Robert Middlekauff and Sacvan Bercovitch to Richard Lovelace, had not been able (as I have been) to write about Mather without contempt.[12] What puzzles me is a question closer to the central concern of this conference: How does Jonathan Edwards escape such disapproving language? Edwards, too, has been portrayed for two centuries as a prodigy who was well along in Latin studies by the time he was eight years old, and who wrote a fine essay on flying or sailing spiders when only eleven. But even before recent scholarship demonstrated that Edwards wrote that essay in his early twenties,[13] he was not portrayed as the kind of infant prodigy who deserved to be kicked about by normal schoolmates. Only rarely has any portrait of his character included his report that "no *new* quarrel" has "broke[n] out betwixt me and any of the scholars" at Yale or his complaint against his classmates' "monstrous impieties and acts of immorality."[14] Nor, in the gravest disappointment of Edwards's clerical life, his dismissal by the congregation he had served for twenty-three years, does his relentless farewell sermon provoke sarcastic disapproval of his vindictiveness—not even when he elevates himself (after a perfunctory disclaimer) to a close parallel with the prophet Jeremiah and the apostle Paul, nor when he repeatedly tells his opponents that Jesus Christ, "before the whole universe" (p. 188), will endorse his position in the Northampton controversy, and will judge the motivation of the pastor and every one of his critics, on the Day of Judgment.[15] In the same sermon Edwards warns a few who have begun to feel some religious awakenings that "the devil will undoubtedly seek to make his advantage" of Edwards's dismissal, and he tells the young people that at the Judgment Day, "when we shall meet before Him," "God will approve and confirm" Edwards's warning "against frolicking (as it is called) and some other liberties taken by young people in the land" (p. 196). Yet this mixture of admonition and self-justification is rarely represented as a trait of Edwards's character.

Edwards, moreover, was capable of writing the kind of private note that has damaged Cotton Mather's reputation. As Patricia Tracy has pointed out, Edwards resolved not to be envious at the time that his father believed one of Jonathan's cousins had been offered the coveted post in grandfather Solomon Stoddard's church. Jonathan resolved "always to rejoice in everyone's prosperity . . . and to expect no happiness of that nature as long as I live."[16] And when he sent off his essay on spiders to Paul Dudley, a fellow of the Royal Society, he cast his hope for publication in the same kind of conventionally fulsome rhetoric, the same false modesty and elaborate decorum, that one finds in some of Mather's prose: "If you think, Sir," Edwards wrote, "that [my observations] are not worthy the taking notice of, with greatness and goodness overlook and conceal [them]": and again, "Pardon me if I thought it might at least give you occasion to make better observations on these wonderful animals, that should be worthy of communicating to the learned world."[17]

Modern scholars may deplore Mather's willingness to blame the Devil for confusing the Lord's People with true and false accusations during the witchcraft craze in 1692; except in Robert Lowell's implicit criticism, I cannot remember reading any modern objections to Jonathan Edwards's comment, in his first "Narrative of Surprising Conversions," on his uncle's suicide: "Satan," Edwards wrote, citing the same biblical text that Mather had used for a sermon on witchcraft, "seems to be in a Great Rage, at the Extraordinary breaking forth of the word of God. I hope it is because he knows that he has but a short time: doubtless he had a Great Reach, in this violent attack of his against the whole affair. We have appointed a day of Fasting in the Town this week, by Reason of this & other appearances of satans Rage amongst us against poor Souls."[18] It is not just the appeal to that biblical text, but the similar way of responding to threatening evidence, that links Mather's and Edwards's statements. Both admit that Satan has taken advantage of a crisis in which the respective minister has taken a controversial position. And in 1735 as well as 1692, for Edwards as well as Mather, blaming Satan for perverting the real meaning of the crisis serves only to verify the millennial significance of the episode.

Before returning more narrowly to the question of character, I would like to consider a few other parallels between Mather and Edwards. Edwards echoes Mather's *Magnalia Christi Americana* when he notes that the Reformation and the discovery of America were providential steps toward "the glorious renovation of the world," which would "make way for the church's latter-day glory," beginning in America.[19] Edwards's xenophobic comments about the French in Canada during the Seven Years' War do not differ markedly from Mather's strictures during the *Decennium Luctuosum*, the grievous decade of the 1690s. Both apocalyptic statements make partisan use of a millennial schedule. Although Edwards was capable, in *The Nature of True Virtue*, of recognizing in national loyalty an expanded form of self-love, his rhetoric in battle could echo the fiercest words of the seventeenth century. As Stephen Stein has noted, Edwards predicted that "the saints," although forbidden ordinary revenge, would do "their utmost for the destruction of popery." The command in Rev. 5:6 to "Reward her even as she rewarded you" does not summon Christians to "revenge upon the persons of men," Edwards says, but followers of Antichrist "shall have that internal pains and torments of mind, that are like judgments that shall come upon them. Antichrist, as he is a body politic, shall forever die an eternal death. There may be papists, vagabonds that shall be the scorn of the world; but there shall never more be a popish polity."[20] The Roman church, Edwards says, is worse than Islam or Judaism; it is like "a viper or some loathsome, poisonous, crawling monster."[21]

Considerable evidence suggests that Mather was at least as effective as Edwards in pastoral visits and in supervising, disciplining, or instructing the young, and that Edwards's alienation from many of the young in his congregation, like his earlier troubles in supervising Yale undergraduates, was even more severe than Cotton Mather's.[22] Here we generally do recognize the contribution of Edwards's personality to the catastrophe of his dismissal. I refer not to the implicitly economic and political issues that Perry Miller and Ola Winslow, respectively, emphasized.[23] Those issues are large enough in their way to have a respectable place beside the questions of theology and church membership that preoccupied Edwards's majestic mind. No, it is Edwards's treatment of midwifery, secretly studied by children of church members, and the pregnancy of an unmarried young woman, whom Edwards commanded to marry the father of her child—it is these petty matters that Ms. Tracy has convincingly tied in a relatively new way to Edwards's character.[24]

The point of my comparisons of Edwards and Cotton Mather is not primarily to gain comfort from demonstrating that Edwards could sometimes be just as puritanically bad. Nor do I chiefly hope to use Edwards's faults as a lever for prying Mather's effigy loose from the gallery of monsters and restoring him to the human race. If we attend to the insights of Tracy and Bushman, and to evidence that we judge similar traits and actions differently in Edwards, Franklin, and Mather, we may see reason to proceed cautiously when we build moralistic judgments into historical portraits. We may then be able to see other parallels in career and character, and to broaden our conception of character itself.

Consider the shape of the two careers. Each of these prodigious boys saw his father and a grandfather exercise strong authority in their respective congregations, and each of the young men joined a powerful progenitor as a colleague before entering his twenty-fifth year. At the age of twenty-six, each of them had to take charge of that progenitor's large congregation—Cotton Mather when his father went to England as agent of Massachusetts in quest of a restored charter; Edwards when Grandfather Stoddard died. Both Edwards and Cotton Mather had extraordinary success in recruiting new church members in these early years, and as Mather's political and social influence flourished until the witchcraft trials, so Edwards enjoyed an extraordinary success in the revival of 1734–35. Stirred by millennial hopes, both Mather (at twenty-nine) and Edwards (at thirty-one) thought they had to face the perplexing, successful counter-attacks of Satan—Mather in spectral evidence and Edwards in his despondent uncle's suicide. Mather knew from the beginning that spectral evidence was unreliable because the Devil could assume the shape of an innocent person, but he was convinced that some specters were agents of guilty witches. In the Great Awakening half a century later, Edwards struggled to define the distinguishing marks of true grace even as he had to admit that some of the marks were indistinguishable from satanic cheats, or self-delusion. Mather hoped that Boston might become, in 1697 and again in 1716, the New Jerusalem; Edwards hoped that the Great Awakening might be "the dawning, or at least a prelude," to the millennium, which would probably begin in America, perhaps in the ideal Christian commonwealth that he was trying to achieve in Northampton.[25] Edwards, like Mather, wrote pamphlets against having "a heterodox minister settled amongst us."[26] And in their forties and fifties, both Mather and Edwards tried unsuccessfully to regain in recalcitrant congregations the heady influence they had enjoyed as young pastors. Mather, of course, was never dismissed by his congregation, but his disappointment was intensified by both the secession of a large group who formed a new church, and a series of petty, yet exhausting conflicts that stood in lugubrious contrast to the grand millennial battles of his twenties.

The great service that Patricia Tracy's book has done is to tie Edwards's character closely to historical circumstances. Her method is much more firmly rooted in quantitative evidence than is my own study of Mather, but her results encourage me to see the value of comparisons across the generations. Tracy shows that Edwards was not above taking a self-pitying tone when he spoke at the ordination of Jonathan Judd, minister to the new congregation at Southampton. At the very time that he was fighting with his own congregation about salary, Edwards warned the new congregation not to pay their new minister "well for a while at first, while the relation between you and him is a new thing, and then afterwards, when your minister's necessities are increased, begin to fail, as it too frequently happens." Here, as Ms. Tracy notices, Edwards concedes that ministers "love to harp on this string" for obvious reasons of self-interest, but he promptly declares that he himself has not "been much in insisting on this duty in my own pulpit . . . ; and blessed be God that I have had no more occasion." Tracy suggests insincerity here, for he had occasion enough. But Edwards at least anticipates her objection. With characteristic rigor, he makes a logical distinction that includes a defiant appeal to his ultimate Authority. He dismisses as irrelevant "whatever any may judge of the secrets of my heart." The truth remains the truth: "it is enough for you to whom I have spoke it, that I have demonstrated that what I have delivered is the mind of God." Against such demonstrations, he warned the new congregation, there would always be some "anti-ministerial men," including church members, to whom it would seem "natural . . . to be unfriendly and unkind towards their own ministers, and to make difficulty for them."[27]

Does not Cotton Mather's desire to be conformed to the example of Jesus seem less peculiar when we remember what Jonathan Edwards, with pointed allusions to his own experience, told Jonathan Judd and the new congregation: that ministers "must suffer—even as Christ did, if necessary—to bring the Gospel to the pharisees"?[28] Is there any fundamental difference between Edwards's admonition about "anti-ministerial men"—or Thomas Shepard's axiom, "He that would live godly must suffer persecution"[29]—and Mather's warning, written for those who try to do good, and ridiculed by Edmund Morgan, "that a man of *good merit* may be treated as "a kind of *public enemy*"?[30] Is there any major difference between Thomas Shepard's succinct command, in the 1640s, "Suspect thyself much,"[31] and Cotton Mather's prescription for responding to insults: "Be always really, heartily, inwardly *loathing yourself*"?[32] Even if we did not have Richard Lovelace's excellent book restoring Mather's writings to their theological context, the comparison to Edwards would supply a good perspective for Mather's pride. Shepard, too, had recorded an almost identical response to the threat of despair. When laboring under an intense awareness of sin, he said, he had been given a divine message: "Be not discouraged therefore because thou art so vile, but make this double use of it: (1) loathe thyself the more; (2) feel a greater need [for] . . . Jesus Christ."[33] And now that we have arrived at the central trait of pride, vanity, self-identification with grandeur, let us compare our three representative figures—how they wrote about their own pride and how they say that they tried to nurture or control it.

All three of these gifted men recognized their vanity and pride in comments that were more than merely conventional, and they all resolved to control or at least disguise their feelings of superiority or anger. Edwards resolved to substitute for his "air of dislike, anger, and fretfulness" an "appearance of love, cheerfulness, and benignity."[34] In an extraordinary passage that still perplexes my students, Edwards also managed to discuss his pride in a way that can easily be misread as blindly claiming (in Franklin's ironic words) to be proud of his humility—or proud of his awareness of his wickedness. A close reading of the syntax— especially in the restored sentence that nineteenth-century editors had deleted from Edwards's spiritual autobiography—shows that Edwards does not claim actually to be the worst sinner in the world. He only means to describe a feeling that he often has, especially when other Christians try to express to him their sense of their own unworthiness. Their expressions, he says, "may be suitable for them," but on these occasions (so I interpret the passage) "it *seems*" to Edwards that "it would be a vile self-exaltation in me not to be the lowest in humility of all mankind." And when "others speak of *their* longing to be 'humbled to dust,'" Edwards says (though the italics are mine) he thinks that he ought "to lie infinitely low before God." He sees the snare in such implicit competition—first when he attributes the apparent enormity of his sins not to his having "a greater conviction of sin than ordinary," but to his feeling that "I *am* so much worse, and have so much more wickedness to be convinced of"[35] (emphasis mine). I find it interesting that these statements come from one of the sentences that had been excised by nineteenth-century editors, not to be restored for modern discussion until Daniel Shea led us back to the text in Samuel Hopkins's biography.[36]

Even without this restored sentence, however, Edwards demonstrates plainly that he sees the dialectical consequence of grace. The very paragraph that begins with his "greater sense of my universal exceeding dependence on God's grace and strength, and mere good pleasure, of late, than I used formerly to have,"—that very paragraph ends with a startling confession: Although nauseated by "the very thought of any joy arising in me, on any consideration of my own amiableness, performances, or experiences, or any goodness of heart or life," he insists that he is "greatly afflicted with a proud and self-righteous spirit, much more sensibly than I used to be formerly. I see that serpent rising and putting forth its head everywhere, all around me."[37]

Those well-known lines about the spiritual dialectic between pride and humility have their institutional counterpart in a meditation that young Edwards wrote about a minister's power to do good—a statement that Patricia Tracy has used to foreshadow her narrative of Edwards's doomed effort to emulate his dominant grandfather's mastery of the congregation. Solomon Stoddard, we recall, was sometimes known as the pope of New England. Here Edwards moves in his customarily methodical progress from step to step—from the pastor's administration of the sacraments, to his choice of who should receive the sacraments, and so to the extension of "my pastoral, or ministerial, or teaching power." If the people "are obliged to hear me," he says, only for ordinary reasons—"only because they themselves have chosen me to guide them, and therein declared that they thought me sufficiently instructed in the mind of Christ to teach them, and because I have the other requisites of being their teacher, then I have power as other ministers have in these days. But if it was plain to them that I was under the infallible guidance of Christ, then I should have more power. And if it was plain to all the world of Christians that I was under the infallible guidance of Christ, and I was sent forth to teach the world the will of Christ, then I should have power in all the world. I should have power to teach them what they ought to do, and they would be obliged to hear me; I should have power to teach them who were Christians and who not, and in this likewise they would be obliged to hear me."[38]

Professor Thomas Schafer has persuaded me that Patricia Tracy's reading of this meditation neglects the context, which remains unpublished. In this meditation and in others, Edwards has been discussing the function of ministers in general, and the power of "popes, bishops, and presbyters" as well. His use of the first person here, as elsewhere in miscellanies on the same subject, may well be merely illustrative, using the pronoun "I" as we often use "you" or "one." Edwards is probably concerned in these months not only with the disciplinary struggles of his father in the congregation at East Windsor, nor especially with Grandfather Stoddard's unchallenged power in Northampton, but also with the defection of Timothy Cutler at Yale from the Congregational to the Anglican church. Surely Edwards meditates here on the nature of ministerial authenticity in any branch of Christianity. His theoretical extension of the young man's power into "all the world" may therefore have no connection to personal "dreams of unlimited power," or to a search for "solace" prompted by his father's weak control in East Windsor.[39]

Yet even if we reject such speculations, we cannot fail to see the competitive implication in this tradition of Christian teaching. One does not want to have teaching power "only as other ministers have in these days." "Difference of power" does exist, Edwards says, "amongst ministers, whether apostles or whatever." As Ms. Tracy clearly sees, the Puritan minister's obligation to have a true vocation, the source of true Christian authority, conflicts with his duty to be humble.

It is in the obligation to be at once proud and humble, distinct from counterfeit Christians and yet self-effacing, that the comparison of Edwards, Franklin, and Mather can be most illuminating. All three men worked out the ethical problem through some version of the doctrine of Christian calling, which both Franklin and Mather enunciate by repeating the biblical proverb (Prov. 22:29) that says a diligent man will stand before kings. "Proud thoughts," Mather confessed in a private meditation, "fly-blow my best performances"; and in his warning that, should the Lord reject him after all, he would be "the direst example of a deluded and exalted hypocrite that ever was," he resolved to abhor himself even in his "enlargements and entertainments."[40] Like Edwards half a century later, Mather commanded himself to "walk softly and sorrowfully as long as I breathe on earth."[41] And just as Franklin would later compare his own methodical efforts at eliminating one fault at a time to weeding a garden, repeating his course in "The Art of Virtue" over and over again, so young Mather (though of course with none of Franklin's self-tolerant humor) perceived that his battle against pride and other sins would be perpetual: "Lord, I here take my *vow*, that I will never give Thee, or my own soul rest, until my dearest lusts become, as bitter as death, as hateful as Hell unto me."[42]

We should not consider it accidental that Benjamin Franklin makes his general statement about vanity in the very first pages of his autobiography, or that humility is the last of his thirteen virtues and the only one (besides order) with which he reports that he had little success. Franklin's habit of humorous understatement introduces vanity not as a dear lust that must become as hateful as Hell to him, but as one of the comforts of life for which we should thank Heaven. He plainly says here at the outset that vanity often does considerable good, presumably by impelling men and women to achievements that benefit themselves and society. His doctrine of enlightened self-interest—seeing that one's own truest interest will ultimately coincide with virtue—implies a recognition of at least some utility in vanity. And his willingness to be content with the *appearance* of humility underlines the point. Not only will he refuse to abase himself in the extravagant language of Thomas Shepard, Cotton Mather, George Whitefield, Jonathan Edwards, and other Christians; Franklin really believes that vanity and ambition, if properly controlled, do considerable good.

What unites Franklin, Edwards, and Mather none the less is the intensity of their striving to drive their amibition or pride in ingenious efforts to do good in the world. All three men were proud and ambitious, and all three were impatient in the face of contradiction. All three were painfully sensitive to criticism; even if one rejects Melvin Buxbaum's or Bernard Bailyn's severe judgment of Franklin's behavior during the affair of the letters purloined from Thomas Hutchinson, one cannot miss the intensity of Franklin's pain and anger when he is forced to endure the abuse of Parliament and the press. Here Franklin seems almost Matherian in his resentment of libels against his virtue and his family name.[43] But it is in the young Franklin's concentration on ingenious ways to express his prodigious gifts, finding means to direct his ambition into acceptably virtuous forms, that he most clearly resembles Mather and Edwards. In the context of Edwards's and Mather's resolutions to try to subject their extraordinarily strong wills to the will of God, their passion to lie low before God and yet to be united to Him, Franklin's resolution to strive for humility by imitating Jesus and Socrates ought to seem less presumptuous (or less humorously ironic) than it did when it infuriated D. H. Lawrence.[44]

In narrating Mather's effort to control his stammer while he was still a young boy at Harvard, I remarked that the key to Mather's developing character was "not only the affliction, the anxiety, the incipient neurosis, but his mighty labor to make the most of it. Who," I asked, "can match the determination of the Puritan determinist?"[45] I believe that this determination, the power of this will to reconcile science and faith (gravely modified in Franklin, of course), ambition and humility, striving and resignation, self-examination and vigorous benefactions in the world— that the power of this will is more important to a comparison of the three men's character than Cotton Mather's shrillness, Franklin's worldly

humor, or the emotional crises that Mather and Edwards suffered. Even
in New England at the beginning of the eighteenth century, there was no
natural law that tied every man's pride and ambition to virtue or to
public service.

It should be no particular novelty to notice in the twentieth century
that Cotton Mather and Jonathan Edwards both had to reconcile their
own ambition with mixed feelings of rivalry and reverence toward their
clerical fathers and grandfathers. And Benjamin Franklin tells us openly
(if only to disarm us) that rivalry with his older brother and resentment of
real or imagined injustice led him to take questionable advantage of an
opportunity to flee his apprenticeship.[46] Does psychoanalysis really
oblige us to assume that the best way of resolving conflicting emotions is
always to express our anger? I think not. Would Cotton Mather have
been a better citizen, a less "odious," "contemptible," and "nauseating"
human being, if he had let it all hang out instead of trying (at admittedly
great cost) to become the best person he could be? If we notice that
Edwards was at least as censorious with his congregation as Mather ever
was with the Second Church in Boston, perhaps we won't scorn Mather's
rebukes as vicious. Perhaps we will read character in the choice of virtue,
service, and self-discipline.

Let us return to style. If we notice that Franklin, for all his delightful
humor, was just as sensitive as Mather and Edwards to attacks upon his
good name, and thoroughly glad to be honored, we ought to be able to
report that Mather was delighted by his election to the Royal Society,
rather than to say gratuitously, with his most recent biographer, that he
was "giddy with delight."[47] But the differences in style and character will
remain. Although they are not my chief subject here, I do want to say a
few words about them before concluding.

Jonathan Edwards persuades me with the substance of his descriptions
of his spiritual life that he lived as intensely, with highs and lows as
exhilarating and depressing, as ever Cotton Mather did. Just imagine, for
example, being present when Edwards could not bear the thought of being
with non-Christians, or when he was overcome with loud weeping, or when
he was moved to sing at length and to proclaim God's glory. Yet, except in
the Applications of some of his revival sermons, his style expresses that
emotion with rigorous control. The intensity of his will, the compulsive
determination in his character, comes through to us in his relentless progression from one step to the next. In this character, then, many of us read
the powerful intellect in the style—in which I include the quality of the
mind, its capacity to order statements so that one seems inexorably to
follow from its predecessor, as well as the clear diction and the rational

tone. The self is expressed on the page, all right, but its intensity seems to be present almost objectively, in the form of irresistible argument.

It would be unjust to deny that Edwards was a much greater thinker than Cotton Mather, and I am convinced that the power and originality of Edwards's mind form an important part of his character. His highest thought, as in *The Nature of True Virtue*, seems to transcend self in every way except an implicit delight in the logic that he displays. Yet I believe that in the rehabilitation (or what Donald Weber calls the recovery) of Jonathan Edwards during the last half-century, one reason many commentators have overlooked some of the less attractive traits and statements that I have dredged up here is respect for Edwards as a thinker. We need to preserve more room even in our scholarly images of the past for what James Baldwin calls "the full weight and complexity of human beings." By reviewing the unattractive and attractive resemblances among Edwards, Franklin, and Mather, we go beyond asking whether Mather's defects were monstrous. We remember that character is complex and that deliberate action, and qualities that memorable people share, may be as important to defining an individual character as the emotional quirks and diary entries that make him unique, or the Oedipal impulses that move below his consciousness. Edwards, Franklin, and Mather, impelled to write voluminously and to strive ingeniously, ambitiously, resolutely for the public good or the glory of God, all lived by the word. They shared values and qualities of character that mark them as fellow American Puritans.

Notes

1. Richard Bushman, "Jonathan Edwards as Great Man: Identity, Conversion, and Leadership in the Great Awakening," *Soundings, an Interdisciplinary Journal* (1969), LII, 15–46; Elisabeth D. Dodds, *Marriage to a Difficult Man* (Philadelphia, 1971); and Patricia J. Tracy, *Jonathan Edwards, Pastor: Religion and Society in Eighteenth-Century Northampton* (New York, 1980).

2. See, for example, Perry Miller, "Benjamin Franklin—Jonathan Edwards," in *Major Writers of America*, ed. Perry Miller (New York, 1962), I, 82–98.

3. See, for example, David Levin, introduction to Cotton Mather, *Bonifacius: An Essay upon the Good* (Cambridge, Mass., 1966); Phyllis Franklin, *Show Thyself a Man: A Comparison of Benjamin Franklin and Cotton Mather* (The Hague, 1969); and Mitchell Robert Breitwieser, *Cotton Mather and Benjamin Franklin: The Price of Representative Personality* (Cambridge, England, 1984).

4. Edmund Morgan, "Heaven Can't Wait," *New York Review of Books*, May 31, 1984, p. 33.

5. Mather, *Bonifacius*, p. 13.

6. *The Diary of Cotton Mather*, ed. Worthington C. Ford (Boston, 1912), I, 234.

7. *The Autobiography of Benjamin Franklin*, ed. Leonard Labaree (New Haven, 1964), p. 44. Further citations of this edition will appear in parentheses in the text.

8. Samuel Eliot Morison, *Harvard College in the Seventeenth Century* (Cambridge, Mass., 1936) I, 82–83.

9. Kenneth Silverman, *The Life and Times of Cotton Mather* (New York, 1984), p. 255. Further citations of this work will appear in parentheses in the text.

10. Morgan, "Heaven Can't Wait," p. 34. Cf. Edmund Morgan, "The Puritan You Love to Hate," *The New York Review of Books*, January 25, 1979, pp. 31–32.

11. Cotton Mather, "Paterna," pp. 3–4. Quoted, with permission from the University of Virginia, from the manuscript in the Alderman Library.

12. See Robert Middlekauff, *The Mathers: Three Generations of Puritan Intellectuals, 1596–1728* (New York, 1971); Sacvan Bercovitch, "Cotton Mather," in *Major Writers of Early American Literature*, ed. Everett Emerson, pp. 93–149; and Richard Lovelace, *The American Pietism of Cotton Mather: Origins of American Evangelicalism* (Grand Rapids, 1979).

13. See *The Works of Jonathan Edwards: Scientific and Philosophical Writings*, ed. Wallace E. Anderson (New Haven, 1980), pp. 6–7.

14. Quoted in Alfred O. Aldridge, *Jonathan Edwards* (New York, 1964), p. 11.

15. "Farewell Sermon," in *Jonathan Edwards: Representative Selections*, ed. Clarence H. Faust and Thomas H. Johnson (New York, 1935), p. 188.

16. Quoted in Tracy, *Edwards*, p. 53.

17. *Scientific Writings*, p. 32. Cf. Edwards's draft, p. 414: "If you think it *Childish* and consider the Rules of Decorum . . . with Greatness *and Generosity to look Down Pity and Conceal* . . ."

18. "Narrative of Surprising Conversions," in Faust and Johnson, *Representative Selections*, pp. 83–84. Robert Lowell's poem "After the Surprising Conversions" paraphrases Edwards's narrative, with ironic emphasis on Satan's alleged descent among the people of Northampton.

19. *The Works of Jonathan Edwards: Apocalyptic Writings*, ed. Stephen Stein (New Haven, 1977), p. 28.

20. Ibid., pp. 120–21.

21. Quoted by Stein, ibid., p. 11.

22. See, for example, David Levin, *Cotton Mather: The Young Life of the Lord's Remembrancer, 1663–1703* (Cambridge, Mass., 1978), pp. 74–77, 90, 96–98, 113, 234–36, 271–73.

23. Perry Miller, *Jonathan Edwards* (New York, 1949); and Ola E. Winslow, *Jonathan Edwards, 1703–1758* (New York, 1940). The two positions, in some

respects antithetical to each other, are succinctly summarized in Tracy (who is of course arguing for her own position), *Edwards*, p. 183.

24. See, for example, Tracy, *Edwards*, pp. 190–92.

25. Jonathan Edwards, *Some Thoughts Concerning the Present Revival of Religion in New England*, quoted in *Apocalyptic Writings*, ed. Stein, p. 26.

26. Quoted in Tracy, *Edwards*, p. 121.

27. Ibid., p. 156.

28. Paraphrased in Tracy, *Edwards*, p. 155.

29. Here Shepard is quoting the second epistle of Paul to Timothy (3:12), in the fifth sermon ["Few are Saved"] of *The Sincere Convert*, in *America in Literature*, ed. David Levin and Theodore L. Gross (New York, 1978), I, 129.

30. Here Mather is quoting "a late French author," in *Bonifacius*, p. 10. Morgan implies that Mather himself wrote it; see Morgan, "Heaven Can't Wait," p. 34.

31. See the fifth sermon, *America in Literature*, I, 123.

32. Quoted in Morgan, "Heaven Can't Wait," p. 34.

33. Shepard, "Autobiography," in *God's Plot: The Paradoxes of Puritan Piety,* ed. Michael McGiffert (University of Massachusetts Press, 1972), pp. 44–45.

34. Quoted in Tracy, *Edwards*, p. 67.

35. Jonathan Edwards, "Spiritual Autobiography," in *America in Literature*, I, 333.

36. See Daniel B. Shea, *Spiritual Autobiography in Early America* (Princeton, 1968), pp. 206–8.

37. *America in Literature*, I, 333.

38. Edwards, "Miscellanies," no. 40, quoted in Tracy, *Edwards*, pp. 64–65.

39. Tracy, *Edwards*, p. 65. Professor Schafer has graciously shown me his transcriptions of half a dozen miscellanies about these subjects, all apparently written in 1723, including at least two passages that clearly use the first person as an illustrative allusion to "anyone" or "one." I have quoted from his transcriptions with the permission of the Beinecke Library. My thanks again to Professor Schafer.

40. See Levin, *Cotton Mather*, pp. 62–63.

41. Mather, *Diary*, I, 43.

42. Ibid.

43. Melvin H. Buxbaum, *Benjamin Franklin and the Zealous Presbyterians* (University Park, Penn., 1975); Bernard Bailyn, *The Ordeal of Thomas Hutchinson* (Cambridge, Mass., 1974).

44. D. H. Lawrence, *Studies in Classic American Literature* (New York, 1923), pp. 12–13.

45. Levin, *Cotton Mather*, p. 37.

46. Franklin, *Autobiography*, p. 70.

47. Silverman, *Life and Times*, p. 254.

4

The Recovery
of Jonathan Edwards

DONALD WEBER

Writing to the aged Benjamin Trumbull in 1818, the Reverend Sereno Edwards Dwight approached the distinguished historian—one of "the few remaining monuments of an earlier age," Dwight deferentially styled him—for information concerning what in 1829 would appear as *The Life of President Edwards*, a mammoth, monumental chronicle and compilation of the life and times of its famous subject, Dwight's great-grandfather. The biographer was just launching his project and, much like current oral historians, Dwight needed to pump his witness with various questions, both factual and impressionistic, that might aid in the process of reconstruction: "Did you ever see Pres. Edwards? . . . Were you ever in conversation with him? . . . Did you ever hear him preach? . . . What was the *feeling of the public* at the time about his dismission? . . . Was his character as high while he was living as it has been since[?]" (italics in original).[1]

Thanks to the work of a host of devoted Edwards scholars, many of whom have written essays for this volume, we have learned new things about Edwards the preacher, the philosopher, the theologian, the ethicist, the religious psychologist. For me, Edwards is most intriguing as a *figure* in cultural history: What lines of intellectual influence radiate out from the center(s) of his thought? Can we speak, in our own time, as did the late eighteenth and nineteenth-century commentators, of an Edwardsian legacy in theology, philosophy, history, and literary imagination? I am concerned here with the recovery, or more accurately, with the appropriation of Jonathan Edwards. In Mark Noll's words, Edwards became "a gigantic object of curious awe to later generations,"[2] inspiring fear and fascination, exerting a cultural weight against which important intellectuals labored to free themselves.

I want to outline this process by examining what might be called four Edwardsian moments: the filial conscience of Samuel Hopkins; the rhetorical reappropriation of Jonathan Edwards, Jr.; the anguished execration of Oliver Wendell Holmes; and the example of Edwards for H. Richard Niebuhr. (Note: these are representative junctures in a cultural history which includes the Unitarian-Orthodox debate, the controversy over "new measures" revivalism, the legacy of Calvinism to American literature, the moment of neo-orthodoxy, and so on.) To establish the context, let me begin with the question of Edwards's contemporary reputation.

According to the findings and arguments of recent scholarship, it seems clear that, well before Hawthorne's famous lament, Edwards was perhaps himself the obscurest man of (theological) letters in America. If asked to comment, he might have added, "most alienated" to the confession as well. Indeed, to judge from the work of Patricia Tracy and Gregory Nobles, on the eve of his notorious expulsion from Northampton Edwards was an "outcast" from both his own congregation and from his ministerial brethren in Hampshire County. In Nobles's view Edwards was "cut off" from his peers and "could expect little or no support from his colleagues."[3] For Tracy, Edwards "never escaped the anachronistic grip of the patriarchal model"; he struggled in vain within the shadowy clutch of grandfather Stoddard. As a result Edwards fell victim to an "emergent class of secular leaders," defeated by an insurgent modernity looming by the mid-eighteenth century.[4] Ironically, of course, the patterns of minister-congregation discord and religious/political fractiousness that doomed Edwards in Northampton were to be far more common *later* in the century. As Donald Scott has shown, Edwards's ministerial generation was remarkably long-lived, often remaining in country pulpits for over fifty harmonious years.[5] Despite his "backward" ideological move in church admissions policy, Edwards's failed power gambit and eventual fall forecasts the *future* of church-pastor relations. Here Perry Miller intuited correctly. In removing (or being removed) to Stockbridge Edwards was, sadly, ahead of the times.

The portrait of alienation is confirmed, we should note, in contemporaneous accounts as well. "Northampton in miserable circumstances," Samuel Hopkins lamented in his "Diary" for April, 1750—at the threshold of confrontation; Edwards's "friends but few & almost discouraged."[6] To the guardians, events were discouraging indeed; to Edwards himself, his plight reflected not merely a local "controversy" between his

theological principles and apostate Northamptom but a general debate
"between me and a great part of New England."[7] Writing to Edwards's
Boston literary agent, Thomas Foxcroft, Joseph Bellamy set forth his
own view of Edwards's design in returning to pre-Stoddardean policies in
a letter that lets us observe the lingering embers of religious debate that
had not yet cooled in the afterflow of the Great Awakening:

> Mr. Edwards has lately sent a piece to the press upon a subject that begins
> to be much discoursed in this country. Mr. *Stoddard's* being against it and
> the *Separates* for it will tend mightily to prejudice many against it as *NEW*
> and *HETERODOX* . . . I am of the opinion that when the book comes out,
> the people will generally be brought over and before all is done I guess it
> will make its way thru the country, and do much towards recovering of it to
> the principles of its first settlers.

Bellamy then turns to matters of the religious marketplace, revealing a
series of striking disclosures about Edwards's popularity. Of the *Humble
Attempt* (1747) he says: "To this day I believe not half the country have
even so much as heard of Mr. Edwards piece [*sic*] upon the Scotland
Concert"; of *Religious Affections* (1746): "As to Mr. Edwards excellent
treatise upon religious affections, I hear that there are yet many books
not sold"; of the work in progress, published as *Qualifications for Communion* (1749): "There is already appeared five men who will take off 250
books if need be, rather than that it shall [be] dropt."[8] Fifty copies! Such
were the displays of intellectual and personal devotion in another age. No
wonder Edwards confessed to his Scottish correspondent, John Erskine,
from the wilderness of Stockbridge: "I am fond of knowing how things
are going on in the learned world." (Dwight, latter-day guardian that he
was, substituted "literary" for "learned" in *The Life*).[9]

The point is that the legendary image of Edwards immersed in a self-
enclosed world of high-level theology, removed from more mundane
concerns—though challenged by Stephen Stein's edition of the apocalyptic writings and my own readings in the sermons—may have, as do all
caricatures, some truth to it. After noting the compositional shift in
Edwards's sermonic habits, from narrative to fragment, Wilson Kimnach
asserts that "Gradually . . . subconsciously . . . unquestionably, Edwards
was withdrawing from Northampton."[10] His closest allies, already self-
authorized, self-appointed defenders of the faith, sensed that their master
needed to become more accessible. Writing to Hopkins in 1756, Bellamy,
with an eye on the theological marketplace, suggested a kind of popular
guide to Edwards, an "Edwards for beginners," to disseminate his basic

ideas. "I have had it in my mind," Bellamy explained, "to propose to correspond with you in a regular manner. Thus—let 2 or 300 questions be stated. You write on one, I on another, for the press, to assist young students in the study of Divinity—Mr. Edwards Books will be the better understood—at present the learned do not understand him—I imagine you and I could set some points in a more familiar light."[11] (Of course Bellamy's *True Religion Delineated* eventually served precisely this function, as H. B. Stowe's grandmother in *Oldtown Folks* tells us.)

But the most fascinating character among eighteenth-century guardians is Samuel Hopkins, whose relentless, indefatigable efforts to protect the legacy began even before the family requested that he preserve the manuscripts and prepare the official "life."

Most of us know Hopkins as Edwards's first biographer and prime architect of the New Divinity, a figure whose theological vision, as Joseph Conforti and William Breitenbach have shown, was no otherworldly retreat from social realities but rather a system of ideas that both challenged and legitimated the dominant ideology of protocapitalist America. We know Hopkins as well from his fervent hankerings after the millennium, along with his heroic agitating for the abolition of slavery. The portrait I wish to sketch is less well known—that of Hopkins the attentive keeper of the flame; a watchman who exerted his self-styled role as guardian for over fifty years.

When the young Hopkins journeyed to Northampton in the winter of 1741, soon after hearing Edwards deliver the famous Yale commencement address on the "distinguishing marks," he was quick to perceive a disjunction between the town's reputation as a city of "famed awakenings" and his own immediate observations. Rather than arrive late and unexpected at the Edwards household, he lodged with a neighboring family who did "not savour spiritual things so well as I thought Northampton people did." The next day he listened to a local preacher "whose discourse was not such as I expected to hear at Northampton which made me afraid that I should miss of my expectations in coming to Northampton."[12] Hopkins's expectations were soon met in the intellectual charisma with which Edwards seems to have enveloped his zealous, judgmental acolyte. Its power persisted, variously reflected from Hopkins's behind-the-scene maneuverings to help Edwards settle in the Indian pastorate, to an unsent letter to Jonathan Mayhew ridiculing the liberal Boston minister's notion of "liberty" and recommending *Freedom of the Will* as proper doctrine,[13] through the famous 1765 biography and beyond. Instead of narrating the full story of Hopkins's continuing efforts of recovery, I would like to highlight two moments that suggest something of the historical pressure the figure of Edwards exerted upon its foremost guardian.

Edwards departed for Princeton in January 1758, leaving Hopkins with many of the now famous manuscripts resting on that curious, many-sided desk (which by the way, may still be viewed, in good condition, at the Stockbridge Library). After Edwards's death in March it was left to Hopkins to see through the press the posthumous treatise on *Original Sin*, which appeared late that year prefaced with a brief, biographical sketch of its author. Of that unexpected appreciation Hopkins reacted in a tone of annoyance, perhaps even anger:

> I hear that Mr. Edwards life & character is affixed to his book on original sin. I am sorry to hear it, for two Reasons. *First*, I am informed that several mistakes are made. *Secondly*, there is a design to publish his life in a more full and correct manner than can be done by any one in Boston, without a better knowledge of that great man's character and conduct than can be expected to be had in Boston without further information: together with some *private writings* of his, which are judged well worthy the sight of the Public. If you should be in Boston timely enough to get it suppressed by your influence, I should look upon it a favour. It was not expected, I believe, that any Gentleman in Boston would have attempted *This* without any desire from the relatives.[14]

Hopkins's bristling response recalls the geographic tensions that lingered residually in the wake of the Great Awakening. Edwards could not be recovered by anyone "in Boston," as Hopkins's troubled refrain sputters out; the unsanctioned sketch obviously subverted his office as literary custodian, usurped his identity as defender of the faith.[15] There isn't enough space to develop fully the intriguing contexts and problems of attribution and content in the preface; the point is that, in Hopkins's imagination at least, the act of *representing* Edwards was fraught with issues personal, geographic, and ideological.[16]

It was personal, too, when in 1802 the 81-year-old patriarch penned, on the spur of the moment, it seems, a concerned letter to Vice President Aaron Burr on a delicate matter of family history. "It is reported, and it is believed by a number," Hopkins gently began, "that you do not believe in divine revelation and discard Christianity. . . ." Invoking Burr's celebrated genealogy, as if to reinsert the infidel back into some providential pattern, Hopkins spoke on behalf of the ancestral shades: "It would be very grievous to me, and I know it would be inexpressibly so to your pious and worthy ancestors . . . to know that one of their posterity, for whom they had so many prayers . . . [who] is possessed of such great and distinguished natural powers of mind, was an infidel . . . and dying so, will be inconceivably miserable forever." This poignant letter may be read as Hopkins's last act of filial piety—his final effort to awaken conviction in an apostate son who denied tradition and figured the end of the Edwardsian line. What was Hopkins's "authority" for indirectly preaching to the vice president (Hopkins opens the letter, "You will probably be surprised ['though it is hoped not offended'].") Apologizing for his presumption, he cites "the intimate acquaintance and friendship which subsisted between me and your grandfather."[17] Long before Stowe translated the spiritual history of New England into the creative achievements of *The Minister's Wooing* and *Oldtown Folks*—in each novel the villain is a fictional type of Burr or Burr himself—Hopkins donned for the last time the Edwardsian mantle to recover a brilliant son who tragically swerved from the original piety of the father. Thus does life *anticipate* art.

The case of Edwards's hereditary son, Jonathan, Jr., is the subject of the next episode of recovery. (Note: The biography of the youngest son, Pierpont, is too hazy and elusive for extended treatment here. Intriguingly, though, he offers perhaps the clearest illustration of Alan Heimert's still provocative argument about Edwardsian Calvinism and Jeffersonian ideology. A Democratic-Republican lawyer from Connecticut, Pierpont lobbied in 1792 against the current vice president, claiming that "a too strong tendency to aristocracy is a trait in Mr. Adams's character." Accordingly, as an ardent "friend of true republican liberty," he urged his correspondent to watch for and "guard against the first advances of tyranny." After the election of 1800, Pierpont redelivered Jefferson's inaugural address to a local Connecticut audience.)[18] As to the career of Edwards, Jr., both nineteenth century and modern commentators have, up till now, had little to celebrate. At the threshold of his ministry, in 1769, William Gordon encouraged Bellamy that among those would-be ministers enrolled in his school of the prophets, the younger Edwards "may give you hope . . . I wish [him] a double portion of his father's spirit and abilities."[19] The son, alas, inherited neither; instead, his biography is a model of the New Divinity men as scathingly limned by Ezra Stiles: a tale of pastor-congregation conflict, separation, and exile. True to the rigors of the clerical ideal, Edwards accepted the call to White Haven (in New Haven) only after the church members revoked their earlier advocacy of the Half-Way Convenant. He was dismissed in 1795, after he refused to soften his doctrinal stand on public confession in the face of dwindling church membership. From all accounts, then, the portrait of the younger Edwards is that of an aloof, abstract "Edwardsian" theologian seemingly impervious to the tremors and shocks that jolted late eighteenth-century America.[20]

My purpose is not so much to rescue Edwards, Jr. from caricature; rather, I want to offer a way to describe the Edwardsian legacy to revolutionary America through the example of the son. Nevertheless, the testament of Edwards, Jr.'s pulpit during the Revolution belies the stereotype of New Divinity otherworldliness; indeed, he preached on virtually every major event, battle, and issue of the war in *precisely* the mode employed by republican preachers (as Nathan Hatch has so compellingly demonstrated):[21] a fast-day sermon on the eve of the first continental congress (1774) that equates the British parliament with the whore of Babylon; a Thanksgiving sermon (from the I Samuel text on the Ebenezer stone, the monument to history that inspired Mather's *Magnalia*) that recounts English monarchical history and applies it to current events; a 1775 fast day sermon that explores the figure of Solomon, whose "observations and experiences in political affairs" are seasonable in times of oppression; a fast after the Battle of Lexington, (inspired by the famous question from Isaiah, "Watchman, what of the night?") that builds on apocalyptic fear—the "night cometh on us in this land"—and ends on a plea for a revival to disperse the "very dull, dead time." "How few awakened? engineering? converted? reformed?" Edwards hurriedly asks towards the close. There are sermons to militia companies and on military victories—St Johnsbury (1775), Burgoyne (1777), Cornwallis (1781)—as well as a sermon preached "when President Washington was in New Haven and present at the delivery" (1789) on, fittingly, fathers and sons.[22]

The first observation to be made is that these revolutionary sermons reveal an Edwardsian minister *immersed* in the times, obsessed (as were all Protestant clergymen) by the events and crises of politics and history. They clearly stand apart from the weekly pattern of pastoral and religious topics, as if the history being enacted had shaken Edwards loose from the atemporal sequence of expounding the morphology of conversion into a world of politics, military maneuvers, and libertarian discourse, which in effect determined the biblical text to be applied to the bewildering whirl of history itself.

I offer this redactive litany to argue that the context for Edwards, Jr.'s revolutionary rhetoric displays not only the idiomatic grafting of Puritan formulae onto Whig ideology (as noted by Hatch) but his immersion in the writings of his father as well—a "seasonable" application of father's ideas for the times. We know that with Hopkins, Edwards, Jr. was the key figure in recovering his father's literary corpus, especially in transcribing and editing the long-awaited *History of the Work of Redemption* for publication in Scotland, in 1774.[23] Writing to Benjamin Trumbull in the summer of 1772, Edwards explained his lack of pulpit etiquette by citing the consuming attention of "Edwardsian" matters: "I have not exchanged with anybody since the Election nor within some time before. I am pretty much hurried in transcribing the work of my father."[24] He did more than simply transcribe, however. The son translated his experience of the Revolution using the grammar provided by the *Work of Redemption.*

Edwards senior, we should note in this respect, interpreted political events in language that, in a later period, would be characteristic of the protestant clergy in general. Exhorting his Northampton congregation in support of the 1746 expedition to Canada, Edwards speaks of God's armies as "not only . . . the instruments of such good to their land and nation but . . . the instruments of the overthrow of a considerable part of mystic Bab[ylon]." Antichrist, in Edwards's scenario, had a foothold in North America, and he viewed the Canadian campaign as a holy effort in the "quelling down [of] the reign of Satan" and the "setting up [the] kingdom of Christ in America." Pursuing a theme he had developed privately in *Apocalyptic Notebooks* (where by recording world events Edwards noted the progress of secular history as forecasts of the penultimate battle with Satan's kingdom) Edwards asserted that these victories "will weaken the kingdom of France, the greatest power that supports antichrist."[25] Edwards's method of interpretation drew from his own model of historical progress, the *History of the Work of Redemption,* which he preached as a sermon series in 1739 and worked on with renewed intensity at the end of his life. A Thanksgiving sermon of 1745 (delivered again in 1757) builds on Edwards's theory of historical "pulsations"—or, as he describes the process in the manuscript notebooks for the *Work of Redemption*: "In each period there has been a gradual increase and diminution, like the waxing and waning of the moon"—as the preacher recalls how God's "wonderful and remarkable providences delivered the nation [in this case Edwards is reviewing the history of England, a frequent subject of the revolutionary pulpit] from the Popish yoke and blessed it with the light of the Reformation." Yet, as every clergyman knew—in 1745 and 1775—England fell. "The nation began very much to depart from the purity of doctrine," Edwards reminded his audience, and this apostasy propelled a saving remnant to settle a new world.[26]

Thus the manuscript notebooks for the envisioned *Work of Redemption* reveal that a good measure of Edwards's antiquarian fascination with cataloguing those "Episodes in the history of the church" (including a detailed chronology of papal reigns) involved the place of New England in the scheme of redemptive history. He even planned sections "concerning the settlement of New England as the more special introduction of the gospel in America." As late as the 1750's, then, Edwards continued to mark the origins of America "as one great thing done to prepare the way" for the millennium.[27]

Significantly, Edwards, Jr. assembled, transcribed, and edited the *Redemption* papers through the early 1770's and the influence of his father's historical vision is unmistakable. A Thanksgiving sermon for November 1774 reviews the reign of English kings with special application to colonial affairs. The "tyranny" of Charles I looks forward to that of the current British; later, James II "introduced popery" to "bring all under absolute tyranny," yet God "stirred up the nation . . . to seek relief"; now however, "the country [is] in great measure asleep," but God "*once* excited the mind of the people remarkable united."[28] (my emphasis). Over and again, patriot preachers called for unity in the face of British oppression—indeed, the fear of collective enslavement was one psychic spur for the Revolution's leveling effect on its participants, both in doctrine and temperament. Keeping the faith, Edwards the younger concluded his Thanksgiving sermon in the tone of the *Work of Redemption* with a clear allusion to the Revival itself, reminding his listeners of God's help in preserving the gospel "in remarkable times in your remembrance."[29]

Still more telling, however, is the persistence of revivalist rhetoric itself. "The [political] links between the revival and the American Revolution" may be "virtually nonexistent," according to Jon Butler's recent revisionary attack on the historical reality of the Great Awakening, but the question of influence cannot be so summarily dismissed in light of the testimony of the Revolution's participants themselves.[30] Through the example of Edwards, Jr. we may observe how the rhetoric of the Awakening was made to fit a new social and political reality. A military sermon of 1775 invokes the famous revival notion of the "distinguishing marks" of the spirit (his father's subject at Yale in 1741 and in an early version of *Religious Affections*). Contrasting true patriots with those "who appear zealous in their country's cause, but only from private selfish motives . . . who are not to be perfectly distinguished by any general marks," Edwards "wish[ed] to see every true son of liberty as much distinguished by the purity of his life and manner as by his wise zeal in the cause of his country."[31]

The juxtaposition of "distinguishing marks" with "sons of liberty" dramatizes the dynamic whereby republican rhetoric blurred with that of religious, effecting an interchange of ideological and affective meanings—what symbolic anthropologists call the ritual process. From this perspective, we might say that the language of the revolutionary pulpit had a "multi-vocal" dimension; an ability to mediate the claims of residual Puritan vocabularies and emerging political discourse to forge an enabling rhetoric that helped people act in history. To detail that process, however, would swerve me from my appointment with Mr. Holmes. For now, let me suggest that the much debated links between the Awakening and the Revolution may reside, not in the realm of abstract theology or political stances, but rather on the level of rhetoric itself.[32]

The next episode in this chronicle of Edwards's impact on American cultural history concerns not recovery and defense but repulsion and attack. To many nineteenth-century writers—especially George Bancroft, Harriet Beecher Stowe, and Oliver Wendell Holmes—Edwards figured the Puritan legacy to their own time: an inheritance which, depending on intellectual outlook and temperament, was either baneful or beneficent. Bancroft, for example, hailed Edwards as his greatest precursor and longed to compose a full-scale biography as (perhaps) an act of cultural rededication. Stowe, on the other hand, traced back to Edwards "the true tragedy of New England life," equating her region's spiritual decline to the "constant wrestling . . . with infinite problems" that, she believed, characterized the debilitating style of Edwardsian theology.[33] The example of Holmes offers yet another telling moment of rebuke, for as he labored against the weight of his own Calvinist father, the generational struggle took the form of a battle with Jonathan Edwards. "This spectre of Calvinism," as Barrett Wendell understood long ago, came to possess the Unitarian doctor, searing its tyrannical spirit "into his brain."[34] Only a metaphorical bloodletting, "driving my inherited Connecticut theology out of me at every pore," could work the personal catharsis that Holmes sought—deliverance from both "the doctrinal boiler at Andover and the rational ice chest at Cambridge."[35] In temperament, Holmes was, I suppose, given to coolness; but on the subject of Jonathan Edwards he heated up, dropping his usual witty, bantering style (as in the memorable characterization, "dear old smattering, chattering, would-be college President Cotton Mather")[36] for the rancorous intensity that marks his encounter with Edwards. The specter of Northampton haunted Holmes ("He had for years," reports Holmes's first biographer, "been interested in that terrible theologian")[37] but, nineteenth-century ghostbuster that he was, he contained Edwards's leering spirit through sheer effort of will and reason.

Holmes grew up within a family psychically split between his father's strict Calvinism and his mother's milder Unitarian faith. (This duality is neatly limned in his parents' letters while Wendell boarded at Andover: the mother usually opens with a gentle, hovering concern for the son's personal well-being; then the father's voice/handwriting takes over, reminding of duties [spiritual and secular], expectations, and the dread of academic failure.)[38] In his memoirs Holmes speaks of the household theology as "mere jargon in my ears" and, with sadness, looks back on the insidious effects of early exposure to the meaningless language of threats and retribution: "No child can overcome these early impressions without doing violence to the whole mental and moral machinery of his being. He may conquer them in after years, but the wrenches and strains which his victory has cost him leave him a cripple as compared with a child trained in sound and reasonable beliefs."[39] Holmes's personal mode of overcoming amounted to a displacement from Abiel to Jonathan; in effect, the father's theology could be more "safely" impugned in the originating shape of the Calvinist father himself.

It is important to recall, in this respect, that Abiel's career ended in controversy and (in Wendell's eyes) embarrassment. The popular annalist of American history, defender of "this American Israel," and memoirist who exhorted the sons to "imbibe [the] spirit and follow [the] example" of the Pilgrim fathers, was expelled from his Cambridge church in a doctrinal dispute with its more liberal members.[40] Rejecting the offer to have the father's life inscribed for posterity (here Holmes consciously avoided the Protestant ritual of ministerial hagiography) the son bitterly recounts his father's fate: "He was sacrificed," Holmes explains; "the two great parties which divided our community crowded against him each from his own side—one pressing upon his Calvinist faith, the other upon his liberal principles." In retrospect, there was little "in his theological career on which I can dwell with pleasure." Though Abiel's "last years were tranquil," the son confesses, "we may try to forget those scenes in which, alas, he suffered."[41]

The return of the repressed would take various forms in "The Moral Bully" and "The Deacon's Masterpiece" (poems marked, as Thomas Wortham reminds us, by a "satirical vigor" and "intensity rarely found . . . in Holmes' other verse");[42] in *Elsie Venner* (one of the so-called "medicated" novels, whose plot undermines the Calvinist notion of inherited guilt); and in the 1880 essay on Jonathan Edwards. Briefly, the Edwards essay is Holmes's own version of the "moral argument against Calvinism." Despite his admiration "for a man who seems to have been anointed from birth," he declares that Edwards's "unwholesome sort of rhetoric . . . led . . . into the use of expressions . . . fitted to disturb the feelings of all persons of common sensibility."[43] Reworking theories of human nature developed from the earlier "Chambered Nautilus," Holmes attacks Edwards's metaphysics for their "disorganizing conceptions," their disrupting "forces" that subvert the *laws of human nature*," thus injuring the "texture of the mind." "The will," he announces in direct rebuttal, is "determined by infinitely varied conditions of the individual."[44] Rather than burying us too deeply beneath Holmes's private philosophy, let me observe that the Edwards essay is more suggestive if read not only as a "projected" assault on the father's religion but also as an indirect account of Abiel's pastoral plight. When Holmes mercilessly derides the "fossil theology" left among the dinosaur-like footprints "along the shores of the Connecticut" we may infer a dual reference, to Edwards and to Abiel's New Haven lineage. And when the son speaks, in a more compassionate tone, of the tragedy of Edwards's expulsion—he "saw the strongholds of his position thwarted by the gradual approach and the actual invasion of later teachings and practices"—we sense the pathos of the father's victimization as well.[45]

In short, Holmes's Edwards is a figure who could be safely reviled by an apostate son self-conscious of his generational burden. "As for the children of clergymen," Holmes observes in "The Pulpit and the Pew," "the presumption is that they will adhere to the general belief professed by their fathers." Defending his own filial break, Holmes offers a poignant rejoinder to those who would charge him with tarnishing the memory of the Pilgrims: "It is an ill-bred and indecent thing to fling a man's father's creed in his face, as if he had broken the fifth commandment in thinking for himself in the light of a new generation."[46]

Of course further episodes could be detailed in this brief cultural history of recovery: the controversy Holmes ignited among the nineteenth-century guardians when, at the end of the Edwards essay, he called for the publication of an Edwards manuscript believed (or so thought Horace Bushnell) to portray him in a softer, more liberal light; the web of legal and familial entanglements among the relatives over possession of the Edwards papers (Professor Thomas Schafer unravels this story in the introduction to his forthcoming edition of the "Miscellanies"); the bicentennial celebrations of 1903, which sought to reinsert Edwards into American history; the stature of Edwards in the recovery of American literature from Wendell to Spiller; Edwards and the rehabilitation of the Puritan tradition, which began, as Henry May taught us long ago, in the 1930s.[47]

Let me conclude, however, with the example of H. Richard Niebuhr, whose "life work," according to Sydney Ahlstrom, amounted to a "daring exploit . . . to rescue Jonathan Edwards from the Puritan dungeon in which secular ignorance and liberal Protestantism had left him."[48] Ahlstrom may have overstated the dramatic aspect of Niebuhr's encounter with Edwards; after all, Niebuhr left no full-scale study of Edwards's theology or metaphysics. Still, "Edwards became one of the most influential figures in Christendom for my father,"[49] reports Dr. Richard R. Niebuhr, and we may begin to gauge the "Edwardsian" dimension of H. Richard Niebuhr's thought if we view his career as a sustained effort to expose the easy pieties and soft-minded anthropology of the social gospel. In his self-styled role as social critic, demanding that his more idealistic brethren acknowledge their shared human "lostness," Niebuhr recognized in Edwards a spiritual ancestor whose voice resonated with the compelling weight of the doctrine of divine sovereignty and the heart-quickening strains of revival.

The Edwardsian note was sounded, albeit indirectly, as early as 1932, in a brief essay titled "Faith, Works, and Social Salvation." Writing amidst "these days of disillusionment and uncertainty"—it is clear, from this perspective, how neo-orthodoxy was a response to psychic and historical disjunction, a sense that events (in the 30s) were spiraling out of control—Niebuhr took liberalism to task for its moral inadequacies, "its misplaced confidence . . . its trust in human self-interest." Rather than relying on human reason as salvific agent, Niebuhr looked to "a more adequate expression" of religious faith, and named it "democracy." "Perhaps democracy," Niebuhr argued in 1932, as "a political expression of faith in the God of history and suspicious of all rationalistic, expert attempts to guide life in pre-arranged grooves, can take on other forms of the form of liberalism." In many ways echoing (and anticipating) Perry Miller's diatribe against the "mechanist" era of the 40s and 50s,[50] H. Richard Niebuhr sought a vision of democracy through an appeal to its "divine agency," manifest politically "in the organic growing together of individuals and societies." This redemptive vision, in turn, offered a way out of current disillusionment, for these faith seekers, as opposed to the all too confident "planners and rationalizers," labored under a still yet unfulfilled prophetic vision of the future, so entrusted "because it is God's end." Thus democracy provides a "redemption by faith" long after the "tired radicals" of the liberal ethos have become "wearied and faint"—after they have "given up the struggle."[51]

Although the Edwardsian aspect is not invoked directly in this early neo-orthodox manifesto, from the perspective of Niebuhr's later writing, especially his very influential *Kingdom of God in America*, it seems clear that the equation of democracy and faith grew out of his own encounter with (to borrow Perry Miller's famous phrase) "the meaning of America." In 1932 Niebuhr could speak of the "road" to the "unity" of "religious democracy" as a journey through "suffering, forgiveness, repentance, restitution."[52] By 1937 he would have appended "revival" as a key element in that spiritual morphology, for in *Kingdom of God* Niebuhr saw himself as a kind of "Jonathan Edwards '*redivivus*,'" reworking, or, better, continuing Edwards's vision of American history "down to our own time." In the process Niebuhr blurred the distinctions between theology and history—"the theology has grown out of the history as much as the history has grown out of the theology," he acknowledged in the preface—and sought to discover the design within American faith-keeping, "the unity beneath the design of American religion."[53]

To seek the pattern within is Niebuhr's project in the *Kingdom of God*; in effect, Niebuhr explained the course of American history to an audience in need of comforting narratives during an era of moral, religious, and economic depression. Of course, from the perspective of modern scholarship Niebuhr's approach appears perhaps too intrinsic; he remains *within* his subject, telling his story too much through the eyes of the historical actors themselves. Still *Kingdom of God* is important, both for its contribution to American religious history and as an *expression* of that history—a work that joined in 1930s recovery of the Puritan legacy and the figure of Jonathan Edwards. And if in 1937 Niebuhr discovered a central motif in the pattern of American culture, it was the thread of revivalism, of awakening, that issued in the triumph of American democracy.

The Great Awakening, in Niebuhr's view, became a kind of cultural touchstone; an originating moment; a "new beginning." The revival was an "awakening to national self-consciousness," he declared in *Kingdom of God*; "it was our national conversion." Edwards, in this respect, became the heroic figure in a drama of national origins, the spokesman for historic Christian doctrines whose relevance and efficacy the Awakening helped to restore. Moreover, the Awakening worked toward a reconciliation between biblical doctrine and the testament of personal experience, rejoining components of Christian life that had been in dialectic opposition since the Reformation. "Scripture without experience is empty," Niebuhr announced in an updated version of a famous passage from *Religious Affections*, "but experience without Scripture is blind." Finally, Edwards and the Awakening ushered in what Niebuhr called "the growth of hope." "Intensely conscious of the great gap which exists between human performance and divine demand . . . between the actuality and the potentiality of human *life*," Edwards "strained" to realize the redemptive moment, to offer a hopeful vision of "the impending future revealed . . . [within] the actual crisis in the present." At this turning point in the religious culture of America (in the 1740s), Edwards "broke the fetters of petrified Puritanism [read: liberalism] and restored dynamic to the Christian church."[54] If by 1960 H. Richard Niebuhr acknowledged an affinity to "Calvin and Jonathan Edwards," that identification issued from a shared desire to break loose from an encrusted, rationalizing theology and (in the process) to revive an energizing spirit to his own time of religious conformity and disillusionment.

By the 1950s, H. Richard Niebuhr would qualify his earlier judgment of the Great Awakening, but not his enthusiasm for the figure of Jonathan Edwards. In the introduction to the Edwards portion of the anthology, *Christian Ethics*, the Revival now had "its bright and its dark sides"; it still remained seminal for "the rise of the democratic spirit" in America, but its excesses led to "despondency," the "undisciplined enthusiasm" of lay preachers, and the tragic blurring of "fanaticism with faith." Edwards, the Awakening's "chief critic and chief defender," emerges as a neo-orthodox precursor, "radically realistic"—Niebuhr's epithet rings with the rhetoric of the 1930s "crisis theology"—rebuking his congregation for its saccharine theology. "What was wrong with believers and unbelievers" in Edwards's age, Niebuhr wrote in 1955, in a sentence inflected with the characteristic Niebuhrian rhythm and tone, "was that they had little ideas about a little God."[55]

Niebuhr's fullest treatment of Edwards, however, remains in manuscript, as a draft of his 1958 speech commemorating the two hundredth anniversary of Edwards's death preached before the First Church of Christ in Northampton.[56] The talk is remarkable, not so much for its effort to recover Edwards from the prevailing "judgment" in theological, literary, and academic circles—Perry Miller and others had, by the mid-50s, already revised that portrait—but rather for the striking affinities between the oration's subject and its orator. Indeed, Niebuhr's "The Anachronism of Jonathan Edwards" might be called his own version of "Sinners in the Hands of an Angry God."

Of course Niebuhr did not preach hellfire and brimstone to his Norhampton auditors in 1958; he did, however, strive to reveal Edwards's contemporaneous relevance despite the deaf ears and hard hearts he would have encountered now. "What hearing could he gain," Niebuhr wondered, "if he stood in this pulpit today, or in any pulpit in America and spoke to us about our depravity and corruption, about our unfreedom and the determinism of our lives . . . about the awfulness of God's wrath?" "Preaching about hell," Niebuhr added, "is always resented by men of so-called liberal mind." Yet Niebuhr recognized in the figure of Edwards a religious imagination that in many ways anticipated—perhaps even prophesied—the apocalyptic anxieties of the nuclear age. By what "right [do we] honor Edwards" today, Niebuhr asked. In reply, the radically realistic preacher offered a vivid portrait of mankind after the holocaust when, "by the failure of a tiny and fragile device," a stray missile "may shoot us into the inferno." "Our feet are standing on slippery places," Niebuhr also warned in the same passage, but the more telling allusion to "Sinners" lies in the translation of the original sermon's doctrinal text, "Their foot shall slide in due time," into an apocalyptic image of man after the nuclear trigger is pulled:

> surviving souls, condemned to live, crawl about scrofulously among the radiations of insidious poison . . . on a planet unfit for habitation within which they must nevertheless inhabit.

Thus Niebuhr's Edwards is not a Parringtonian anachronism but rather a fellow neo-orthodox social critic whose visions of humanity's limits and the tendencies of historical "progress" spoke powerfully to the religious sensibility of the 1950s. History changed our minds about Edwards, Niebuhr explained; "We have seen evil . . . as he saw it, not because we desired to see it, but because it was thrust upon us."[57]

By 1960, in his autobiographical response to the *Christian Century* series, "How My Mind has Changed," Niebuhr could claim a wholesale spiritual affinity with Calvin and Edwards, figures whom Niebuhr contrasted with those liberal theologians "who *thought* they were taking history seriously" (my emphasis). Again, as in the earlier manifesto, the Edwardsian note may be observed indirectly, in the overtones which resound in Niebuhr's critical stance toward the mass revivalism of the 1950s. Surveying his own career, Niebuhr remained resolute, despite the whirl of events, to his "fundamental convictions about the sovereignty of God, the lostness of men . . . and the gift of forgiveness through faith." But the current religious stir seemed inauthentic, from Niebuhr's Edwardsian perspective. "The religious revival we are said to have had in recent years has been, so far as I can see, less a revival of faith in God and hope for glory than a revival of desire for faith and a hope for hope." In its place Niebuhr looked forward to what he called a "resymbolization" of God's "message"—a new language of faith and spirit that, like its historical antecedents, the Reformation and the Great Awakening, would issue in "pregnant words," "new words" of a divinely appointed prophetic era. The current times did not seem to augur well for such a moment of *kairos*: "unless the human spirit is revived within itself," Niebuhr warned at the end of his career, advances in space technology or cold war rapproachement would avail not; "nothing very important for mankind will happen."[58]

Still, with Edwards, Niebuhr continued to look for the design and pattern of American religious history, to listen for the transfiguring, resymbolizing power of the Word. In Edwards, Niebuhr discovered a fellow critical realist: each sought the palpable meaning of America in the *testament* of American history.

Of course, each generation reads the major figures of its cultural heritage in its own image. If Edwards seemed retrograde for Parrington in the Progressive era he emerged from Perry Miller and the Niebuhrs in the 1950s as a contemporary.[59] The act of recovery still goes on, as the various scholars from various disciplines gathered together in this volume richly demonstrate. Edwards still compels; he engages us as we seek a foothold on the slippery, multiple facets of his thought, career, and legacy. The figure of Jonathan Edwards thus continues to speak powerfully to those who listen attentively to his words in our own time.

Notes

1. S. E. Dwight to Benjamin Trumbell, 15 Dec. 1818, Yale University Library. On the same day Dwight wrote J. W. Edwards, the son of Jonathan Edwards, Jr., reporting that he had "found nothing to my purpose" upon examining "the trunk in the garret" that he had hoped would be filled with materials. (S. E. Dwight to J. W. Edwards, 15 Dec. 1818, Yale University Library.)

2. Mark A. Noll, "Moses Mather (Old Calvinist) and the Evolution of Edwardseanism," *Church History* 49 (1980), 285. The context of Noll's phrase is significantly different from my own sense of Edwards's legacy: "The possibility must exist that Edwards and his reconstruction of Calvinism were [*sic*] more than a gigantic object of curious awe to later generations—condemned to the intellectual insignificance of those who have proved themselves unfit for the American environment by failing to survive."

3. Gregory H. Nobles, *Division Throughout the Whole: Politics and Society in Hampshire County, Massachusetts, 1740–1775* (New York and London, 1983), 72, 67.

4. Patricia J. Tracy, *Jonathan Edwards, Pastor: Religion and Society in Eighteenth-Century Northampton* (New York, 1980), 192. I treat Tracy more fully in "The Figure of Jonathan Edwards," *American Quarterly* 35 (1983), 556–64.

5. Cf. Donald M. Scott, *From Office to Profession: The New England Ministry, 1750–1850* (Philadelphia, 1978), chap. 1, especially pp. 3–4.

6. Samuel Hopkins, "A Journal or Diary," 2 April 1750, Gratz Collection, Historical Society of Pennsylvania (HSP).

7. Jonathan Edwards to Thomas Gillespie, 2 April 1750, Trask Library, Andover-Newton Theological School (ANTS).

8. Joseph Bellamy to Thomas Foxcroft, 6 May 1749, Houghton Library, Harvard University. Foxcroft's emendation.

9. Jonathan Edwards to John Erskine, 7 July 1752, Trask Library, ANTS. Dwight's purposeful misquoting may be found in *The Life of President Edwards* (New York, 1829), p. 499.

10. Wilson H. Kimnach, "The Literary Techniques of Jonathan Edwards," Ph.D. Diss., University of Pennsylvania, 1971, p. 181.

11. Joseph Bellamy to Samuel Hopkins, 30 Jan. 1756, Gratz Coll., HSP. From manuscript correspondence it seems clear that Bellamy was the acknowledged repository of Edwards's writings. "I have not yet read Mr. Edwards books on the affections," confessed Nathaniel Hazard to Bellamy, "or have I read any of his on original sin; you told me you could let me have some of them; I should be glad of Half a Dozen for my self & friends." Nathaniel Hazard to Joseph Bellamy, 7 April 1760, Bellamy Papers, Hartford Seminary (HS). Before Hopkins's 1765 *Life* appeared, Bellamy offered to edit a collection of miscellanies: "a volume of Miscellanies out of Mr. Edwards would sell better than any thing—had I liberty & should I have health, I should be willing to collect & prepare for the press such a volume." Bellamy to Hopkins, 11 Jan. 1764, Bellamy Papers, Yale University Library.

12. Samuel Hopkins, "A Journal," p. 15, Gratz Coll., HSP.

13. Cf. Hopkins's "A Journal or Diary," passim; Samuel Hopkins to Jonathan Mayhew (never sent), [1754?], Bellamy Papers, HS.

14. Samuel Hopkins to Gideon Hawley, 19 Sept. 1758, Bellamy Papers, HS. Hopkins's concern was echoed by Foxcroft in a letter to Bellamy: "Mr. Edwards's book is at last got thro the press, and is in binding, as fast as possible. I want to know what you are proposing to do about his MSS and the memoirs of his life. It won't do to put him out with the very defective preface to this book." Thomas Foxcroft to Joseph Bellamy, 23 Sept. 1758, Gratz Coll., HSP.

15. In his *Memoir of Hopkins* (Boston, 1852), p. 216, the nineteenth century-guardian E. A. Park reinforced this view: *Original Sin* was "the first printed volume for which Mr. Hopkins felt any responsibility" (p. 215). Park also describes Hopkins's frustration in offering Edwards to the public: "After several . . . works of Edwards for the press, the disinhearted editor became satisfied that they would not be sold, and he therefore turned his mind to other projects" (p. 219). Park also quotes a letter from Hopkins, 24 March 1762, about the sales of the proposed volume containing *The Life* and a selection of sermons: "The Printer is waiting for subscriptions, very few of which come in" (p. 217).

16. I treat the subject more fully in "The Image of Jonathan Edwards in American Culture," Ph.D. Diss., Columbia University, 1978.

17. Samuel Hopkins to [Aaron Burr],? 1802, Yale University Library.

18. Pierpont Edwards to [?], 4 Oct. 1792, Gratz Coll., HSP; David Austin, *Republican Festival* (New Haven, 1803).

19. William Gordon to Joseph Bellamy, 14 July 1769, Bellamy Papers, HS.

20.Robert L. Ferm's *Jonathan Edwards the Younger* (Grand Rapids, 1976) offers another version of this portrait.

21. Cf. Nathan O. Hatch, *The Sacred Cause of Liberty* (New Haven, 1977); the only discussion of Edwards Jr.'s revolutionary sermons I am aware of is that by Wesley C. Ewert, "Jonathan Edwards the Younger: A Biographical Study," Th.D. Diss., Hartford Theological Seminary, 1953, 78–86.

22. Jonathan Edwards, Jr., Papers, Hartford Seminary, sermon 390 (31 Aug. 1774); sermon 400 (2 Nov. 1774); sermon 412 (1 Feb. 1775), p. 2; sermon 420 (19 April 1775); pp. 2, 7; sermon 448 (11 Nov. 1775); sermon 537 (20 Nov. 1777); sermon 741 (13 Dec. 1781); sermon 1109 (18 Oct. 1789). Subsequent references to numbered sermons are also in this collection.

23. The 1774 edition of *Work of Redemption* realized a long-standing desire of (for example) John Erskine's: "Tho I long to see Mr. Edward's confutation of the different branches of Arminianism," he told Bellamy, "yet I more long to see his intended history of man's redemption. From such a pen upon such a subject, something highly valuable may be expected. May a kind providence preserve from danger a life so important!" John Erskine to Joseph Bellamy, 24 March 1755, Bellamy Papers, HS. The millennial expectancy tapped by *Redemption* is conveyed by David Austin, in his preface to *The Millennium* (Elizabethtown, N.J., 1793) which "hail[s] the approach of MILLENNIAL DAY!" (p. iv).

24. Jonathan Edwards, Jr., to Benjamin Trumbull, 7 July 1772, Trumbull Papers, Yale University Library. Cf. Ferm, *Edwards the Younger*, p. 141, which quotes a letter from an Edwards opponent concerning the son's zealous activities as editor and transcriber of the father—a loyalty which may have had something to do with the son's pastoral difficulties.

25. Jonathan Edwards, *ms* sermon on Neh. 4:14 (June, 1746), Beinecke Library, Yale University; Jonathan Edwards, *ms* sermon on Rev. 7:11 (1 July 1746), Beinecke Library, Yale University. For a discussion of Edwards's apocalyptic thought, see Stephen J. Stein's introduction to *Apocalyptic Writings* (New Haven, 1977).

26. Jonathan Edwards, "History of Redemption Notebook 'A'," p. 37, Edwards mss, sermon 5 Dec. 1745 (preached again Nov. 1757), Beinecke Library, Yale University. For a description of the "Redemption Notebooks" see John F. Wilson, "Jonathan Edwards's Notebook for 'A History of the Work of Redemption" in *Reformation, Continuity and Dissent: Essays in honour of Geoffrey Nuttall*, ed. R. B. Knox (London, 1977), 239–54.

27. Edwards, "History of Redemption Notebook 'A', " pp. 34, 35.

28. Edwards, Jr., sermon 400, pp. 7, 8.

29. Edwards, Jr., sermon 400, p. 9.

30. Jon Butler, "Enthusiasm Described and Decried: The Great Awakening as Interpretive Fiction," *Journal of American History* 69 (1982), 324. On the persistence of terms from the Great Awakening in late eighteenth-century America, see Sacvan Bercovitch, *The American Jeremiad* (Madison, 1978), 130–31 (on John Adams) and Emory Elliott, "The Dove and the Serpent: The Clergy in the American Revolution," *American Quarterly* 31 (1979), 188–89 (on Jefferson).

31. Jonathan Edwards, Jr., sermon 454 (22 Dec. 1775), pp. 24, 32, Hartford Seminary.

32. I discuss the ritual aspect of Revolutionary pulpit discourse in *Rhetoric and History in Revolutionary New England* (New York, 1988), which treats the example of Jonathan Edwards, Jr., in more detail.

33. Harriet Beecher Stow, *Oldtown Folks* (Boston, 1869), 378.

34. Barrett Wendell, *A Literary History of America* (New York, 1900), 422, 419.

35. John T. Morse, Jr., *Life and Letters of Oliver Wendell Holmes*, vol. 2 of 2 vols. (Boston and New York, 1896), 226. The passage is from a letter to Stowe, 29 May 1869.

36. Oliver Wendell Holmes, *The Autocrat of the Breakfast-Table* (1858) in vol. 1 of *Works* (Boston, 1891), 67.

37. Morse, *Life and Letters*, vol. 2, 11.

38. See Abiel Holmes to Oliver Wendell Holmes, 27 Feb. 1824, Houghton Library, Harvard University.

39. Morse, vol. 1, *Life and Letters*, 39–40.

40. Abiel Holmes, *Sermon on the Freedom and Happiness of America* (Boston, 1795) (Holmes goes on to quote Barlow's "Vision of Columbus," p. 31); Holmes, *A Discourse . . .* (Cambridge, Mass., 1806), 28. Eleanor Tilton describes Abiel Holmes as "a rather mild kind of Puritan, a lukewarm Calvinist." *Amiable Autocrat: A Biography of Dr. Oliver Wendell Holmes* (New York, 1947), 27.

41. Oliver Wendell Holmes to Rev. William Jenks, 21 Feb. 1838, quoted in Tilton, *Amiable Autocrat*, 147, 148.

42. Thomas Wortham, "Oliver Wendell Holmes," in *American Writers: A Collection of Literary Biographies*, ed. Leonard Unger (New York, 1979), p. 302.

43. Oliver Wendell Holmes, "Jonathan Edwards," in *Pages from an Old Volume of Life*, in vol. 8, *Works*, pp. 366, 370. The Edwards essay appeared originally in the *International Review* 10 (1880), 1–28.

44. Holmes, "Jonathan Edwards," pp. 383, 379.

45. Holmes, "Jonathan Edwards," pp. 399, 367.

46. Oliver Wendell Holmes, "The Pulpit and the Pew," in *Pages from an Old Volume of Life*, pp. 421, 422. In the same letter to Stowe which contains the famous passage, "I do not believe you or I can ever get the iron of Calvinism out of our souls" (note the cathartic metaphor) Holmes asks, "*Can* I love a father who lets me ruin myself?" (Holmes's emphasis). Morse, *Life and Letters*, vol. 2, 246, 250.

47. These various "Edwardsian moments" in American cultural history are discussed more fully in Weber, "The Image of Jonathan Edwards."

48. Sydney E. Ahlstrom, "H. Richard Niebuhr's Place in American Thought," *Christianity and Crisis* 23 (25 Nov. 1963), 213.

49. Conversation with author, 7 August 1985. I am indebted to Dr. Richard R. Niebuhr for clarifying the nature of the Edwardsian legacy to H. Richard Niebuhr. On the relationship between Edwards and Niebuhr see Leo Sandon, Jr., "Jonathan Edwards and H. Richard Niebuhr," *Religious Studies* 12 (1976), 101–15.

50. I refer to Perry Miller's essay of 1961, "The Responsibility of Mind in a Civilization of Machines," in John Crowel and S. J. Searl, Jr., eds., *The Responsibility of Mind in a Civilization of Machines: Essays by Perry Miller* (Amherst, Mass.: 1979), 195–213.

51. H. Richard Niebuhr, "Faith, Works, and Social Salvation," *Religion in Life* 1 (1932), 429, 430.

52. Niebuhr, "Faith, Works . . . ," 430.

53. H. Richard Niebuhr, *The Kingdom of God in America* (New York, 1937), xvi, xiii, xi.

54. Niebuhr, *Kingdom of God*, 126, 109, 135–6, 139, 172.

55. Waldo Beach and H. Richard Niebuhr, eds., *Christian Ethics: Sources of the Living Tradition* (New York, 1955); 384, 389, 383.

56. H. Richard Niebuhr, "The Anachronism of Jonathan Edwards," H. Richard Niebuhr Papers, Harvard Divinity School. I am indebted to Dr. Richard R. Niebuhr for allowing me access to this unpublished work.

57. Niebuhr, "The Anachronism of Jonathan Edwards," 3, 4, 12, 13, 14, 16. Sandon excerpts part of this address in "Jonathan Edwards and H. Richard Niebuhr," 112–3.

58. H. Richard Niebuhr, "How My Mind has Changed," *Christian Century* 77 (March 2, 1960), 249, 250, 251.

59. The connections among Perry Miller, the Niebuhrs and the response to Edwards in the 1950s are narrated in Donald Weber, "Perry Miller and the Recovery of Jonathan Edwards," Introduction to Perry Miller, *Jonathan Edwards* (Amherst, 1981), v–xxv.

*Edwards in
Cultural Context*

5

The Rationalist Foundations of Jonathan Edwards's Metaphysics

NORMAN FIERING

I

John Norris (1657–1711), the rector of the Anglican church at Bemerton, England, late in the seventeenth century, is a figure known, for the most part, only to specialists in early English philosophy. Yet he has two claims to fame. Norris was the very first critic in print of John Locke's *Essay Concerning Human Understanding*—his astute *Reflections* on the *Essay* came out within a year of the *Essay's* publication in 1690—and he was the most distinguished and accomplished of Nicolas Malebranche's British disciples, if we exclude Bishop Berkeley.[1]

The two facts about Norris go together. A disciple of the French Cartesian philosopher Malebranche could be expected to find much lacking in Locke's *Essay*. Norris was by no means a doctrinaire or an intemperate critic of Locke. He described himself at the end of his *Reflections* on the *Essay* as an "Admirer" of the work and as one who "would not part" with the *Essay* "for half a *Vatican*." referring, we may suppose, to the great wealth of the papal seat.[2] But for all his appreciation of the treasures Locke afforded the reader, Norris judged Locke to be a poor reasoner, and he found intolerably frustrating Locke's outright refusal to deal with some of the central metaphysical and ontological issues of the day.

The most fundamental of Norris's criticisms, perhaps, pertained to Locke's use (or misuse) of the word "idea," a term that had been wrested by the force of Descartes's genius from centuries of relative tranquility within Platonism and made into a watchword of the new philosophy. In the thirty years preceding the publication of Locke's *Essay*, few philosophical topics were more actively debated than the status of "ideas".[3] Malebranche, Arnauld, Spinoza, Leibniz, and numerous lesser writers were involved in this controversy, for the obvious reason that its resolution appeared to have enormous significance for theology and religion, for law, for theories of human nature and psychology, and for metaphysics in general. It is not surprising, then, that almost the first point that Norris made in opposition to Locke was the observation and complaint that Locke

> ought *first* to have Defined what he meant by Ideas, and to have acquainted us with their *Nature*, before he proceeded to account for their Origination. For how can any Proposition be form'd with any certainty concerning an Idea, that it is or is not *Innate*, that it does or does not come in at the Senses, before the meaning of the Word Idea be stated, and the nature of the thing, at least in general, be understood?[4]

Locke's "*first*, and indeed *main* Business," Norris insisted, should have been "to have given us an account of the Nature of Ideas." This omission Norris considered "a *Fundamental* defect" of the *Essay Concerning Human Understanding*.[5]

Locke did define ideas up to a point, Norris acknowledged: "Whatsoever the Mind perceives in itself, or is the immediate Object of Perception, that I call Idea," Locke wrote,[6] more or less following the Cartesian definition, which had transferred the emphasis in the meaning of the term "idea" from a divine archetype to almost any object of mental activity. But by Norris's lights, Locke failed altogether to assign an ontological status to ideas. Are ideas "Real Beings," Norris asked? And if they are real beings, are they substances or modifications of substances? And if they are substances, are they material or immaterial?[7]

Locke was no fool, of course; his strategy included a deliberate avoidance of the kinds of questions about ideas that were uppermost in Norris's mind. Although Locke himself had divided all so-called complex ideas into the three categories of modes, substances, or relations, he did not apply these categories to the term "idea" itself and ask where it properly fit. Locke was deeply distrustful of metaphysical speculation, and the *Essay*, as has often been pointed out, was primarily devoted to showing the *limits* of human understanding. His intent, as he said, was to clear the ground a little, to remove some of the rubbish that lies in the way of knowledge, and to indicate how far man's intellect could safely reach.[8] "I shall not . . . trouble myself," Locke wrote, to examine wherein the essence of mind consists, "or by what motions of our spirits or alterations of our bodies we come to have any *sensation* . . . or any *ideas* in our understandings; and whether those ideas do in their formation . . . depend on matter or not." "Meddling with things exceeding [human] comprehension" was to be avoided above all, along with the vanity of letting "loose our thoughts into the vast ocean of Being" before the processes of understanding were clarified.[9]

Whatever the inherent merits of Locke's celebrated program for keeping the Antaeus of knowledge with his feet on the ground, it is essential to recognize, when considering the influence of the *Essay*, that Locke's self-imposed intellectual asceticism would have left most American readers as unsatisfied as it had left John Norris. It is all too easy to picture Locke's readers in America or elsewhere as enmeshed in Scholastic cobwebs, hoping desperately for release from imprisonment in medieval ignorance, which supposedly Locke's "plain, historical method" wondrously dispersed. Locke was indeed refreshingly plain-speaking and original; but to those schooled in the philosophical debates of the last half of the seventeenth century he was also irritatingly incomplete.

II

Jonathan Edwards's discovery of Locke has been described as a kind of epiphany. According to one biographer, upon reading the *Essay* "the boy of fourteen grasped in a flash . . . that Locke was the master-spirit of the age," and the encounter was "the central and decisive event in [Edwards's] intellectual life."[10] Another account calls Edwards flatly a "Lockean philosopher" and claims that the *Essay* provided "the general framework within which [Edwards] worked."[11] Still another authority writes that Edwards "quickly accepted most of the Lockean philosophy," although he notes more moderately that Edwards "did not hesitate to disagree with Locke on specific points."[12]

One of the basic contentions of this essay is that it is misleading to categorize Edwards as a Lockean, especially when this categorization implies—along the lines of the familiar but questionable dichotomy— that Edwards is allied with the English empiricists as opposed to the Continental rationalists.

Edwards's reading of Locke's *Essay*, or the reading of the *Essay* by any other American in the early eighteenth century, did not occur in an intellectual vacuum. The extraordinary philosophical storm in the Atlantic world of the late seventeenth century in logic, metaphysics, and epistemology had reverberated on American shores.[13] Coming after Francisco Suarez, therefore, the *Essay Concerning Human Understanding* might have seemed dazzlingly novel, a work refreshingly sui generis. Coming after Descartes, Hobbes, Malebranche, Spinoza, Arnauld, Leibniz, and the Cambridge Platonists, Locke's *Essay* was simply one of the major voices in a monumental philosophical colloquy.

There is no reason to believe that Edwards read Hobbes, Spinoza, or Leibniz, although it is quite possible that copies of the periodical *Acta Eruditorum*, to which Leibniz contributed regularly, were circulating in the colonies.[14] Edwards certainly had derivative information about much more philosophy than he had actually read. In some of his very earliest notes he refers to Hobbes's materialism as being in error, yet it is a virtual certainty he had not read a word of Hobbes directly.[15] Edwards studied the famous Port Royal logic by Nicole and Arnauld, and Antoine LeGrand's equally interesting Cartesian logic, before he read Locke, and he probably encountered various works by Henry More and Jean LeClerc in his college years also. Edwards may not have read Malebranche's *Search After Truth* before he read Locke's *Essay*, but LeClerc's *Ontologia* and *Pneumatologia*, both first published late in the seventeenth century, reviewed many of the philosophical positions then current, including Malebranche's major teachings, and we know that LeClerc was an academic favorite in New England.[16] Various of John Norris's works are found so widely dispersed in British America that it would be no surprise to learn that Edwards had read the *Theory of the Ideal and Intelligible World* at any particular date in the second decade of the eighteenth century.[17]

But these facts are beside the point. What we must assume in general is that when Edwards read Locke's *Essay*—it is now believed this happened when he was a postgraduate tutor at Yale in his early twenties—he did so with certain well-established philosophical proclivities that were the outgrowth of prior thought and training in Cartesian philosophy (defined broadly enough to include Henry More), as well as training in rather sophisticated Protestant Scholastic theology. In short, Edwards did not come to Locke as a brilliant pre-Cartesian reasoner who was suddenly captivated by the "new philosophy," anymore than Locke himself wrote without benefit of the whole range of innovative Cartesian-influenced thinking in the late seventeenth century, however much he himself may have tried to create the impression that he was autonomous.[18]

Recent scholarship has seriously undermined the belief that Edwards's reading of Locke was as decisive as Perry Miller assumed it was. The next task facing Edwards scholars, however, is the difficult one of reconstructing the development of the youthful Edwards's leading ideas without Locke's *Essay* as the major catalyst. My central purpose here is to show that many of Edwards's most characteristic philosophical ideas can be traced to intellectual principles and trends that long antedated Locke's *Essay* and in fact had essentially theological roots. Edwards's philosophical idealism or immaterialism, his occasionalist theory of causation, his conception of intuitively certain spiritual and moral knowledge (the sense of the heart),[19] his assumption that the created universe is perfectly orderly and harmonious and governed by nearly invariable laws, his psychological determinism, and many other Edwardsian notions were assembled out of elements of thought and belief that did not depend in any way on Locke's *Essay*.[20]

To assume that Edwards was in some way derivative from Locke, either by direct positive influence or even by way of negative reaction against Locke, is a serious error, I believe, and gives rise to a profound misclassification of Edwards as a thinker,[21] for Edwards belongs not with Locke but with Locke's rivals, with Norris and Bishop Berkeley and Malebranche in a group that Louis Loeb in a fine recent book has called the "theocentric metaphysicians," a sub-branch of the so-called Continental school.[22] It is significant that all the members of this group were clergymen and determined to introduce philosophy that not only was perfectly compatible with Christian dogma but that would deliberately employ philosophy, in Henry More's phrase, to build stronger fences around theology.[23]

Loeb's basic criteria for including a philosopher in the "genre" of Continental metaphysics (which is the genus of which theocentric metaphysics is a species) are three: the denial that certain kinds of causal relations obtain (between matter and spirit, spirit and matter, or matter and matter); the attribution of considerable metaphysical importance to the problem of such relations; and the belief that the standard of knowledge is strict demonstration based upon intuition and deduction.[24] The theocentric metaphysicians in particular emphasized the divine determination of all events and denied that material substance, if it exists at all, is capable of independent activity or causal efficacy. Edwards fits perfectly into these criteria, of course, whereas Locke hardly belongs at all, although, as Loeb argues, there was more "rationalism" in Locke's *Essay* than is sometimes appreciated.[25]

The main elements of Edwards's metaphysics can be derived, I believe, from five general principles—in some cases these are more like attitudes or cultural convictions than axioms—all of which had come down to him from traditions or sources that are completely independent of Locke's influence (sources such as Scholastic theology, both Protestant and Catholic, Cartesian academic writings, Cambridge Platonism, and certain Newtonian writings). These five inherited principles were: the affirmation of total divine sovereignty, entailing among other things the position that events in the universe are entirely free of contingency; a belief in divine concurrence in events and in the continuous conservation and re-creation of the existing world; a commitment to teleology at the ultimate level of explanation—everything exists for some divine purpose; acceptance of the Neoplatonic typological system that posited divine archetypes and ectypal representations on earth; and the rejection of the Cartesian position that the essence of matter is extension. One might also mention in this context a sixth Edwardsian conviction that was so general and endemic it hardly needed to be articulated, namely, an unalterable opposition to materialism or to teachings that could lead to materialism. With this background in place, Edwards's point of view was consolidated, there is reason to believe, by his reading of Malebranche in the early 1720s.

My intention in the balance of this article is to look briefly at the background and context of each of these five conventional notions. It should hardly be necessary to emphasize that none of these ideas belonged exclusively to Edwards in New England in 1720. He had no privileged access to literature unavailable to others in his milieu. Edwards's uniqueness lay not in his having read Locke before anybody else in America but in his being a daring and acute philosophical speculator who shared the (perhaps naive) trust common in his time that modern philosophy—that is, philosophy beginning with Descartes—could be turned to the advantage of orthodox religion. This widely shared, optimistic vision of the potential usefulness of the new philosophy for Christian apologetics would become hopelessly snarled by the time Hume wrote his *Dialogues Concerning Natural Religion* in the middle of the eighteenth century, but Edwards did not anticipate this outcome. It is especially important to recognize that despite the pietism evident in Edwards's thought, he was no Schleiermacher or Kierkegaard, writing out of disillusionment with rationalist metaphysical systems. On the contrary, as a man of his time he was captivated by such systems, no less than Malebranche, Leibniz, and Henry More.

The first three of Edwards's presuppositions that I have cited—divine sovereignty, divine concurrence, and the belief in a purposeful universe—were all venerable theological ideas, and they are so closely related they could well be treated as a single complex of elements. The dogma of divine sovereignty, when held strictly, eliminated contingency from the universe; without contingency God must be responsible directly or indirectly for all events, which implies concurrence. And because God is an infinitely wise spirit, as well as being omnipotent, all of the creation must be ultimately explicable as an expression of His purposes, which in large part are intelligible to man.

The intensity and thoroughness with which Edwards adhered to the doctrine of divine sovereignty were notable even in his own day.[26] Physical science and metaphysics were completely intertwined in this conviction, and Edwards seems to have enjoyed entertaining awesome speculations on the direct application to phenomena of God's power and wisdom. He apparently took it as a proper task in natural philosophy

> to shew how the motion, rest and direction of the least atom has an influence on the motion, rest and direction of every body in the universe. . . . Everything that happens with respect to motes or straw, and such little things, may be for some great uses in the whole course of things throughout eternity. . . . The least wrong step in a mote may, in eternity, subvert the order of the universe.

We must "take notice," Edwards continued, "of the great wisdom that is necessary in order thus to dispose every atom at first, as that they should go for the best throughout all eternity," including "by an exact computation," a "nice allowance" for "the miracles which should be needful."[27] God must know "the exact number of particles of dust," Edwards believed, "the exact dimensions and weight of every atom, the exact distance of every, yea, of every part of every one from every other; yea, from every part of all others in the universe."[28] Many theologians stressed divine sovereignty; Edwards's concrete application of the idea was extraordinary.

The traditional religious doctrine of divine concursus, or concurrence, made God a participant in every event but still left ample room for secondary causes, especially in the case of human action, where overemphasis on divine sovereignty and agency ran the hazard of implicating God in human sin. To the pious mind a still stronger version of this teaching was also powerfully appealing; the doctrine of continuous creation, or re-creation, which stressed the necessity and immediacy of divine intervention every moment and every instant. This ancient teaching, it should be noted, was implicit in the New England Puritan tradition. In 1677, the president of Harvard, Urian Oakes, in a sermon in Cambridge spoke as follows: "The Issues and Events of Undertakings do in some respect, ordinarily, depend upon the Sufficiency of Second Causes." On the other hand, secondary causes, "though of the greatest sufficiency . . . have not the certain Determination of Successes & Events in their own Hands." For there is "no Contingency, or Emergency, or Accident so casual, but it is ordered and governed by the Lord." "God hath the absolute and infallible Determination of the Successes and Events of all the Operations & Undertakings of created Agents & Second Causes, in his own Power." The Creature, Oakes wrote, "cannot be the absolute first Cause of any physical action." God not only predetermines second causes, "He concurs with them in their Operations," to the point that "there can be no real Effect produced by the Creature without it." Moreover, God not only concurs with the use, he also concurs with the *effect*. He "most immediately, intimously, and without Dependence upon these Causes by which He acts, produce[s] the Entity, or Esse of the Effect." Created agents, then, by Oakes's reckoning "are, as it were, God's Instruments, that act as they are acted by Him," and God produces both the cause and the effect.[29]

From such theological literature, which possibly could be traced back to late Medieval nominalism, it was a small step to full acceptance of the more secularized position expressed by Descartes, that the distinction usually made between the *original creation* and the *sustenance of the world after the creation from moment to moment* is purely a distinction of reason. For it is "perfectly clear and evident," Descartes wrote, that " . . . in order to be conserved in each moment in which it endures, a substance has need of the same power and action as would be necessary to produce and create it anew."[30] Thus, however much secondary causes may come into play, the stable orderly *existence* of the sequence of events is continuously and directly dependent upon divine will.[31] This teaching develops easily into an occasionalist theory of causation in which it is assumed that the concatenation of events follows predictable causal sequences, but a prior event in any sequence is not in itself causal or autonomously efficacious. With God producing both cause and effect, autonomous or actual cause and effect relations in the world, where one event is a sufficient cause of another, become superfluous.[32] The harmony and regularity of natural physical laws, then, are essentially an expression of God's love of order. Edwards and Malebranche shared this view of causation.

The doctrine of continuous conservation, the belief, that is, that the world is re-created every moment, does not necessarily give rise to an occasionalist theory of causation, but if such a theory is available and impressively presented, as it was by Malebranche, it would be highly attractive to a person with the combination of piety and logicality found so prominently in Edwards. Like Malebranche, Edwards began with the conviction that the deepest truths of philosophy are rooted in religious revelation, such as the revelation of God's sovereignty.[33]

Very early in his career Edwards expressed the belief that "the universe is created out of nothing every moment." "If it were not for our imaginations, which hinder us," he wrote, "we might see that wonderful work performed continually, which was seen by the morning stars when they sang together."[34] Edwards moved smoothly from the belief that "the existence of things every moment ceases and is every moment renewed"[35] to a highly formal definition of "cause" as that, "after or upon the existence of which, or the existence of it after such a manner, the existence of another thing follows."[36] This definition left plenty of room for God's substantive role. At the same time that Edwards decided that the "laws of nature in bodies" were simply "the stated methods of God's acting with respect to bodies, and the stated conditions of the alteration of the manner of his acting," he also noted "that what divines used to say concerning divine concourse [i.e. concurrence] had a great deal of truth lay at the bottom of it."[37]

Edwards began with a belief like that of Urian Oakes's that God produces both the cause and effect and does so in regular sequence. By the time his philosophy had ripened a little, he was a full-fledged occasionalist: "In natural things means of effects in metaphysical strictness are not the proper causes of the effects, but only occasions. God produces all effects but yet he ties natural events to the operation of such means or causes them to be consequent on such means according to fixed, determinate, and unchangeable rules which are called the laws of nature."[38] Occasionalism was the vehicle most available to Edwards for shattering belief in the autonomy of nature, a mechanistic universe, and the independence of second causes. It also opened the way to Edwards's immaterialism.

Divine sovereignty implied not only the absolute, immediate government of all that is, but also wise and purposeful government. Edwards's imagination never for a moment admitted the possibility of absurdity in the universe. It was utterly outside of his reckoning that anything in the universe was meaningless. Terror of God's judgment was certainly part of Edwards's experience, but never the modern anxiety that there may be, in fact, no judgment at all, no ultimate rectification. Hence, all his life he reasoned teleologically with perfect comfort and confidence and used such reasoning as the basis of long series of demonstrations.[39]

Edwards's often reiterated belief that existence, or being, implies consciousness seems to have been originally a philosophical amplification of the basic confessional tenet that the purpose of the Creation is the manifestation of the glory of God, with the creation of men and angels supremely important in this scheme. One can follow in Edwards's writings step by step the transformation of this familiar theological dogma into idealist metaphysics, a process not unlike that we have just seen in the development of his occasionalist theory of causality. "'Tis certain that God did not create the world for nothing," Edwards wrote in one of his earliest notes. "'Tis most certain that, if there were no intelligent beings in the world, all the world would be without any good at all; for senseless matter, in whatever excellent order it is placed, would be useless if there were no intelligent beings at all, neither God nor others. . . . What could this vast universe of matter, placed in such excellent order and governed by such excellent law, be good for if there was no intelligence that could know anything of it? Wherefore, it necessarily follows that intelligent beings are the end of the creation, and that their end must be to behold and admire the doings of God and magnify him. . . . "[40] This is the Westminster Confession made into a philosophical demonstration by use of teleological reasoning.[41]

A little later the argument is more refined. "Men, or intelligent beings, are the consciousness of the creation, whereby the universe is conscious of its own being. . . . Now except the world had such a consciousness of itself, it would be altogether vain that it was. If the world is not conscious of its being, it had as good not be as be." Moreover, this consciousness must be eternal, for if it is destroyed, "it is in vain that ever it has been."[42] Existence is logically dependent on consciousness.

This strict relationship between being and consciousness was constructed by Edwards, first of all, through an interpretation of divine purposes within the context of what is known about God from revelation. The universe does not exist for nothing; that fact we know as a revealed truth. Whatever the purpose of the universe is, it requires consciousness for that purpose to be a purpose. Without intelligence to perceive it, the whole concept of "purpose" is meaningless. On dogmatic grounds there must be a purpose; therefore there must be consciousness.[43] Then, in some early Augustinian-type thoughts on the Trinity, Edwards attempted to demonstrate that consciousness and being are related not only theologically but also ontologically. He began by arguing that knowledge in man and God is essentially the same, both existing by ideas. All that mankind can mean by knowlege involves ideas. Whatever God may somehow know without ideas is unintelligible to us. The difference between ideas in God and ideas in humans is first of all that God's ideas are "infinitely perfect," whereas human knowledge is merely an "image" of the divine. Second, God's knowledge can only be the immediate idea of Himself, which necessarily includes knowledge of all things, without reference to anything external to Himself; whereas human knowledge is based upon the apprehension of ideas of things external to the human mind. Human knowledge is therefore not immediate as God's knowledge is.[44]

God's knowledge of Himself, being perfect, must be a replication of Himself, Edwards argued, for "an absolutely perfect idea of a thing is the very thing; for it wants nothing that is in the thing, substance nor nothing else. . . . Whatsoever is perfect and absolutely like a thing is that thing."[45] The second person of the Trinity, Christ, is God's idea of Himself, and this infinite and all-encompassing idea also constitutes the ideal world of which human knowledge is but an image and shadow. Edwards had already argued that "nothing has any existence, any way at all, but in some consciousness or idea." When or if there is no human consciousness of a thing, it exists or continues to exist in divine idea, which being perfect must be real and in fact *is* the thing itself (more truly than human consciousness of a thing can be). "Things as to God exist from all eternity alike," Edwards wrote; "that is, the idea is always the same, and after the same mode. The existence of things, therefore, that are not actually in created minds, consists only in power, or in the determination of God that such and such ideas shall be raised in created minds upon such conditions."[46] It is at this point that Edwards sounds so much like Bishop Berkeley.[47]

It should be noticed in this context that Edwards's frequent statement that the created world is an emanation of Christ was not simply a pious metaphor or some type of mystical vision. As the second person of the Trinity, which is God's idea of Himself and hence the idea of all that is, Christ is truly all being, including created being. In John Norris's words—there are many similar in Edwards—the beauty of the world is "truly *Divine*. For 'tis the Beauty of him that is the Brightness of his Father's Glory, and the express Image of his Person. . . . Tis a Beauty purely *Intellectual*, the Beauty of Truth, of Order, of Reason, of Proportion, and of Wisdom."[48] In a note on the Logos written not too long after the reflections on the Trinity from which I have already quoted, Edwards commented: the notion of the Logos, "more confirms me in it . . . that the existence of all corporeal things is only ideas."[49]

To pause for a moment and sum up, on grounds nearly entirely theological and from powerful currents of ideas in the late seventeenth century unrelated to Locke's writings, Edwards was able to formulate definite beliefs about the ideal foundations of being and to adopt the doctrine of continuous creation and the occasionalist theory of causality, concepts that are not only highly characteristic of his thought, but fundamental to it.

III

In a recent book on Malebranche's influence in England, Charles McCracken refers to the French philosopher's decisive influence on the immaterialist speculations of Pierre Bayle, Arthur Collier, and George Berkeley.[50] These three saw that Malebranche's notion of the vision of all things in God made matter superfluous. "If Edwards read either Norris or Malebranche when at Yale," McCracken writes, "such an idea may also have struck him; if he did not read them, then he is the only immaterialist of the period to work out the idea of immaterialism in complete independence of the Malebranchean doctrine of the vision of all things in God." As I have already indicated, I am inclined to believe that Edwards's immaterialism was in fact ultimately dependent on his reading of something by, or inspired by, Malebranche—it could have been some discussion of Malebranche's ideas in periodical literature—but we cannot appreciate how primed Edwards was for this discovery without looking at the last two of his presuppositions that I cited earlier, namely: his acceptance of the Neoplatonic system that posited divine archetypes and ectypal representations on earth, and his critique of the argument that the essence of matter is extension.

The suffusion of New England Puritan philosophical theology with Platonic idealism has by no one been better described than by Perry Miller;[51] therefore, the argument does not require a great deal of elaboration here. The principal source of Platonist theory in New England, perhaps, was a work entitled *The Logicians School-Master*, a Ramist text by the obscure Cambridge University teacher Alexander Richardson that was in standard use at seventeenth-century Harvard; but the Platonist influence also came in from a variety of other angles. It was widely held among the Puritan reformers, as it was among the Puritans' contemporaries in the Cambridge Platonist group, that Platonism and true Christianity were especially compatible, whereas Aristotelian metaphysics led all to easily to materialism and atheism.

Hardly any one can be named, the theologian William Ames asserted, "who having previously professed the Peripatetic philosophy, later received the truth of the Christian faith."[52] Platonism, on the other hand, when suitably interpreted, reinforced belief in a God of rational order who is intelligible to man, which was the nearly universal view of God among Calvinists—various stereotypes to the contrary notwithstanding.[53]

The dominant epistemological theory in seventeenth-century New England divided the universe of knowable things into the three orders of divine archetype, entypal object representing the archetype, and ectypal innate idea in the human mind. The natural material world has hidden in it, therefore, the great eternal system of ideas, although this world appears to man in fragmented form at first. The task of *scientia*, or systematic knowledge, is to reconstruct the world mentally in accordance with the archetypes. When the task is complete, if it ever can be, the human mind thus informed will correspond to the divine mind in detail, as it does potentially at any time. The mind of man, now a shattered mirror reflecting the archetypes fragmentarily and chaotically, will one day be truly an image of God.[54]

Those at seventeenth-century Harvard who adhered to this Platonist epistemology varied from the tradition only in their emphasis on God as *act* rather than *idea*. The divine archetypes, William Ames said, differ from Platonic ideas in that they are properly guides to action, exemplars that exist for the purpose of practical application, not objects for passive discovery or contemplation. They are the rules by which God Himself acted in the creation of the world.[55] Perhaps with the same intent, Edwards sometimes used the phrase "constitution of God" as synonymous with the phrase "law of nature." In any case, as Wallace Anderson has observed, Edwards conceived of the general laws of nature as "ontologically prior to the objects and events of the world."[56] Edwards saw the universe as a rationally ordered system of ideas or rules in accordance with which everthing is created and all events occur.

The bearing of Platonic concepts—which were pervasive in early New England—on the development of Edwards's thinking is fairly obvious, but one point deserves special attention: the relationship between Platonic idealism and the immaterialism that Edwards espoused.

The historical relationship between idealism and the emergence of immaterialism is a complicated problem, but one thing is certain: it is a mistake to assume that John Locke's critique of innate ideas, which gave the coup de grace to the Platonic conception of a basic correspondence between the human mind and the divine mind, was an essential step in the process that led to either Berkeley's or Edwards's metaphysics. It is true that for those who were committed to a spiritualized theory of knowledge and metaphysics, as Berkeley and Edwards were, immaterialism was a satisfying substitute after Locke for a destroyed Platonist innatism. For although it could not be said after Locke's critique that the human mind contains innate ideas, the mind nevertheless has, according to Berkeley and Edwards, direct access to divine ideas without the necessity for sensory mediation as described by Locke or for material representation. The bridge to immaterialism was provided by Malebranche's analysis of how external objects are known, not by Locke's.

The first seven chapters of the second part of book III of Malebranche's *Search After Truth*, comprising only about thirty pages, constituted a turning point in the history of philosophy. This was the case not because of the necessary rightness of the answers Malebranche provided but because of his superb joining of the issues. It was here that Malebranche enunciated his theory of the vision of all things in God, but only after considering each of the alternatives to this theory of knowledge and demonstrating their implausibility. One can comprehend Malebranche's radical solution to the problem of knowledge only after having fully understood the deficiencies of all of the other theories.

The ideas we have of bodies, our knowledge of the external world, Malebranche argued, can be gained in only one of five ways: the bodies themselves may emit "species" that resemble them, which was the prevailing Scholastic view; the soul of man may have the capacity in some unexplained way to produce ideas of things out of the impressions made upon it by bodies, as though man were himself a God able to create and destroy real beings; our ideas may be created with us from birth, and as needed appear to us with God's aid, which was the Platonic solution; the essence of all objects may be perceivable within the mind itself without need of anything outside;[57] or, finally, the soul may be united with God and thus dependent upon God for all of its thoughts, which was Malebranche's view.

Malebranche accepted the Platonic premise that God has in Himself the ideas of all the beings He has created.[58] As in the Augustinian notion of the Trinity that Edwards espoused, Malebranche assumed that those ideas which God has of the world are not different from Himself, and thus that "all Creatures, even the most Material and Terrestrial, are in God," although in a spiritual manner that we cannot comprehend. If we then posit, as Malebranche did, that the mind of man is a spiritual creation that is also archetypically in God, or part of God's idea of Himself, it follows that the mind of man is in some sense in union with the mind of God, and though not itself part of the divine essence, yet capable of seeing directly the spiritual or ideal world itself, without the necessity of the intermediation of material entypes and without the supposition of innate ideas.[59] God is "the place of Spirits, as Space is the place of Bodies," Malebranche wrote, and it is by vision in God that the spirit or mind of man discovers, according to the will of God, what it knows of created things.

Like Edwards, Malebranche hastened to point out that this truth about the spiritual nature of all knowledge, its independence from matter, makes little practical difference, for it can truly be said that "we do not so much see the Ideas of things, as the things which those Ideas represent." When we see a square, for instance, "we do not say that we see the Idea of that Square, which is united to the Mind, but only the Square which is without us."[60] Edwards similarly wrote:

> We would not, therefore, be understood to deny that things are where they seem to be, for the principles we lay down . . . do not infer that. Nor will it be found that they at all make void natural philosophy, or the science of the causes or reasons of corporeal changes; for to find out the reasons of things in natural philosophy is only to find out the proportions of God's acting. And the case is the same, as to such proportions, whether we suppose them only mental in our sense, or no. Though we suppose that the existence of the whole material universe is absolutely dependent on ideas, yet we may speak in the old way, and as properly and truly as ever.[61]

Like Edwards, too, Malebranche cited a corollary of this theory, namely that all knowledge, even the most seemingly natural, is "an immediate Gift from Heaven," the product solely of what God chooses to unveil of created things. Of the totality of knowledge we of course know very little, God giving us, aside from revelation, only ideas of "things that happen according to the Order of Nature."[62] It should be clear from these few remarks on Malebranche that virtually nothing in Locke's *Essay Concerning Human Understanding* constituted an essential step in the transition from Platonism to immaterialism. Malebranche had already asserted that bodies are known by ideas only; that the primary and secondary qualities of bodies are both mental, the one as divine idea, the other as a mode of the human mind; and that the notion of innate ideas, however conceived of, is fallacious insofar as it is premised on some alleged independence of human knowledge from the immediate action of divine will from moment to moment. "The mere exertion of a new thought is a certain proof of God." Edwards wrote:

For certainly there is something that immediately produces and upholds that thought. Here is a new thing, and there is a necessity of a cause. It is not in antecedent thoughts, for they are vanished and gone; they are past, what is past is not. But if we say 'tis the substance of the soul, if we mean that there is some substance besides that thought that brings that thought forth, if it be God, I acknowledge it; but if there be meant something else that has no properties, it seems to be absurd.[63]

IV

One might well ask at this point, Why has Edwards in the past been associated with English empiricism at all? Why has he so often been discussed as a product of the revolution in philosophy effected by Locke and Newton? The reasons, I think, are two: first, it has often been assumed, wrongly, that Edwards's immaterialism, his denial that matter exists as an independent substance, was a subjective idealism, that is, a philosophical position derived initially from the insight that Locke's sensationalist epistemology brings into question the independent existence of the primary qualities of matter as much as the secondary; and second, Edwards has been grouped with Locke and Newton because he appears to have sided with the Newtonians and the corpuscularians against Leibniz and the Cartesians in the controversy over the existence of void space. The Cartesian tenet that extension is the essence of matter and that therefore space, which is extended, must be in some sense material was one of the trademarks of Continental rationalism. According to this teaching, the effects of gravity must be explained in mechanical terms. Edwards, however, was an antimechanist who, like the Newtonians, regarded causal action-at-a-distance (as in the instance of gravity) as a possibility, or at least as an acceptable description of events. Since Newton was able to calculate the laws of celestial dynamics with great precision yet without making an allowance for the friction or resistance of the so-called plenum, there was no reason to assume the plenum existed.[64] Physical causation could occur in a natural void, it seemed. The results of experimental philosophy seemed to indicate that the plenum, or a material space, was a redundancy, its existence mathematically superfluous.[65]

Despite this empirical evidence for action-at-a-distance, however, Leibniz and others pressed the Newtonians on the issue, seeing in the empiricist approach a revival of "occult forces," and particularly pointing

to the absence of sound metaphysical doctrine in England. In consequence, the English empiricist view hardened and was presented almost
as though it were a satisfactory metaphysics in itself, rather than avoidance of metaphysical questions. Locke and Newton became paired as the
proponents of true and productive philosophy in opposition to the vain
and fruitless speculation that occurred on the Continent. Meanwhile, the
very real theoretical problems with Newtonian corpuscularianism, especially that of action-at-a-distance, a supposition which necessarily followed from the supposition of a void between atoms, were rationalized
away, usually by unsystematically calling in theology.

This monumental controversy, more than any other issue, has served
to sustain for historians a polarity between English empiricists and
Continental rationalists. How did Edwards fit into it? We know that the
Irishman Berkeley and the American Edwards have commonly been
assimilated into the English empiricist group, but what are the facts?

Edwards was not a Cartesian mechanist, but neither was he one who
believed that metaphysics, i.e., "hypothetical" philosophy, could or
should be bypassed. However, his belief in continuous creation and his
occasionalist analysis of causation removed action-at-a-distance as a
serious problem at one level. Indeed, the workings of gravity as proposed
by antimechanical empiricists like Newton served to validate the occasionalist theory of causation.

Regarding the nature of matter, Edwards was not a Newtonian in the
conventional sense, but he also did not side with the Cartesians. It must
be remembered, first of all, that it was not *only* the Newtonians who
rejected the Cartesian conception of matter as fundamentally extension.
Pierre Gassendi and Henry More, on strictly a priori grounds, also
challenged the Cartesian conception. In other words, it was not only
English empiricists who were anti-Cartesian; there were *rationalist* metaphysicians who were anti-Cartesian on this subject as well. When one
looks at the development of Edwards's thought, it turns out that he
opposed the Cartesian conception of matter in Cartesian terms, that is, as
a rationalist, and not as a British empiricist or as one who was determined to sharply set off experimental evidence against "merely" hypothetical conclusions.

More than twenty years ago, in a pathbreaking article, Wallace Anderson argued convincingly that Edwards's immaterialism had rationalist,
not empiricist, foundations.[66] Beginning with an analysis of atoms as
paradoxically both extended and indivisible, Edwards concluded, first,
that it is indivisibility, not extension, that defines the essential quality of

the smallest particles, and, second, that indivisibility is equivalent to solidity or impenetrability. The "extension" of an atom is in fact an irrelevant consideration. What is it, then, that makes an atom solid or impenetrable? To answer "matter" or "substance" begs the question, since these concepts have already been reduced to solidity as the basic characteristic. The question is, what makes solidity solid, or from whence the solidness of solidity? The answer, Edwards concluded on a priori grounds, can only be God, who chooses in his wisdom to imbue certain parts of space with impenetrability. "The constant exercise of the infinite power of God is necessary to preserve bodies in being," Edwards wrote. "It follows that solidity results from the immediate exercise of God's power, causing there to be indefinite resistance in that place where it is." And it follows, too, that "all body is nothing but what immediately results from the exercise of divine power in such a particular manner. . . . The substance of bodies at last becomes either nothing, or nothing but the Deity acting in that particular manner in those parts of space where he thinks fit. So that, speaking most strictly, there is no proper substance but God himself."[67] Material substance, therefore, is just as much spirit as mental substance is.

Somewhat later, probably after having read Locke and maybe even after having gained some knowledge of Berkeley's thought, Edwards did do a phenomenalistic analysis of our knowledge of the external world (not a subject of concern to him at first), arguing that what we know of matter is only by color perception and touch, which is knowledge through our senses and therefore inescapably subjective or mental.[68] Through touch we encounter resistance, which is a sensation or an idea and is therefore mental. The material world is therefore ideal, in the sense that our knowledge of it is by idea and is in fact the communication of ideas to us by God. This phenomenalistic analysis, however, was not the basis of Edwards's immaterialism. For by the time Edwards did this analysis he already knew what matter *is* in essence, namely, God in a particular manifestation. But this later and secondary stage in Edwards's thinking can be classified as subjective idealism rather than as immaterialism.

Subjective idealism was useful to Edwards, perhaps, because it articulated nicely with his earlier belief that being or entity implies consciousness, either finite or infinite.[69] Yet we must insist that the immaterialist thesis based on the deduction that matter is spiritual substance, or the will of God exerted to create certain characteristics in space, notably solidity, impenetrability, or resistance—using the term "resistance" here not as a subjectively perceived attribute or tactile sensation but as a rationalist explanation of physical phenomena based on inference—antedated Edwards's subjective idealism. To state this point somewhat differently, Edwards arrived at the belief that bodies were *spirit* before he concluded that they were also *mental*. The resistance presented by a material object was an ontological characteristic of bodies in Edwards's thinking before it was a perceptual characteristic.[70]

It is important to note that this ontological conception of bodies as spiritual energy, taking the idea broadly, was very much in the air in the late seventeenth century, and Edwards may have picked it up in one or another of its forms from a variety of sources.[71] In an early unpublished essay, "De Gravitatione," Newton himself was guided by compelling theological commitments to suggest that God "by the sole action of thinking and willing, can prevent a body from penetrating any space defined by certain limits."[72] A world constituted "of this kind of being," Newton noted, ". . . would seem hardly any different" from a world with matter.

It is usually assumed that Newton came to this idea from reading Henry More, whom Edwards had also studied. Indeed, no other writer had as much influence on American academic philosophy between 1690 and 1720 as More. More himself, however, did not regard matter as spiritual substance. On the contrary, matter in his view is completely dead and motionless, but in his criticism of the Cartesian argument that the essential characteristic of matter is extension, More pointed out that the "miraculous force of resistance (*renixus*)" is not contained in the idea of extension, which means that extension is not conceptually adequate as the primary characteristic of matter upon which all else is dependent.[73]

Not only must matter be something more specific than extension, but extension is not exclusively an attribute of matter. For More believed that spirit, too, is extended, and that in truth all being is extended. Despite the totally antithetical properties of spirit and matter for More—matter is intrinsically devoid of perception, life, and motion, and is impenetrable, whereas spirit has the intrinsic properties of perception, life, and self-motion, and is both penetrable by matter and interpenetrable by itself—spirit can move matter, and it is only the activity of spirit that accounts for all motion in the material world. Both matter and spirit, then, are extended, but matter happens to have, in More's words, the "miraculous force of resistance," hence its impenetrability, which spirit lacks. It is not hard to see how Edwards could have come to the conclusion, after reading More's *Enchiridion Metaphysicum* and other works by him, that God could just as easily endow spirit with the miraculous force of resistance as He could create an independent material substance. In the same way that Malebranche's analysis of the origins of knowledge led Berkeley and others to conclude that the supposition of matter was superfluous, so Henry More's analysis of the properties of extension, both material and spiritual, could have led Edwards to conclude that extended matter was a superfluous supposition.[74]

It is striking that Leibniz also, by a different route, suggested early that extension did not suffice as the essential characteristic of matter. In a 1695 essay in the *Acta Eruditorum* Leibniz wrote: "There is something besides extension in corporeal things; indeed, . . . there is something *prior* to extension, namely, a natural force everywhere implanted by the Author of nature—a force which does not consist merely in a simple faculty such as that with which the Scholastics seem to have contented themselves but [a force] which is provided besides with a striving or effort which has its full effect unless impeded by a contrary striving. This *nisus* sometimes appears to the senses, and is in my opinion to be understood on rational grounds, as present everywhere in matter, even where it does not appear to sense. But if we cannot ascribe it to God by some miracle, it is certainly necessary that this force be produced by him within bodies themselves. Indeed, it must constitute the inmost nature of the body, since it is the character of substance to act, and extension means only the continuation or diffusion of an already pre-supposed acting and resisting substance. So far is extension itself from comprising substance."[75] There are major differences between the power of God in bodies discerned by Leibniz and the power of God in bodies discussed by Newton, but these examples should nevertheless serve to illustrate the degree to which rationalist speculation with direct bearing on the idea of immaterial matter was circulating during Edwards's formative years.

To summarize and conclude, Edwards's intellectual heritage and his own intense religious experience predisposed him toward philosophical positions that magnified God's power and glory, such as the occasionalist doctrine that made all knowledge of the physical world the immediate product of divine will and treated natural phenomena as representations of divine spirit and order.[76] Edwards would not have had to read much of Malebranche, or even much about Malebranche's thought, to have been quickly convinced of its suitability for enhancing his own philosophical and theological goals. That Edwards studied Locke's *Essay* closely, was stimulated by it, and learned from it is not at issue. But the notion that the *Essay* played a key functional role in the development of Edwards's metaphysics is not sustainable. An accurate picture of the foundations of

Edwards's thought requires that he be grouped with the theocentric, rationalist metaphysicians who have often wrongly been considered alien to the Anglo-American tradition in eighteenth-century philosophy.

Notes

I am indebted to Charles McCracken for a close reading of this essay that substantially improved it.

1. John Norris, *Cursory Reflections Upon a Book Call'd, An Essay Concerning Human Understanding* (London, 1690). Norris is treated in Frederick J. Powicke, *A Dissertation on John Norris of Bemerton* (London, 1894) and Flora MacKinnon, *The Philosophy of John Norris of Bemerton*, Philosophical Monographs of the Psychological Review, no. 2 (Baltimore, 1910); I have not read Richard Acworth, *La Philosophie de John Norris* (Paris, 1975).

2. Norris, *Cursory Reflections*, 43.

3. See, e.g., Richard A. Watson, *The Downfall of Cartesianism, 1673–1712: A Study of Epistemological Issues in Late 17th-Century Cartesianism* (The Hague, 1966), and John W. Yolton, "As In a Looking Glass: Perceptual Acquaintance in Eighteenth-Century Britain," *Journal of the History of Ideas* XL (1979), 207–34.

4. Norris, *Cursory Reflections*, 3.

5. Ibid., 3–4.

6. The quote from Locke is Norris's and is not exact. In bk. II, chap. viii, sec. 7, Locke wrote: "Whatsoever the mind perceives in itself, or is the immediate object of perception, thought, or understanding, that I call idea." I am using the Alexander Campbell Fraser edition of Locke's *Essay*, originally published in 1894 and reprinted by Dover Publications in 1959.

7. Norris, *Cursory Reflections*, 22–24.

8. Locke, *Essay*, "Epistle to the Reader".

9. Locke, *Essay*, "Introduction", secs. 2,6,7.

10. Perry Miller, *Jonathan Edwards* (New York, 1949), 52.

11. Morton White, *Science and Sentiment in America: Philosophical Thought from Jonathan Edwards to John Dewey* (New York, 1972), 35.

12. Elizabeth Flower, and Murray G. Murphey, *A History of Philosophy in America* (New York, 1977), 140.

13. For information on this subject, including further bibliography, see Norman Fiering, "Early American Philosophy vs. Philosophy in Early America," *Transactions of the Charles S. Pierce Society* 13 (1977), 216–37; *Moral Philosophy at Seventeenth-Century Harvard: A Discipline in Transition* (Chapel Hill, N.C. 1981), chaps. 5 and 6; and *Jonathan Edwards's Moral Thought and Its British Context* (Chapel Hill, N.C., 1981), chap. 1.

14. See Fiering, "The Transatlantic Republic of Letters: A Note on the Circulation of Learned Periodicals to Early Eighteenth-Century America," *William and Mary Quarterly* 3rd ser., 33 (1976), 642–60.

15. In "Miscellanies," letter f, Harvey G. Townsend, ed., *The Philosophy of Jonathan Edwards from His Private Notebooks* (Eugene, Oreg., 1955), and "Things to be Considered," Long Series, no. 26, Wallace E. Anderson, ed., *Jonathan Edwards: Scientific and Philosophical Writings* (New Haven, Conn., 1980), Edwards refers to Hobbes. Letter f was written ca. 1723. In *Freedom of Will*, written thirty years later, Edwards said explicitly that he had never read Hobbes.

16. Bishop Berkeley also read LeClerc in his formative years and corresponded with him. See A. A. Luce, *Berkeley and Malebranche: A Study in the Origins of Berkeley's Thought* (Oxford, 1934), 12, 16, 71. We know that Samuel Johnson of Connecticut read LeClerc (he called him "J. Clark") in 1716, and LeClerc's works were part of the curriculum at Harvard twenty years earlier.

17. Anderson, ed., *Jonathan Edwards*, contains an excellent 130-page introduction by Anderson that reviews much of what is known about Edwards's early reading. Neither LeClerc nor LeGrand is given sufficient attention in this introduction, however.

18. On Cartesianism in England, see: Sterling P. Lamprecht, "The Role of Descartes in Seventeenth-Century England," in *Studies in the History of Ideas*, ed. Dept. of Philosophy, Columbia University (New York, 1935), II, 181–240; Marjorie Nicolson, "The Early Stages of Cartesianism in England," *Studies in Philology* 26 (1929), 356–74; and Charlotte S. Ware, "The Influence of Descartes on John Locke," *Revue Internationale de Philosophie* 4 (1950), 210–39.

19. This particular subject is not addressed in this essay. See, however, Terrence Erdt, *Jonathan Edwards: Art and the Sense of the Heart* (Amherst, Mass., 1980), chap. 1, which relates Edwards's "sense of the heart" more to a Calvinist tradition than to Locke, and James Hoopes, "Jonathan Edwards's Religious Psychology", *Journal of American History* 69 (1983), 849–65, which carefully sifts Edwards's relation to Locke on the matter of "sense."

20. The two best essays on the development of Edwards's metaphysics are chapter 3 in Elizabeth Flower and Murray G. Murphey, *A History of Philosophy In America*, 2 vols. (New York, 1977) and Wallace E. Anderson's excellent introduction to Anderson, ed., *Jonathan Edwards: Scientific and Philosophical Writings*, the most complete study thus far. Both of these works go a long way toward correcting the Locke bias in so much interpretation of Edwards, but in my estimation not far enough. Flower and Murphey's comment that Edwards's "attitude toward Locke was more critical [than it was toward Newton], and while he quickly accepted most of the Lockean philosophy, he did not hesitate to disagree with Locke on specific points," should be reversed: Edwards may have agreed with Locke on a few specific points, but he did not accept Locke's philosophy in spirit or substance. Anderson is more definite: "If the articles in 'The Mind' reflect Edwards's first exposure to Locke's work, then we can no longer think of Locke's influence upon him as though it were the intellectual ravishment of a schoolboy busy at his logic lessons." Edwards's discussions in "The Mind" are "well anchored by the metaphysical principles that Edwards had

already settled, and he was not likely to be blown far from those moorings. . . . In most questions where Edwards may be seen responding to Locke, we find he either rejects or consciously modifies Locke's express claims" (p. 33). Anderson goes on to demonstrate Edwards's divergence from Locke on numerous specific issues, but Locke nevertheless looms disproportionately large in Anderson's account of Edwards's intellectual growth.

21. White, *Science and Sentiment*, treats Locke as more of a rationalist than he is commonly assumed to be, and thus relates Edwards to Locke somewhat unconventionally, but nevertheless it still seems to me to be incorrect to call Edwards a "Lockeian philosopher" (p. 32) and to claim that the *Essay Concerning Human Understanding* provided "the general framework within which [Edwards] worked" (p. 35).

22. Louis E. Loeb, *From Descartes to Hume: Continental Metaphysics and the Development of Modern Philosophy* (Ithaca, N.Y., 1981), 29–30.

23. More at one time defined his purpose as being not "to Theologize in Philosophy, but to draw an Exoterick Fence, or exteriour Fortification about Theologie." (Quoted in William C. DePauley, *The Candle of the Lord: Studies in the Cambridge Platonists* [London, 1937], 119–20.) All of the theocentric metaphysicians were similarly motivated. See Leroy E. Loemker, *Struggle for Synthesis: The Seventeenth-Century Background of Leibniz's Synthesis of Order and Freedom* (Cambridge, Mass., 1972), 58–60, "philosophy as apologetic." Charles J. McCracken, *Malebranche and British Philosophy* (Oxford, 1983), 211, makes the point effectively: "The chief goal of the philosophical labours of both Malebranche and Berkeley was the same: to recall Christian philosophy to a recognition of the total and immediate dependence of all things on God."

24. Loeb, *Descartes to Hume*, 320, 37–56.

25. The historiography of seventeenth- and eighteenth-century philosophy is in a period of revision at present, with results that are bound to lead to a more accurate conception of early American philosophy. Loeb's *From Descartes to Hume* is a sustained attack on what he calls the gross distortions inherent in the "standard framework" of interpretation. This standard framework has three main elements, and the rejection of each of them has important bearing on how Jonathan Edwards is understood. The three claims of the standard framework that Loeb rejects are as follows: (1) "that Berkeley, Descartes, Hume, Leibniz, Locke, and Spinoza are the most important figures of the period prior to Kant"; (2) "that these figures divide into two competing schools, the Continental Rationalists and the British empiricists"; and (3) "that within each group successive figures apply the school's basic (Rationalist or Empiricist) principles with increasing rigor to a common body of problems, ultimately carrying them through to their 'logical conclusions'" (pp. 13–14). The obvious resurgence of interest in Malebranche in the past few years, with the first translation of the *Search After Truth* into English in nearly three hundred years (by Thomas M. Lennon and Paul J. Olscamp [Columbus, Ohio, 1980]), and at least two new monographs on his philosophy published in the 1980s in addition to Loeb's revival of Malebranche, is a dramatic

symptom of the turnaround that is occurring. See *Philosophical Books* 24 (1983), 17–22, a review of recent Malebranche literature by H. A. S. Schankula.

26. See "Miscellanies," nos. 16 and 29, in Townsend, ed., *Jonathan Edwards*.

27. From Edwards's "Things to be Considered," Long Series, no. 14, in Anderson, ed., *Jonathan Edwards*, 231; see also nos. 15–17.

28. Ibid., 246, no. 49.

29. Perry Miller and Thomas H. Johnson, eds., *The Puritans*, rev. ed. (New York, 1963; orig. publ. 1928), II, 353, 358–59. William Ames, Peter Sterry, and many other Puritans adhered to the doctrine of "continuata Creatio," uniting the act of creation with God's preserving and governing of it. The doctrine is discussed learnedly in J. E. McGuire, "Boyle's Conception of Nature," *Journal of the History of Ideas* 33 (1972), 523–42. See also, McGuire's "Force, Active Principles, and Newton's Invisible Realm," *Ambix* 15 (1968), 202.

30. Meditations, III, in *The Philosophical Works of Descartes*, ed. Elizabeth S. Haldane and G.R.T. Ross, 2 vols. (Cambridge, 1931), I, 168, quoted in Loeb, *Descartes to Hume*, 211.

31. Cf. McGuire, "Force", 198, for additional references to Descartes. McGuire notes that this doctrine was common among the medieval Arabic philosophers.

32. I am using the term "occasionalist" in the loose sense, which includes Hume's skeptical "constant conjunction" with Malebranche's divine determination of events.

33. According to Malebranche, the "New Philosophy . . . destroys all the Pretences of the Libertines, by the establishing its very first Principle that perfectly agrees with the first Principle of the Christian Religion, namely that we must love and fear none but God, since none but He alone can make us happy. . . . As Religion declares that there is but one true God, so this Philosophy shews that there is but one true Cause." (*Search After Truth*, trans. Thomas Taylor, bk. VI, chap. ii, p. 57.) "Christian Philosophers ought to wage an uninterrupted war with prejudices . . . and particularly those of so dangerous importance as that of the Efficacy of Second Causes." (*Search After Truth*, trans. Thomas Taylor, "Illustrations," 173.)

34. "Things to be Considered," Long Series, no. 47, in Anderson, ed., *Jonathan Edwards*, pp. 241–42.

35. Townsend, ed., *Jonathan Edwards*, "Miscellanies," no. 125.

36. "Mind," no. 26, in Anderson, ed., *Jonathan Edwards*, 350. See also "Of Atoms," prop. 2, corol. 4 and corols. 12–15.

37. "Of Atoms," prop. 2, corol. 15, 13. Corol. 16 has: "Hence we learn that there is no such thing as mechanism, if that word is taken to be that whereby bodies act upon each other, purely and properly by themselves." (Anderson, ed., *Jonathan Edwards* 215–16).

38. "Miscellanies," no. 629, from the manuscript transcripts of Thomas Schafer, Beinecke Library, Yale University. Edwards can be distinguished from more empiricist, nominalist corpuscularians like Robert Boyle by his belief in

immanent laws of nature, or divine rules. According to McGuire, "Boyle's Conception of Nature," Boyle believed that causal relations were a direct result of divine agency, as did Edwards, but unlike Edwards he maintained that the concept of law is projected upon nature as a result of human recognition of similarities in phenomena. The uniformity and coherence of natural phenomena abstracted by man are not necessarily expressions of God's ideas, or representative of the "constitution of nature," in Edwards's phrase. Borrowing from McGuire's distinction between Leibniz and Boyle, it may be noted that Edwards's God and the world He creates are intelligible because God acts in accordance with reason and logic. Although we cannot deduce natural laws a priori, in Edwards's view they are explicable by the principle of sufficient reason or by teleological interpretation.

39. See "Miscellanies," nos. 1, 3, and 20, in Townsend ed., *Jonathan Edwards.*

40. "Miscellanies," letter gg, in Townsend, ed. *Jonathan Edwards.*

41. "Miscellanies," nos. 3, 87. Cf. n. 71, below.

42. "Miscellanies," nos. 1 [one], 20.

43. Working independently, I find myself confirming Anderson's conclusions about the relationship of Edwards's faith to his metaphysics on this point. See Anderson, ed., *Jonathan Edwards,* 78–79.

44. "Miscellanies," no. 94, in Townsend ed., *Jonathan Edwards.* Edwards's conception of the Trinity in this note is very close to Bartolomaus Keckermann's in *Systema Sacrosanctae Theologiae* (Geneva, 1611), as excerpted in Heinrich Heppe, *Reformed Dognmatics . . .,* ed. Ernst Bizer, trans. G. T. Thomson (London, 1950), pp. 106–8.

45. "Miscellanies," no. 94. Cf. Nicolas Malebranche, *Search After Truth,* trans. Richard Sault (London, 1694), bk. III, p. 2, chap. v: "It is certain that there was none but God alone before the World was Created, and he could not produce it without Knowledge and without Ideas: Consequently those Ideas which God had of the World, are not different from himself; and thus all Creatures, even the most Material and Terrestrial, are in God, though in a manner altogether Spiritual, which we cannot apprehend. God therefore sees all Beings in himself, in considering his own Perfections which represent them to him." Cf. also the Ramist conception of God and God's reflection of Himself in James Fitch, *The First Principles of the Doctrine of Christ* (Boston, 1679), a work widely read in New England.

46. "Mind," no. 36, in Anderson, ed., *Jonathan Edwards.* Cf. also, no. 40: "Since all material existence is only idea, this question may be asked: In what sense may those things be said to exist which are supposed, and yet are in no actual idea of any created minds? I answer, they exist only in uncreated idea. . . . But, it may be asked, how do those things exist which have an actual existence, but of which no created mind is conscious . . . ? I answer, there has been in times past such a course and succession of existences that these things must be supposed to make the series complete, according to divine appointment of the order of things. . . . The supposition of God which we speak of is nothing else but God's

acting in the course and series of his exciting ideas, as if they, the things supposed, were in actual idea." Edwards's belief in this "system and series of ideas" that constituted the divine mind was much like that espoused by John Norris.

47. See Berkeley, *A Treatise Concerning the Principles of Human Knowledge*, Part 1, secs. 6, 22–23, 45, and 48.

48. John Norris, *An Essay towards The Theory of the Ideal or Intelligible World*, Part I (London, 1701), p. 429. Cf. also Ralph Cudworth, *True Intellectual* (1678) pp. 546ff.

49. "Miscellanies," no. 179, in Townsend, ed., *Jonathan Edwards*.

50. *Malebranche and British Philosophy* (New York, 1983). McCracken kindly allowed me to read the appendix, which is on Malebranche's influence in America, in manuscript.

51. Perry Miller, *The New England Mind: The Seventeenth Century* (Boston, Mass., 1939; rpt. 1961), 154–80.

52. Quoted in Keith L. Sprunger, *The Learned Doctor William Ames: Dutch Backgrounds of English and American Puritanism* (Urbana, Ill., 1972), 141.

53. The divine Plato had to be rescued from false interpretations that failed to connect him to the *prisca theologia* the ancient teaching of Moses that passed to the Greeks through the Egyptians. See, e.g., Fiering, *Moral Philosophy at Seventeenth-Century Harvard*, 280. See also, John H. Muirhead, *The Platonic Tradition in Anglo-Saxon Philosophy: Studies in the History of Idealism in England and America* (New York, 1931).

54. Cf. Fitch, *First Principles*, which was influenced by Richardson. Samuel Parker's anti-Platonist work, *A Free and Impartial Censure of the Platonick Philosophie* (1666) commented on the Platonists' supposition "that the Truth of all Beings consists in a conformity to their *Archetypal Ideas*, whereby they mean some General Patterns, by which all the Individuals of each Species are framed." Parker also referred to the Platonist belief that "God has hang'd a multitude of these little Pictures of himself and all his creatures in every man's understanding." See G. A. J. Rogers, "Locke, Newton, and the Cambridge Platonists on Innate Ideas," *Journal of the History of Ideas* 40 (1979), 191–205.

55. Cf. Lee W. Gibbs, *William Ames: Technometry* (Philadelphia, 1979). Richardson wrote: "ens is the subject of all Arts," but the arts are not about God himself. They are about what comes from God. Every art is "an eternall rule in the Idea of God." God governs his creation by "the rules of Art, for so every rule of Art is a Statute-law of God, by which hee made the things, and whereby hee governes the things." Every true rule of art "is eternall" and is true insofar as it "answers to that Idea that is in [God]."

56. See "Mind," no. 10 (Anderson, ed., *Jonathan Edwards*). Charles McCracken points out that Edwards's notion of God's "constitution" is identical to Malebranche's conception of God's "general will." See also Fiering, *Jonathan Edwards's Moral Thought*, 70–80, 93–104, and Anderson ed., *Jonathan Edwards*, 109.

57. Cf. Edward, Lord Herbert of Cherbury, *De Veritate*, trans. with an introduction by Meyrick H. Carre (Bristol, Eng., 1937).

58. *Search After Truth*, bk. III, pt. 2, chap. vi, p. 47.

59. Edwards, like Malebranche, struggled all his life with the question of why God bothered to create sense organs. See, e.g., "Mind," no. 34 (Anderson, ed., *Jonathan Edwards*): "We need not perplex our minds with a thousand questions and doubts that will seem to arise as to what purpose is this way of exciting ideas [i.e., through created events]. . . . It is just all one as to any benefit or advantage, any end that we can suppose was proposed by the Creator, as if the material universe were existent in the same manner as is vulgarly thought. For the corporeal world is to no advantage but to the spiritual, and it is exactly the same advantage this way as the other [i.e., for created ideas to be bypassed]; for it is all one as to anything excited in the mind." Cf. also, "Mind" no. 40: "If material existence be only mental, then our bodies and organs are ideas only; and then in what sense is it true that the mind receives ideas by the organs of sense, seeing that the organs of sense themselves exist nowhere but in the mind? Answer: Seeing our organs themselves are ideas, the connection that our ideas have with such and such a mode of our organ is is no other than God's constitution that some of our ideas shall be connected with others according to such a settled law and order, so that some ideas shall follow from others as their cause." Cf. also, "Mind," no. 51, and "Miscellanies," no. 1340, in Townsend, ed., *Jonathan Edwards*.

60. *Search After Truth*, bk. III, pt. 2, chap. vi, p. 48.

61. Cf. "Mind," no. 34, (Anderson ed., *Jonathan Edwards*). This conclusion brings Edwards close in practical terms to Spinoza's doctrine that the order and connection of ideas is the same as the order and connection of things.

62. *Search After Truth*, bk. III, pt. 2, ch. viii, p. 68.

63. "Miscellanies," no. 267, (Townsend, ed., *Jonathan Edwards*.) Anderson, ed., *Jonathan Edwards*, 105, sums up Edwards's theocentric views admirably in the following passage but fails to note how closely Edwards agreed with Malebranche on all of these points: "Edwards holds that all the objects and events in nature received their existence from God: ideas of sensations are immediately communicated by God, the order of phenomena by which bodies are solid objects is wholly determined by God, and even every new thought in a mind depends for its occurrence upon God."

64. The issues are very informatively discussed in J. E. McGuire, "Body and Void and Newton's De Mundi Systemate: Some New Sources," *Archive for History of Exact Sciences* 3 (1966), 206–48.

65. Contrary to the popular impression, Newton engaged in a great deal of metaphysical speculation, which he called, unpejoratively, hypothetical philosophy, and to which he had no aversion whatsoever, but he did assert unambiguously that to cling to any hypothetical position that is contradicted by experimental philosophy is a profound error. McGuire, "Body and Void," 221, quotes from an unpublished Newton manuscript: "One must pass from experimental philoso-

phy to the efficient and final causes of things and from all these to the nature of imperceptible things and finally to hypothetical philosophy." See also, McGuire, "Force, Active Principles, and Newton's Invisible Realm," *Ambix* 15 (1968), 173: Newton believed "in an ontology richer and more complex than any version of the mechanical philosophy."

66. Wallace Anderson, "Immaterialism in Jonathan Edwards's Early Philosophical Notes," *Journal of the History of Ideas* XXV (1964), 181–200.

67. (Anderson, ed., *Jonathan Edwards*). "Of Atoms," 215.

68. See "Mind," no. 13, no. 27, no. 40, no. 51, in Anderson, ed., *Jonathan Edwards*.

69. "Miscellanies," no. 247 (Townsend, ed., *Jonathan Edwards*): "For God to glorify Himself is to discover [i.e., uncover] Himself in His works or to communicate Himself in His Works, which is all one. For we are to remember that the world exists only mentally, so that the very being of the world implies its being perceived or discovered." Cf. Anderson, ed., *Jonathan Edwards*, 79.

70. I am following the lead here of George Rupp, "The 'Idealism' of Jonathan Edwards," *Harvard Theological Review* 62 (1969), 209–26, who asserts that Edwards's "alleged idealism has its roots not only in epistemological considerations but directly in his ontology as well." On the term "spirit," McGuire's warning is well taken: "spirit" as used "in the seventeenth and early eighteenth century, is notoriously slippery and ambiguous." Newton could "move from spirit of vitriol to electric spirit, through animal, aerial, and aethereal spirits, to angelic spirits, and God. If Newton were not fully conscious of the subtle shifts in meaning it mattered little; for his abiding concern was to assert the existence of the non-material in the world . . . : he and the seventeenth century made no clear distinction between the 'spirituous' and the 'spiritual'." (McGuire, "Force, Active Principles, and Newton's Invisible Realm," *Ambix* 15 (1968), 186.

71. Edwards's statement in "Things to be Considered," Long Series, no. 23[a] (Anderson, ed., *Jonathan Edwards*), that "it is universally allowed that gravity depends immediately on the divine influence" is suggestive of his reading in English Newtonian theological arguments. Edwards continued: "and because it may be proved that solidity and gravity are in a good sense the same, and resolvable into each other; and because solidity has been proved to be the very being of a body: therefore we may infallibly conclude that the very being, and the manner of being, and the whole of bodies depends immediately on the divine power."

72. "De Gravitatione et Aequipondio Fluidorum," has been printed in the original Latin and in English translation in *Unpublished Scientific Papers of Isaac Newton*, ed. A. Rupert Hall and Marie Boas Hall (Cambridge, 1962). It is put into context in J. E. McGuire, "Force, Active Principles, and Newton's Invisible Realm," *Ambix* 15 (1968).

73. Henry More, *Enchiridion Metaphysicum, sive, de Rebus Incorporeis* (London, 1679), 321. Précis of this work used by Harvard students at the end of the seventeenth century still survive in manuscript.

74. It is known that in the early 1660s Newton took notes from Henry More's *Immortality of the Soul*, which was included in *A Collection of Several Philosophical Writings of Dr. Henry More* (London, 1662). See Richard S. Westfall, "Foundations of Newton's Philosophy of Nature," *British Journal for the History of Science* 1 (1962), 171–82. More's *Enchiridion Metaphysicum* was not published until 1671, making it too late to have influenced Newton's earliest speculations on immaterial matter. Edwards is more likely to have read the *Enchiridion* than the *Immortality of the Soul*, because of the use of the former work as a text at Harvard. On Edwards's indirect "Harvard" education, see Fiering, *Jonathan Edwards*, chap. 1. Criticism of the Cartesian doctrine that extension is the essence of matter was widespread in England as elsewhere, and Edwards may have borrowed ideas concerning it from a number of sources. Samuel Clarke, for instance, in notes to his Latin translation of Rohault's *Physics*, published in London in 1697 and 1702, wrote: "It does no more seem to follow from hence; that, because we conceive extension before any other properties of matter, and that those properties can't be conceived to exist, without first conceiving extension; therefore extension is the essence of matter; then it follows from hence, that existence is conceived before all other properties of matter, and therefore existence is the essence of matter. . . . Not extension, but solid extension, impenetrable, which is endued with a power of resisting, may . . . be more truly called the essence of matter" (pt. I, chap. vii, sec. 8, n.) (Quoted in Lamprecht, "The Role of Descartes in Seventeenth-Century England," 219–20.) Rohault's *Physics* was well known in New England. For other similar instances, such as John Ray's *Wisdom of God* (1691), an immensely popular work, see Lamprecht.

75. G. W. Leibniz, *Philosophical Papers and Letters*, ed. and trans. Leroy E. Loemker, 2nd ed. (Dordrecht, 1969), 435–44.

76. Edwards's immaterialism, his occasionalism, and his belief in continuous creation are so closely conjoined that it is impossible to tell which came first. In "Things to be Considered," Long Series, no. 47, this unity is apparent: "Since . . . body is nothing but an infinite resistance in some part of space caused by the immediate exercise of divine power, it follows that as great and as wonderful a power is every moment exerted to the upholding of the world, as at first was to the creation of it; the first creation being only the first exertion of this power to cause such resistance, the preservation only the continuation or the repetition of this power every moment to cause this resistance." (Anderson, ed., *Jonathan Edwards*, 241).

6

Jonathan Edwards's
Pursuit of Reality

WILSON H. KIMNACH

As the instigator of "surprising conversions" in Northampton, Massachusetts, during the mid-1730s, and as one of the leading exhorters of the Great Awakening in 1740, Jonathan Edwards has laid claim to the place of foremost American preacher. Inspiration of the New Lights in his own day and of succeeding generations devoted to "heart religion," Edwards has been renowned and reviled as the prototype of the revivalist. At the same time, he has been credited and blamed for having established the taste for philosophical theology among adherents of the New Divinity, as he has become identified with the last flowering of dogmatic Calvinism. In his own lifetime and since, he has been claimed as eponym by various parties, while other parties have defined themselves by their opposition to him. For the many who only glance now and then at one of his sermons—and one is usually *the one*—the voice of Edwards is loud and clear but often seems to issue from another world. Last of the Puritans or first of the American Evangelicals, Edwards's piety and intellectual stature have made him the perfect representative man.

But it is in the conscious pursuit of reality that Edwards most differentiates himself from other preachers and ecclesiastical leaders on both sides of the issue of the Great Awakening and in subsequent movements. Indeed, it is in this that he is to be differentiated from some of his most devoted followers.

By "pursuit of reality," at least two levels of activity on Edwards's part are implied: first, a sustained evaluation of the nature of human experience; second, a method of preaching. Edwards explored the determinants of life, such as the relationship between man and nature, and the contrastive code of language which had been given to man as a seeming alternative to nature; moreover, he developed a style of preaching that dramatized this exploration even while he propounded conventional doctrines. The pursuit was thus conducted in public and in private, in published and in private writings. The account of his extraordinary effort will inevitably involve the piecing together of many disparate materials as we seek the fundamental nature of this activity in his thought and expression.

Perhaps it is best to consider first the activity of his mind during the formative period including his New York pastorate, the Yale College tutorship, and his first year or two in Northhampton. It was, after all, during this period that Edwards began to grapple with the problem of the pursuit of reality in his private life. In his "Diary," notebooks such as the "The Mind" and "Miscellanies," as well as in sermons, one can observe the struggle to define the nature of reality to his own satisfaction. He seems never to have seriously questioned the fundamental doctrines of his faith once he accepted the doctrine of election; indeed, it would be a mistake were we to view him primarily as a dogmatist.[1] The great test of mind and character he undertook was, from the start, concerned not so much with the truth of doctrine as with its reality.

This preoccupation with religion as experience is reflected in many of the earlier private writings in which Edwards explored his hopes and fears, or attempted to shape his very psychic being. In the "Diary" and "Resolutions," as well as in such pieces as his early "Natural Philosophy" notes, including his rules for writing a treatise, the hallmark of Edwards in not the mere pious soul-searching of the traditional Puritan, though that is there, nor the fevered ambition of the bright young man on the rise, though that is there too, but the manifold reaching and grasping after a multitude of diverse particular thoughts, impulses, and experiences that apparently represented so many potential openings into the complex edifice of life. The jumble is impressive: "rational philosophical truths" and the highest aspirations cheek by jowl with dietary strictures and hints on handling an audience, and of course the diary reveals contrarieties in abundance, since the life pursued had to be brought into coherence through repeated countermeasures. Perhaps the early years are best reflected by the sixth resolution: "To live with all my might, while I do live." That sentiment, above all others, expresses the essential Edwards at the onset.[2]

The intensity of Edwards's mentality might have found a number of outlets within the intellectual playgrounds defined by "natural philosophy" and "divinity" in the eighteenth century academy, but his purpose was not merely to collect data on nature or to speculate endlessly upon theological abstrusities. Rather, Edwards early launched upon a series of imaginative speculations concerning the constitution of natural world, with the idea of decisively ascertaining God's relation to his physical creation. Having finally settled upon the immaterialist position that the world exists as it is known by God, and that what we know as substance is the present power of God's intention in a particular time and place, it was not long before Edwards turned to the work of completing the cycle commonly divided between the "objective" and the "subjective":

Friday, Feb. 12, 1725. The very thing I now want, to give me a clearer and more immediate view of the perfections and glory of God, is as clear a knowledge of the manner of God's exerting himself, with respect to Spirits and Mind, as I have, of his operations concerning Matter and Bodies.[3]

The search for knowledge of the precise operation of God upon "Spirits and Mind," in particular, was to preoccupy Edwards during the remainder of his life, however distracted he may have been by the course of events during brief periods. For the "manner of God's exerting himself" was nothing less than absolute reality, given Edwards's conception of the nature of the creation, and he was determined to discover that ultimate power in all aspects of the creation, but particularly as revealed in the drama of redemption, as his very raison d'être. Man, he came to believe, was created to complete the circuit of cognition through which God realized himself, although only those redeemed in Christ would be able to participate in that ultimate fulfillment.

As a preacher in the Puritan tradition, a pastor and teacher whose "prophesying" constituted the heart of his office as one of "Christ's ambassadors," Edwards had a call not only to share the fruits of his meditations with his parishioners, but to do all in his power to enable them to follow in his spiritual steps. For Edwards, this meant leading his people according to the traditional tenets of the New England Way, and in the most general sense he was a conservative with no innovative impulses—unless the undoing of Stoddardean innovations constitutes innovation. Yet Edwards also was nothing if not extraordinary, and the Way as interpreted by his preaching must always have been the occasion of superlative experiences and responses.

The people of East Windsor are credited with an early recognition of the character of his preaching: "*Mr.* [Timothy] *Edwards* was, perhaps, the *more learned* man, and more animated in his manner. Yet *Mr.*

Jonathan was the deeper preacher."[4] Compared to his father, the Reverend Timothy Edwards, whose efforts had been the occasion of significant religious awakenings among his people and whose sermon manuscripts reveal a mastery of Scripture citation if not much remarkable secular learning, the younger Edwards was immediately perceived to be a *searcher*. Small wonder, then, if Solomon Stoddard, critic and instructor of preachers, saw in his grandson one who might actually inspire what he himself noted had become the spiritually weary community of Northampton. In any event, within a year after his Northampton ordination, Edwards made explicit declaration of the ground upon which he would conduct his holy warfare. In a yet unprinted sermon addressing the limits of preaching to awaken, Edwards insists: "The reason why men no more regard warnings of future punishment, is because it don't seem real to them." He continues, "this opposition of nature to divine truth causes that the being of God and another world don't seem real to them."[5] This issue was central and crucial to Edwards, for in all matters of religion, a mere acquiescence in abstract validity was the same as no acceptance at all.

For divine truth to be real in human experience, Edwards concluded, it had to overcome "the prejudices of nature" in specific ways. "There are these two things in realizing a thing, or necessary in order to things seeming real to us: believing the truth of it, and having a sensible idea or apprehension of it."[6] As is so often the case in Edwards, the answer is not only not simple, but it involves factors that are frequently deemed to be in some respect antithetical. Here, rational conviction and sensation are explicitly linked in Edwards's pulpit discourse for the first time, defining a position to which he would adhere for the remainder of his life.

For the sake of clarity, I will now do a little Ramistic dichotomizing, considering first Edwards's notion of the role of reason in relation to faith, and then the role of sensation.

That "truth" that anchors belief is, according to three entries in Edwards's notebook, "The Mind," primarily a consistency of ideas within the mind.[7] It is the awareness that all fits that gives the confidence of having ascertained the truth. But consistency implies plurality, a series of data within which consistency or inconsistency may be defined. Thus the structure of ideas implied by logic—indeed, even the "old logick"—is necessary to the establishing of either truth or falsehood. The old Ramistic sermon form to which Edwards adhered and which he vehemently defended, probably with the comments of the Earl of Shaftesbury in mind, in the preface to his *Discourses on Various Important Subjects*, enabled him to *arrange* data in impressive array.[8] The very distribution of

ideas under the heads permitted extensive deductive analysis and distribution of parts. And as Edwards points out in a "Miscellanies" entry
entitled "Spiritual Knowledge, Faith," "Belief of the truth may be saving
that doth most directly depend on rational arguments. . . . Rational
arguments give opportunity for [believing the truth of divine doctrines],
they give opportunity for such a belief with a less degree of grace. They
give opportunity for a fuller and more established belief . . ."⁹ While the
rational argument which advances the truth may not adduce saving
grace, it may indeed shape a more fortuitous occasion for it.

Yet another aspect of higher truths of real significance for Edwards is
their complexity; indeed, the higher the truth the more complex. As the
first entry on "Excellency" in "The Mind" makes clear, reality is a matter
of relationship for Edwards: the higher the truth the greater the extent of
relationships involved.¹⁰ Rational exposition within sermons is thus a
means of enlarging the awareness of extensive relationships within spiritual reality. The belief that is the result of a reasoned consent to highly
complex relationships among seminal theological ideas is a more adequate belief, a higher exercise of common grace, and thus a nearer
approach to supernatural grace.

In fine then, Edwards insists upon the necessity for a defining, differen-
tiating, and structuring of the elements in a rational scheme as requisite
to establishing a convincing truth. The more extensive the network of
relationships defined, moreover, the more substantial the authenticating
context which establishes truth. It is in the light of this convction that
Edwards intended to culminate his career in the vast works entitled "A
Rational Account of Christianity" and "A History of the Work of Redemption." Yet at the same time that Edwards seems to strive for the
most exhaustive rationalistic realization of spiritual truth, he insists that
such an achievement does not alone constitute more than metaphysical
validity: in order for the attainment of reality, one must also possess a
"sensible idea or apprehension of it."

The concept of a "sensible idea" is one of the most insistent of Edwards's preoccupations, occurring in discussions ranging beyond rhetoric
to epistemology and ontology. In its inception, however, it seems to have
been directly related to a not unfamiliar need for any scholar or thinker.
Perhaps the earliest reference to a version of it occurs in the "Diary":

Saturday night, June 8 [1723] at Boston. . . .

One thing, that would be of great advantage to me, in reading to my profit,
would be, the endeavouring, with all my might, *to keep the image and*

picture of the thing in my mind, and be careful that I do not lose it, in the chain of the discourse.[11]

To somehow gather up a complex sequence of ideas from an abstract theological discourse so that a configuration as vivid and sustained as a visual sense impression is achieved, and more than that, is maintained during the continuation of the argument, is Edwards's not unheard-of goal. He wants to "get the picture." Later writers might invoke the integrative power of the imagination for such a solution, but Edwards rather consistently reserves the word "imagination" for self-deceptive mental activities, in the manner of pre-Romantic writers generally. Still, in our post-Romantic idiom it would be appropriate to say that he is demanding higher imaginative effort of himself.

This preoccupation with imaginative apprehension approximating sense impression became more pronounced as Edwards undertook his pastoral vocation and began to assess the practical problems related to efficacious preaching. From the earliest entries in "The Mind" notebook, Edwards tended to understand the mind as a sense organ. For instance, in entry [16], "Consciousness," he stresses that the mind "feels" ideas, abstract ones as well as those originating in sense impressions or actions. But in later meditations on the way of the mind with ideas, he is even more insistent upon the capacity of the mind to apprehend reality through ideas. In a meditation upon the Trinity in his "Miscellanies," we find the following:

> Seeing the perfect idea of a thing is to all intents and purposes the same as seeing the thing. It is not only equivalent to seeing of it but it is seeing of it; for there is no other seeing but having an idea. Now, by seeing a perfect idea so far as we see it we have it, but it can't be said of anything else that in seeing of it we see another speaking strictly except it be the very idea of the other.[12]

In a later "Miscellanies" entry, we find these further reflections:

> Spiritual Knowledge. When the ideas themselves appear more lively and with greater strength and impression, as the ideas of spiritual things do [in] one that is spiritually enlightened, their circumstances and various relations and connections between themselves and with other ideas appear more, there are more of those habitudes and respects taken notice of, and they also are more clearly discerned, and therefore hereby a man sees the harmony between spiritual things and so to be convinced of their truth. Ratiocination without this spiritual light never will give one such an

advantage to see things in their true relations and respects to other things
and to things in general.[13]

Not long after this, Edwards wrote the meditation on "Spiritual Knowledge," entry 489, which led in turn to the publication of the doctrine in
A Divine and Supernatural Light in 1734. The evolution of thought
issuing in that sermon embodies the growing conviction that the human
mind, participating in an ideal cosmos within the mind of God, as it
were, has the potential to experience as sensation ideas that relate to
spiritual subjects and that therefore cannot be apprehended through
the ordinary senses. Such experiencing of ideas that can be no more than
ideas in the mind of God would of course be to have a conception
equivalent to that in God's mind, perhaps excepting only the scope. One
would then necessarily be in direct communion with reality. Perhaps the
most interesting implication of this conception is the easy and logical
union of idealism and sensationalism. The process of achieving sensible
ideas of divine realities is also strikingly anticipatory of the Romantic
conception of the imagination, particularly the "esemplastic imagination" of S.T. Coleridge, except for the crucial denial of imaginative
autonomy by Edwards—or the failing hope for cosmic unity among the
Romantics.[14]

By the late 1730s—perhaps at about the time that he was preparing his
"Personal Narrative"—Edwards wrote the now well-known "Miscellanies" entry 782, "Sense of the Heart." Here he attempts to clarify and
systematize the whole gamut of spiritual awareness, from a mere gossip-
ing in signs to the efficient apprehension of divine reality. By this time
Edwards had determined that although words normally relate only partially and externally to all but the simplest concepts, man could hope to
achieve much higher levels of awareness through disciplined meditation
and, ultimately, through a divine act:

> The special work of the Spirit of God or that which is peculiar to the saints
> consists in giving the sensible knowledge of the things of religion with
> respect to their spiritual good or evil which indeed does all originally
> consist in a sense of the spiritual excellency, beauty, or sweetness of divine
> things, which is not by assisting natural principles but by infusing some-
> thing supernatural.[15]

Between the mere tokens Edwards designates as "signs" and the divinely
illuminated vision of utterly compelling beauty, there exists a field of
progressively expanding awareness available to men through the com-

mon work of the Spirit. Here, one might hope for that knowledge which fixes the mind as visual images fix the eye, too complex for complete understanding, yet vivid and enduring, the result of meditation and spiritual instruction.

Through the exposition of the data of life in so rational and orderly a way that a cosmic order is defined, while maintaining a vocabulary so concrete, or at least specific, as to induce the virtual visualization of the subject, Edwards hoped to lead his people along the narrow and difficult road to reality. Moreover, given his firm adherence to the ideal world, his task consisted more in reconciling mentalities than in mediating between some ultimately alienated Self and Other, or mental and material worlds. The Divine Being suffuses and sustains all, save the small grotto of the unregenerate heart.

But Edwards's utter dedication to the pursuit of reality did not permit him or his flock much rest in this conforting vision. In practice, the theater of the preacher's operation posed many difficulties. It was language, after all, that constituted his medium, and language as it came to hand, shaped by the experience of natural men in a fallen world. Because of the prejudices of conventional thinking it was hard enough to instill a few "rational philosophical truths" concerning the mechanics of the physical world, but to deal with the ultimate reality of the Deity was indeed daunting. Edwards readily admitted that words are generally inadequate to the challenge of defining complex or esoteric reality:

> Language is indeed very deficient, in regard of terms to express precise truth concerning our own minds, and their faculties and operations. Words were first formed to express external things; and those that are applied to express things internal and spiritual, are almost all borrowed, and used in a sort of figurative sense. Whence they are most of 'em attended with a great deal of ambiguity and unfixedness in their signification, occasioning innumerable doubts, difficulties and confusions in inquiries and controversies about things of this nature. But language is much less adapted to express things in the mind of the incomprehensible Deity, precisely as they are.[16]

Even in his private meditations, as in this entry in "The Mind," concerning the relationship of the soul and the brain, Edwards continually manifests a sense of the severe linguistic limitations under which he must operate:

> . . . But we have got so far beyond those things for which langue was chiefly contrived, that, unless we use extreme caution, we cannot speak, except we speak exceedingly unintelligibly, without literally contradicting

ourselves.—*Coroll.* No wonder, therefore, that the high and abstract mysteries of the Deity, the prime and most abstract of all beings, imply so many seeming contradictions.[17]

Finally, one had to be wary of his own powers, limited as they may be, lest he erect a private tower of Babel in the very earnestness of his pursuit:

> We may go so far in abstraction, that, although we may thereby, in part, see Truth and Reality, and farther than ever was seen before, yet we may not be able more than just to touch it, and to have a few obscure glances. We may not have strength of mind to conceive clearly of the Manner of it. We see farther indeed, but it is very obscurely and indistinctly. We had better stop a degree or two short of this, and abstract no farther than we can conceive of the thing distinctly, and explain it clearly: otherwise we shall be apt to run into error, and confound our minds.[18]

Whether in private writings, published treatises, or in the central activity of preparing sermons, Edwards invariably professes such a degree of verbal humility. Even in the midst of a true hellfire sermon he would occasionally remind his auditory that the discourse was circumscribed by accommodation to the human mind through the use of similitudes—not that that should be any comfort, he assured them, the reality being far worse than the power of rhetoric or poetry to suggest.

In his primary vocation as preacher of the gospel, then, Jonathan Edwards strove to bring his congregation to an "ideal apprehension and sensible knowledge of the things of religion."[19] This effort which constituted nothing less than the unremitting pursuit of ultimate spiritual reality was severely compromised, as he himself repeatedly insisted, by the degraded hearts and dulled understandings of his auditors, the severe limitations of conventional language, and of course his own noteworthy inadequacies as an orator. It was not only an imperfect world; it was a fallen world in which he labored, and the very theology he advocated specified the hopelessness of a large percentage of his listeners, as well as his own helplessness to *cause* the redeeming light to penetrate the hearts of the saints in any case. But as an occasionalist—whether a Malbranchian or merely an old-fashioned Puritan—Edwards trusted in a "fitness" in God's world that would likely crown extraordinary efforts in the pulpit with successful seeking in the pews, whatever the cultural and psychological obstacles.

The character of Edwards's extraordinary pulpit efforts, including the literary continuation of published sermons, tracts, and treatises that have sustained his influence down to the present, has been studied both narrowly and broadly by numerous scholars, myself included. I do not intend to significantly enlarge such technical appreciation at this time; however, in concluding I would like at least to note those aspects of his preaching that appear to have been most directly related to this pursuit of reality and thus, in my estimation, should be considered among his distinguishing traits as a master of the sermon. These traits are specificity, unity, and intensity.

Edwards's power of specification is one of his most prominent traits, evident in virtually all of his writing, whether the subject be souls or spiders. Much of this power results from visual imagery, though tactile and other forms of imagery are also employed. Himself possessed of an intensely particularistic and concrete imagination, Edwards was impressed with the power of imagery to seize and direct attention—to "fix the mind," as he would say. Although he was fully aware that most images are merely "something external or sensible that we are wont to make use [of] for signs of the ideas of the things themselves . . . more easily excited than ideas of spiritual or mental things which, for the most part, can't be [fully realized] without attentive reflection,"[20] he persisted in the belief that "there is a great and remarkable analogy in God's works . . . God does purposely make and order one thing to be in agreeableness and harmony with another . . . why is it not reasonable to suppose He makes the whole as a shadow of the spiritual world?"[21] Indeed, in a more confident mood, he avers, "The works of God are but a kind of voice or language of God to instruct intelligent beings in things pertaining to Himself."[22] Of course, Edwards devoted many years to collecting "The Language and Lessons of Nature," or *Images or Shadows of Divine Things*, as the published notebook has come to be known, at the least an impressive collection of interpreted images. These, combined with the vast array of images he took from the Scriptures, including those designated as types, composed an extensive arsenal of specificative devices.

Remarkable in Edwards's imagery is the simplicity of most images: flower, sun, foot, water, tree, and so forth. They are for the most part general, if not abstractions. More remarkable is the dynamic quality of most images: they do not designate single entities so much as relationships. Thus the flower basks in the sun, the foot slips toward the pit, the tree stands by the water, and so forth: an important and inevitable quality when Edwards's ontology is considered. Reality itself is a matter of perceived relationship.

Beyond imagery, the unusual analytical powers of Edwards are a source of clarity in exposition. The power of specification in his discourse, "Justification by Faith Alone," achieved through precise logical division and exposition with little reliance on other rhetorical devices, is a thing of beauty. No wonder the elaborate forensic discourse is reputed to have been Edwards's own favorite sermon. In his adherence to this particular kind of rational exposition within a formal structure deriving directly from the "old logic," Edwards differentiated himself both from the radical New Lights and from liberals such as Jonathan Mayhew. But it was a form that only he could sustain on a masterly level, however much his Edwardsian successors might seek to emulate him.

Related to his logical analysis is Edwards's ability to define his intended subject. Here, perhaps the most distinctive procedure is his clearing the field through negation of alternatives prior to declaring that which is affirmed. In pieces ranging from *A Divine and Supernatural Light* to the *Treatise Concerning Religious Affections*, Edwards succeeds in presenting those troublesome "high and abstract mysteries" in the splendid isolation of logical silhouette. In a complementary strategy, Edwards isolates his entire sermon from the personal and social context in which it is inevitably enmeshed, not through negation but through silence. Except in the most urgently occasional of occasional sermons, such as those dealing with military expeditions, there is no explicit context to distract one jot from the intense pursuit of the point, but pastor and congregation are ironically drawn more closely and intimately together in the vortex of the sermon's intensity as a result of their not being formally differentiated. Only an occasional "you" or "they" keeps personal relationships evident, but hardly ever is an "I" required.

While Edwards's power of specification may constitute his most obvious trait, hardly less important to his achievement is the unity of effect which results largely from his ability to clarify and sustain relationships among crucial terms and concepts. Perhaps his greatest strength in this area is the result of his mastery of Scripture. As Samuel Hopkins wrote in his biographical sketch, "[Mr. Edwards] studied the Bible more than all other books, and more than most other divines do."[23] Edwards was a textuary in an age of textuaries, and while he may not have quoted Scripture as frequently as his father, he exploited it brilliantly. Perry Miller once accused Edwards of drawing "the baldest, most obvious doctrine" from his chosen text,[24] but it is not so bald or obvious when we consider that the doctrine often *preceded* the choice of the text. Who would have thought of "Their foot shall slide in due time"?

But it is not the selection of texts, the interpretation of texts, or the massing of texts that is so impressive; rather it is the integration of the text and its context within the discourse that forges a verbal and ideational unity. Like many a Bible-saturated preacher, but with infinitely more art, Edwards deployed an idiom which synthesizes his dialect and that of the Word of God, giving additional subliminal sanction to all that he asserts. His variations upon this technique seem innumerable, but an easily described one occurs in his sermon on Job 31:3.[25] The text selected reads, "Is not destruction to the wicked? and a strange punishment to the workers of iniquity?" In this case Edwards responds to the text and frames a doctrine incorporating the most "workable" word from it: "It is a strange punishment that God has assigned to the workers of iniquity." "Strange," a common enough word then as now, but always vaguely exciting too, is worked into the verbal fabric of the discourse, subtly at first, but with increasing emphasis. As the sermon progresses, the vivid images of an awakening sermon are brought forth in abundance: "billows of the mighty deep rolling over the soul . . . killed with thunder . . . those perpetual streams of brimstone . . ." and so forth. Engrossed in the variety of images and metaphors, the listener/reader finally encounters the clause, "they will have a strange and wonderful sensation of misery under God's wrath," the word "strange" resounding ever so lightly. But it returns again and again: "The bodies of the wicked, after the Resurrection, will be strange, hideous Kinds of bodies; there will be a strange crew at the left hand of Christ at the Day of Judgment. . . . such a strange punishment as being suitable to such a strange and monstrous evil . . . the torments being principally spiritual and consisting in the horrors of the mind makes it appear like some strange fable or dream," and so on to the final peroration at the sermon's conclusion: "and if you continue in this state that you are now in, as you are a strange sort of sinner so your punishment will be distinguishingly strange." There are secondary verbal resonances, also, as when Edwards urges that, if one is to avoid "strange punishment" in the next world, he must be "singular" in this. Such verbal techniques— and that described here sounds more obvious when abstracted from its context—are remote from the baroque wordplay of an Edward Taylor, nor do they resemble eighteenth century wit, but they contribute to a fusion of the verbal fabric of the Bible and the vocabulary of everyday life, combining truth and reality, as Edwards would put it, in a curiously modern way.

Beyond unifying the words of the Bible and those of life, Edwards continually strove to bridge the imaginative gap separating the eternal world of spiritual reality and the Lockean world of sensation in which natural men live. Although he possessed a rich vocabulary of symbol and metaphor, Edwards was clearly dubious about attention-getting tropes that could become enjoyable and distracting resorts in themselves. He evidently preferred to at least attempt bringing his listeners as close as possible to the reality, granted their limitations of experience and imagination. Thus he employed the *a fortiori* or "what is more" technique to erect analogical bridges between the material and spiritual worlds, or time and eternity. He patiently labors in many memorable passages to hoist mere humans—himself included—to meditative awareness of the barely thinkable. Those who have read his sermons remember it: holding a finger in a candle for a moment, several moments, an hour, a day, a year, ten thousand years, and so on, without losing the sensitivity of the first moment. Time, the great isolator, is a prime target of this technique:

> Consider that if you do go to hell, hell is certainly near. How near, you can't tell, but in the general that it is near you may be certain. If you should live fifty years longer, how soon will they be gone! How soon is the revolution of the year finished, and how soon are fifty of them numbered! It would terrify you if you knew you was to burn at the stake, or [be] roasted to death by the Indians fifty years hence. It would appear near to you; you would be ready to count the months and the days.[26]

And to be fair, there are probably just as many positive meditations such as this:

> If the natural sun of this lower world be so bright and glorious, how glorious is the sun of the Heavenly world, in comparison of which this world is but a dark dungeon? And if the very inhabitants that are enlightened there by the rays of Christ's glory do themselves shine as the sun, how brightly then does He shine who is a sun to them, and does as much exceed them in glory as the sun exceeds our bodies?[27]

With the intensity of an inchworm, the mind climbs ever onward and upward, striving to come to imaginative terms with the infinite and the divine. In a sense, Edwards's intention is to analyze metaphor, to uncover that hidden basis in truth and reality that gives it validity.

Similar in essential impact is the most pervasive of all Edwards's literary devices, repetition. Simple and incremental repetition, sanctioned in Edwards's eyes by Hebrew poetry, are employed widely and effectively for the same end: to induce a maximum of contemplation with a minimum of verbal deflection from the subject of meditation. Thus Edwards is inclined to employ repetition not only when exhorting and inculcating, but likewise in the most contemplative passages. By restating, the preacher achieves both increased emphasis and the sense of continuity in time, dramatizing both the importance and the endurance of the subject handled.

Such dramatic effect is also inherent in another convention to which Edwards clung in a time of change. The sermon as he composed it consists of a tripartite form: Text, Doctrine, and Application, however many installments are required by the preaching of a long sermon in the pulpit. The form dramatizes the preacher's act of mediation by its structure, placing doctrinal development between scriptural interpretation and practical exhortation. Perhaps more important is the explicitly structured relationship among the eternal Word of God, human reason and learning, and the heart which regulates moral conduct. Although preachers in Edwards's day were already departing from what many associated with "logic chopping" and mechanical literary form, Edwards exploited the capacity of the old form for sustaining rigorous analysis and dramatizing the essential relationships among the Word, human intelligence, and conduct.

Tensions created within the sermons by these sustained relationships—verbal, conceptual, and structural—are the source of much of that terrific intensity which imparts a certain suspense even when Edwards is examining a familiar theme in a traditional manner. Moreover, the striking effect of his discourses, with their centripetal unity of many carefully analyzed elements, confirms his notion of higher reality as a vast web of perceptions.

Specificity and unity, I suppose, when taken together predicate intensity. Only the dynamism of the pursuit of that ultimate end beyond the self is not necessarily implied. So I must mention the intensity, the condition of pursuit which suffuses virtually everything Edwards wrote, but particularly the sermons. It is in the syntax of his sentences: those insistent, agglutinative sequences of phrases and clauses, pressing urgently on, periodically leaping with brilliant insight or pausing to double back in the act of analysis. At this point we go beyond technique to the man, or at least the mentality. I am reminded of a poem by Francis Thompson entitled "The Hound of Heaven," which depicts Christ pursuing the fleeing sinner "down the nights and down the days . . . down the arches of the years . . . down the labyrinthine ways of my own mind . . ."[28] Except that in Edwards's case it is the man who pursues, and he pursues not only Christ but an ultimate reality *through* Christ. He was a kind of Christian scientist, if I may appropriate a name, or a Christian philosopher, as he would have put it, from first to last.

Of course Edwards could never fully realize that ultimate reality as a scientist, nor could he have expressed it as a preacher had he done so, for that reality would have been no less than the mind of God and all within it. On the other hand, Edwards insists that the nature of reality for us humans is not that of a place but rather that of an orientation, a relationship, or in his idiom, that of being's perception of and consent to Being. His entire effort as a preacher was thus to enlarge the scope of individual awareness. Moving from negation to affirmation within the cycles of preaching programs, he strove to reestablish the authority of the Christian vision and to refresh the language of orthodoxy.[29]

Notes

1. The account of Edwards's acceptance of the doctrine of election is given in his "Personal Narrative," edited by Samuel Hopkins in *The Life and Character of the Late Reverend Mr. Jonathan Edwards, President of the College at New-Jersey* (Boston, 1765), pp. 24–25.

2. S. E. Dwight, *The Life of President Edwards* (New York, 1830), p. 68.

3. "Diary," quoted in Dwight, *Life*, p. 105.

4. John A. Stoughton, *"Windsor Farmes": A Glimpse of an Old Parish* (Hartford, 1883), p. 43.

5. MS sermon on Gen. 19:14, Beinecke Library, Yale University.

6. Ibid.

7. "The Mind," nos. [6], [10], and [35], in *The Works of Jonathan Edwards: Scientific and Philosophical Writings*, ed. Wallace E. Anderson (New Haven, 1980), pp. 340–42, 355.

8. The structuring of thought according to the scheme of Peter Ramus—referred to by Edwards as the "old logick"—in the sermon form inherited by Edwards is stoutly, even militantly defended in the preface to his *Discourses on Various Important Subjects* (Boston, 1738), pp. iv–v. The tone of these remarks suggests a reply to a particular challenge. It is probable that Edwards recalled the remarks of Anthony Ashley Cooper, third Earl of Shaftesbury, in his *Characteristics* (London, 1711), *3*, 113: "Fashion is indeed a powerful Mistress, and by her single Authority has so far degraded the carving Method and Use of *Solids*, even in Discourse and Writing, that our religious Pastors themselves have many of 'em chang'd their Manner of distributing to us their spiritual Food. They have quitted their substantial Service, and uniform Division into *Parts* and *Under-Parts*; and in order to become fashionable, they have run into the more savoury way of learned *Ragout* and *Medley*. 'Tis the unbred rustick Orator alone, who presents his clownish Audience with a *divisible Discourse*. The elegant Court-Divine exhorts in Miscellany, and is asham'd to bring his *Two's* and *Three's* before a fashionable Assembly."

Edwards had read and cited the *Characteristics* years before in his memoranda on style (see Anderson, *Scientific Writings*, p. 194). Shaftesbury's glib assessment must have rankled as he prepared his "collected sermons" for the world to see, including the somewhat gratuitous footnote to the stylish Tillotson. Edwards clearly wanted everyone to know that he neither wrote nor thought as he did through ignorance of alternatives.

9. "Miscellanies," no. 630. For "Miscellanies" text I have used a transcription prepared by Thomas A. Schafer and deposited in the Beinecke Library, Yale University. Each passage quoted has been checked against the original MS.

10. Anderson, *Scientific Writings*, pp. 332–38.

11. Quoted in Dwight, *Life*, p. 87.

12. "Miscellanies," no. 260.

13. "Miscellanies," no. 408.

14. For "esemplastic" and Coleridge's conception of the imagination, see J. Shawcross, ed. *Biographia Literaria* (London, 1962), 1, lxiii, 107ff.

15. "Miscellanies," no. 782.

16. *The Works of Jonathan Edwards: Freedom of the Will*, ed. Paul Ramsey (New Haven, 1957), p. 376.

17. "The Mind," no. [35], in Anderson, *Scientific Writings*, p. 355.

18. "The Mind," no. [8], Anderson, p. 341.

19. "Miscellanies," no. 782.

20. Ibid.

21. "Shadows of Divine Things," MS, no. 8 in the Beinecke Library, Yale University.

22. "Shadows" MS, no. 57.

23. Hopkins, *Life*, p. 47.

24. Perry Miller, *Jonathan Edwards* (New York, 1949; rpt. New York, 1963), p. 48.

25. MS in the Beinecke Library, Yale University.

26. Sermon on Luke 16:24, MS in the Beinecke Library.

27. Sermon on Ps. 24:7–10, MS in the Beinecke Library.

28. *The Works of Francis Thompson* (New York, [1913]), 1, 107–13.

29. That Edwards normally preached a cycle of sermons is clearly suggested in the preface to *Discourses* (1738) where he discusses the selection of sermons for the volume (p. v).

7

The Spirit and the Word:
Jonathan Edwards
and Scriptural Exegesis

STEPHEN J. STEIN

I

In his perceptive study of the development of the principles of modern biblical interpretation, Hans Frei charts the emergence of a new way of reading the narrative sections of the Bible at the turn of the eighteenth century, a period he describes as the "starting point" for modern theology.[1] The traditional approach to such texts in western Christianity—in his terms, the "precritical" approach—rested on a "strongly realistic" reading of the narratives as literally and historically reliable. This stance assumed that the texts describe actual historical events, that they constitute one larger story in a normal time sequence, and that the narratives are consistent with the extrabiblical experience of the reader. The precritical approach frequently depended heavily upon "figuration or typology" to extract this unity and meaning.[2]

According to Frei, the precritical mode broke down in the eighteenth century. The relationship between the literal meaning of the biblical stories and the historical reality of the events was destroyed. Commentators increasingly distinguished between the "depicted biblical world" and the "real historical world." The narrative, the reality, and the meaning became separable in the minds of exegetes. Correspondingly, figural interpretation came under a blistering attack from those who maintained "the elementary assumption that a propositional statement has only one meaning." Modern historical criticism arose in the aftermath of these developments.[3]

Jonathan Edwards was relatively untouched by these changes. His lifelong pattern of biblical interpretation conforms closely to the precritical approach described by Frei. Edwards not only reflected the precritical mindset, but he also mounted a formidable defense of typological interpretation and, in fact, extended its range and application. He was not part of any emergent school of historical criticism. At the same time, it is clear that Edwards was responding to the transitional age in his views on the authority of Scripture and in his actual interpretation of narrative texts. An examination of his pattern of biblical interpretation will enable us to position him tentatively with respect to the hermeneutical developments of his day and also to understand why he considered his investment in scriptural study so important to his overall theological program. In a distinctive way the analysis of Edwards as a scriptural exegete joins an old debate concerning his modernity, suggesting on exegetical grounds that neither those who would enroll him in the ranks of modern thinkers nor those who would place him in the pantheon of fundamentalist theologians are correct.

II

Edwards's most significant early statements concerning the interpretation of the Bible appear in the "Miscellanies." In entry no. 6, written in early 1723, he describes "a strange and unaccountable kind of enchantment" in biblical history which, despite its simplicity, is "most pleasant, agreeable, easy and natural," combining an aesthetic attraction with a witness to the truth. This appeal of "Scripture history" is, in part, a product of the fact that the Bible "sets forth things just as they happened, . . . in such a natural method, that one seems to be actually present. . . ." The readers are, as it were, caught up in the action themselves. The details of the narrative lead their minds "naturally and easily" so that they are able to trace "the whole transaction." Even the smallest child can understand.[4] That does not guarantee, however, that the scriptural expressions are always intelligible, a fact Edwards addressed in an earlier entry by pointing to the richness and complexity of biblical language. One hundred pages would be required to express what is "implied" in the simile, "Ye are the temple of the Holy Ghost," he wrote. In other words, the "lively pictures" employed in Scripture represent by indirection a "vast volume" of ideas that "we are not able to behold directly."[5]

The tension between the natural appeal of the biblical text and the potential mystery of its meaning defines certain hermeneutical possibilities for Edwards. Edwards had been nurtured in a context saturated with typological exegesis, and he embraced it as a standard interpretive device. In 1723, he recorded in his "Diary" his pleasure in "reading the scriptures" and "in writing on Types of the Scripture."[6] His first written comments on the Bible drew upon familiar examples of typology, which he defined very broadly. In the spring of 1724, he noted that God "shadowed forth spiritual things" by such diverse types as aspects of the ceremonial law, "transactions" in the life of Christ, and "innumerable things in human affairs." The "wisdom of God" has seen fit to order "things natural, that they livelily represent things divine and spiritual"— a deeper meaning not always clear to the readers.[7] Sometimes the "same portion of Scripture" will have great effect, appearing "astonishingly glorious" and "wonderful," expressing an "admirable majesty, coherence, and harmony." On other occasions, the same text may appear "insipid, mean, impertinent, and inconsistent." The difference is in the mind of the readers, who when they possess "ideas of things spiritual" are able to see in God's Word spiritual things, "sweetly" corresponding and harmonizing with the words of the text. In that sense the "Word of God is said to be written in the hearts of believers."[8] It is therefore the presence of the Spirit which makes possible a full understanding of the words of the biblical narrative which are themselves of divine authority."[9]

Edwards spent a lifetime in pursuit of a full understanding of the Bible. In 1739 he wrote of his youthful years, "I had then, and at other times, the greatest delight in the holy Scriptures, of any book whatsoever."[10] That pattern probably remained true for the last twenty years of his life. Samuel Hopkins, his first biographer, declared that Edwards had "studied the Bible more than all other books."[11] Five months before his death, Edwards summarized in his own words his established pattern of study and his plans for the future. In his letter to the trustees of the College of New Jersey, he sketched the prospectus for a "great work" of divinity to be called "a *History of the Work of Redemption.*" In it he intended to deal with all aspects of Christian theology in an "historical order," examining successively the divine dispensations, including history and prophecy in the biblical and post-biblical periods. Edwards planned to introduce the "parts of divinity in that order which is most scriptural and most natural," thereby demonstrating "the admirable contexture and harmony of the whole." The historical mode, he still believed in 1757, was "most beautiful and entertaining."[12]

III

In the same letter, Edwards went on to describe a second project tied even more closely to his pattern of biblical study. (This one has received much less scholarly attention than the former.) Edwards contemplated "another great work" to be called the *"Harmony of the Old and New Testament."* In three parts, it was to deal successively with prophecies of the Messiah and their fulfillment, with types of the Old Testament and the ways in which they agreed with their antitypes in the gospel of Christ, and with the doctrinal and theological harmony between the Old and New testaments. Concerning this exegetical project, Edwards wrote, "In the course of this work, I find there will be occasion for an explanation of a very great part of the holy Scriptures. . . ." According to his own assessment, he had already "done much" towards the completion of this work.[13] How much is rather clear, for in the years between his first entries in the "Miscellanies" and his letter to the trustees at Princeton he had invested heavily in his favorite pursuit, the study of Scripture. The results of that study are extant in his manuscripts and published works.

Edwards's exegetical writings may be divided into four categories on the basis of their intended audience. The largest consists of commentary on all parts of the Bible written in his private notebooks for his own use. The "Miscellanies" includes some such material, but the bulk of it is located in "Notes on the Scriptures" and in "Miscellaneous Observations on the Holy Scriptures." The former manuscript series includes more than five hundred numbered entries on different biblical texts, arranged simply by the order in which they were written between 1723 and 1758.[14] The latter, known also as the "Blank Bible," consists of a small printed Bible with interleaved sheets ruled in two columns for writing commentary on adjacent texts. It contains perhaps as many as ten thousand separate entries, ranging across the canon, written in random fashion between 1730 and 1758.[15] Edwards also filled a separate manuscript with commentary on the book of Revelation, and he used the "Miscellanies" to collect materials dealing with both prophecies and types of the Messiah.[16] These private notebooks represent the core of his reflections on Scripture.

The next largest concentration of exegetical materials is in Edwards's sermons, more than eleven hundred of which remain today.[17] Most of these contain a section of scriptural exposition. Some draw directly on materials in the scripture notebooks; others do not. Edwards used his preaching as further occasion for reflection on biblical texts. In the sermons pastoral considerations led to the improvement or application of scriptural truths. The audience for these materials was comprised of Edwards's congregations at New York, Northampton, Stockbridge, and elsewhere.

Third, Edwards also prepared works for publication which include extensive biblical argumentation, some drawn from his notebooks and sermons and some appearing to be original to the published texts. For example, in the treatise on *Religious Affections*, he supported the argument that "gracious and holy affections have their exercise and fruit in Christian practice"—the twelfth sign—with extensive citations from both the Old and New testaments.[18] More than a third of Edwards's publication on *Original Sin* is devoted to "observations" on particular biblical texts which "proved" for him that traditional doctrine.[19] Even works regarded primarily as philosophical contain extended exegetical sections. More than half of *The End for Which God Created the World* is concerned with "what is to be learned from the Holy Scriptures" on the matter.[20] The audience for these writings was the contemporary theological world.

Finally, Edwards's plans for future publications featured biblical materials. Both the "History of Redemption" and the "Harmony" were to be essentially exegetical theological undertakings. Among his papers are several small notebooks dealing with types, history, and the harmony of the testaments, which contain working notes for his future projects.[21] It appears that Edwards intended to incorporate biblical reflections from his notebooks, sermons, and theological publications. The audience for the projected works was his contemporary theological world as well as future generations.

Edwards's exegetical legacy includes all four of these categories of biblical writings which comprise a set of ever-wider circles, each necessarily embracing the text, Edwards the exegete, his audience, and the context of the times. These circles center on the text itself which Edwards examined for its potential usefulness to each of his different audiences. The circles intersect with one another, however, for it is virtually impossible to separate the acts of study, reflection, application, argumentation, and speculation for him. The categories overlap in usage.

IV

Edwards's pattern of interpreting biblical texts is more difficult to characterize. He was not preoccupied with the traditional post-Reformation emphasis upon the literal sense of the text, even though it was basic for him and he frequently mounted theological arguments on that basis. As I have pointed out elsewhere, his ultimate interest was in the spiritual sense of Scripture—what I might now call the "spirit-given" sense of the text—that which is the product of the indwelling presence of the divine in the exegete.[22] His confidence about this sense of "inspiration" led him to creative, imaginative heights in some of his commentary. The sheer volume of his biblical writings, however, makes all simple characterizations suspect until more research has been done on this aspect of his thought. Despite the quantity of his writings on the Bible, there is an amazing paucity of serious scholarship dealing with it. The contemporary renaissance of interest in Edwards has hardly touched this dimension of his work.[23]

The form and structure of Edwards's biblical writings might be compared with those of the publications of earlier commentators whose works he knew well. As a young man, Edwards became acquainted with several authors who set out to write commentary upon one or the other testament or the entire Bible. The model they provided may have been an informing guide as Edwards pursued a "full understanding" of the Scriptures. References to the massive folios of Matthew Poole and Matthew Henry—both English dissenters—appear early in his "Catalogue" of reading.[24] Edwards's actual use of these commentaries was spotty in the early years but increased with the passage of time. Poole's *Synopsis Criticorum* and his *Annotations* and Henry's *Exposition of the Old and New Testaments* contain prodigious amounts of textual exposition, citation of authorities, theological reflection, and speculation.[25] The six volumes of Philip Doddridge's *Family Expositor* on the New Testament might be added later as another contemporary model.[26] Edwards eagerly studied each of Doddridge's volumes as they became available. All of these commentators linked the task of interpretation with religious application. The "Blank Bible" bears some formal resemblance to this genre.

But Edwards's goal was not to write another commentary on the whole Bible. He undoubtedly knew that an American had already done that and had been unsuccessful in securing a publisher. Cotton Mather's "Biblia Americana"—a kind of American *Synopsis Criticorum*—had been written and rewritten, but never published, perhaps in part because of the celebrated works of Poole and Henry.[27] Edwards's "Harmony" was to be organized along very different lines and written in a "most entertaining and profitable" method. He hoped it would lead its readers "to a view of the *true* [emphasis mine] spirit, design, life and soul of the scriptures, as well as their *proper* [emphasis mine] use and improvement."[28] Edwards's plans for the "Harmony" provide important clues for understanding and organizing the content of his biblical writings.

In the first part of the "Harmony," Edwards proposed to deal with prophecies of the Messiah, specifically comparing references to the messianic redemption and kingdom in the Old Testament with one another and with their fulfillments in the New Testament. He believed that he could demonstrate "the universal, precise, and admirable correspondence" between the predictions and New Testament events.[29] The theme of prophecy, a major motif in Edwards's biblical writings, has been overlooked by many scholars except those who have equated it with prophetic eschatology and millennialism—a far more limited notion. (Even the important studies of Sacvan Bercovitch manifest this tendency.)[30] Edwards displayed a disposition to read everything in the Old Testament in terms of a New Testament referent. The intent of the Spirit of God in employing the language of prophecy, he believed, was to represent things pertaining to the gospel. According to Edwards, the poetic images used by the ancient "penmen" under the "fire of grace" "very exactly described the affairs of the . . . Christian church" and, in fact, agreed "more properly" with them than with the doings of the Jews. Thus the affairs of the "Jewish church," to use Edwards's phrase, were most naturally a "shadow and representation" of the things of the gospel.[31]

By his willingness to employ the process of analogy liberally, Edwards was able to turn the entire text of the Old Testament into a massive anticipation of Christ and his work of redemption. The christological emphasis came at the expense of Jewish history. Edwards sounded the same note at the beginning of his collection of prophecies of the Messiah. "That there was some one individual person," he wrote, "that was often prophecied of from age to age, that should come & be the head & king & deliverer of God's people, and the great means of their happiness in the latter days is manifest, by comparing the different prophecies in different ages."[32] Gen. 3:15, Isa. 9:6–7, Zechariah 9:9—these and hundreds of other passages have direct and primary reference to Christ, his salvation, and the establishment of his kingdom. Prophecy therefore allowed Edwards to organize the content of the entire Bible around Christ and to bind together the two testaments as coordinate witnesses to his work of redemption.

In the second part of the "Harmony," Edwards planned to examine the types of the Old Testament as "representations of the great things of the gospel of Christ" and their agreement with their antitypes in the New Testament.[33] His definition of a type was liberal and inclusive. In the

"Miscellanies" he noted that God had consistently chosen the inferior things in the world to "shadow forth" spiritual things. Thus, he wrote, "almost everything that was said or done, that we have recorded in Scripture from Adam to Christ, was typical of Gospel things. Persons were typical persons; their actions were typical actions; the cities were typical cities; the nations of the Jews and other nations were typical nations; their land was a typical land; God's providences towards them were typical providences; their worship was typical worship; their houses were typical houses; their magistrates, typical magistrates; their clothes, typical clothes, and indeed the world was a typical world."[34] In this way God chose to instruct those whom he created. Edwards's fascination with typology has attracted more scholarly attention than perhaps any other aspect of his biblical interests. Even Perry Miller, whose antipathy to the scriptural dimension of Edwards's work was substantial, dealt with typology in the introduction to his edition of the *Images or Shadows of Divine Things*. Miller proposed that Edwards's extension of typology and his collection of types in the world of nature constituted "an exaltation of nature to a level of authority coequal with revelation"—a mistaken judgment, in my view, which conveniently allowed Miller to link Edwards with Emerson's naturalism and which has produced a long and distinguished but potentially misleading scholarly tradition.[35] In fact, Edwards never waffled on the primacy of Scripture as the principal source of divine revelation, nor on the usefulness of biblical typology as an interpretive device.

In his later years Edwards set to work on a systematic statement concerning typology. His views rested on the judgment that it had always been God's common method of revelation "to exhibit . . . future things by symbolical representations," that is, by types. In particular, God had chosen this means to reveal the Messiah and his work of redemption. Thus the types of the Messiah point to Jesus and his kingdom. Edwards regarded typology as a matter of "great IMPORTANCE." The types are for instruction and therefore, he wrote, "we must endeavour to understand them, even those of them that are no where explained in scripture." Although he was sensitive to the potential abuses of typology, Edwards thought it was unfair (and well he might) to accuse those with a "teeming imagination" of such abuses. On the contrary, he pointed out that the "principles of human nature render TYPES a fit method of instruction." Types tend "to enlighten and illustrate, and to convey instruction with impression, conviction, and pleasure, and to help the memory."[36] But the antitype was an even clearer revelation. The types of the Old Testament were "obscure and dark," he wrote. "The light that was plainly to reveal

gospel things came after Christ, the substance of all the ancient types."[37]
The second section of the "Harmony" featured Christ as the center of the
Bible by opening the types and showing him to be the principal subject of
both testaments and of type and antitype.

The third part of Edwards's projected scriptural work was to focus
upon the harmony of the Old and New testaments in "doctrine and
precept."[38] This exegetical concern of Edwards has never received any
sustained attention. Calvinistic doctrine seemingly has little of the attraction that prophecy and typology display for scholars today. The most
useful document shedding light on Edwards's intentions for this part of
his work is his small notebook entitled "The Harmony of the Genius
Spirit Doctrines & Rules of the Old Testamt and the New," a product of
the last ten years of his life.[39] Not that he came to a conviction concerning
the harmony at a late point. On the contrary, the harmony of the
testaments is a pervasive theme in his biblical writings. Edwards's earliest
comment on the Canticles in the "Notes on the Scriptures" points to
"Christ's incarnation" as an accomplishment of the poet's wish for famil-
iarity with his beloved, for "the Son of God . . . is come down unto us in
our nature," he wrote.[40] The "Harmony" notebook shows the mature
Edwards trying to identify issues on which the harmony existed. The first
entry is a doctrinal proposition: "Faith in God The Ground Condition of
Gods Salvation Protection deliverance &c." It is followed by a cluster of
Old Testament passages supporting that idea. Other entries itemize moral
precepts such as "Love to Enemies. Forgiving Injuries, doing Good for
Evil, &c." and "not hoarding up Treasure for future Time in This world,
but Laying out what we have to Spare for pious & Charitable Purposes."[41]

Edwards also used the "Blank Bible" to take note of passages illustrating the doctrinal and moral unity of the Old and New testaments. In
almost every case—whether in the interleaved Bible or the "Harmony"
notebook—the final referent is a New Testament concept. For example,
Edwards explained the phrase in Gen. 22:8, "God will provide himself a
lamb," as "an Instance of the Harmony" between the two testaments. It is
reasonable, he maintained, that God would provide the sacrifice by
which sins against himself were atoned. Edwards noted carefully that
Abraham, of course, had no thought of Christ being such a sacrifice, but
only of Isaac. However, the mind of the Holy Ghost had respect to Christ
as the sacrifice. Thus for Edwards the narrative of the sacrifice of Isaac
becomes confirmation of the divine role in Christ's redemption.[42] Edwards cited the example of Joseph's discretion in taking the pregnant
Mary as his wife (Matt. 1:19) as evidence that the Christian virtues of

meekness and gentleness "were duties under the law and before X came."[43] Similarly, in commenting on the beautitudes in the Sermon on the Mount, he stated that "the Religion & vertues & duties that Christ taught were the Same that was taught in the old T. & the Spirit of the Gospel & Temper of the Christian Church is the Same with the Spirit that Gods Church was of under the Old Testament."[44] For Edwards Christ's experience was the key to the doctrinal propositions expressed implicitly and explicitly in the Old and New testaments and to their "proper use and improvement."

V

Several observations are now in order concerning these biblical materials. First, Edwards's projected "Harmony" involves his plans for a tripartite witness to the centrality of Christ in both the Old and New testaments. Prophecy, typology, and doctrine represented different approaches to the biblical text, but they all converged in the person and work of Christ, according to Edwards. Prophecy required the passage of time, typology demanded correspondence and analogy, doctrine translated into proposition, but all three drew the reader of the biblical text into the heart of the gospel for Edwards, namely, Christ's work of redemption.

Second, in this christological focus Edwards found the "genius and spirit" of the Scriptures, its "true spirit, design, life and soul," or in the categories of Hans Frei, the unity and meaning of the Bible. Here perhaps we need to recover some sense of the generative force or power involved with Edwards's use of the word "genius." The "genius" of Scripture points to its "life and soul," which for him was the figure and spirit of Christ, the heart of the biblical text.

The fact that Edwards regarded his method of interpretation as "natural" and "fitting" confirmed for him the congruence between the narrative pattern of Scripture and the everyday experience of the reader. Again, to use Frei's categories, Edwards's reading of the text placed him squarely in the precritical camp. Historical events were real, even if they were subject to infinite typological redaction. The scriptural narratives formed one continuous account in time, even if the temporal framework finally collapsed into a single significant moment of revelation in Christ. And the texts conformed to the everyday experiences of the readers, even if those experiences found ultimate meaning only in relationship to the activities of Christ.

Much work remains to be done in the study of Edwards as an exegete. Norman Fiering has recently placed Edwards's moral philosophy into its larger intellectual context.[45] We need equivalent studies for his biblical writings. We need to recover the world of seventeenth- and eighteenth-century exegesis, which was populated not only by Poole, Henry, Mather, and Doddridge, but also by Arthur Bedford, Humphrey Prideaux, John Locke, Henry Hammond, John Owen, Thomas Manton, Thomas Sherlock, and a host of other figures who were part of Edwards's intellectual context.

It is likely that when we know more about that world and Edwards's engagement with it we will discover subtle ways in which he reflected the currents of his day. After all, his comments on the sacrifice of Isaac recognized the interpretive limitations of the historical and logical situation, but the quest for a "fuller understanding" pushed him to another spiritual level of meaning. In his own way he was beginning to separate the narrative, the reality, and the meaning. But at the same time he defended mightily his liberal construction of typology. In other words, Edwards was not ready to separate word and spirit in the interpretation of Scripture.

Notes

1. Hans W. Frei, *The Eclipse of Biblical Narrative: A Study in Eighteenth and Nineteenth Century Hermeneutics* (New Haven, 1974), p. 51.

2. Ibid., pp. 1–65.

3. Ibid.

4. "Theological Miscellanies," no. 6, entitled "Scripture." Here and elsewhere in this chapter the text of the "Miscellanies" (MSS, Beinecke Library, Yale University) is cited from transcriptions and editions prepared by Thomas A. Schafer of McCormick Theological Seminary.

5. "Miscellanies," no. dd, entitled "Scripture."

6. "Diary," August 28, 1723, in Sereno E. Dwight, ed., *The Works of President Edwards with a Memoir of His Life*, 10 vols. (New York, 1829–30), I, 94.

7. "Miscellanies," no. 119, entitled "Types." See also no. 139, entitled "Difficulties in Religion."

8. "Miscellanies," no. 126, entitled "Spiritual Understanding of the Scriptures."

9. "Miscellanies," no. 22, entitled "Jehovah."

10. "Personal Narrative," in Samuel Hopkins, *The Life and Character of the Late Reverend Mr. Jonathan Edwards* (Boston, 1765), reprinted in David Levin, ed., *Jonathan Edwards: A Profile* (New York, 1969), p. 32.

11. Levin, ed., *Edwards*, p. 40.

12. Dwight, ed., *Works*, I, 569–70.

13. Ibid., p. 570.

14. "Notes on the Scriptures" (MSS, Beinecke Library, Yale University) has been edited in canonical order by Sereno E. Dwight in Dwight, ed., *Works*, IX, 113–563.

15. The "Blank Bible" is in the Beinecke Library, Yale University. A few of the entries were included in *Selections from the Unpublished Writings of Jonathan Edwards, of America*, ed. Alexander B. Grosart (Edinburgh, 1865).

16. "Notes on the Apocalypse" (MS, Beinecke Library, Yale University). See *The Works of Jonathan Edwards*, vol. 5, *Apocalyptic Writings*, ed. Stephen J. Stein, (New Haven, 1977), pp. 95–305. See also "Types of the Messiah," in Dwight, ed., *Works*, IX, 9–111.

17. The manuscripts are in the collections of the Beinecke Library at Yale University and the Hills Library at Andover Newton Theological School.

18. *The Works of Jonathan Edwards*, vol. 2, *Religious Affections*, ed. John E. Smith (New Haven, 1959), pp. 383–461.

19. *The Works of Jonathan Edwards*, vol. 3, *Original Sin*, ed. Clyde A. Holbrook, (New Haven, 1970), pp. 221–349.

20. Jonathan Edwards, *Dissertation on the End for which God Created the World*, in *The Works of President Edwards*, 4 vols. (New York, 1843), II, 222–57.

21. "Notebook on the Types" (MS, Hills Library, Andover Newton); "Notebooks on the History of Redemption" (MSS, Beinecke Library, Yale University); "The Harmony of the Genius Spirit Doctrines & Rules of the Old Testamt & the New" (MS, Beinecke Library, Yale University).

22. Stephen J. Stein, "The Quest for the Spiritual Sense: The Biblical Hermeneutics of Jonathan Edwards," *Harvard Theological Review* 70 (1977), 99–113. See also Stein, "Jonathan Edwards and the Rainbow: Biblical Exegesis and Poetic Imagination," *New England Quarterly* 47 (1974), 440–56.

23. Exceptions to this pattern are Conrad Cherry, *The Theology of Jonathan Edwards: A Reappraisal* (Garden City, N.Y., 1966); and Karl Dieterich Pfisterer, *The Prism of Scripture: Studies on history and historicity in the work of Jonathan Edwards* (Frankfurt, 1975). See also below, nn. 30 and 35.

24. Jonathan Edwards, "Catalogue" (MS, Beinecke Library, Yale University), letter sheet and p. 1.

25. Matthew Poole, *Synopsis Criticorum aliorumque Sacrae Scripturae Interpretum*, 5 vols. (London, 1669–76); and *Annotations upon the Holy Bible*, 2 vols. (London, 1683–85). Matthew Henry, *Exposition of the Old and New Testaments*, 5 vols. (London, 1710).

26. Philip Doddridge, *The Family Expositor: or, a Paraphrase and Version of the New Testament: With Critical Notes; and a Practical Improvement of each Section*, 6 vols. (London, 1739–56).

27. Concerning the "Biblia Americana," see Kenneth Silverman, *The Life and Times of Cotton Mather* (New York, 1984), especially pp. 257–60.

28. Dwight, ed., *Works*, I, 570.

29. Ibid.

30. See Sacvan Bercovitch, *The Puritan Origins of the American Self* (New Haven, 1975); and *The American Jeremiad* (Madison, Wisconsin, 1978).

31. "Miscellanies," no. 251, entitled "Prophecy of the Old Testament."

32. "Miscellanies," no. 891, entitled "Christian Religion. Prophecies of the Messiah."

33. Dwight, ed., *Works*, I, 570.

34. "Miscellanies," no. 362, entitled "Trinity."

35. Perry Miller, ed., *Images or Shadows of Divine Things by Jonathan Edwards* (New Haven, 1948), p. 28. See also Miller, "From Edwards to Emerson," *New England Quarterly* 13 (1940), 589–617; Ursula Brumm, "Jonathan Edwards and Ralph Waldo Emerson," in *American Thought and Religious Typology* (New Brunswick, N.J., 1970), pp. 86–108; Bercovitch, *Puritan Origins*, pp. 157ff., and *American Jeremiad*; and Mason I. Lowance, Jr., "From Edwards to Emerson and Thoreau: A Reevaluation," in *The Language of Canaan: Metaphor and Symbol in New England from the Puritans to the Transcendentalists* (Cambridge, Massachusetts, 1980), pp. 277–95.

36. "Types of the Messiah," Dwight, ed., *Works*, IX, 9, 109–11.

37. "Notes on the Scriptures," Dwight, ed., *Works*, IX, 544–45.

38. Dwight, ed., *Works*, I, 570.

39. See above, note 21, "Harmony."

40. Dwight, ed., *Works*, IX, 373.

41. "Harmony," pp. 1–2, 6–8, 18.

42. "Blank Bible," p. 23.

43. Ibid., p. 658.

44. Ibid., p. 660.

45. Norman Fiering, *Jonathan Edwards's Moral Thought and Its British Context* (Chapel Hill, N.C., 1981).

8

History, Redemption, and the Millennium

JOHN F. WILSON

Although the title, "History, Redemption, and the Millennium," appears to promise a comprehensive disquisition about a major aspect of Jonathan Edwards's thought, my paper will deal less with Edwards himself than with his interpreters or the uses to which he has been put. I take as justification for this broadening of the scope of my concern the theme of this volume, which suggests it will be an assessment of Edwards in relation to "the American experience" in general. I shall take up this assignment by turning to an essay that early contributed to the recovery of interest in Jonathan Edwards and his thought so prominent during the last several decades. I refer to C. C. Goen's discussion, "Jonathan Edwards: A New Departure in Eschatology," which appeared in *Church History* twenty-five years ago.[1] The Goen essay, surely notable because it was written by a graduate student, is all the more remarkable because it has proved to be immensely influential over the succeeding years. Part of its influence has been due to its codification of a particular interpretation of Jonathan Edwards's thought; it has exerted perhaps even greater influence by identifying Jonathan Edwards as a central figure in the development of postmillennial thinking in American culture. It is not too much to say, I think, that Goen's essay was a foundation stone for Alan Heimert's large, controversial study of early American culture, *Religion and the American Mind*, as well as the immensely significant—and less controversial—*Redeemer Nation* by E. L. Tuveson.[2] Perhaps more important still in the world of scholarship is the litany of citations of the Goen piece in articles and books about Jonathan Edwards and American culture published since 1960. I suggest we begin by charting the argument that Goen sets out in his essay.

The article emphasizes at its outset that Edwards's thought with respect to eschatology was comprehensive and generally in line with the broad Christian tradition regarding the understanding of "last things." According to Goen, Edwards "saw clearly that the redemption which proceeded from the heart of a just and merciful God was being realized progressively in the drama of history and would be consummated on the grand scale of eternity."[3] Here, Goen suggests, Jonathan Edwards "introduces a radical innovation which had decisive consequences for the future." This was, precisely, his "millennial speculations."[4]

Goen focuses in the essay upon Edwards's distinction between the suffering state of the church, which expressed the standard Protestant construction of the Christian era as moving toward the completion of redemption, and the prosperous state of the church, that is, "a golden age for the church on earth, within history, and achieved through the ordinary process of propagating the gospel in the power of the Holy Spirit." This Goen denominates a "historical millennium."[5] He traces out in some detail the structure of a course of redemption that would justify this postmillennial view—Jonathan Edwards, of course, does so systematically in his sermon series that we know as *A History of the Work of Redemption*.[6]

But what concerns Goen more is the issue of how imminent Edwards thought this event might be. While traditional arguments deriving from Dan. 12:7 and Rev. 12:14 ordinarily located the beginning of the millennium either in the middle of the nineteenth century (by adding 1260 years, the three and one half "times," to 606) or very early in the twenty-first century (by adding the same 1260 years to 756), it is certain that Jonathan Edwards thought manifestations of the Awakening in his own lifetime (in the 1730s and 1740s) might in fact be harbingers of the millennium or possibly even the beginnings of the event itself. This is clear from his correspondence with Scottish divines in the 1740s as well as from his tract, *The Humble Attempt*, of 1747, evidence C. C. Goen uses to advantage.[7]

Goen goes on to argue through reference back to Calvin that this idea was "new." Indeed, he finds no hint of postmillennialism in the Westminster Confession of the 1640s, the standard English Puritan codification of Puritan thinking. He does detect a shadow of it in the Savoy Declaration of 1658 and more strikingly in the New England creeds, first the Cambridge Platform of 1648 and again in the Saybrook Platform of 1708.[8]

Having acknowledged these immediate beginnings of postmillennial-ism in the later Puritan tradition of Old England, and even more New England, Goen turns to emphasize the contribution to Edwards's think-ing made by Daniel Whitby, Charles Daubuz, and especially Moses Lowman. The latter in particular, in his *Paraphrase and Notes on the Revelation* (1737), seems to have influenced Edwards directly and deeply. We have evidence for this in a number of Edwards's writings. But the crucial point in Goen's argument is that, however dependent Edwards was on these writers, he himself became "America's first major postmil-lennial thinker."[9] Whatever its eventual impact upon "radical utopian-ism" and "manifest destiny," the origin of this American heresy, Goen argues, was in Jonathan Edwards's deviations from orthodoxy, however sharply he may have limited them.[10]

Now let me bring into focus my concern about the Goen article. I am not inclined to argue at length with his analysis either of Edwards's construction of the course of redemption, or of the role of a millennium within history as described in his writings on the subject. Perhaps I would stress more than Goen does Edwards's tentativeness on the matter, which flows from his emphasis on divine agency in redemption, rather than standing as a prominent doctrine in its own right. Nor am I inclined to take issue with the location Goen assigns to the millennium in Edwards's thought. It is present throughout numerous Miscellanies over many years as well as in the *Work of Redemption*. Nor will I argue with the emphasis Goen places on Edwards's use of Lowman, essentially as an eighteenth century commentator upon apocalyptic literature and its interpretation, although it does seem to me that Lowman reinforces opinions Edwards had already arrived at rather than introducing him to new positions.

What does concern me about the article, first, is Goen's failure to make more of the precursors to Edwards who opted for a "historical millen-nium." After all, if the Savoy Declaration, the Cambridge Platform, and the Saybrook Platform even hinted at it in creedal form, this conviction must have had a more general currency than Goen seems prepared to grant in his essay. This leads to more searching questions about the status of this interest in millenarianism in pre-Edwardsian New England and England. Second, I am inclined to argue that factors beyond Edwards's contribution must be stressed in assessing the post-Edwardsian signifi-cance of this optimistic construction of the millennium. This is to say, Goen may be read as overemphasizing Edwards's role in the development of postmillennialism in American culture. For when others began to strip away the context in which Edwards had set out his own development of this particular thesis, certainly the tone, and possibly the content, became significantly changed. In short, while I believe Goen's representation of Edwards's position to be largely correct, I think he does not properly delineate for us its background (thereby making Edwards seem more innovative than he was) nor does he trace the foreground or consequent development of postmillennialism in a way that helps to identify why, when the comprehensive framework utilized by Edwards as a setting for his postmillennialism was stripped away, his original argument became reduced to a religious version of the doctrine of providence. In the remainder of this essay I shall speak to those two issues.

For reasons that I hope will become clear, let me consider the issues—first, Goen's interpretation of Jonathan Edwards in relationship to his background, and second, his view of Edwards's relationship to nine-teenth century postmillennialism—in reverse order. I do so because it is important to take account of the cultural transformation that occurred between the seventeenth and the nineteenth centuries if we hope to understand why apparently similar or at least related positions, in this case with respect to eschatology, were in fact substantially different in the two periods. In the analogy of the archeological dig, we must work backwards through layers of cultural deposit in order to understand how change took place forward through time.

When we focus on the postmillennialism of the nineteenth century, and especially its widespread and prominent role in popular circles, we must recognize the enormous influence of the cultural "sea change" that we identify as the Enlightenment. Thanks to Professor May's marvellous study, we have a much surer grasp of how the Enlightenment entered American culture in different ways at different points in time.[11] But what concerns me now is not so much the several generations of the official Enlightenment that he has identified, either in their separateness or in their interrelationship. Rather my concern is with their comprehensive impact upon the culture, the sum-total revision of modes of thought with respect, in this particular case, to religion, that took place as a result of the Enlightenment. Here even Professor May's "didactic Enlightenment" is too formally defined a stratum or episode for our purposes. To chart the impact of the Scottish Common Sense school, for example, even as purveyed through the preaching fostered by the academies, does not bring out the crucial issue.[12] Perhaps the most effective way of making the point is to use the example of Thomas Paine. In this I have in mind not so much the content of Paine's thought about religion as the mode of thinking that he exhibits as he discusses it. He applies to it the same practical, commonsense approach that he brings to all subjects. As a result, he reduces his thought on religion, as on everything else of consequence, to an essentially literalistic level.

Paine's view of religion is, of course, like that of other Enlightenment thinkers such as Gibbon, one of scepticism toward all revealed religion.[13] He takes the Bible seriously, so to speak, but as a record of the superstitions of ancient peoples as well as of their ideals. He sees it as a kind of record of their consciousness as they lived in their pre-enlightened and pre-Enlightenment condition. For Paine, effective knowledge upon which humans could operate had to be essentially rational knowledge, cast in basically propositional terms. I want to suggest that while Paine's explicit attitudes toward religion aroused tremendous hostility among religious folk of the late eighteenth and nineteenth centuries, there is a sense in which he may have had the last laugh. For while rejecting the content of his views, popular religious positions—prominently including the espousal of premillennialism as well as postmillennialism—adopted their *form*. This is to say, religious positions increasingly became cast in terms of propositional ways of thinking. While at high cultural levels, among the Princeton theologians, for example, scientific modes of argumentation prevailed, at more popular levels, commonsense, literalistic modes became the norm. In either case, the great, rich, internally complex Christian tradition of the West, including those elements that bore on eschatological issues as well as on prophetic, ecclesiological, and creedal positions, among others, became filtered through the mindset of the Enlightenment. Consequently they were either reduced to propositional form and thus believed to be concerned only with the mundane world, or held to be essentially unintelligible. Of course the residue, that which was filtered out in this fashion, consisted precisely of those modes of knowledge that we recognize as poetic, symbolic, figurative, and so forth. In short, a truncated Enlightenment-derived view of human nature and destiny, especially with respect to religious issues, became the operative model even among those who explicitly rejected the content of the Enlightenment's views of humankind. In no subject is this ironic development more evident than with respect to the issue of "last things."

So when C. C. Goen makes of Jonathan Edwards "America's first major postmillennial thinker" he may not be wrong—although we have yet to explore how Edwards stood in relationship to his forebears—but he is failing to signal that nineteenth century postmillennial traditions adapted Jonathan Edwards's ideas even as they adopted them—and thereby reduced to a broadly Enlightenment-derived frame of reference, using essentially propositional modes of thought, a position which for

Edwards was embedded in a much richer and far more traditional and complex cognitive world. Compare, for example, his expansive spiritual typology, which reminds the reader of Bach variations as they repeatedly explore given themes, with the literal claims made by nineteenth century exegetes of virtually every school. Edwards may have been appropriated by the postmillennialists of the nineteenth century and they may have looked to him as their fountainhead, but their appropriation of him was on their terms, not on his. Their terms, I am suggesting, had more kinship with those of Thomas Paine than with those in which Edwards pursued his intellectual endeavors. Taken abstractly, there is nothing surprising in this—indeed there is an inevitability about it; for any act of appropriation entails some translation. But critical historical studies have the burden of registering exactly what changes were taking place in, with, and under apparent continuities, as well as what unobserved continuities existed in, with and under manifest changes. That Jonathan Edwards's thought is a source for nineteenth century postmillennialism is beyond dispute, but it is equally important to record how his thought was selectively adapted and was basically transformed in that adaptation.

This brings us to our second major issue in this archeological dig. How did Edwards's thought about a "historical millennium" stand in relationship to earlier tradition? In general, I do not take quite so casually as C. C. Goen the fact that creedal statements developed by the English Independents and the Massachusetts Bay and Connecticut Colony Puritans suggest possible departures from the Westminster standards on precisely the point under discussion, namely how the return of Christ might be related to a "golden age" of the church prior to the end of history. After all, both the English Independents and the New England Puritans knew well the price they might pay for diverging from the broader Puritan movement, and they were not reserved about touting their divergences—indeed we know how thoroughly they studied these divergences so as to frame their own positions more effectively. This should alert us to pay special attention to the distinctions they espoused as they explained their creedal pecularities to themselves and to others.

What did, then, lie behind the creedal peculiarities that in Goen's view formed at least a background to the emphasis on postmillennialism in Jonathan Edwards's thought? Modern scholars have explored eschatological issues as they developed in the late sixteenth century Reformed community so thoroughly in the last several decades that I will not attempt to delineate the issues here.[14] While the mainstream of Puritanism continued to adhere in general to an orthodox point of view (that is to say, teaching broadly consistent with that of John Calvin), many of those committed to reforming the English church in the seventeenth century at least entertained variations on the pattern of expectations about the end of the world as codified in the Westminster standards. But speculation about a millennial era, often believed to be prefigured in the reform then taking place under Protestant auspices, became prominent in the course of the 1630s and 1640s—and not only among sectaries and those without position, influence, and classical education. The "dissenting brethren" of the Westminster Assembly all shared to some degree in these explorations of a better future grounded in the present. Indeed, it is one of the marks of the Independents in the middle decades of the century that they looked for a purer age of the church within history, and more than a few leaders of the New Englanders stood committed to the same position.[15]

Of course the chief point is that variant constructions of the penultimate period of Christian history did not stand alone. Rather, they were tied up with issues like beliefs about the degree of Spirit presence and direction among the faithful in their congregations, the reality of the presence of Christ in his churches, the prefiguration in scripture of the course of redemption, and, above all, the desire to construct churches complete in themselves, populated by "visible saints"—in a phrase, to bring the visible church militant as close to the invisible church triumphant as humanly possible. The Cambridge Platform (1648) spoke to this when it identified a "spiritual union and communion common to all believers" that achieved expression in ecclesiastical-political union and communion.[16] So the direct headship of Christ over the contemporary church is posited by the Platform as a fundamental given of the entire New England ecclesiological experiment. I think it wrong to suppose that millennial speculations stood free of or took place without some grounding in this basic claim of the New England order concerning the presence of Christ as already sought and experienced among them.

With this as background, it is not accidental that in Jonathan Edwards's ministry the experience of Spirit action and Awakenings that began in the 1730s and continued into the 1740s should have prompted his interest in signs of such action and speculation about the penultimate epoch of history, in addition to renewed emphasis upon the purifying of the local congregation. These were all aspects of the same issue for him— as they were for the seventeenth century Independents in England and the New England Saints who handed down the tradition to him.

Casting the subject we are exploring in these terms helps us to recognize how directly Edwards grew out of the soil tilled so thoroughly in New England. It is also a reminder that, in our analogy of the archeologi-

cal dig, our transition back through the Enlightenment era has taken us
into a culture where the rules of the game are very different. The truths
that stand as individual propositions in the nineteenth century—about
such things as church order or the end of history—turn out in more
traditional perspectives to have pronounced interrelationships. And earlier propositions cast in literal terms, if they can be found, always have
allusions, resonances, and counterparts which Thomas Paine, exemplar
of Enlightenment thinking about religion, would have insisted be
stripped away to disclose their real meaning. Mason Lowance made an
inspired choice for the title of his recent book—he called it *The Language
of Canaan*.[17] This master metaphor makes it plain that Puritan thought
about collective destinies was antipropositional and rooted in the figural
traditions that proceeded from the Bible and continued to suffuse Western intellectual history.

How does this perspective relate to millenarianism and ecclesiology in
seventeenth and eighteenth century England and the New England colonies? I would maintain that claims about Christ's presence in his churches
were not propositions to be proved or disproved, but truths axiomatic to
church communities that evoked understandings of the self and of history
based on biblical precedents and promises. So the basic distinction upon
which so much turned in the nineteenth century among the literal-
minded—whether Christ would return before the millennium (yielding
premillennialism), or after it (constituting postmillennialism)—was foreign to the seventeenth and eighteenth centuries. For the earlier period,
Christ was both present now and to be more thoroughly present later. In
short, a rigid distinction between premillennialism and postmillennialism
cut against the grain of how thinking about "last things" was carried on.
But Christ's reality in and for the church was understood to be authentic
both now and later. Indeed, he constituted the common denominator
between these periods and was the grounds of assurance that the visible
saints of New England were the earnests or firstfruits of the redemption
that they believed was coming to fulfillment in their own future. This was
a claim to eschatology as realized in the Christian community that
preceded C. H. Dodd's modern interpretations of early Christianity.[18]

Once we have returned through the Enlightenment, so to speak, to the
richer world of religious discourse that preceded it, we recognize that the
distinction between premillennialism and postmillennialism that comes
to have so much currency in the nineteenth century—largely dividing
populist from relatively elite religious circles—had much less significance
in earlier religious thought. Perhaps it would be more accurate to say that
rather than constituting mutually exclusive positions, the formulations or

images were thought to represent related aspects of the same reality. Pre-Enlightenment modes of thinking permitted believers both to hold that Christ was with them individually and collectively in the present and yet also that he would be the more effectively with them later. He was, so to speak, present, but would surely be even more present later. What made this possible—indeed we might even say necessary—was their use of image, metaphor, and especially figuralism in understanding their religious life in relationship to the Scriptures. These strategies were staples of Reformed exegesis as it came to terms with the basic Protestant commitment to the literal or historical reading of the Bible. It follows that contemporary scholars interested in earlier religious thought should take seriously the contribution made by more strictly literary scholars who have explored for us the transformation of language that took place between the seventeenth and nineteenth centuries, a transformation that had its primary location in the religious usages of the time. Of course Sacvan Bercovitch's work has been exceptionally influential in this endeavor.[19]

Against this background, and taken in a technical sense, there is no doubt that Jonathan Edwards stands as a remarkably rational and lucid exponent of postmillennial views, although set within a comprehensive scheme of redemption that was deeply and thoroughly grounded in the Scriptures. This means that at different times Edwards could and did stress different and sometimes even contradictory interpretations of specific biblical passages. These views did not exclude a final apostasy before the Last Judgement. But Edwards believed the faithful could and should be confident that their period of visible sainthood would pass over eventually into eternal communion with God as the work of redemption was being completed. These specific ideas, which are often thought of as speculative, seem to me better viewed as expressions of Edwards's ecstatic side. They were, and this is the important point, scarcely new in his time or to him. They lie at the heart of the English Independency of the seventeenth century and are an expression of the impulse to visible sainthood so central to New England Puritanism. Jonathan Edwards may have put them forth, in the context of the Awakening, with a greater clarity than did earlier writers, but I do not think that the substance of his claims with respect to a purer age for the church was so markedly innovative.

Edwards's thought on postmillennialism represented, therefore, nothing remarkably new until the Enlightenment transformed it. That transformation reduced it to literalistic formulations. In consequence, positions that had been much richer, nuanced, and multivalent became expressed in the limited logic of modern propositions. So while I suggest that C. C. Goen is essentially correct in portraying Jonathan Edwards's specific delineation of the course of redemption, and in emphasizing that it included a period in which the church could expect to prosper before the Last Judgement, his discussion is at least open to misconstruction with respect to two additional issues which have had consequences for placing Edwards's thought and assessing its significance. First, Edwards's formal position was far less innovative in the context of New England Puritanism and Independency in England than Goen suggests. Second, a marked discontinuity exists between Edwards's position, rooted as it was in pre-Enlightenment modes of thought, and the nineteenth century, postmillennial position claimed by Goen to derive from his ideas. There is no question that Edwards's writings and thought contributed significantly to the nineteenth century position. But that contribution was made not in Edwards's terms but in terms defined by the revolution in human consciousness we know as the Enlightenment.

Notes

1. *Church History* 28 (1959), pp. 25–40.
2. (Cambridge, Mass., 1966) and (Chicago, 1968), respectively. Alan Heimert began his second and central chapter, titled "The Work of Redemption," with a reference to Goen's essay (see note 1, p. 59). E. L. Tuveson cited the essay in compiling a list of prominent American religious authors, beginning with Edwards, who wrote on millennialism (see note 2, p. 53).
3. Goen, "Jonathan Edwards," p. 25.
4. Ibid.
5. Ibid., p. 26.
6. *A History of the Work of Redemption* was published in Edinburgh by John Erskine. Erskine had edited into the form of a treatise a transcription made by Jonathan Edwards, Jr., in New Haven of sermon booklets from which his father had preached a sermon series in 1739, more than thirty years earlier. While it is clear that Edwards senior intended to return to treat the work of redemption in a systematic fashion, and that his point of departure would have been this series of sermons, exactly *what* he would have done in developing this magnum opus is less evident. Erskine's edition has provided almost a "Rorschach Test" for interpreters of Edwards. Goen's analytical summary of Edwards's outline of the periods of the Christian era is certainly a faithful representation of the scheme that is used in the sermon series (see Goen, "Jonathan Edwards," p. 26).
7. Goen, "Jonathan Edwards," pp. 29–33.
8. Ibid., pp. 33–35.

9. Ibid., pp. 35–37, 38

10. Ibid., p. 39.

11. Henry F. May, *The Enlightenment in America* (New York, 1976).

12. Other recent studies of the Enlightenment's introduction to America include that of Lefferts A. Loetscher, *Facing the Enlightenment and Pietism* (Westport, Conn., 1983).

13. See *The Age of Reason* and *The Age of Reason, Part Second* in *The Complete Writings of Thomas Paine*, ed. Philip S. Foner (New York, 1945), vol. 1, pp. 463–604.

14. The following titles suggest the many dimensions of this literature: Bryan W. Ball, *The English Connection* (Cambridge, 1981); B. S. Capp, *The Fifth Monarchy Men* (Totowa, N.J., 1972); Paul Christianson, *Reformers and Babylon* (Toronto, 1978); Christopher Hill, *Antichrist in Seventeenth Century England* (London, 1971); Christopher Hill, *The World Turned Upside Down* (New York, 1972); V. Norskov Olsen, *John Foxe and the Elizabethan Church* (Berkeley, 1973).

15. Williston Walker, *The Creeds and Platforms of Congregationalism* (New York, 1893) remains useful. It was reissued in 1960 (Philadelphia and Boston).

16. See Walker, *Creeds and Platforms*, p. 205 (1960 edition).

17. (Cambridge, Mass., 1980).

18. Dodd's interpretation occurs in such studies as *The Parables of the Kingdom* (New York, 1935) and *History and the Gospel* (London, 1938).

19. Among many titles in this literature the following have special relevance: Sacvan Bercovitch, ed., *Typology and Early American Literature* (Amherst, 1972); Sacvan Bercovitch, *The Puritan Origins of the American Self* (New Haven, 1975); Ursula Brumm, *American Thought and Religious Typology* (New Brunswick, N.J., 1970); Barbara Lewalski, *Protestant Poetics* (Princeton, 1979); Mason Lowance, *The Language of Canaan* (Cambridge, Mass., 1980).

9

The Puritans and Edwards

HARRY S. STOUT

The title of my essay—"The Puritans and Edwards"— is one of those beguilingly simple phrases that in a disturbingly brief period of time can recall virtually the entire corpus of colonial New England religious studies. Edmund Morgan tells us, only half in jest, that there will soon be one published book for every forty colonial New England families. Similarly, in a recent reference guide to Edwards scholarship, M. X. Lesser records over eighteen hundred books, articles, and dissertations, including a majority completed in the past forty years.[1] In short, if any subject has enjoyed more sustained and concentrated study than the Puritans in New England, it would be Jonathan Edwards.

With so much scholarly attention devoted to the Puritans and Edwards it is not surprising that the interrelationship between the two has been the subject of frequent examinations. Equally predictable is the fact that the conclusions have differed widely. Writing in the 1920s and 1930s, "progressive" historians led by Vernon Parrington had no problem lumping the Puritans and Edwards together as one continuous and repressive "anachronism" retarding America's progress to enlightened liberalism. At the other extreme was Perry Miller's 1949 intellectual biography of Edwards, which concluded that Edwards was so far ahead of his time that our own is barely catching up. So successful was Miller's rehabilitation that a generation of scholars set themselves to explore the question of Edwards's "modernity."[2]

Over the past decade, more balanced assessments have appeared that seek to place Edwards in his eighteenth century American and British context. While conceding Edwards's genius and confirming his standing as America's first great philosopher, they also point to the many ways in which his thought moved along the plane of seventeenth and eighteenth century Puritan theology. In one important respect, however, Miller's revisionists agree with him in separating the Puritans and Edwards. Both find that Edwards repudiated the "national" covenant of his Puritan predecessors. The term national covenant was first used by Perry Miller to distinguish the Puritans' sense of two covenants. One covenant—the "covenant of grace"—referred to individuals and personal salvation in the life to come. The other covenant—the national covenant—applied to nations and governed their temporal success in this world. In early Puritanism these two contradictory covenants—one of faith, the other of works; one unconditional, the other conditional—existed in creative tension. By 1740, if not sooner, they became hopelessly shattered and divided into two opposing parties. One group (the "liberals" or "rationalists") emphasized corporate morality and God's outward covenant with New England. The other group (called "pietists" or "evangelicals") rejected the "federal theology" and focussed their preaching solely on personal salvation and the life to come.

As America's foremost evangelical theologian, Edwards fell into the camp of those who rejected that national covenant. Indeed, according to Miller, Edwards initiated the evangelicals' rejection of federal theology: "Every New Englander before Edwards was a 'Federalist,' and because [Edwards] put aside all this sort of thinking, he became a new point of departure in the history of the American mind." Surprisingly, this view has gone virtually unchallenged. In the most complete analysis of Edwards's thoughts on the covenant to appear since Miller, Conrad Cherry concludes that the federal theology "did not assume for [Edwards] the same importance for an understanding of the saints' social and political life as it had for his forefathers."[3]

In the remarks to follow I will suggest that Edwards was even more a Puritan than Miller or his revisionists concede. In fact, he was every bit the federal theologian that his Puritan predecessors were. Throughout his career as pastor and teacher he adhered exactly to the logic and tenets of the national covenant and reiterated them in exactly the same terms as did his predecessors in the New England pulpit. Nor was he alone among evangelicals. A corollary to my thesis is that evangelicals generally accepted the federal logic and applied it to their own New England in times of great national trial and stress. Indeed, the federal theology enabled evangelicals and rationalists to come together on a common footing when faced with external enemies.

That historians have missed the connections between Edwards and the federal theology is owing largely to the types of evidence they consulted. For the most part, scholars have approached Edwards's preaching from the vantage point of his published sermons. With the exception of a handful of ordination sermons, these printed works were exclusively "regular" or Sunday sermons that had as their central theme the great drama of salvation. Comments on the national convenant and corporate morality were generally considered inappropriate for Sunday preaching, and naturally did not appear in the text. The appropriate time for social commentary and discussion of covenant conditions was election day or a fast day when communities met during the week to hear about the current state of God's covenant with New England.[4] Unlike many rationalist ministers who often had their fast (or election) sermons published, Edwards never published a fast sermon, nor was he ever invited to deliver an election sermon. As far as the printed record is concerned, then, Edwards never preached on the federal covenant.

For the most part Edwards and his fellow evangelicals preferred to publish selections from their regular Sunday sermons. But this does not mean that they did not deliver fast sermons in times of great calamity or national uncertainty, any more than it means that rationalists did not preach salvation on Sundays. To the contrary, evangelicals delivered fast sermons on weekdays with the same faith and seriousness with which rationalist ministers delivered conversion sermons on Sundays. Edwards was no exception.[5] When his fast and thanksgiving sermons are examined in their entirety it becomes apparent that Edwards, together with his rationalist counterparts, approached New England as a "peculiar" nation who, like Israel of old, enjoyed a special covenant relationship with God.

Edwards absorbed the logic and terminology of federal covenants from an early age, when he sat under the ministry of his father, Timothy Edwards. Like his son, Timothy Edwards was widely recognized as an evangelical preacher who concentrated on the New Birth. But in times of national or local crisis he wielded the logic of the fast, with its distinctive jeremiad, as efficiently as any other minister of his age. In an unpublished fast sermon delivered in 1709 following "Our fatal disappointment in our expedition against our French and Indian Enemies," Timothy explained that defeat came as a result of New England's sin. When God's people failed to acknowledge their corporate dependence on Him, then, Timothy explained:

> [God] trys afflictions and the Rods of anger. He makes use of many angry frowning dispensations. [He] chastens, corrects em and sends calamitys

and Judgments of various Kinds and Sorts . . . to bring e'm back from their Sinfull Wanderings unto the Straight path of their duty . . . especially those of e'm that he has taken nearest himself, and thus he dealt with that sinfull and Rebellious people of his, the children of Israel.[6]

Threats like this were frightening. But from the parallel with Israel, New England could also take hope. Disappointments in defeat were different from utter destruction; they were not signs of divine desertion so much as urgent calls to reformation: "Sincere Repentance and hearty and Real returning unto God is the proper voice and Loude call of the Judgments of God . . . the Judgments of God do with a Loud voice call upon a Sinfull and disobedient people to Repent and Return unto the Lord." If God's people sincerely reformed, then according to the logic of the federal covenant, they could depend on victory in the end.

Contained in Timothy's fast sermon were all the elements of federal rhetoric that Jonathan would later employ in his own pulpit. First was the parallel with Israel. National covenants did not cease with Israel, but would continue to the end of time. The people of New England were such a covenant people, but their corporate standing beford God was precarious. God was angry at them because of their sins. If they refused to repent, their trials and calamities would become progressively more severe and culminate in divine desertion. But if they repented and reformed their lives, God would be merciful and deliver them. What at first glance seems to be a rhetoric of condemnation and guilt turns out on further analysis to be the necessary first step to deliverance and triumph.[7]

Jonathan's first surviving fast sermon manuscript came soon after his ordination at Northampton in 1726. Within a year of that date New England experienced the "Great Earthquake" of November 1727. The quake began, according to several accounts, with a "flash of light," which was then followed by a "horrid rumbling" and "weighty shaking" that continued to reverberate throughout the evening. Weymouth's Thomas Paine recalled how: "The motion of the Earth was very great, like the waves of the sea . . . The strongest Houses shook prodigiously and tops of some Chimnies were thrown down . . . It affected the People of N-E, especially those near the Center of it, with more Fear Amazement than ever is thought to have befallen the Land since it had that Name." Awakened sleepers poured into the streets in huddled groups, certain that the day of judgment had come. The aftershocks continued for nine days which, Paine observed, "mightly kept up the Terror of it in the People, and drove them to all possible means of Reformation."[8]

On the day following the earthquake, fasts were called spontaneously throughout the land and repeated several times in the ensuing weeks. In Northampton Edwards mounted the pulpit and preached from Jon. 3:10: "And God saw their works that they turned from their evil way and God repented of the Evil that he had said he would do unto them and he did it not."[9] While in regular sermons Edwards's primary concern was the individual soul, his concern on this occasion was the temporal estate of New England, which he believed was governed by its corporate covenant with God. Even as his text was devoted to the nation of Nineveh and God's mercy to it because it repented, so also was his concern that day with the nation of New England and the warning contained in its earthquake.

Like the other ministers in 1727, Edwards perceived both natural and supernatural meanings in the great earthquake. On the one hand, he drew from the most recent scientific literature to explain that earthquakes were not in themselves miracles but natural convulsions that occurred when bodies of water met with "subterraneous Fires" in underground caverns to produce rumblings at ground level.[10] On the other hand, Edwards explained, God also used earthquakes to warn a covenant people: "earthquakes and lights in the heaven may often have natural causes yet they may nevertheless be ordered to be as a forerunner of great changes and Judgments." Such was clearly the case with New England's recent convulsion, leading Edwards to the doctrine that, "when God gives a sinful people warnings of impending judgments, the only way to have them averted is reformation."

A little later in the sermon, Edwards made plain that he was speaking in temporal and collective terms to the people of Northampton, not in eternal terms, and in so doing illustrated the different ends and logics of the two covenants:

> If a nation or people are very corrupt and remain obstinate in the Evil way God generally if not universally exercises these threatenings. God is more strict in punishing of a wicked people in this world than a wicked person. God often suffers particular persons that are wicked to prosper in the world and discharges them to judgment in the world to come. But a people as a people are punished only in this world. Therefore God will not suffer a people that grow very corrupt and refuse to be reclaimed to go unpunished in this world.

Here it was appropriate to think of New England "as a people" in temporal terms of rewards and punishments. Corporate morality could not win or merit eternal salvation, but it could ensure success on earth.

With temporal logic firmly in mind, Edwards returned again to the earthquake and rehearsed the corruptions that gave rise to the divine warning. The earlier revivals of his grandfather had clearly passed, leaving Edwards to conclude that "our Land is very much defiled." In particular Edwards cited an "abundance of cheating and injustice" that had increased since his arrival in Northampton a year earlier. Equally offensive was an increase in swearing and insensitivity to the great concerns of religion. This insensitivity was "especially among the young People" who most needed to consider the state of their souls. Too many of the inhabitants had grown "secure in riches." Therefore, "God shows us that we are in his hand every moment by this shaking the foundation of the Earth . . . [He could] plunge us down to the Pit when he pleases."

In his regular preaching Edwards used the language of destruction and "the Pit" to drive sinners to conversion. Here, however, he employed similar terminology to encourage a corporate turning away from sin to avoid further punishments "in this world." As with personal repentance, hypocrisy was the sin most to be avoided in outward shows of repentance and humiliation. Mere external observance of the fast was not enough if New England was to escape temporal punishments: "Tis only their Reformation that will prevent them [from destruction] . . . A peoples praying that Judgments may be averted is insufficient for a people to pray . . . and all the while to go on sinning and provoking God." The severity of the earthquake confirmed how God's patience was being pushed to the breaking point: "God has a long time been warning us and has been waiting to be gracious to us . . . And yet there has been no general Reformation. We have kept many days of fasting and humiliation . . . and have pretended to humble ourselves for our backsliding. But yet [we] have not grown any better." If New England did not repent as a people, then God would annul his covenant and there would be no defense. Individuals in New England might still be saved for eternity (that was another story and another covenant), but they could not escape destruction in this earthly life: "And how can you expect . . . that you can escape the wrath of that God that can shake a whole land and make the Earth to tremble . . . Do you flatter yourself that God may bring judgments upon this land, yet you shall escape the publick calamities?" Clearly the answer was no. All must repent and reform before it was too late. The wicked must turn to God or face "the cold arms of death and the hot flames of hell."

Throughout the 1730s and 1740s most of the grievances facing New England were internal. Apart from occasional attacks from the Indians, New England's borders were safe, and the chief concerns in these years were natural calamities like drought, fire, disease, and pestilence, and internal discord over questions of revival and the New Birth. Already in 1736 Edwards employed a fast sermon to plead for harmony and the elimination of a "party spirit among us." While differences of opinion were inevitable, "yet there is no necessity of making parties and raising tumults because of this . . . How much more comfortable and pleasant living is in a society that lives in Love and Peace than when [there is] perpetual contention."[11]

Despite New England's precarious peace in the 1730s and 1740s all recognized the possibility of war and presented it as the divine affliction most to be avoided. With the possibility of war everpresent, congregations needed to be constantly reminded of their national standing before God. Edwards was no exception.

At a fast sermon delivered in March 1737, Edwards outlined federal theology and its temporal corollaries. Ancient Israel was the model and prototype for all subsequent covenant people, so Edwards turned to 2 Chron. 23:16 for his text: "And Jehoiada made a covenant between him, and between all the people, and between the king, that they should be the Lord's people." That text, Edwards explained in his opening remarks, occurred at a point in Israel's history when they had turned away from worshiping false idols and returned to God. Earlier, Judah had worshiped Baal, and God had allowed the enemy nations to attack His people for their idolatry. Now they had returned to God, renewed the covenant, implored his mercy, and received outward blessings in return. In brief compass, Edwards explained to his listeners what was meant by a covenant people:

> [S]ome are distinguished of God as a Covenant People. So were the people that were spoken of in the Text. God entered into Covenant with Abraham and Isaac and Jacob and brought them out of Egypt and in a Solemn manner entered into Covenant with them in the [desert] and separated them from the [other] nations on the earth to be a Covenant people a peculiar People to the Lord.[12]

As a covenant people, Israel could depend on divine protection and "Temporal Blessings," as long as they honored the terms of God's people. Indeed, Edwards went on, it was the enjoyment of "covenant blessings" that distinguished covenant peoples from profane societies.

From ancient Israel, Edwards turned to New England, observing that the federal theology did not cease with the Old Testament but continued throughout history. Citing God's promise in Exodus 19:6, Edwards assured his listeners that, "if you keep my covenant ye shall be unto me . . .

an holy nation." Clearly New England was such a people, called of God to be a "peculiar people":

> We have been greatly distinguished by God as a covenant people. God has distinguished us by making known his covenant to us. We have been in a very [clear] manner a Land of Light . . . The land of our forefathers has been a land of such light . . . You are a people that have been distinguished of god as covenant people for a long time and have been distinguished in the means that god has used with you.

With such blessings, the lessons to be learned in the fast were obvious: "Hence learn such causes we have to lament the degeneracies and corruptions of this land." Through fasting Edwards hoped to inculcate true humbling, which, as earlier, he distinguished from "hypocritical fasting." If God's people were to continue receiving the blessings of the land they must heed the words of their pastors and repent: "You are a People that have been distinguished of God as a Covenant People for a long time. You have for a long time enjoyed the Preaching of God's Word and the visibility of the Gospel in a steady course." Only by honoring that word and reforming the evil in their communities could God's people expect to continue receiving temporal rewards and prosperity. If they failed to acknowledge the words of God's prophets on days of fasting and humiliation they would surely suffer the same fate as Israel at the hands of neighboring enemies. Even now, Edwards warned, there were "great numbers of papists" to the North, creating in North America an ominous "mixture of dark with light."

As long as peace prevailed on New England's borders, fast sermons were usually centered on calls for internal harmony and repetitions of the terms for temporal and material blessings. All of this changed in the spring of 1745, when New England forces mounted an assault on the French fortress at Louisbourg. From that point on, Edwards's generation of ministers faced an ongoing regime of wars and rumors of wars. Fast days would be called with renewed urgency in New Light and Old Light congregations alike, and the chief concern was no longer internal contention, drought, or blastings, but national survival. The stakes were high in the mounting struggle between France and England for control of the New World, and nowhere were they higher than in New England, where the harshest fighting was sure to take place. The new circumstances charged the old rhetoric of the fast with a new urgency.[13] If New England was to survive its long ordeal for liberty and self-determination, it must remain a covenant people.

In articulating the terms of victory, Edwards and other New Light ministers proved to be as quick to claim federal promises as were their Old Light counterparts. For Edwards, no less than for the rationalists, New England was a "visible People of God;" a "city set on a hill" that was under great obligations to its covenant God. On the eve of the Louisbourg expedition Edwards delivered a serious of sermons on Lev. 26:3–13 that had as their overriding theme the message that "temporal blessings" accrue to a people of God. Included in those blessings were martial promises. God's people could depend upon "safety . . . with reference to enemies," and eventually they would inherit "the blessings of peace."[14] Edwards's April 4 "fast for success in [the] expedition against Cape Breton" followed the traditional formula in defining a righteous war and then promising ultimate victory. From 1 Kings 8:44 he demonstrated how "a people of God may be called to go forth to war," and that such action was "lawful and a duty." With flawless logic he pressed the point that "if it be lawful for a particular person to defend himself with force, Then it is lawful for a nation of People made up of particular persons." In situations where God's people were threatened it was up to them to look to God for deliverance because "God and he only determines the event of war and gives the victory." If they went to war in dependence on God and honored the terms of his covenant, then they could claim the victory: "God is ready in such a case to Hear the prayer of his People and give them success."[15] Like his earlier fasts, Edwards's Louisbourg fast was unoriginal; it offered nothing new in terminology or logic. When facing outward enemies and the horrors of war, Edwards, like his peers, instinctively fell back on federal promises in their simplest, most elemental form.

Throughout the spring of 1745 all ears eagerly awaited news from Louisbourg. On May 21, following another series of fast sermons, New Englanders rejoiced to learn the·"news from Cape Breton that ye royal Battery is taken [and] ye english army encamped before ye Town."[16] Through a fortunate set of circumstances, including good sailing weather and French miscalculations, the New England troops were able to set in a siege and wait out the outnumbered and undersupplied French. Finally, on June 17, the unthinkable happened: pressed by dwindling goods and constant bombardment the "Gibraltar of the New World" fell and passed to the command of the colonial commander William Pepperell. The impossible had been achieved. With no assistance from England, New England troops had succeeded in humbling one of the most powerful French fortresses in the New World and, in the process, had fixed their self-image as a divinely assisted people of war.[17]

News of the surrender did not reach Boston until July 3, at the same time that many ministers were convening there for the annual college commencement. The ensuing celebration was unrestrained. Westboro's Ebenezer Parkman witnessed "all manner of Joy thereat . . . The Bells were rung, Guns fired etc. Commencement was rendered the most gladsome Day." Thomas Prince later recalled how, "when the Tydings came . . . we were like them that dream: our mouth was fill'd with Laughter, and our Tongue with Singing." Throughout the evening the sky over Boston was illuminated by bonfires and fireworks. Religious controversies which as late as April 6 were, in Parkman's words, "hotter than ever," melted away as all New England joined to celebrate the victory. Over the next two weeks, towns and churches throughout New England gathered for thanksgiving sermons and services of celebration.[18]

Like the earlier fast sermons, thanksgiving sermons were quick to portray the victory in apocalyptic terms and ascribed success to God's historic covenant with New England. No other explanation seemed adequate to explain the "train of providences" accompanying the New England troops on their feared expedition. Again, differences between rationalists and evangelicals disappeared in the occasional pulpit. Following news of the surrender, Edwards turned to history for comparable achievements. So magnificent a victory, he concluded, came "the nearest to a parallel with God's wonderful work of old, in Moses', Joshua's, and Hezekiah's time, of any that have been in these latter ages of the world."[19]

Edwards's chief antagonist, Charles Chauncy, used similar terms to describe the recent events. The colonists' victory "in this part of the dominion of Antichrist" was so stupendous, that the only historical precedent for Chauncy—as for Edwards—was ancient Israel: "I scarce know of a conquest, since the days of *Joshua* and the *Judges*, wherein the finger of god is more visible. . . . let the inspired language of *Moses*, and the *whole Body of the Jewish Nation*, be ours upon this memorable occasion."[20]

In a sermon preached in Northampton following the safe return of twenty soldiers in his congregation in August 1745, Edwards again traced the train of remarkable events attending the colonial victory that were, he believed, "enough to convince any infidel" that God fought "for his people that go forth to war and returns them to the people and House of God in prosperity." Later that month Edwards employed his quarterly lecture on Psalm 111:5 ("he will ever be mindful of his convenant") to explain how "God is engaged to do great things for his people," and that he "never fails in any instance of faithfulness of the covenant engagements he has entered into." The exhortation portion of his sermon notes were left blank for extemporaneous enlargement, save for the simple phrase, "to exhort all to be mindful of their covenant with God."[21]

So monumental was the Louisbourg victory in building New England's self-confidence and sense of mastery that in annual Thanksgiving sermons in the following fall ministers again reiterated the glorious victory. Again, Edwards was no exception to the general pattern. For his thanksgiving day discourse on December 5, 1745, Edwards selected Jeremiah 51:5: "For Israel hath not been forsaken, nor Judah of his God, of the Lord of hosts; though their land was filled with sin against the Holy One of Israel." That prophecy, Edwards explained, came at a time in Israel's history when Babylon was about to be destroyed and the children of Israel "set at liberty from their Captivity."[22] The destruction of Babylon, moreover, "was an evidence that God had not forsaken his people." From there Edwards reiterated the familiar conclusion that all nations were not alike in the sight of God; some were set aside to be in a "special Relation" to him as a professing people: "A professing people are a covenant people of god and stand in special relation to him as his People in distinction from others that are not in covenant with him as it was of Israel of Old." Such professing peoples did not stop with Israel but continued into the New Testament period and throughout history. New England was such a people and could claim God's promise "to guard them from their Enemies and . . . keep them from being swallowed up by them." In his mercy God sustained covenant relations with a nation until they absolutely rejected him, thus leading Edwards to the doctrine that "the mercy of God towards a professing people is very wonderful when he don't forsake them tho their land be filled with sin against him." Quite simply, God will not forsake a covenant people unless they first forsake him.

From the model of Israel contained in his text, Edwards turned the application portion of his sermon to a consideration of New England. "How wonderful God's mercy is to our nation and Land for this that is spoken of in the Text and doctrine seems to be the case with us." Despite grievous sins and lapses in piety, New England remained a covenant people. To locate them in the vast history of redemption, Edwards proceeded to trace the history of professing peoples from England to New England. In the grand manner of the election sermon preacher, he unveiled the long train of covenants that culminated with the birth of New England. Beginning with the apostasy of Rome and the papal "AntiChrist," he turned to movements for reform in England, first with John Wycliff, and moving through Henry VIII. Despite the contrary ambitions of Queen Mary, Edwards continued, England continued on a

Reformed course under Elizabeth and thwarted "a grand design formed by the Papish party in Europe to bring the Protestant nations under the yoke of the church of Rome." Again there was peace and prosperity until the reign of King James, when "England began in many respects to be false against the holy one of Israel." Increasingly through the reign of King Charles "the nation began very much to depart from the Purity of doctrine," leading to calls for reform sounded by the "Puritans as they were called." The Puritans suffered "great cruelty" and persecution by the Church of England. Many escaped to New England, and just "when the nation seemed to be on the brink of Ruin God was pleased wonderfully to appear and bring about a great Reformation." Through the English Revolution, reformation appeared in "the Assembly of Divines" meeting at Westminster and the confession of faith they produced.

From English Revolution and the Westminster Confession, Edwards turned to England in the eighteenth century. Queen Anne's War between 1702 and 1713 was, he observed, a dangerous time that brought the nation "back to brink of Ruin," but again they were spared and peace returned. Now under the reign of King George I there was freedom of religion and "Liberty of Conscience," allowing God's people to thrive both in England and, more importantly, in New England. In Northampton, Edwards reminded his congregation of the great revival in 1735 and the "more general Revival of Religion" that came later. Despite regrettable lapses in piety and immorality the revivals ensured God's continued presence in New England and promised victory over "the French nation."

Throughout 1746, Edwards continued to use fast days to justify war as both a natural right and sacred duty. In June 1746 he employed a text from Neh. 4:14 ("remember the Lord, which is great and terrible, and fight for your brethren, your sons, and your daughters, your wives, and your houses") to establish the doctrine that: "When a people of God are molested and endangered by injurious and bloody enemies; for them cheerfully to exert and expose themselves in a war tending to their defence of safety is a good work and a duty they owe to God, their country and themselves." Besides temporal success Edwards saw in war with France an apocalyptic significance whereby "Tis to be hoped that the time of his own throne is approaching."[23]

While victory over France was certain so long as New England remained a covenant people, the timing was not certain. No one saw the 1748 treaty with France as anything more than an armistice, postponing for a time the dreaded struggle that was sure to follow. Formal peace did nothing to solve the territorial disputes between France and England, nor did it ease the hatreds—both national and religious—that had been accumulating for over a century. Rationalists and evangelicals would continue to divide strenuously over questions of pulpit style and theology, but there was an overriding concurrence over enemies in this world that released energies for common action. All believed that, as God's covenant people, New Englanders had a glorious mission to uphold in this world, and that mission required the preservation of their civil and religious liberties against external enemies. These liberties were interconnected in New Englanders' minds, and both were essential to their corporate identity as the New Israel. It did not matter which was threatened: remove one and the other was sure to follow. When that happened, God's Word would cease to reign supreme, and New England would relinquish its special covenant.

During the interwar years between 1749 and 1754, Edwards struggled furiously against the tide of "Arminianism" as it found expression in the Half-Way Covenant (or Stoddardeanism) and the denial of original sin. His well-known opposition to the policy of open communion initiated by his grandfather was so uncompromising that it earned him a dismissal from his Northampton congregation and resettlement among the Stockbridge Indians in 1751. Yet throughout his opposition to the Half-Way Covenant, he never wavered in his acceptance of the federal theology, and his conviction that New Englanders were a special people who enjoyed peculiar blessings and responsibilities in this world. Fast sermons that were delivered in the 1740s to his Northampton congregation were repeated verbatim in the 1750s.[24] Throughout he approached New England as a people bound in covenant, whose blessings and calamities would be commensurate with their performance of covenant conditions.

By March of 1755 it was clear to Edwards and other colonial leaders that New England's armistice with France was about to end. To the members of his Stockbridge congregation, set on the outer rim of English civilization, the dangers of renewed war were especially frightening. At a special fast day called in March 1755, Edwards repeated a sermon he delivered in 1744 "on occasion of war with France." It is, Edwards began, "owing to the protection of heaven that our nation and land have not been destroyed before now by the same kind of Enemies with those that . . . now oppose [us]."[25] With war again approaching, the one lesson frightened New Englanders had to remember was that "sin above all other things weakens a people in war." When "vice prevails among a people," defeats were sure to follow, because among professing peoples, success or failure "corresponds to" their covenant keeping. If they break the covenant, then "destruction by the sword of the enemy is a most just . . . Recompence for the Rebellion of a people against god." Conversely, a turning back to God in Northampton or in Stockbridge would prompt God to deliver his people and, "in a special manner to show his Hand in the government of the world in disposing [of] the Enemies of War."

Within three months of Edwards's fast sermon, New England's time of trial reappeared. In July 1755, at the very time that Edwards was completing his dissertation on *True Virtue* and beginning his massive defense of *Original Sin*, General Edward Braddock and his British regulars were decisively defeated on the banks of the Monongahela River by a combined force of French and Indian troops. Thus began the fourth and final war for North American hegemony. In New England, one out of every three men able to bear arms was enlisted for service—a figure far exceeding other regions and other colonies. Before the Seven Years' War (or French and Indian War) was over, virtually every New England family had one member engaged in what would become the largest war fought to that time on North American soil.[26]

The spectacular shouting matches between rationalists and evangelicals disappeared in the face of renewed war with France. In keeping with previous wartime experiences, New Englanders were brought together by war, and the chief instrument of cohesion was the local sermon sounded on days of fasting and troop musterings. From the commencement of hostilities, the clergy were united in stirring martial resolve and specifying the terms and nature of divine assistance. In this war, as others, they did not discourage armed conflict but encouraged it for nationalistic and prophetic reasons. Their rhetorical task on weekday fasts and artillery addresses was twofold. First, they had to establish the justice and necessity of war with France in terms drawn both from secular writings on civil liberties and property rights, and from Scripture prophecies foretelling terrible wars between God's New Israel and the forces of Anti-Christ. Second, they had to prepare their people for the possibility of short-term defeats and great sufferings before victory would be ultimately won. Temporary defeats signaled the need for repentance and dependence on God; victories confirmed New England's chosen status as the unconquerable people of God. In either case the national covenant was confirmed.

Of the righteousness of New England's cause there could be no doubt. Despite its many wars, ministers insisted that New England was not a militaristic culture pursuing armed conquest for the sake of vain glory. Its wars were just, fought in defense of life, property, and civil and religious liberty. At a fast service in July 1755, Edwards repeated a sermon he delivered earlier on the eve of the Louisbourg expedition underscoring the doctrine that "it is lawful and duty in some cases for one nation to wage a war with another . . . Reason and the light of nature shows it . . . it follows from the law of self-preservation."[27] Clearly war with France was such a case. In 1755 as in 1745, "it is of vast importance to us that the expedition should be [a] success on many accounts." God's people must be fervent in their prayers, but they must also be willing to lend their arms in the sacred cause. In closing, Edwards sought "to excite all to seek to God for success in this . . . Enterprise."

However just the "enterprise," success was not immediately forthcoming. Following Braddock's defeat, Anglo-American forces suffered one disappointment after another. So devastating were the defeats that in a fast sermon from 1756, Edwards turned to Psalm 60:9–12 ("Give us help from trouble, for vain is the help of men"), to establish the consoling doctrine that "it becomes a people after defeat in war to relinquish all other dependence and to look to him for help."[28] The times, Edwards conceded, were dark. "It is now a time distinguished from all others that ever have been in the Respect that this [is] a time wherein the civil and Religious Liberties of the British Plantation in America and all that is dear to us [is] being threatened." But the times were not hopeless. Despite temporary setbacks and smaller armies, Edwards assured his listeners that "the race is not to the swift," and that even as God delivered his people Israel in time of distress, even so would he continue to provide "a peculiar Encouragement for God's people." New Englanders could be sure that immediate losses in battle were not a final sentence of doom, because Scripture clearly foretold the downfall of Anti-Christ.[29]

Edwards's death on March 22, 1758 prevented him from witnessing the final victory over France, though he would certainly not have been surprised. Like other thanksgiving preachers in 1759 and 1760, he would have ascribed triumph to New England's covenant with God, and their ongoing status as a "peculiar people." That same image of a chosen people would sustain New Englanders through their next crisis in the controversy with England. Had Edwards lived to witness the unfolding conflict with England, he would have certainly supported the "sacred cause" of liberty and turned his pen to calls for moral reformation and promises of national success. Such calls for national reformation and triumph would never have displaced Edwards's primary concern with the great and all-consuming question of personal salvation in the world to come, but they would have assumed a crucial significance in questions bearing on New England's temporal estate in this world. The covenant made that inevitable.

If anything is clear from the foregoing analysis of Edwards's fast and thanksgiving sermons, it is that he was a child of New England's inherited covenant. The federal covenant—unlike questions of epistemology, psychology, and moral philosophy—was not a philosophical problem for Edwards, but part of the taken-for-granted reality in which New England society grew and took shape. In fact, *no* eighteenth century established minister dared to deny the federal covenant and New England's attendant identity as a special people with a messianic destiny. The external threats were too direct and the fears of national extinction too real for any to challenge this master organizing principle of New England culture. If the formulaic terms of covenant promise and chosen peoplehood sound hopelessly repetitious and formal—not to say plain wrong—it must be remembered that in New England they gained force with retelling and success. Quite simply, New Englanders, like "Americans" later, never lost the big battles. As long as they continued to win, the covenant was validated and the myth lived on. The vision of a redeemer nation and a covenant people was dazzling, and none, including Edwards, could escape its glare. As one voice among thousands, Edwards helped perpetuate that quintessentially Puritan notion of a righteous city set high upon a hill for all the world to see. That notion apparently has yet to run its course. In this sense, we continue to inhabit a world formed largely by the Puritans and Edwards.

Notes

1. See Edmund S. Morgan, "The Historians of Early New England," in Ray Allen Billington, ed., *The Reinterpretation of Early American History: Essays in Honor of Jonathan Edwin Pomfret* (New York, 1968), 41–42; and M. X. Lesser, ed., *Jonathan Edwards: A Reference Guide* (Boston, 1981).

2. See V. L. Parrington, *Main Currents in American Thought*, vol. 1, *The Colonial Mind* (New York, 1927; rpt. 1954), 153–62; and Perry Miller, *Jonathan Edwards* (New York, 1949). For a fine summary of the debate over Edwards's "modernity," see Donald Weber's introduction to the new edition of Miller's *Edwards* (Amherst, 1981).

3. Perry Miller, *Jonathan Edwards*, 76, and "The Marrow of Puritan Divinity," reprinted in *Errand Into the Wilderness* (New York, 1965), 50, 98. See also Conrad Cherry, "The Puritan Notion of the Covenant in Jonathan Edwards' Doctrine of Faith," *Church History* 34 (1965), 329, and *The Theology of Jonathan Edwards: A Reappraisal* (Garden City, N.Y., 1966), 109.

4. The major distinctions in form, content, and function between regular (Sunday) sermons and occasional (weekday) sermons have not been sufficiently

emphasized in studies of Puritan preaching. For a discussion of the very different purposes and logics of these two categories of sermon, see Harry S. Stout, *The New England Soul: Preaching and Religious Culture in Colonial New England* (New York, 1986), 13–31.

5. I am grateful to James F. Cooper, Jr., for assistance in compiling the listing of occasional fast and thanksgiving sermons in the Edwards Papers at Yale University's Beinecke Library. In all, 68 sermon manuscripts survive, of which 26 were thanksgiving sermons, and 42 fast sermons. These sermons span Edwards's careers in Northampton and Stockbridge from 1727 through 1757.

6. Timothy Edwards's sermon notes are printed in John A. Stoughton, *"Windsor Farmes": A Glimpse of an Old Parish* (Hartford, 1883), 143, 122, 126.

7. Sacvan Bercovitch discusses the ways in which Puritan rhetoric was simultaneously condemnatory and optimistic in *The American Jeremiad* (Madison, Wisc., 1980).

8. Thomas Paine, *The Doctrine of Earthquakes* (Boston, 1728), preface. The earthquake fasts are described in W. D. Love, *The Fast and Thanksgiving Days of New England* (Boston, 1895), 185–95.

9. Jonathan Edwards, "Sermon on Jonah 3:10," 21 December 1727, Edwards Papers, Beinecke Library. All subsequent references to Edwards's unpublished sermons are taken from the Beinecke collection unless otherwise noted.

10. John Barnard, *Two Discourses Addressed to Young Persons* (Boston, 1727), 78. The conventional logic of earthquake sermons is summarized in Maxine Van De Wetering, "Moralizing in Puritan Natural Science: Mysteriousness in Earthquake Sermons," *Journal of the History of Ideas* 43 (1982), 417–438.

11. Jonathan Edwards, "Sermon on Acts 19:19," 1 April 1736.

12. Jonathan Edwards, "Sermon on 2 Chronicles 23:16," March 1737.

13. The significance of the Louisbourg campaign is discussed in S. E. D. Shortt, "Conflict and Identity in Massachusetts: The Louisbourg Expedition of 1745," *Social History (Histoire Sociale)* 5 (1972), 165–185.

14. Jonathan Edwards, "Sermon on Leviticus 26:3–13," 28 February 1745.

15. Jonathan Edwards, "Sermon on 1 Kings 8:44ff," 4 April 1745.

16. Recorded in G. L. Walker, ed., *Diary of Rev. Daniel Wadsworth, 1734–1747* (Hartford, 1894), 123.

17. See S. E. D. Shortt, "Conflict and Identity in Massachusetts."

18. Frances G. Walett, ed., *The Diary of Ebenezer Parkman, 1703–1782* (Worcester, 1974), 3 July 1745, p. 120, and 6 April 1745, p. 114; and Thomas Prince, *Extraordinary Events . . .*, 2nd ed. (Boston, 1747), 34.

19. Jonathan Edwards, *An Humble Attempt*, reprinted in Stephen Stein, ed., *Apocalyptic Writings*, vol. 5, *The Works of Jonathan Edwards* (New Haven, 1977), 362.

20. Charles Chauncy, *Marvelous Things* (Boston, 1745), 11, 20.

21. Jonathan Edwards, "Sermon on 2 Chronicles 20:27–29," August 1745; and "Sermon on Psalm 111:5," August 1745.

22. Jonathan Edwards, "Sermon on Jeremiah 51:5," 5 December 1745.

23. Jonathan Edwards, "Sermon on Nehemiah 4:14," June 1746. See also Edwards's thanksgiving sermon, "Sermon on Exodus 33:19," August 1746.

24. See, e.g., Jonathan Edwards, "Sermon on Joshua 7:12," 28 June 1744, repeated March 1755; "Sermon on Jeremiah 51:5," repeated November 1757; "Sermon on Exodus 33:9," repeated November 1754; "Sermon on 1 Kings 8:44," 4 April 1745, repeated July 1755; "Sermon on Isaiah 33:19–24," 16 October 1746, repeated July 1756.

25. Jonathan Edwards, "Sermon on Joshua 7:12".

26. On the costs of war in New England, see Fred Anderson, "A People's Army: Provincial Military Service in Massachusetts During the Seven Years' War," *William and Mary Quarterly* 40 (1983), 499–527.

27. Jonathan Edwards, "Sermon on 1 Kings 8:44ff."

28. Jonathan Edwards, "Sermon on Psalm 60:9–12," 28 August 1755.

29. For equations of France with Anti-Christ, see Nathan O. Hatch, *The Sacred Cause of Liberty: Republican Thought and the Millennium in Revolutionary New England* (New Haven, 1977), 41–42, and Thomas M. Brown, "The Image of the Beast: Anti-Papal Rhetoric in Colonial America," in Richard O. Curry and Thomas M. Brown, eds., *Conspiracy: The Fear of Subversion in American History* (New York, 1972, 1–20).

10

"A Flood of Errors": Chauncy and Edwards in the Great Awakening

AMY SCHRAGER LANG

In March of 1743, Charles Chauncy, one of the most vocal opponents of the revival then sweeping the American colonies, wrote to his brother Nathaniel announcing the publication of Jonathan Edwards's long awaited defense of the Great Awakening, *Some Thoughts Concerning the Revival of Religion in New England.* "Mr. Edwards's book . . . upon the good work is at last come forth," Chauncy began, "And I believe will do much hurt; and I am the rather inclined to think so, because there are some good things in it." Unlike many of his fellow revivalists, Edwards suffered from a dangerous tendency toward moderation, dangerous, as Chauncy explained, because "Error is much more likely to be propagated, when it is mixed with truth. This hides its deformity and makes it go down the more easily."[1] As a self-appointed guardian of orthodoxy,[2] Chauncy took it upon himself to expose to the world the particular "deformity" which lurked in Edwards's insidious book. Six months after the appearance of *Some Thoughts Concerning the Revival,* Chauncy published his answer to Edwards under the title *Seasonable Thoughts on the State of Religion in New England.* Mimicking not only the name but the five-part structure of *Some Thoughts,* Chauncy undertook to refute Edwards's argument point by point.

Right from the start, however, Chauncy's book diverges from the pattern established by *Some Thoughts.* While Edwards opens his book with a brief apology for his presumptuousness in attempting such a work and a short exposition on freedom of expression, *Seasonable Thoughts* begins rather ponderously with a thirty page account of the "ANTI-NOMIANS, FAMILISTS and LIBERTINES, who infected these churches, above an hundred years ago . . ." A patchwork of lengthy quotations from such contemporary authorities as Thomas Welde, John Winthrop, and Edward Johnson, the preface to *Seasonable Thoughts* tells the story of the conflict between Anne Hutchinson and her followers and the ministers and magistrates of the Bay Colony during the first years of settlement. This story Chauncy offers as "very needful for *these* days; the LIKE SPIRIT, and Errors, prevailing *now* as they did *then*."[3] A reminder of the events of the 1630s would "prepare" his readers for his treatise on the evils of the present revival and would moreover "power-fully tend to undeceive" those beguiled by error.

Aligning himself with Hutchinson's opponents, Chauncy glosses over the dramatic changes in both doctrine and church polity which had occurred in the hundred years since the antinomian controversy and insists upon his own orthodoxy. Of course, Edwards, too, by raising the banner of the New Jerusalem, hoped to establish himself as the Puritans' heir apparent. It has been pointed out that Edwards, in his *Treatise Concerning Religious Affections*, quotes Thomas Shepard more often than any other writer. But interestingly, while Edwards resorts to "right religion" and to the prophetic history of New England to support his claims, Chauncy turns to the "methods," both social and ecclesiastical, of the first generation. He finds in the accounts of Anne Hutchinson not only the type of the revivalists but the measures to be taken against them and a mirror of his own fervent need to save the New World from the agents of Satan.

Chauncy's avowed purpose in writing the preface and the effect of the preface on our reading of *Seasonable Thoughts* are, however, two differ-ent things. While the story of Anne Hutchinson is meant to caution us against antinomian error, the preface goes beyond this to indicate the terms of argument, both explicit and implicit, on which the whole of *Seasonable Thoughts* depends. The preface defines the appropriate method of judging the Awakening; it asserts the centrality of language as sign in the debate between Old and New Light; and, perhaps most interestingly, it links language and gender in ways which illuminate the social distance between the revivalists and their opponents.

Chauncy's use of the antinomian controversy as the type of enthusiasm in America has not escaped the notice of students of the Great Awaken-ing. Some scholars have dismissed the preface to *Seasonable Thoughts* as "predictable."[4] Others have found in it evidence of a pervasive rhetoric of generational conflict.[5] As minister to Boston's First Church, the site of

Hutchinson's rebellion, Chauncy regarded himself as the lineal descendant of the earliest defenders of orthodoxy. By mingling his voice with those of the first generation, the argument goes, he meant to cast himself as yet another reproving "father." Still other students of the Awakening, from Perry Miller on, have exploited the symmetry of Chauncy's analogy: just as the antinomian controversy ushered in the age of Puritanism in America, so, in the view of some historians, the Great Awakening signaled its end. Limited as the comparison may be, these two conflicts, both of them centered on the means of conversion, have provided a suggestive frame for discussions of the rise, reign, and ruin of American Puritanism.

These readings tend, however, to obscure the point of Chauncy's comparison, which is far less oblique than our interpretations of it have tended to be. The theological link between the antinomian controversy and the Great Awakening lay, Chauncy believed, in the problem of visible sainthood, of the proper relation between the private, invisible experience of grace and its outward manifestation. With respect to the question of works and grace, Edwards and the revivalists, he thought, had fallen prey to the old errors. Their emphasis on religious affections, their reliance on invisible witness and verbal testimony, their manifest disrespect for authority, all opened the way to rejection of the Law. Both the antinomian and the awakened abandoned outward signs of sanctity and went, as Chauncy explained elsewhere, "into the way of judging from men's hearts." This way, he believed, "tends to nothing . . . but to destroy the peace of the churches, and fill the world with contention and confusion." "We have no way of judging," he insisted, "but by what is outward and visible: Nor are we capable of judging any other way."[6] To a mind like Chauncy's, this conclusion highlighted not the fallibility of man's judgment but the certain connection between inner experience and outward show, between the felt and the seen—or the spoken. To separate the grace of God from the holy life was, he was certain, to "separate between those things which God has joined together."

The visibility of God's intentions meant, among other things, that the Awakening could be judged by its appearance. The optimistic interpretation of the revival as a prelude to the millennium, recorded by apologists like Jonathan Edwards, depended on the assumption, dubious at best, that what looked like disorder was, in fact, the quickening of the Spirit. Chauncy was sure that Edwards misread the signs of the times; his doctrinal errors were recapitulated in his misinterpretation of social phenomena, and that, in turn, was reflected in his misuse of language. As far as Chauncy was concerned, order, peace, tranquility, and obedience characterized God's work. To identify a period of patent hysteria as the millennium begun to come down from heaven was to misrepresent, to misname the event.

As a cautionary tale, the story of Anne Hutchinson suffers no major revision in Chauncy's hands; on the contrary, his use of direct quotation (not to mention his impeccable sources) insures against any alteration in the narrative or its interpretation. What is striking, however, in Chauncy's use of the story is his explicit acknowledgment of a rhetorical divide separating Old and New Light along much the same lines that separated Hutchinson and her accusers. In other words, the problem with Edwards is not that he *is* an antinomian but that he *sounds* like one—or rather, that he writes out of a set of assumptions about the availability of meaning which are, for Chauncy, inextricably tied to a particular misinterpretation of doctrine, a misinterpretation which achieved its fullest expression in America in the antinomian controversy.[7]

In effect, the preface to *Seasonable Thoughts* proposes the interpretation of signs as the point on which Chauncy and Edwards divide, both as theologians and as writers. Chauncy means to pit the logic of Edwards's defense of the revival against a more persuasive logic of his own. But since Edwards's logic seems to him to deny any necessary coincidence of visible and invisible, Chauncy must refute Edwards's direct claims by addressing the largest assumption that stands behind these. In order to show that Edwards has misinterpreted the revival, in other words, Chauncy must establish the very possibility of interpretation. His intention is to repudiate Edwards's representation of the universe as fraught with a meaning which limited man can neither comprehend nor articulate, and to demonstrate instead that what we see is sufficient for all our purposes.

It is hardly surprising, in view of this, that Chauncy shows an overwhelming interest in the language of the antinomian crisis and of the Great Awakening *as* language, for language links the two moments, and language, likewise, measures the distance between the revivalists and their opponents. "Few," he insists, "will venture to disown a *Likeness* between the Disturbances *then* and *now*: They are indeed surprisingly familiar; insomuch, that, if I had not spoken in Language, Part of which was in Print, *fifty*; and Part, *eighty* Years ago, some I doubt not, would have imagined, I had purposely gone into the Use of certain *Words* and *Phrases*, to make *former* Times look like the *present*."[8] On the face of it, Chauncy's point is a simple one: had he not quoted from the chronicles of the first generation, he would surely have been accused of falsifying the past in an effort to shore up his analogy. Instead, he has demonstrated an essential connection between antinomian controversy and Great Awakening by showing that they *sound* alike. Language forces an analogy between the heretics of 1636 and those of 1740: "The *old* ANTINO-MIANS," he tells us, "began . . . with much the same Language about the *Law* and *good Works*, that is now in Use: And . . . gradually . . . they arriv'd at those Heights of Extravagance, for which they have justly been stigmatized . . . Is there no Danger," he asks, "lest this should be the case, with many, in these Days?"[9] As far as Chauncy was concerned, the power of language was perfectly clear, and the danger the language of revivalism posed was more apparent with every new expression of awakening.

The preface to *Seasonable Thoughts*, then, assumes the existence of two languages—one belonging to the revival, the other to those whom Chauncy considered spokesmen for the truth. Further, it assumes a fixed relationship between language and doctrine. To speak the language of revivalism is, ipso facto, to partake of the doctrinal errors of the New Lights. Chauncy himself is perfectly aware of these implications. "Had I wrote [the ensuing treatise] to please my self," he explains, "it would have been without those numerous Quotations, which, I am sensible, have not only taken up a great Deal of Room, but made the Book less agreable to many Readers . . . My design herein," he goes on, "was to make it evident, that the *Divines*, in most Esteem, in these Churches, for their *Piety* and *Soundness* in the *Faith*, have spoken in much the same Language, upon the Things now in Agitation, with those who have been called *Opposers of the Work of God*, and charg'd with *leading Souls to Hell* . . . "[10] This is partly self-defense. Reviled as an "opposer" himself, Chauncy hopes to submerge his own voice in the multitude of those renowned for their piety; his credibility depends on his words being indistinguishable from those of the estimable divines he quotes.

This gathering of voices has a larger significance as well. Chauncy finds in the unanimity of his sources—both contemporary and historical— confirmation of the correspondence between sign and meaning. If, presented with the same evidence, independent witnesses arrive at the same interpretation, the possibility of order in the world is restored. The visible is not only meaningful but stable in its meaning, and authority—the monolithic authority of a particular language and the social authority of the fathers who speak it—thereby reinstated. In asserting the ambiguity of signs, the revival, Chauncy believed, had forfeited the possibility of an orderly universe. In its place, the Awakening raised the specter of a world of radical individualists, attentive only to their private experience, arrogant in their self-trust and incapable of Christian community. The opposers answered the clamor of revival in one voice and, thus, proved truth of their position; ambiguity, dissension, idosyncrasy were banished to the side of revivalism.

Chauncy's attention to language is not, of course, limited to the preface. Rather, it is an obsessive concern of *Seasonable Thoughts*. Again and again, Chauncy draws our attention to language as sign and to the revival's apparent repudiation of signs. In describing the dangers of itinerancy, for example, Chauncy asks, "what is the Language of this going into *other Men's Parishes*? Is it not obviously this? The *settled Pastors* are Men not qualified for their Office . . . Or, the Language may be, we are Men of *greater Gifts, superiour Holiness, more Acceptableness to God* . . . " The point is oddly stated. This issue, it would seem, is not simply the "going into other men's parishes" but the violation of a traditional language of deference entailed by so extreme a breach of decorum. The real challenge to the authority of the settled ministry—the itinerants' intrusion into the pulpit—is subsumed into the problem of how that act is represented in language—or, rather, the problem of the act *as* language—and that language, for all its apparent ambiguity, is a charged one. To speak uncharitably of the ministers, as Chauncy explains, makes "the *Relation*, between *Pastors* and *People*, a *meer Nothing, a Sound without Meaning*."[11] The right relation between pastor and people, in other words, is signified by a language of respect. To dispense with that language, as the itinerants surely did, is to violate the relationship between minister and congregation, and that violation contains in it the possibility of a wholesale inversion of the order of things.

If, as Chauncy proposes, the pastoral relationship is made real and apparent by its embodiment in language, then, clearly, language has the power to undo that relationship. To the itinerants the existence of a language of pastoral authority did not prove the existence of the thing itself, but that it did not was only, in Chauncy's view, further evidence of the danger of their position. To the itinerants, Chauncy argues, language is only language. But if the dismissive words of the itinerants, as much as their intrusion into the parishes, reduced the relation between minister and flock to "sound without meaning," these words, by the same token, asserted their own power.

This brings me to my point (or rather, to Chauncy's), which is that for Edwards language is, in large measure, sound without meaning. That is, for Edwards, words, like other forms of visible evidence, are accidental and ultimately inadequate signifiers. While Edwards does not address the problem of language directly, his view of the ambiguity of all such signs is apparent both from the logic and the language of part 1 of *Some Thoughts*—the response to which occupies three of Chauncy's four hundred pages. Edwards's argument against *a priori* judging, one of the "foundation errors" of the Old Light position, for example, illustrates the unreliability of visible evidence. At the outset, Edwards insists that we can judge God's glorious work only from the "effect wrought," and not from "the way it began, the instruments . . . employed, the means that have been made use of, [or] the methods that have been taken . . . in carrying it on."[12] At first glance, this assertion looks surprisingly like Chauncy's claim that we know God's work by its "fruit." But clearly Edwards means something quite different, for the "effect" to which he refers is not a visible one but an immediate, sensory one.

Lest we mistake his meaning, Edwards offers us an analogy from the natural world. We know that the wind blows, Edwards points out, because "we hear the sound, we perceive the effect." We do not wait, he goes on, "to be satisfied what should be the cause of the wind's blowing from such a part of the heavens, and how it should come to pass that it should blow in such a manner, at such a time."[13] In other words, we infer cause from effect, but the only *reliable* effect is wholly private. Our senses tell us that the wind is blowing, and, likewise, the "new sense" lent by conversion reports God's presence.

The wind analogy is intended simply to make the case for *a posteriori* judging, but like most of Edwards's analogies, this one is interesting both for what it says and what it only intimates. In this particular instance, we begin to see the larger problem with which Edwards is grappling if we draw out the implications of his analogy. Certain as I am that the wind is blowing, I cannot prove that I hear or feel it. I can only attest to my felt experience—and I may, of course, lie. If the wind should happen to ruffle my hair, you might infer, if not wind, at least the movement of air. But this visible evidence is not to be depended on. The wind may blow, after all, without ruffling my hair and, from this, you might wrongly infer an absence of wind. You can achieve my level of certainty only if you, too, feel the wind. In no case need your inference effect my conviction.

The fact, as Edwards caustically remarks, that "God has not taken that course [in carrying out his work] . . . which men in their wisdom would have thought most advisable" is nothing to the point. God's ways are mysterious and his work in America extraordinary. As far as Edwards was concerned, to pry into the origins of the revival or to question its appearance, was to "expose ourselves to the calamity of those who pried into the ark of God."[14] Some deny God's work because they lack the "sense" with which to perceive it; others refuse the evidence of their senses; and still others, like Chauncy, willfully usurp God's prerogative by demanding that the revival conform, in its outward appearance, to

their idea of it. But for Edwards knowledge of God's presence is immediate, internal, invisible. It is not, however, universal. But ironically, to
those like Edwards, for whom the truth of the revival was self-evident,
fell the task of testifying to the "effect wrought" by means of a system of
visible signs as unreliable in their way as any other. The nature of
religious experience as Edwards understands it renders it wholly private,
yet his defense of the revival demands that he transcribe this experience
in language. The language he devised for this purpose was one which lent
enormous power to its speaker.

One of the places in which Edwards attempts to find a language
commensurate with the experience of grace is in the spiritual biography
of Sarah Pierpont, the nameless, genderless "example of evangelical
piety" of *Some Thoughts*. The language of Edwards's account of his
wife's religious experience is similar to that of his own *Personal Narrative*. Mistrustful of visible signs as evidence, and believing, moreover,
that the nature of religious affection cannot be inferred from its conformity to a conventional sequence of conversion,[15] Edwards is left with a
language stripped both of temporal and concrete referent. In an early and
characteristic passage from the "example," Edwards recounts his "subject's" renewed "sense of the holiness of God, as of a flame infinitely pure
and bright, so as sometimes to overwhelm soul and body."[16] Here, as
elsewhere, Edwards employs a language of intimation and approxima-
tion, a language predicated on the inadequacy of language. Repetitious,
abstract, and conventional, Edwards's words offer, at best, only a faint
glimmer of his wife's "sense" of ineffable holiness. But the very failure of
language on one front allows for its success on another. Edwards's self-
proclaimed inability to represent the stirrings of grace in human language
reminds us of the inexpressible power of God and the limitations of fallen
man at the same time that it works to empower his speech. The ambiguous relationship between word and meaning pushes Edwards toward
figurative language. Turning him into a poet of sorts, it lends his words
the power we take to reside in poetry. All meanings are hidden, but any
sign can bear meaning. Whereas Chauncy limits the pool of signifiers,
Edwards expands it.

Writing about the *Personal Narrative*, Daniel B. Shea, Jr., has suggested that Edwards is faced there with the problem of rendering "the
perceptions of the 'new sense' with an instrument so imperfect as human
language and so indiscriminate in itself as to be the common property of
both spiritual and natural man."[17] Not even the sensationalist vocabulary
to which Edwards repeatedly turns in his effort to impart religious truth
can overcome the limitations of this "instrument." Words cannot bespeak

God. Needless to say, for Chauncy, who firmly believed that we should concern ourselves only with visible evidence of God's work—which evidence he defined in the most traditional terms as obedience of all sorts—Edwards's tendency to use *"loose, general* and *indefinite* Words, which People may put a Meaning to, just as they are led by their Imaginations"[18] was deplorable. The "fatal consequence" of a language to which "People," that is, anyone, could put their own meaning was so obvious as to demand the restraint of "some men's tongues with Bit and Bridle."[19]

Of course there is a paradox in all this. Chauncy, for all his attention to language, is highly mistrustful of men's declarations concerning their spiritual condition. The work of God is "secret" and can be judged "only from the *Outward* Discoveries of it." Nonetheless in a world rife with hypocrisy, some outward signs are more reliable than others. Thus Chauncy insists, somewhat platitudinously, that *"Action* speaks louder than Words," though clearly the confluence of word and deed speaks loudest of all. Edwards is more generous, or perhaps more resigned. Precisely because he begins from the proposition that language is inadequate to the task of describing the things of God, he is far more willing to accept verbal testimony. At the same time that affectionate religion, by its very nature, devalues the visible signs of grace, it places a premium on the conversion relation, for imperfect as it is, language is the only instrument men have with which to record a "new sense." Like the old antinomians, then, Edwards seemed to Chauncy to deny outward signs, whether of sin or sanctity, and to elevate the witness of the spirit recorded in a language the unreliability of which Edwards was the first to admit.

Inasmuch as antinomianism builds from a radical mistrust of signs, Chauncy's preface gives us access to the central issue in *Seasonable Thoughts.* His explicit theological argument is reiterated in an implicit one about the efficacy of signs, in which words stand as archetypal signifiers and their use stands as evidence of the doctrinal sympathies of the user. In this sense, the problem of antinomianism informs the whole of *Seasonable Thoughts.* But Chauncy's use of the story of Anne Hutchinson illuminates the subtext of *Seasonable Thoughts* as well as its surface.

Despite the prominence (in both senses) of the male Hutchinsonians, the story of the antinomian controversy, particularly as it is told by the writers Chauncy quotes, is the story of a woman and, more particularly, the story of a woman who, in the words of one of her judges, "stept out of [her] place." "You have," Hugh Peters explained to Hutchinson, "rather bine a Husband than a wife . . . a preacher than a Hearer . . . a Magistrate than a subject."[20] In the terms I have been using, Hutchinson embodies the problem of signification: her usurpation of male roles is the visible emblem of her erroneous theology. But beyond this, the fact that the story of the antinomian controversy is the story of a *woman* heretic alerts us to the possibility that gender, as it stands for a constellation of culturally ascribed characteristics, is an issue in the Great Awakening.

Both Chauncy and Edwards were acutely aware of the disproportionate numbers of women, children and young men among the newly converted. For Chauncy, this preponderance of "*Children, young People* and *Women* whose Passions are soft and tender, and more easily thrown into a Commotion" was proof positive of the questionable nature of the revival. After all, he argues, "*Men* may as easily be overcome by the Power of the HOLY GHOST, as *Women* . . . what should then be the Reason that they should be, as it were, overlook'd . . ."[21] The rise of exhorters not merely young, but illiterate—"*Lads*, or rather *Boys: Nay,* Women and Girls: yea *Negroes*"—could only "portend *Evil* to these Churches." The case of women exhorters was the simplest to answer: to allow women to preach was, in Chauncy's view, to "give up all Pretence to the *Scripture* as our Rule." As to the young, the illiterate, the black, by exhorting they took "upon them to act the Part that is proper to another."[22] Women who acted like men, boys who spoke like ministers, blacks who preached like whites—these were not merely evil tendencies but visible signs of the heretical nature of the revival and the threat it posed to the standing order.

Edwards, of necessity, took a different position. While he associates the errors of the revivalists with their youth and inexperience, he rejects both the notion that only "silly women" and children experience divine joy in the manner of the revivalists, and the idea that the revival is discredited by either its youthfulness or its femininity. He wonders, in fact, whether "God has [not] begun at the lower end, and . . . made use of the weak and foolish . . . mere babes in age and standing" so as to "chastise the deadness, negligence, earthlymindedness and vanity . . . of the ministers. . . ."[23] While for Chauncy what links women, children and boys is their "silliness," their susceptibility to error, for Edwards they are related by their powerlessness. The are a "lower end" lacking "standing" in the world. And while censoriousness does not become them, they are not to be silenced: "tis beautiful in private Christians, though they are women and children, to be bold in professing the faith of Christ . . . without any fear of men, though they should be reproached as fools and madmen, and frowned upon by great men, and cast off by parents and all the world."[24] To argue, as Chauncy did, that the converts' lack of standing made their awakening suspect was to argue once again, in a new way, that signs—this time signs of status—were more important than felt experience.

Edwards's account suggests that the new converts were drawn from a relatively disempowered portion of the population. This dovetails neatly with the information modern historians offer about the newly awakened in the 1740s. While women continued to be admitted to the churches in greater numbers than men, historians record a significant increase in the rate of male conversion and in the numbers of youthful converts during the Great Awakening.[25] Richard Bushman has proposed that for these young men, evangelical religion "cleared the air of tensions. Men admitted that they had lusted after wealth, condemned themselves, and afterwards walked with lighter hearts. They ended the long struggle with the social order by denying its power to save and hence to condemn."[26] J. M. Bumstead has pointed to a decline in economic opportunity for young men living in towns suffering the pressure of increased population on the availability of land.[27] Philip Greven has suggested that increased mobility and the consequent anxiety of displacement experienced by young men in this period prepared the way for conversion.[28] In larger schematic terms, James Henretta has located the Great Awakening at a transitional moment in the morphology of New England society when the traditional patriarchal forms founded on an abundance of land and characterized by limited mobility gave way to a new order marked by overcrowding, a relative dearth of land, increased mobility, and the lessening of paternal authority.[29]

These accounts of the young male convert ignore the fact that there is a basis for the association of such young men with women and that that association was confirmed in certain external ways. Like women, young men were apparently relegated to the galleries of the churches. Like women, unmarried men paid neither taxes nor ministerial rates. And like at least some women during the Revival, these men were called upon to "step out of their places," both literally and figuratively. By their very conversion, one might say, these young men threatened to displace their "fathers." Given what we know of the young male convert, the appeal of Edwards's theology—and more especially, the tremendous appeal of the language of revivalism—makes sense. Its insistence on experience, its attention to feeling, and its appeal to women have caused Edwards's language and, more broadly, the language of evangelicalism to be characterized as feminine, "feminizing,," or even sentimental.[30] But clearly the same characteristics that served to empower women in this language may be seen as empowering the "lower end" of the male social scale as well. Edwards's language, by exalting invisible signs of grace, diminishes the importance of outward marks of status. Election is sealed not by altered behavior nor by outward signs of God's favor but by the birth of a new self to which the convert can testify only in "*loose, general* and *indefinite* Words*.*" Edwards's emphasis on the testimony of the hopeful does not imply an antinomian disregard for the Law—in fact, if anything it restores that tension between works and grace so useful to the first generation of American Puritans—but by elevating the invisible, his language does empower the individual convert in ways that have nothing to do with his position in a hierarchical social order.

For all the attention paid by historians to the new male convert during the Great Awakening, it may be more useful, finally, to regard these converts as so many more "women" constrained not by their sex but by the conditions attending their lives in the 1740s. In that case, the story of the American Jezebel with which Chauncy begins *Seasonable Thoughts* can be seen as a cautionary tale twice over. It urges the revivalists to beware of the language of antinomianism because of both its theological implications and its social ones. Moreover, it brings together gender and class. The "woman" is once again taken to embody the danger of lawlessness inherent in the repudiation of signs, but this time with an expanded significance, for to deny the import of the visible is, potentially, to empower those *visibly* disempowered. The example of Anne Hutchinson, Chauncy believed, would teach the revivalists to keep both their words and themselves in place.

Notes

1. Quoted in Edwin S. Gaustad, *The Great Awakening in New England* (New York, 1957), p. 90.

2. Letter from Chauncy to Ezra Stiles, quoted in Gaustad, *Great Awakening*, p. 153: "I wrote and printed in that day more than 2 volumes in octavo. A vast number of pieces were published also as written by others; but there was scarce a piece against the times but was sent to me, and I had a labour sometimes of preparing it for the press. I had also hundreds of letters to write, in answer to letters received from all parts of the country."

3. Charles Chauncy, *Seasonable Thoughts on the State of Religion in New England* (Boston, 1743), title page.

4. *Works of Jonathan Edwards*, ed. C. C. Goen (New Haven, 1972), IV, 82. Certainly Chauncy was neither the first nor the only antirevivalist to find the specter of antinomianism in the heresies of the New Lights; the designation "New Light" itself refers back to the seventeenth century dispute.

5. Donald Weber, "Joshua and the Fathers: The Rhetoric of Generational Conflict in the Great Awakening," (unpublished paper).

6. Charles Chauncy, *Enthusiasm Described and Caution'd Against* (Boston, 1742), p. v.

7. For a discussion of denotation as an issue in the trial of Anne Hutchinson, see Patricia Caldwell, "The Antinomian Language Controversy," *Harvard Theological Review* 69 (July–October, 1976), 345–67

8. *Seasonable Thoughts*, p. xxvi.

9. Ibid, p. 278.

10. *Seasonable Thoughts*, pp. xxviii–xxix.

11. Ibid.,p. 50–51. It is worth noticing how diffuse the boundary between act and language is in Chauncy. Acts are often described as language, and language as act. It is not clear, for example, whether the language of "going into other men's parishes" refers to the language that *accompanies* the act or the "language"—that is, the *significance*—of the act itself.

12. Jonathan Edwards, *Some Thoughts Concerning the Revival of Religion in New England, Works*, IV, 293.

13. Edwards, *Some Thoughts*, p. 294.

14. Ibid., p. 294.

15. Edwards did, however, believe that it was not unreasonable to assume that God would work according to a logic similar to that of the morphologies of conversion. Se *Religious Affections* in *Works*, ed. John E. Smith, I, 151.

16. *Some Thoughts*, p. 336.

17. Daniel B. Shea, Jr., in *The American Puritan Imagination*, ed. Sacvan Bercovitch (New York, 1974), p. 166.

18. *Seasonable Thoughts*, p. 397.

19. *Seasonable Thoughts*, p. 369.

20. *The Antinomian Controversy, 1636–38: A Documentary History*, ed., David D. Hall (Middletown, 1968) pp. 382–3.

21. *Seasonable Thoughts*, p. 105.

22. Ibid., pp. 226–7.

23. *Some Thoughts*, p. 295.

24. Ibid., p. 427.

25. See Gerald F. Moran, "Conditions of Religious Conversion in the First Society of Norwich, Connecticut, 1718–44," *Journal of Social History*, v, 3 (Spring, 1972), 331–43, and "The Puritan Saint: Religious Experience, Church Membership, and Piety in Connecticut, 1636–76" (unpub. diss. Rutgers, 1974). See, too, Cedric B. Cowing, "Sex and Preaching in the Great Awakening," *American Quarterly* (1968) 624–44.

26. Richard Bushman, *From Puritan to Yankee* (New York, 1967), p. 194.

27. J. M. Bumstead, "Religion, Finance and Democracy: The Town of Norton as a Case Study," *Journal of American History* 57 (March 1971), 830–31.

28. Philip Greven, *Four Generations: Population, Land, and Family in Colonial Andover* (Ithaca, 1970), p. 279ff.

29. James Henretta, "The Morphology of New England Society in the Colonial Period," *Journal of Interdisciplinary History* 2 (Autumn, 1971), 379–98.

30. See Barbara Eaton, "Women, Religion and the Family: Revivalism as an Indicator of Social Change in Early New England" (unpub. diss, Berkeley, 1975); Philip Greven, *The Protestant Temperament* (New York, 1977), p. 124ff; Nancy Cott, *The Bonds of Womanhood* (New Haven, 1977), p. 126ff.

The Legacy of Edwards

11

Piety and Moralism: Edwards and the New Divinity

WILLIAM BREITENBACH

Edwards versus the New Divinity

Over the years the New Divinity has taken its lumps from historians. Repeatedly Jonathan Edwards's most loyal disciples have been condemned as his betrayers. Either scholars have insisted that the great colonial theologian had no true intellectual heirs or they have perversely fingered Ralph Waldo Emerson as his actual if illegitimate issue. There are at least two reasons for this astonishing line of argument. It satisfies our taste for pathos by portraying Edwards as an isolated, ignored, tragic genius. More practically, it spares us the joyless and dispiriting chore of reading and understanding many daunting volumes by those prolix men of God: Joseph Bellamy, Samuel Hopkins, Stephen West, Jonathan Edwards, Jr., Nathanael Emmons, Timothy Dwight, Asa Burton, and Nathaniel William Taylor—to name only the most important New Divinity theologians.

The betrayal interpretation comes in a couple of versions. The first, and still the most common, characterizes the Edwardsians as arid metaphysicians and austere hyper-Calvinists who systematized Edwards's thought, but in so doing drained it of its warm and vital piety. These theological Doctors Rappaccini, killing what they hoped to protect, ultimately found themselves alone in their studies with the bloodless corpse of a rigid and unpopular Calvinism. The second version describes the New Divinity ministers as liberalizers and moralizers who were intent upon accommodating Edwards's Calvinistic creed to the humanitarian spirit of the day, even if that meant compromising the essentials of his faith. In the end they found themselves, to paraphrase Joseph Haroutunian, with a Calvinism that was neither objectionable nor Calvinistic. The contradiction between these two arguments should have alerted scholars—especially those scholars who advanced both versions at once—that something was amiss. In fact, both accounts simply parrot the charges leveled against the New Divinity by its Old Calvinist opponents, who were hardly the most reliable commentators. Both accounts fail to comprehend the aims and achievements of the Edwardsian school of theologians.[1]

This paper will venture another appraisal of Edwards and the New Divinity. It will argue two things: First, that the so-called peculiarities and innovations of the New Divinity reveal Edwards's most creative and important contributions to New England theology. Admittedly there were differences between the master and his disciples, but it is evident nonetheless that the leading tendencies of Edwards's system can be discovered by tracing the trajectory of his ideas in the theology of his New Divinity successors. The second argument is that this Edwardsian theology, for all its originality, should be seen as maintaining the fundamental commitment of New England Puritanism to the reconciliation of grace and law. Historians misunderstand the New Divinity because they obstinately continue to impose the piety-versus-moralism paradigm on eighteenth-century New England religious history. This interpretation, familiar to all students of American religion, describes a pure theocentric piety descending from the crags of Calvinism by way of covenant theology and worldly prosperity into the meadows of moralism, Arminianism, and Unitarianism, and finally losing itself—some would say, finding itself—in the swamps of Transcendentalism. Given this plot, there are only the two conventional roles for the New Divinity to play: the reactionary Calvinist partisan resistance, doomed but defiant, fighting futilely on in the hills; or the Calvinist quislings, cravenly collaborating with the moralistic lowlanders.[2]

Fortunately there has recently occurred within Puritan studies a revision that calls into question the validity of the piety-versus-moralism model. For one thing, a number of scholars have documented the *variety* of theological positions held by New England Puritans. This discovery of diversity makes older assumptions about the inevitable organic evolution of a universally accepted covenant theology into Arminian moralism seem too simplistic.[3] For another thing, historians have recognized that

Reformed theology, even in its pristine formulations, did not set piety against moralism. The Reformed theologians most influential in New England were clear in affirming that divine sovereignty does not contravene human freedom or abolish man's activity as a rational, voluntary agent; that grace does not violate the integrity of man's natural faculties; and that regeneration does not substitute for but rather inaugurates holiness and obedience in the saint. Indeed, many of the supposed signs of legalism and moralism in the Puritans' covenant theology were perfectly legitimate expressions of Reformed theology, and not deviations from it. The *dominant* New England theological tradition, the clerical orthodoxy, was one of piety *and* moralism.[4]

It is within this tradition that Edwards and the Edwardsians belong, extending a line that stretches forward to them from Beza to Perkins to Ames to Shepard. It is wrong to see Edwards as sweeping aside a compromised federal theology in order to restore a severe, uncorrupted, theocentric Calvinism. Rather, he and his followers occupied the familiar middle ground, defending it against the extremes of Antinomianism and Arminianism.

Edwards and the Great Awakening

The commitment of Edwardsians to piety and moralism is apparent in the emergence of their theological system during the period of the Great Awakening. In the 1730s Jonathan Edwards was primarily concerned with defending Calvinist doctrines against those who denied the reality or the necessity of a sovereign and supernatural work of grace on the souls of sinners. His first published work, *God Glorified in the Work of Redemption* (1731), was a rebuke to Arminians, who claimed that men are only partially dependent on God's grace for the achievement of their salvation.[5] He continued the attack in 1734 by preaching a series of sermons on "Justification by Faith Alone," in which he declared that God justifies believers without regard to any qualification in them. In particular, he assailed neonomian "modern divines" who contended that a merciful God has abolished the original law and substituted a milder one requiring only imperfect, sincere obedience. Such a doctrine, Edwards charged, robbed God of his sovereignty in dispensing grace by selling salvation for the price of the sinner's defective virtue.[6]

Arminians were also the targets in another representative work of this period, *A Divine and Supernatural Light* (1734). This sermon set out to prove that sinners cannot save themselves, even with the assistance of common grace. According to Edwards, the common grace available to all men can do no more than aid existing natural principles in the soul, whereas the Spirit's gift of saving grace infuses entirely new supernatural principles or habits into the soul.[7] Edwards's point in all three of these works was to show that grace is the free gift of a sovereign God, compatible with but beyond the grasp of natural human capacities. He always scrupulously warned against Antinomian distortions of his ideas, but clearly his preoccupation in the 1730s was with disproving Arminian notions, which threatened to render grace less gratuitous.[8]

Naturally Edwards saw the Great Awakening, with its striking conversions, as a divine confirmation of the doctrines of grace that he had been preaching in the 1730s. However, not everyone was equally pleased. The extravagances and imprudences of itinerant preachers and their awakened audiences gave many observers pause, especially when these excesses were defended by what seemed to be enthusiastic pretensions to immediate revelations and impulses from the Spirit. Ministers leery of the anticlericalism of the Revival predictably began to detect theological errors in the revivalists. New Englanders sorted themselves into Old Light and New Light parties and started to wrangle about whether the religious stir in their land was truly the work of God. This debate over the authenticity of the Revival quickly narrowed into a dispute about the nature and evidence of true conversion.

By 1743 the Old Lights had concluded that many of the ostensible conversions were nothing but enthusiasm compounded with Antinomianism. Critics of the Awakening pointed to converts' claims that their inward impressions and impulses came by the immediate influence of the Spirit, and that these signs enabled them to know indubitably that they were saved, so that they did not need to seek further for evidence of their justification. Old Lights acknowledged that there is such a thing as a supernatural operation of the Spirit on the souls of sinners, but they insisted that these mental agitations and perturbations were not it. Old Lights were certain that the Spirit does not subvert the Word by issuing new revelations. Furthermore, they believed that God deals with humans as reasonable creatures, making use of knowledge to illuminate the intellect so that true converts always keep their passions and affections under the control of their sanctified reasons. Moreover, the Old Lights denied that conversion is always sensible and perceptible. Hence they judged that the best and safest evidence of a true conversion comes not from internal motions or the immediate witness of the Spirit but from a change in the conduct of the believer's life. In sum, to critics of the Revival, the New Light errors seemed to differ little from those of previous Antinomian groups such as the Hutchinsonians and the French Prophets.[9]

Edwards's works in the early 1740s were attempts to defend the Awakening against these Old Light attacks. In *The Distinguishing Marks of a Work of the Spirit of God* (1741), he set out to prove the Revival to be God's work by demonstrating the authenticity of the conversions experienced during it. At the same time, Edwards recognized that the religious upheaval was attended with unfortunate irregularities, which did not deserve defending. Edwards concluded that the Revival was in fact genuine, but he took the opportunity to curb Antinomianism and enthusiasm by proclaiming that holiness and love are better proofs of conversion than are the extraordinary gifts of the Spirit.[10]

In *Some Thoughts Concerning the Present Revival* (1742), Edwards carried forward his moderate defense of the Great Awakening. This important work made two significant contributions to the revival debate. First, in response to the Old Lights' allegation that New Light conversions were merely high tran,ports of the passions, Edwards committed himself to a voluntaristic interpretation of the psychology of conversion. He asserted that holiness has its seat in the heart or will rather than in the understanding, and that holy affections are therefore the substance of true religion. Hence the raised emotions of the converts were readily explained: conversion is more than just the enlightenment of the reason by doctrinal truth. The second important theme of *Some Thoughts* was the clear condemnation of New Light enthusiasm, which Edwards increasingly considered a threat to the Awakening as grave as the opposition of the Old Lights. He was particularly critical of the self-centered pride of these who claimed that God guides his saints by immediate revelations. Such extraordinary gifts of the Spirit are graceless, he argued, because they require no change of heart in the sinner. True religion involves new holy affections of the heart, not new inspirations in the understanding. Thus Edwards was able to use his psychological theory of heart religion to distinguish true conversion from both the intellectualistic moral suasionism of Old Light rationalists and the intellectualistic enthusiasm of New Light illuminati.[11]

The debate over the marks of real and counterfeit conversions only grew more acrimonious as the Awakening petered out in the mid-1740s. Old Lights' denunciations and moderates' admonitions provoked extreme New Lights like Andrew Croswell to present a theological defense of their version of conversion. These extremists—call them Antinomians for the sake of convenience—believed that the Old Lights belittled the witness of the Spirit in order to substitute works for faith as the ground of justification. Croswell's main concern was to emphasize the sufficiency of Christ's imputed righteousness above any human qualification in the process of justification. For him, saving faith was the faith of assurance— a person's certain belief that Christ's righteousness is applied to him for his pardon. Croswell called this faith "particular faith," because the first thing a person believes in faith is that Christ has saved him in particular. Obviously, this explanation of justification made conversion experiences both discernible and self-authenticating. Indeed, the theory of particular faith made doubt sinful, for a believer always has exactly as much assurance as he has faith. Croswell was especially critical of those who instructed converts to seek assurance in the observation of their "good Frames, and good Duties." He warned that such advice supplanted Christ with works, by implying that converts cannot tell when they have been converted. To Antinomians like Croswell, a believer's confident presumption that he is saved was not a sign of enthusiasm but a mark of grace.[12]

Clearly Edwards had his work cut out for him as he prepared his *Treatise Concerning Religious Affections* (1746). He needed to show that conversion is a supernatural change in sinners involving more than just an enlightened understanding and improved behavior. Yet he also needed to show that Antinomians improperly slighted the importance of holy practice when they focused all their attention on an intense, self-certifying moment of conversion. *Religious Affections* brilliantly met the challenge. In it Edwards made three main points about the signs of true conversion. The first point was that gracious affections are exercises of the inclination (or will or heart) made possible by a supernatural influence. This influence occurs when the Spirit dwells within the soul, communicating holiness as a supernatural principle or foundation for holy action. The presence of this vital principle gives the heart a new sense (or taste or disposition) that enables the saint to recognize, relish, love, and consent to the excellency of divine things. Edwards's intention here was to refute Arminians both by showing that gracious affections differ in kind from the exercises of natural principles and by demonstrating that saints possess a kind of intuitive evidence of the reality of religion (and of the Spirit's operations) unavailable to the unregenerate. Yet significantly, Edwards went on to turn the point against enthusiastic New Lights as well. The new sense acquired by the saints also differs entirely from the immediate revelation of a particular promise, which is a kind of knowledge that is wholly natural. According to Edwards, the true witness of the Spirit is not some revelation of one's pardon but rather the enstamping of holiness—the spirit of life—on one's heart. Hence the most immediate evidence of redemption available to saints is not, as Croswell would have it, the assured *belief* that Christ has saved them from their sins but rather the intuitive sense of their *love* to God. Croswell had insisted that saints must believe themselves saved before they see any good thing in themselves; Edwards here demanded that saints must exercise love before they see themselves saved.[13]

The second main point in *Religious Affections* was that the saints' gracious love to God is not based on calculations of self-interest but instead arises from a disinterested relish for God's intrinsic excellency and loveliness. Edwards had begun to recognize that both Arminians and Antinomians—or as he labeled them, legal and evangelical hypocrites—shared a fundamentally selfish approach to conversion. Neither required any greater love to God than that attainable by a heart inclined to self-love. Arminian "converts" love God because they believe that he has benevolently agreed to bestow salvation in return for their imperfect endeavors. Antinomian "converts" love God because they first believe that he loves them and has forgiven their sins. Both types of hypocritical love are fundamentally mercenary or interested. They both derive from some prior expectation of benefits that extorts the sinners' consent. Edwards insisted, however, that gracious love be disinterested, that it be exercised because the inherent beauty of God's moral excellency attracts the heart in a voluntary and unselfish consent. Saints first love God because he is a lovely God. Hypocrites do not see God as lovely, so they can love him only after seeing that he loves them.[14]

The third main point in *Religious Affections* was that gracious affections manifest themselves in Christian practice. For Edwards, grace is an abiding principle of holy *action* in the heart. He gave his analysis of conversion this voluntaristic slant primarily because he wanted to condemn the Antinomians who disdained the evidence given by sanctification. Edwards's argument in Signs Six through Twelve was that true saints treat their conversion experiences as the commencement and not the culmination of their redemption. He was able to differentiate his call for holy obedience from the Arminians' reliance on external morality because he defined grace as a *supernatural, internal* principle of action. Yet he was also able to show that holy practice is a better and more essential sign of grace than all of the extraordinary discoveries, revelations, and promises claimed by the Antinomians.[15]

Religious Affections was perhaps the most important work in the development of the Edwardsian "new" divinity. It completed Edwards's shift to a balanced viewpoint, from which he looked on legal and evangelical hypocrites with equal and impartial disgust. In addition it identified the characteristics common to Arminians and Antinomians. Both erred by defining grace primarily as an illumination or inspiration conveyed to the natural understanding. Both required of converts no better inclination of heart than self-love. Edwards's recognition of the fundamental similarity of the two counterfeit schemes pushed him toward an increasingly voluntaristic explanation of religious psychology, for only in the heart and will could he locate a kind of religious experience involving both a supernatural transformation and holy action.

Edwardsian Divinity

During the late 1740s and early 1750s Edwards elaborated and applied these themes. His *Life of David Brainerd* (1749) was a skillful transcription of *Religious Affections* into a biographical format. Brainerd's religion was neither an Arminian process of self-improvement nor an Antinomian persuasion of pardon. He had a striking and sensible conversion experience, but he reported in good Edwardsian fashion that at the critical moment his soul was so "delighted" with God's excellency and loveliness that he did not think about his own salvation. And afterwards, he did not rely on this momentary experience for assurance; instead, he hit the road as a missionary, finding his hopes for heaven in the evidence of his holy life. Lest anyone miss the point, Edwards emphasized the dying Brainerd's debate in Boston with a person (perhaps Croswell himself?) who championed the selfish and Antinomian doctrine of particular faith.[16]

In 1752 Edwards preached an important sermon entitled *True Grace Distinguished from the Experience of Devils*. In it he continued his attempt to reduce Arminianism and Antinomianism to a common denominator by showing that all the attainments of legal and evangelical hypocrites fall short of true grace because they do not involve a change of heart. The highest degrees of outward moral virtue, the clearest speculative knowledge of divinity, and the most extraordinary discoveries of pardon, he observed, all arise from either natural understanding or a heart biased to self-love.[17] Especially interesting was Edwards's hint that the Fall damaged only the heart or will and not the natural understanding. Edwards began to situate religion exclusively in the heart and will, because he realized that a voluntaristic psychology worked equally well against Arminian rationalism and Antinomian inspirationalism.[18]

Edwards's attempt during this period to alter the terms of church membership should also be seen in the context of his dual struggle against these two enemies. In *Religious Affections*, after noting that gracious affections display themselves in holy practice, he had suggested that this evidence might be used by others to identify saints and, by implication, to screen candidates for admission to the church. Edwards's rejection of Stoddardeanism has been generally, and correctly, seen as the extension of the Revival's experimental religion into the ecclesiastical realm. Striking conversion experiences made it no longer necessary to admit to full membership people who exhibited only good behavior without any clear evidence of rebirth. Thus the success of the Awakening enabled Edwards to repudiate practices that made concessions to Arminian moralism.

Yet it also should be recognized, as Edwards himself insisted, that his new policy was not based on the Antinomians' claim that saints possess a spirit of discerning. Indeed it was in great measure to control enthusiastic relations of conversion experiences by Antinomians that Edwards instituted the new standards for admission. True, he hoped that abandoning open communion would provoke conversion experiences in those who had been content to rely on their outward morality. But he also hoped that it would bring enthusiasts under the supervision of skillful clerical guides. By subjecting such giddy converts to "some public regulation," ministers could compel them to seek evidence of redemption in their godly exercises and affections, rather than exclusively in their conversion experiences.[19]

By the early 1750s the dust from the Great Awakening had settled, revealing a transformed theological landscape. There now existed a defiant party of Antinomians who advanced a theory of justification aimed at exalting Christ's imputed righteousness and denying any human work or qualification.[20] At the other extreme were the avowed Arminians. So as better to fish in troubled waters, Anglicans after 1744 shifted their quarrel with the standing order from the tedious dispute about the antiquity of episcopacy to a new theological issue. Alleging that the doctrines of election and sovereign grace discouraged all effort, undermined morality, and promoted Antinomianism, Anglicans offered their openly Arminian doctrines of free will, good works, and common grace as a refuge from the pernicious moral implications of Calvinism.[21]

By the end of the decade, some of the Old Lights had had enough. Upset by the antimoral tone of revival Calvinism, distressed by the New Lights' hostility to a religion of the reason, these theological liberals began to form an Arminian party within the Congregationalist churches. Their exasperation is captured in the title of the sermon that signaled the emergence of their movement: Lemuel Briant's *The Absurdity and Blas-*

phemy of Depreciating Moral Virtue (1749). In this sermon Briant complained that Calvinists spoke of election and grace in such a way as "to destroy all moral Agency" by implying that nothing on the part of sinners is necessary for salvation. He criticized the notion that believers need not be righteous themselves "because they have the perfect Righteousness of Christ imputed unto them." Briant insisted that true religion "suspends our whole Happiness upon our *personal* good Behaviour." Charging that Calvinists' exhortations to sinners contradicted their own doctrines, he proposed a more consistent creed, which would recognize that God's grand design is "to promote the moral Rectitude and Happiness of his Creatures." Such a creed would also recognize that God grants his creatures enough freedom and ability to perform their duty.[22]

Things were now in a pretty pickle. If there had not been a real Arminian threat before the Awakening, the Awakening itself had created one, and it had begotten an Antinomian threat to boot. The appearance of outspoken Arminianism within the New England churches was the final influence in shaping the Edwardsian system. For the remainder of his life Edwards sought to defend Calvinism's doctrines of election, depravity, and sovereign grace against the Arminians' accusations that these tenets destroyed moral accountability and subverted the motives to virtue. He realized that to defeat Arminianism, he had to devise a Calvinistic theology free from any taint of Antinomianism. Edwards's perception of the vulnerability of traditional New England Calvinism to charges of Antinomianism pushed him in creative new directions during the 1750s.

He took his first step in *A Careful and Strict Enquiry into the Modern Prevailing Notions of that Freedom of Will, Which Is Supposed to be Essential to Moral Agency* (1754). In many ways the treatise on the will was simply a more systematic and philosophical explanation of the ideas set forth in *Religious Affections*. His aim in this work was to demonstrate that man is at once determined and accountable. Successfully proving this would answer Arminians' grumblings that Calvinism is essentially Antinomian.

Edwards began the argument by stating that acts of will are preferences or prevailing inclinations of the soul. (This definition completely equated the heart with the will, and thereby connected *Freedom of the Will* with Edwards's earlier writings on heart religion.) Edwards noted that a person never wills contrary to the prevailing inclination of his soul; that is, he never chooses what he does not prefer or love.[23] After this explanation of the workings of the will, Edwards went on to describe necessity, which he said comes in two varieties. There is a natural necessity, which is a certainty arising from the force of natural, involuntary causes. When a person is prevented from doing something by natural necessity, his inability is excusable because it results from a defect or obstacle extrinsic to his will. However, there is also a moral necessity, which is a certainty arising from moral, voluntary causes like the "habits and dispositions of the heart." If a person is prevented from doing something by moral necessity, his inability is moral, consisting in a disinclination to do it. Consequently moral inability is always voluntary—it is a "cannot" that is really a powerful "will not." Indeed, technically speaking, it is not even an inability; it is an unwillingness or disinclination. According to Edwards, depravity is just such a disinclination. It is a general and habitual form of a necessary but voluntary inability to love God.[24]

With these definitions of willing and necessity, Edwards rescued Calvinism from the censures of Arminians. The Arminians claimed that Calvinism denies man his liberty, but what higher freedom could they demand than a person's power to do as he pleases? The necessarily sinful exercises of the unregenerate are perfectly voluntary, and so are as free as they can be. Since their inability is their unwillingness, the greater their inability—that is, the stronger their disinclination to do their duty—the more culpable they are. They have all the natural ability they need to love God; nothing is wanting but a will to love him. But they never do love him until they receive by grace a new habitual inclination of heart.[25] Edwards's argument reconciled freedom and necessity, proving that sinners are at once guilty and helpless. In so doing, he managed to save the doctrines of total depravity and sovereign grace from the Arminian attack. But it is important to note that Edwards also saved these doctrines from the Antinomians by demonstrating that depravity is voluntary and that the sinner's only obstacle to performing his duty to God is his disinclination to do it.

Having shown that sinners are accountable agents despite their depravity, Edwards could go on to affirm that God properly and justly inflicts the penalty of the law upon those who fail to obey it. The emphasis on the authority of the law and on the eternal punishment of sinners, which became pronounced in Edwardsian theology during the 1750s, was directed at both the neonomian Arminians, who suggested that God abates the law by accepting sincere though imperfect obedience, and the Antinomians, who suggested that Christ releases sinners from the obligation of the law. Arminians wanted to justify sinners by a milder law; Antinomians, without the law. The Edwardsians were beginning to believe that they alone preached the gospel *and* law.[26] It was at this point that they began to stress an argument made by Edwards in both *Religious*

Affections and *True Grace Distinguished from the Experience of Devils:* one of the signs of grace is a hearty approval of and cordial submission to the law. In other words, true converts always love the beauty of the law's severity and willingly consent to God's justice in the damnation of sinners *before* they believe that they are pardoned. This test, though it was roundly and inaccurately derided as a requirement that saints be willing to be damned, was simply a description of the convert's gracious disinterested love to God's law and justice. It was the opposite of the Arminians' neonomianism and the Antinomians' faith of assurance, both of which offered salvation to selfish sinners on cheaper terms than the law required.[27]

The same commitment to grace *and* the law can be seen in Edwards's *Dissertation on the Nature of True Virtue*, written in the mid-1750s. Historians have long recognized Edwards's intention in this work to refute secular moralism. He did so by defining virtue as disinterested love to being, so that only the holiness of regenerated saints can be said to be truly virtuous. All apparent virtue in the unregenerate, however useful it may be in human society, falls short of this rigorous standard because it can be reduced to some form of self-love or some involuntary natural principle like conscience, understanding, or instinct. So much for the Arminians. But it should be apparent by now that the composition was also aimed at the Antinomians. To the Arminians Edwards said that virtue to be true must be gracious. To the Antinomians he said that grace to be true must be virtuous. If it is true that one must have a conversion experience to become virtuous, it is equally true that conversion experiences, however intense, are nothing without benevolence. The mark of a saint is not a revelation of pardon; it is love to being. Nor is this love a selfish gratitude for rescue from deserved punishment; it is a disinterested love to being in general. Edwards specifically criticized the notion that love to a particular being—for instance, the self-love that is the basis of particular faith—has any virtue except insofar as it is grounded in love to the comprehensive system of being in general. A true saint's love to God comes before his love to himself. In *True Virtue*, as in his other works, Edwards showed that Arminians and Antinomians both set gospel against law when they tried to pass off counterfeit religion for true. He insisted, by contrast, that the highest standard of obligation remains in force.[28]

As the Arminians continued to pound away at the Calvinists, the debate widened to include such matters as the character of the God who enforces this rigorous law. Arminians argued that God is a benevolent being who seeks the happiness of his creatures. To their way of thinking, the Calvinists blasphemed God by portraying him as a cruel and malevolent being. In the 1750s Edwards set out to vindicate the character of the Calvinists' God. In *Freedom of the Will* he demonstrated that God is a necessarily holy being. In *True Virtue* he showed that holiness in God is identical to holiness in man: in both cases, it is a disinterested benevolent love to being in general. In his *Dissertation concerning the End for which God Created the World*, a companion piece to *True Virtue*, Edwards proved that God is benevolent and not selfish when he seeks his own glory rather than the happiness of his creatures. Because the infinite God in effect is being in general, he is as obliged to love himself as his creatures are to love him.[29] God seeks his glory in the manifestation of his moral attributes, including his justice. Hence God's justice is not at odds with his benevolent love but rather the expression of it. The introduction of sin into the universe is the occasion for the display of God's benevolent justice. Thus, as one of Edwards's disciples was to put it, sin is an advantage to the universe. God is benevolent to permit it and benevolent to punish it. This reasoning led Edwards to conclude that Calvinistic doctrines did not discredit God's benevolence but declared it. The legalism so typical of Edwardsian theology emerged as a response to the coincident threats of neonomianism and Antinomianism.[30]

A related issue was the fairness of imputing Adam's original sin to his posterity, making that transgression the ground of their innate sinful depravity. In the course of a controversy begun in 1757 by Samuel Webster's *A Winter-Evening's Conversation upon the Doctrine of Original Sin*, Arminians objected to the Calvinistic belief that Adam's descendants are liable to punishment for his original sin. Webster focused on the plight of infants who die at birth. Surely, he declared, Calvinists are wrong to say that God condemns them to hell for Adam's sin alone. According to Webster and his Arminian allies, sin and guilt are personal and nontransferable. They charged that the Calvinistic explanation of original sin was Antinomian because it tended to undermine people's sense of personal moral accountability.[31]

Of course, New England's Antinomians saw no problem with the idea that the imputation of Adam's sin condemned them, because they believed with equal fervency that the imputation of Christ's righteousness saved them. Indeed they positively preferred to direct attention away from personal performances and qualifications toward the union of sinners with Adam and saints with Christ. But moderate Calvinists like Peter Clark could make only weak and defensive responses to Webster. The covenant theology committed them to the doctrine of immediate imputation, but at the same time they were plainly uncomfortable about the damnation of infants, an eventuality implying that people are guilty before they become personally sinful. These sheepish Calvinists tried their best to avoid the harsh implications of their creed. Clark, for example, said that though dying infants are liable to eternal punishment for Adam's sin, God will not doom them to it.[32]

Once again Edwards sought to find a middle ground between the extreme positions of Arminianism and Antinomianism. He championed the Calvinistic doctrine of original sin by demonstrating that it does not jeopardize personal moral responsibility. In his final work, *The Great Christian Doctrine of Original Sin* (1758), Edwards argued that identity depends solely on God's sovereign and arbitrary constitution. Just as God, who upholds the universe at every instant by a continual creation, constitutes the moments of an individual's life into a single unit, so too does he choose for certain purposes to constitute all mankind into a single identity. Such is the case of Adam and his posterity in the matter of the first sin. Because of mankind's constituted unity with Adam, Adam's descendants are liable for his sin—not simply because it is legally imputed to them by virtue of some convenantal relationship but because they participate in it. As Edwards put it, "the sin of the apostasy is not theirs, merely because God *imputes* it to them, but is *truly* and *properly* theirs, and on that ground, God imputes it to them." Edwards refused to recognize a distinction between imputed original sin and personal sin. Hence he could maintain, like the Arminians, that all sin is personal sin. No one can excuse his guilt by casting the blame for his depravity back on Adam. But at the same time Edwards could assert that the bond between Adam's sin and the depravity of his posterity is as strong as God's sovereignty. Thus Edwards reconciled Calvinistic determinism and personal responsibility. Indeed, relinquishing the covenantal explanation of imputed sin permitted him to make an extraordinarily bold assertion of God's sovereignty. And yet his magnifying of the divine power made possible a fuller and clearer statement of individual moral accountability.[33]

After Edwards

From the early 1740s, when he began to recognize that enthusiastic Antinomianism was as great a menace to true religion as moralistic Arminianism, Edwards dedicated himself to a single, sustained purpose—the defense of Calvinism against extremists of both sides. Over the next two decades Edwards fashioned a theology incorporating both piety *and* moralism, a theology thoroughly Calvinistic yet uncorrupted by Antinomian tendencies.

By 1758 most of the important New Divinity principles had already emerged to public view in the writings of Edwards. They included the following tenets: (1) God is a benevolent being who is necessarily limited by his holiness. Benevolence in God is the same as benevolence in man. (2) God displays his benevolence in permitting and punishing sin. (3) All sin is personal. There is no imputed sin distinct from personal sin. (4) The seat of holiness and sin is in the heart or will. Acts of holiness and sin are free and voluntary. (5) Grace is a divine operation on the heart, not on the natural understanding. Depravity is confined to the heart, and the natural understanding is left unimpaired by the Fall. (6) The gracious affections of the heart consist in disinterested love to God for his intrinsic amiableness. Any conversions based on self-love are counterfeit. (7) Love to God precedes faith in the order of justification, or, put another way, the first act of justifying faith is love, not belief or assurance. (8) Evangelical repentance—a cordial and willing consent to the beauty of the law that damns sinners—precedes pardon. (9) The evidence of justification is to be found in the lively actings of a holy temper of heart, and not in the experience of conversion itself. Sanctification rather than assurance is the most significant result of conversion. (10) Sinners are accountable moral agents because they have a natural ability to exercise holiness even though they sin by a moral necessity. (11) Because sinners' inability to love God is a voluntary disinclination, they may justly be commanded to do so immediately. (12) These principles can be applied in a practical way to ecclesiastical affairs as tests for the admission of members to communion and as discouragements from a complacent and lethargic reliance on the means of grace.[34]

When Joseph Bellamy and Samuel Hopkins assumed the leadership of the Edwardsian party in the 1760s, they remained true to Edwards's principles. The New Divinity was Edwardsianism responding to new challenges. Three controversies in particular led to the christening of Edwardsian theology as a "new" divinity. The first struggle, which occurred in the late 1750s and early 1760s, was with the followers of James Hervey, a British theologian who wrote a popular work on justifying faith entitled *Theron and Aspasio* (1755). Hervey's argument, a variation on the doctrine of particular faith, appealed to extreme New Lights and Separates in New England who wanted to direct sinners to Christ, but who also wanted to avoid a blatantly Antinomian statement of justification. Hervey contended that in saving faith sinners believe that they are pardoned. Their belief is not based on any evidence or grounds in themselves to indicate that God loves them, for there is no evidence. God does not love them until they believe that he loves them. But by their believing that he loves them, it becomes true that he loves them. Consequently they are obliged to believe without seeing any evidence of qualification in themselves. Hervey thought that he had cleverly evaded both the Arminian error of assuming that there is a qualification in the believer prior to pardon, and the Antinomian error of assuming that elect sinners are justified before they have faith.[35]

Bellamy led the opposition to this scheme, which he labeled "refined Antinomianism." His arguments committed the Edwardsian theology even more fully to the notion that religion is a matter of the heart and will rather than the intellect. In responding to Hervey, Bellamy and other Edwardsians realized that they had to confine regeneration to the will if they hoped to explode the Antinomian doctrine that faith is a belief or persuasion or assurance of forgiveness. Hervey also forced Bellamy to be more explicit about the order of exercises in conversion. Edwardsians began to state more insistently that regeneration first changes the temper of heart so that holy acts (particularly disinterested love to God and willing consent to the law) precede justification. Bellamy and company either used the word "faith" to denote love, or else, if they continued to define faith as belief, placed faith after holy love and evangelical repentance in the order of exercises. In reaction to Hervey, Edwardsians stressed even more the requirement that converts exercise a willing submission to the law before they are pardoned. It was particularly important to uphold both grace and law at the time of Hervey's popularity, because Arminians were then loudly complaining that Calvinism excuses believers from their obligation to be righteous.[36]

The second important controversy after Edwards's death involved the doctrines of a Scottish critic of Hervey named Robert Sandeman. Sandeman, who acquired a considerable following in New England during the 1760s, believed that Calvinists, even "refined Antinomians" like Hervey, conceded too much importance to human qualifications in justification and thereby detracted from the sufficiency of Christ's imputed righteousness. Sandeman attacked Hervey for requiring sinners to do even so much as to *think* themselves saved. This, he said, was succumbing to justification by works. Sinners have nothing to *do* except believe with a bare speculative or notional belief that the gospel is true. Hence preachers who exhort sinners to do anything—pray, attend worship, do good deeds, or whatever—are legalists. In fact, Sandeman's main targets were not the Arminians but rather those Calvinists who placed great emphasis on the means of grace.[37]

His criticisms came at an awkward moment for New England Calvinists. At that time they were desperately responding to the Arminians' accusations that Calvinism eliminated all motives for sinners to try to be good. Typically, non-Edwardsian Calvinists had replied to the Arminians by saying that though there are no *promises* of grace in return for the best efforts of the unregenerate, there are *encouragements* that sinners who strive will be saved. But this was precisely the sort of Calvinism that Sandeman derided as a disingenuous version of justification by works. Edwardsians quickly recognized that Sandeman was right to call this kind of Calvinism inconsistent. If the efforts of sinners please God in any way so as to attract grace, sinners are saved by works. If, on the other hand, even the best efforts of sinners are abominable to God, Calvinists should be honest enough to admit that sinners who diligently strive are no more likely to be saved than if they neglect the means of grace altogether.[38]

Accordingly, when Samuel Hopkins wrote *An Enquiry concerning the Promises of the Gospel* (1765) as an answer to Jonathan Mayhew's Arminian book *Striving to Enter in at the Strait Gate* (1761), he flatly declared that everything done by a sinner before regeneration is wicked and totally unacceptable to God. Moreover, Hopkins said that while the sinner remains unconverted, the more he attends the means of grace, the more he aggravates his guilt. Of course, non-Edwardsian Calvinists immediately reproached Hopkins for advocating the "new" divinity of Sandeman. And indeed Hopkins had been influenced by Sandeman's perception that Calvinists who emphasized the means of grace often preached a formalistic, legalistic, and unevangelical religion.[39]

But Hopkins was no Sandemanian. He was an Edwardsian. Whereas Sandeman was an intellectualist, Hopkins was a voluntarist. Sandeman rejected the strivings of the unregenerate because he believed that the sinner has nothing to *do* to obtain salvation—Christ's righteousness does all. Hopkins, by contrast, rejected the strivings of the unregenerate not because strivings are acts but because they are the wrong kind of acts. They are acts of sinful self-love, while God demands acts of disinterested holy love. Because Hopkins was an Edwardsian voluntarist, he did not conclude that the unregenerate have nothing to do but passively wait for forgiveness. They have plenty to do. It is their immediate duty to love God and be holy. So long as they attend the means of grace, stuffing their understandings with speculative knowledge about God and yet continuing to love themselves more than him, they do less than their duty and only compound their guilt. Here was the crucial difference between Hopkins and Sandeman. Hopkins could condemn an inactive reliance on the means of grace, because the Edwardsian theory of the will told him that the unregenerate have a full natural ability to do their entire duty, which is to be holy. The only thing preventing them is their voluntary and culpable disinclination to do it. The problem with Calvinists who encouraged unregenerate strivings was that they implied that sinners lie under some excusable inability to love God. Hopkins believed that this attitude invited sinners to pull up short of conversion.[40]

Hopkins's examination of unregenerate doings managed to answer the Arminians, who claimed that New England's Calvinists were all Antinomians, and the Sandemanians, who claimed that New England's Calvinists were all Arminians, and he was able to achieve this victory without resorting to the evasive, equivocal, and unevangelical preparationism preached by many moderate Calvinist ministers.[41]

The third important controversy in the 1760s involved standards for admission to full membership in the churches. In their rejection of Stoddardean theories of church membership, the Edwardsians were applying their voluntaristic psychology of conversion to ecclesiastical affairs. The Stoddardean willingness to accept moral sincerity as a sufficient qualification for communion seemed to Edwardsians to be an unevangelical practice. It allowed the unregenerate to stop short of their duty. Just as the Edwardsians denied that God makes promises to unregenerate strivings, so too did they deny that the sacraments can be a means of grace. Consequently they restricted membership to those who could give evidence of a gracious change of heart. Stoddardeanism implied that sinners can do no more than own the covenant, live moral lives, and wait for grace; Edwardsianism demanded that sinners exercise the gracious love of which they are capable before they are permitted to enjoy the privileges of saints.[42]

It was the combination of Hopkins's rejection of unregenerate strivings and the Edwardsians' restrictions on church membership that provoked non-Edwardsian Calvinists to array themselves into an opposition party. The "old Calvinists," as they styled themselves, accused the Edwardsians of preaching a "new divinity." These Old Calvinists were a coalition of former New Lights and ex-Old Lights who suddenly realized that they had a lot more in common with each other than they did with the Edwardsians. In particular what they shared was a refusal to locate religion exclusively in the heart, will, and affections. Plainly they were annoyed by the outrageous new doctrines. But the perplexed Old Calvinists did not know what to make of them. Sometimes the Edwardsians seemed to be too harsh and rigid—as when they said that people should be thankful for God's permission of sin; or that sinners grow worse when they use the means of grace; or that regeneration is a divine operation on the will without any enlightenment of the understanding; or that converts should love a damning God; or that nothing short of disinterested love to being is truly virtuous. To the Old Calvinists, these tenets seemed to be Antinomian or worse! But other times the Edwardsians seemed to be too lax—as when they said that there is no imputed sin, only personal sin; or that the understanding is left undamaged by the Fall; or that depravity is nothing more than voluntary disinclination and unwillingness; or that sinners have the complete natural ability to repent and be holy. These notions seemed patently Arminian![43]

So the frustrated Old Calvinists attacked the New Divinity men for being both Arminians and Antinomians, for being at once humanistic moralists and austere hyper-Calvinists. For their part, the New Divinity preachers smugly proclaimed that they had discovered the solution to the problems bedeviling Calvinism. They believed that they alone could preach a consistent Calvinism, balancing grace and law, piety and moralism. Indeed their pride in their clever system often led them to take a perverse delight in expressing their doctrines in the most provocative way possible, stressing the extremes of divine sovereignty and human ability. What is more, they gloried in their evangelical success, for they soon learned that they could drive their congregations to conversions by preaching the sinner's helplessness and his guilt. And they were particularly proud that their revivals were orderly affairs that bred converts who were sanctified, not enthusiastic.[44]

By the 1770s there had occurred a fundamental reordering of New England Calvinism. In place of the New Light-Old Light divisions of the Great Awakening stood four theological parties: Antinomians, Arminians, Old Calvinists, and New Divinity Edwardsians. At a time when Arminians and Antinomians seemed intent upon pulling grace and works apart, the New Divinity sought to maintain New England Calvinism's traditional commitment to both piety *and* moralism. But the New Divinity did not come out of the blue. It came out of Edwards.

Notes

1. Edward H. Davidson's *Jonathan Edwards: The Narrative of a Puritan Mind* (Cambridge, Mass., 1968; orig. pub. 1966), 134, 146, contends that Edwards had no true heirs. See also Mark A. Noll, "Moses Mather (Old Calvinist)

and the Evolution of Edwardseanism," *Church History* 49 (1980), 285, 285 n. 49. Perry Miller argues for a connection between Edwards and Emerson in his essay "From Edwards to Emerson," in *Errand into the Wilderness* (New York, 1964; orig. pub. 1956). Similar claims are made in William A. Clebsch, *American Religious Thought: A History* (Chicago, 1973), 65–66; Terrence Erdt, *Jonathan Edwards: Art and the Sense of the Heart* (Amherst, Mass., 1980), 84–90; Conrad Cherry, *Nature and Religious Imagination: From Edwards to Bushnell* (Philadelphia, 1980), 1–2; Ursula Brumm, "Jonathan Edwards and Ralph Waldo Emerson," in *American Thought and Religious Typology* (New Brunswick, N.J., 1970), 86–108; Sacvan Bercovitch, *The Puritan Origins of the American Self* (New Haven Conn., 1975), 152–63; Mason I. Lowance, Jr., "From Edwards to Emerson and Thoreau: A Reevaluation," in *The Language of Canaan: Metaphor and Symbol in New England from the Puritans to the Transcendentalists* (Cambridge, Mass., 1980), 277–95. Miller may have taken the hint from Harriet Beecher Stowe, who wrote of Edwards, "He was the first man who began the disintegrating process of applying rationalistic methods to the accepted doctrines of religion, and he rationalized far more boldly and widely than any publishers of his biography have ever dared to let the world know. He sawed the great dam and let out the whole waters of discussion over all New England, and that free discussion led to all the shades of opinion of our modern days. Little as he thought it, yet Waldo Emerson and Theodore Parker were the last results of the current set in motion by Jonathan Edwards." *Oldtown Folks*, ed. Henry F. May (Cambridge, Mass., 1966; orig. pub. 1869), 260. The most influential proponent of the betrayal thesis has been Joseph Haroutunian, *Piety versus Moralism: The Passing of the New England Theology* (New York, 1970; orig. pub. 1932), xxiv–xxxi, and *passim*. Other examples of this interpretation can be found in Ola Elizabeth Winslow, *Jonathan Edwards, 1703–1758: A Biography* (New York, 1940), 327–28; Conrad Cherry, *The Theology of Jonathan Edwards: A Reappraisal* (Garden City, N.Y., 1966), 216–17; James Carse, *Jonathan Edwards and the Visibility of God* (New York, 1967), 183; and William J. Scheick, ed., *Critical Essays on Jonathan Edwards* (Boston, 1980), xii, xx. The suggestion that New Divinity ministers were cold-blooded hyper-Calvinistic systematizers can be found in Herbert W. Schneider, *The Puritan Mind* (Ann Arbor, 1966; orig. pub. 1930), 155, 208; Edmund S. Morgan, *The Gentle Puritan: A Life of Ezra Stiles, 1727–1795* (New Haven, Conn., 1962), 313–315; Morgan, "The American Revolution Considered as an Intellectual Movement," in Arthur M. Schlesinger, Jr., and Morton White, eds., *Paths of American Thought* (Boston, 1963), 11–33; Donald Meyer, "The Dissolution of Calvinism," *ibid.*, 77–78; Sidney Earl Mead, *Nathaniel William Taylor, 1786–1858: A Connecticut Liberal* (Hamden, Conn., 1967; orig. pub. 1942), 16–18; Alan Heimert, *Religion and the American Mind: From the Great Awakening to the Revolution* (Cambridge, Mass., 1966), 349, 353; Robert L. Ferm, *Jonathan Edwards the Younger, 1745–1801: A Colonial Pastor* (Grand Rapids, Mich., 1976), 61–66, 174–75; William G. McLoughlin, *New England Dissent, 1630–1833: The Baptists and the Separation of Church and State* (Cambridge, Mass., 1971), II, 730–34; Stephen E. Berk, *Calvinism versus Democracy: Timothy Dwight and the Origins of American Evangelical Orthodoxy* (Hamden, Conn., 1974), 15, 29, 55–58, 71; Cedric B. Cowing, *The Great Awakening and the American Revolution: Colonial Thought in the 18th Century* (Chicago, 1971), 197–98; and Clebsch, *American Religious Thought*, 14–15, 55, 64. Those who see the New Divinity as moralizing and legalizing Edwards include Haroutunian, *Piety versus Moralism*; Richard J. Purcell, *Connecticut in Transition, 1775–1818*, (Washington, D.C., 1918), 42; Berk, *Calvinism versus Democracy*, 59–61; Roland Andre Delattre, *Beauty and Sensibility in the Thought of Jonathan Edwards: An Essay in Aesthetics and Theological Ethics* (New Haven, Conn., 1968), 218–19 n. 5; and Cherry, *Nature and Religious Imagination*, 9–10, 66–82. The paraphrase of Haroutunian comes from *Piety versus Moralism*, 281. Some writers attempt to deal with the discrepancy between the two versions of betrayal by speaking of two wings of the New Divinity movement—a hyper-Calvinistic Hopkinsian wing and a milder Edwardsian-Bellamyan wing. See Berk, *Calvinism versus Democracy*, 54–73; and, for a nineteenth-century statement, Edward A. Lawrence, "The Old School in New England Theology," *Bibliotheca Sacra* 20 (1863), 311–49. My disagreement with this theory should become evident.

2. The most powerful statement of this paradigm can be found in the works of Perry Miller. The argument is stated succinctly in the essay "The Marrow of Puritan Divinity," in *Errand into the Wilderness*.

3. For example, see Philip F. Gura, *A Glimpse of Sion's Glory: Puritan Radicalism in New England, 1620–1660* (Middletown, Conn., 1984); and Stephen Foster, "New England and the Challenge of Heresy, 1630–1660: The Puritan Crisis in Transatlantic Perspective," *William and Mary Quarterly*, 3d ser. [hereafter *WMQ*] 38 (1981), 624–60.

4. Excellent discussions of the recent reinterpretation of Puritanism and the Reformed tradition can be found in David D. Hall, "Understanding the Puritans," in Herbert J. Bass, ed., *The State of American History* (Chicago, 1970), 331–49, and Michael McGiffert, "American Puritan Studies in the 1960's," *WMQ* 27 (1970), 36–67. In addition to works discussed in these essays, I have found the following works especially helpful: Norman Fiering, "Will and Intellect in the New England Mind," *WMQ* 29 (1972), 515–58; William K. B. Stoever, *"A Faire and Easie Way to Heaven": Covenant Theology and Antinomianism in Early Massachusetts* (Middletown, Conn., 1978); and R. T. Kendall, *Calvin and English Calvinism to 1649* (Oxford, 1981; orig. pub. 1979). The last of these argues that although Puritans (Kendall calls them experimental predestinarians) *did* differ significantly from Calvin, they agreed with other Reformed theologians, notably Beza. In my essay I use the word *Calvinist* as Edwards did, for distinction's sake, without any implication that Calvinists always agreed with Calvin.

5. Jonathan Edwards, *The Works of President Edwards* [revised Worcester edition] (New York, 1869), IV, 169–78.

6. Ibid., IV, 64–132. The phrase "modern divines" appears on page 77.

7. Ibid., IV, 438–50, especially 441–42, 448.

8. His warnings against Antinomian distortions can be found in, *ibid.*, IV, 128, 174–75, 450.

9. The best accounts of the Great Awakening in New England are Edwin Scott Gaustad, *The Great Awakening in New England* (Chicago, 1968; orig. pub. 1957); Richard Bushman, *From Puritan to Yankee: Character and the Social Order in Connecticut, 1690–1765* (Cambridge, Mass., 1967); C. C. Goen, *Revivalism and Separatism in New England, 1740–1800: Strict Congregationalists and Separate Baptists in the Great Awakening* (New Haven, Conn., 1962); and Joseph Tracy, *The Great Awakening: A History of the Revival of Religion in the Time of Edwards and Whitefield* (Boston, 1842). Old Light complaints about the enthusiasm and Antinomianism of the New Light converts can be found in the following works: *The Wonderful Narrative: or a Faithful Account of the French Prophets* (Boston, 1742); Charles Chauncy, *Enthusiasm Described and Caution'd Against* (Boston, 1742); Chauncy, *Seasonable Thoughts on the State of Religion in New England* (Boston, 1743); *The Testimony of the Pastors of the Churches . . . Against Several Errors in Doctrine, and Disorders in Practice* (Boston, 1743); and Benjamin Doolittle, *An Enquiry into Enthusiasm* (Boston, 1743). Good statements of the Old Lights' intellectualist conception of conversion can be found in Chauncy, *Enthusiasm*, and William Hart, *A Discourse concerning the Nature of Regeneration* (New London, Conn., 1742). Old Lights were intellectualists because they assumed that man's moral agency depends on his being a rational creature and a "cause by counsel." By this they meant that the understanding judges the good according to the motives presented to it, and the will (or rational appetite) moves the soul to embrace that good. Old Lights believed that regeneration accordingly must involve a change in the understanding as well as in the will. First there has to be an illumination of the intellect so that it can see and value Christ in his true excellency as a Savior of sinners. This illumination occurs by the influence of the Spirit, which presents the quickening truth to the understanding with an efficacious moral power. After presenting divine truths in their proper light to the understanding, the Spirit renovates the will by inclining it to desire and embrace that which the understanding judges to be good. Because Old Lights thought that regeneration involves the participation of the understanding, they viewed the New Lights' sudden and violent conversions as violating man's moral agency by making grace a physical and forcible operation on the passive convert. Old Lights preferred to think of regeneration as effectual calling, which implied that the Spirit invites and persuades sinners by the light of truth. Their interpretation allowed more room for human participation in the process of redemption, especially since God conveys light through the instrumentality of appropriate means. It was very easy for this intellectualist explanation of regeneration to slip into Arminianism and Pelagianism, as Norman Fiering has noted in "Will and Intellect," 550–51.

10. Jonathan Edwards, *The Great Awakening*, ed. C. C. Goen, in *The Works of Jonathan Edwards*, vol. IV (New Haven, Conn., 1972), 278–80.

11. Ibid., 296–300, 432–33, 436.

12. Andrew Croswell, *What is Christ to Me, If He Is Not Mine?* (Boston, 1745), reprinted in Alan Heimert and Perry Miller, eds., *The Great Awakening: Documents Illustrating the Crisis and Its Consequences* (Indianapolis, 1967), 505–15. The quotation is on page 512. I use the word *Antinomian* as loosely as I use the word *Calvinist*. It should be noted that Croswell denied that his doctrines were Antinomian. Antinomians, he said, claim that an elect sinner is forgiven before faith, whereas he asserted that forgiveness comes with faith (see page 510). Indeed, in this Croswell did differ from the seventeenth-century Antinomians of Boston, who declared that union with Christ precedes any human act, including the act of faith, which follows justification and reveals it. See Stoever, *"Faire and Easie Way"*, and David D. Hall, ed., *The Antinomian Controversy, 1636–1638: A Documentary History* (Middletown, Conn., 1968), 3–20. Still, Croswell can fairly be classified as a "refined Antinomian"—to use Joseph Bellamy's phrase. In my essay *Antinomian* refers to those who (1) interpret justification in such a way as to deny the value of human acts and works as the main evidence of pardon; (2) define faith as the faith of assurance (the faith that one has been justified, based on the immediate light and direct witness of the Spirit), so that the conversion experience is self-authenticating; and (3) set the gospel against the law by implying that calls for sanctification and morality are signs of legalism. By this construction Croswell was clearly Antinomian. So were many of the New Light Separates, whose confidence in their ability to form pure churches of the saints rested on the faith of assurance. See Joseph Tracy, *The Great Awakening*, 317; Goen, *Revivalism and Separatism*, 12–17, 40–48, 148–54, 159–67; and J. M. Bumsted and John E. Van de Wetering, *What Must I Do To Be Saved? The Great Awakening in Colonial America* (Hinsdale, Ill., 1976), 110–14. Since this paper was presented, a first-rate article on Croswell and the New Light Antinomians has appeared. See Leigh Eric Schmidt, "'A Second and Glorious Reformation': The New Light Extremism of Andrew Croswell," *WMQ* 43 (1986), 214–44.

13. Jonathan Edwards, *Religious Affections*, ed. John E. Smith, in *The Works of Jonathan Edwards*, vol. II (New Haven, Conn., 1959), 197–239 especially 200, 205–08, 229, 233–39. See also 266–91 (Fourth Sign), and 291–311 (Fifth Sign). Thomas A. Schafer has noted that Edwards emphasized love rather than assurance in his definition of justifying faith. See Schafer, "Jonathan Edwards and Justification by Faith," *Church History* 20 (December 1951), 55–67, especially 57–63.

14. See Edwards, *Religious Affections*, 240–66 (Second and Third Signs), especially 240, 244–46. Edwards borrowed the names legal and evangelical hypocrites from Thomas Shepard. See *Religious Affections*, 173. It is striking that Edwards often referred to self-interested love as being coerced or forced, and to disinterested love as being voluntary. For example, in *True Grace Distinguished from the Experience of Devils* (1752), he said, "This sight of the beauty of divine things will excite true desires and longings of soul after those things; not like the

longings of devils, or any such forced desires, as those of a man in great danger of death, after some bitter medicine that he hopes will save his life; but natural, free desires, the desires of appetite—the thirstings of a new nature, as a newborn babe desires the mother's breast." Edwards, *Works* [revised Worcester edition], IV, 470.

15. Edwards, *Religious Affections*, Sixth through Twelfth Signs, especially the Twelfth Sign, 383–461. Edwards distinguishes his notion of Christian practice from that of the Arminians on pages 422–24.

16. Jonathan Edwards, *The Life and Diary of the Rev. David Brainerd* (1749), in *The Works of President Edwards*, ed. Edward Williams and Edward Parsons (New York, 1968), III, 554–55, 92–93, 537, 296–97. The quotation is on page 555.

17. Edwards, *Works* [revised Worcester edition], IV, 467.

18. Ibid., IV, 451–73. The suggestion that the Fall left the understanding undamaged can be found on page 454. Edwardsians claimed that any darkening of the sinner's understanding is the effect of moral depravity in the heart, and is not itself moral depravity. Edwards could afford to abandon the understanding to his opponents because he had managed to smuggle cognitive functions into the heart and will. Since the saint's new sense of heart is a new taste or relish for the excellency of divine things, gracious affections always carry with them an apprehension of the truth and divinity of the divine things relished. Love must involve a recognition of loveliness, for there can be no love where no loveliness is seen. See Fiering, "Will and Intellect," 532–33.

19. Jonathan Edwards, *An Humble Inquiry into Rules of the Word of God concerning the Qualifications Requisite to a Complete Standing and Full Communion in the Visible Christian Church* (1749); and *Misrepresentations Corrected, and Truth Vindicated, in a Reply to the Rev. Mr. Solomon Williams's Book* (1752) can be found in Edwards, *Works* [revised Worcester edition], I, 83–292. See especially 86–87 and 190.

20. Croswell remained the principal spokesman for this party. To support their position on justification, Antinomians in the 1740s and 1750s began to reprint the writings of British theologians of a similar mind, especially the "Marrow-Men" of the Scottish Secession Church. Works by Ebenezer and Ralph Erskine were reprinted in Boston regularly during these two decades (1742, 1743, 1744, 1749, 1759). Thomas Boston's *The Nature and Necessity of Regeneration* had a Boston printing in 1743, and *The Marrow of Modern Divinity* was itself reprinted there in 1743. Also see the appendix containing material by Boston and the Erskines in Croswell's *A Narrative of the Founding and Settling the New-Gathered Congregational Church in Boston* (Boston, 1749).

21. The Anglicans' attack on Calvinism was led by Samuel Johnson and John Beach. See Johnson, *A Letter from Aristocles to Authades, concerning the Sovereignty and the Promises of God* (Boston, 1745); Johnson, *A Letter to the Rev. Jonathan Dickinson in Defence of Aristocles and Authades* (Boston, 1747); and Beach, *A Sermon, Shewing, that Eternal Life is God's Free Gift, Bestowed*

upon Men According to their Moral Behaviour (Newport, 1745); Beach, *God's Sovereignty and His Universal Love to the Souls of Men Reconciled* (Boston, 1747); Beach, *A Second Vindication of God's Sovereign Free Grace Indeed* (Boston, 1748); and Beach, *An Attempt to Prove the Affirmative Part of that Question, Whether there Be any Certainty that a Sinner under the Advantages of the Gospel and Common Grace, Striving with All His Might . . . Shall Obtain Such a Measure of Divine Assistance as is Necessary to Fit Him for Eternal Salvation* (Boston, 1748).

22. Lemuel Briant, *The Absurdity and Blasphemy of Depreciating Moral Virtue* (Boston, 1749). The quotations are on pages 7, 8, 7, and 23–24. Briant's sermon provoked hostile responses from Calvinists, including John Porter, Samuel Niles, Thomas Foxcroft, John Cotton, and Samuel Dunbar. Ministers sympathetic to Briant's position included Jonathan Mayhew, Charles Chauncy, John Brown, John Bass, Ebenezer Gay, William Balch, and John Tucker. For accounts of the emergence of the Arminian or Liberal party, see Conrad Wright, *The Beginnings of Unitarianism in America* (Hamden, Conn., 1976; orig. pub. 1955); and Charles W. Akers, *Called unto Liberty: A Life of Jonathan Mayhew* (Cambridge, Mass., 1964).

23. Jonathan Edwards, *Freedom of the Will*, ed. Paul Ramsey, in *The Works of Jonathan Edwards*, vol. I (New Haven, Conn., 1957), 137–48.

24. *Ibid.*, 149–62. The quotation is on pages 156–57.

25. *Ibid.*, 163–66. The phrase "nothing is wanting but a will" appears in a slightly different context on page 162.

26. For an example of Edwards's concern for the authority of the law during this period, see his "Endless Punishment of Those Who Die Impenitent," which Norman Fiering says was written about 1755. Norman Fiering, *Jonathan Edwards's Moral Thought and Its British Context* (Chapel Hill, N.C., 1981), 238–39 n. 107. "Endless Punishment" can be found in Edwards, *Works* [revised Worcester edition], I, 612–42.

27. Edwards makes the point about willing consent in *Religious Affections* 274, and in *Works* [revised Worcester edition], IV, 459. Joseph Bellamy emphasized cordial submission in *The Law Our Schoolmaster* (1756), which can be found in *The Works of Joseph Bellamy, D.D.*, ed. Tryon Edwards (Boston, 1850), I, 363–416, especially 363–65, 385, and 400–401.

28. *Dissertation on the Nature of True Virtue* (1765), ed. William K. Frankena (Ann Arbor, Mich., 1960). Norman Fiering discusses *True Virtue* as a response to British secular moralists, whose theories in effect constituted a non-Calvinistic "counter-religion." See Fiering, *Jonathan Edwards's Moral Thought*, 8–9, 322–61, especially 356–61. Conrad Cherry perceptively notes that *True Virtue* was aimed at both Arminians and Antinomians. See Cherry, *Theology of Edwards*, 176–85.

29. Edwards argued that God's moral excellency is necessary in *Freedom of the Will*, 277–280, 375–96. He showed that true virtue is identical in God and man

in *The Nature of True Virtue*, 23; and he demonstrated that God is not selfish when he seeks his own glory in *The End of Creation*, in *Works* [revised Worcester edition], II, 193–257, especially 215–20.

30. Edwards said that God's purpose in creation is the exertion and manifestation of his attributes, in *Works* [revised Worcester edition], II, 204. He contended that those who interpreted God's benevolence to mean a compassion for particular creatures misunderstood the nature of benevolence. For a discussion of Edwards's views on God's justice, see Fiering, *Jonathan Edwards's Moral Thought*, 200–260, especially 222–25, 238–44, 253–60. For the views of Edwards's disciples, see Joseph Bellamy, *Four Sermons on the Wisdom of God in the Permission of Sin* (1758) in Bellamy, *Works*, II, 3–96; Bellamy, *The Wisdom of God in the Permission of Sin, Vindicated* (1759) in Bellamy, *Works*, II, 97–155; and Samuel Hopkins, *Sin, through Divine Interposition, an Advantage to the Universe* (1759), in *The Works of Samuel Hopkins, D.D.* (Boston, 1852), II, 491–545.

31. Samuel Webster, *A Winter-Evening's Conversation upon the Doctrine of Original Sin* (Boston, 1757). Webster's pamphlet continued the controversy between Arminians and Calvinists begun by Lemuel Briant. Webster received support from Charles Chauncy and Edmund March. For accounts of this controversy, see Wright, *Beginnings of Unitarianism*, 83–90; H. Shelton Smith, *Changing Conceptions of Original Sin: A Study in American Theology since 1750* (New York, 1955), 37–46; and Haroutunian, *Piety versus Moralism*, 15–42.

32. Peter Clark, *The Scripture-Doctrine of Original Sin, Stated and Defended* (Boston, 1758). Clark made his point about infants in his *Remarks on a Late Pamphlet, Entitled, "The Opinion of One That Has Perused the Summer-Morning's Conversation"* (Boston, 1758), 31. Another evasive statement by a Calvinist can be found in Samuel Niles, *The True Scripture-Doctrine of Original Sin Stated and Defended* (Boston, 1757), 102.

33. Jonathan Edwards, *Original Sin*, ed. Clyde A. Holbrook, vol. III in *The Works of Jonathan Edwards* (New Haven, Conn., 1970), 407–408, 389–91. The quotation is on page 408. Also see Daniel T. Fiske, "New England Theology," *Bibliotheca Sacra* 22 (1865), 494–503; George Park Fisher, *Discussions in History and Theology* (New York, 1880), 356, 379–80, 393–404; and Enoch Pond, *Sketches of the Theological History of New England* (Boston, 1880), 60–61.

34. For evidence that these principles were considered to be the distinguishing marks of the New Divinity, see Hannah Adams, *A View of Religions, in Two Parts*, 3d ed. (Boston, 1801), 128–34; Ezra Stiles, *Extracts from the Itineraries and Other Miscellanies of Ezra Stiles, D.D., LL.D., 1755–1794. With A Selection from His Correspondence*, ed. Franklin Bowditch Dexter (New Haven, Conn., 1916), 412; *Essays on Hopkinsianism* (Boston? c. 1820), 12–26; Pond, *Sketches of Theological History*, 60–63; Jonathan Edwards, Jr., *The Works of Jonathan Edwards, D.D., Late President of Union College*, ed. Tryon Edwards (Andover, Mass., 1842), I, 481–92; and Edwards A. Park, *Memoir of Nathanael Emmons* (Boston, 1861), 428.

35. For an account of Hervey's life, see *The Dictionary of National Biography, s.v.* "James Hervey."

36. Joseph Bellamy, *Theron, Paulinus, and Aspasio; or, Letters and Dialogues upon the Nature of Love to God, Faith in Christ, Assurance of a Title to Eternal Life* (1759), in *Works*, II, 157–267. See especially 222. Edwardsians believed that non-Edwardsian Calvinists, if they were to remain true Calvinists, could not avoid adopting a scheme similar to Hervey's because they also defined faith as intellectual persuasion and also placed justification before repentance. See Bellamy, *A Blow at the Root of the Refined Antinomianism of the Present Age* (1763), in *Works*, I, 524–25; and Stephen West, *Sketches of the Life of the Late Rev. Samuel Hopkins, D.D.* (Hartford, 1805), 133–35.

37. On Sandeman and the Sandemanians, see Williston Walker, "The Sandemanians of New England," *Annual Report of the American Historical Association for the Year 1901*, I (1902), 133–62; *Contributions to the Ecclesiastical History of Connecticut* (New Haven, Conn., 1861), 284–85; Ezra Stiles, *The Literary Diary of Ezra Stiles, D.D., LL.D.*, ed. Franklin Bowditch Dexter (New York, 1901), I, 101, 259, 502; II, 171, 228; and *The Dictionary of National Biography, s.v.* "Robert Sandeman" and "John Glas."

38. Jedidiah Mills had distinguished *encouragements* from *promises* in the course of his dispute with Anglican Arminians in the late 1740s. See Mills, *A Vindication of Gospel-Truth, and Refutation of Some Dangerous Errors, in Relation to that Important Question, Whether There Be Promises . . . of Special Grace . . . to the Unregenerate, on Condition of Any Endeavours, Strivings, or Doings of Theirs Whatsoever?* (Boston, 1747), 45, 75, 77.

39. Hopkins's *Enquiry* can be found in his *Works*, III, 183–275. See page 263 for his assertion that awakened sinners grow worse while using means.

40. It is worth noting that Hopkins published Edwards's manuscript on *True Virtue* in the midst of his own dispute over unregenerate strivings. Edwards's demonstration that only regenerate saints can be truly virtuous lent support to Hopkins's argument that all endeavors by sinners are abominable in God's eyes because they are tainted by sinful self-love. Hopkins charged that non-Edwardsian Calvinists seemed to suppose sinners under an excusable inability to repent and embrace the gospel, in his *Works*, I, 502.

41. The following quotation from the *Enquiry* summarizes Hopkins's position: "Many public teachers, therefore, seem to make a great mistake here. Instead of calling upon all to repent and believe the gospel, as the only condition of God's favor and eternal life, the most they do, with relation to unregenerate sinners, is to exhort and urge them to these doings, which are short of repentance. They teach them to use means in such a manner as rather tends to defeat the proper end of means, and so as that they become a means of blinding their eyes, rather than of instruction; it tends to lead them to rest in means, and make a Savior of them. . . ." Hopkins, *Works*, III, 272.

42. Bellamy led the attack on Stoddardeanism with a series of publications in

the 1760s and early 1770s. His principal opponents were Moses Mather, Ebenezer Devotion, and William Hart.

43. The Old Calvinist coalition included such former New Lights as Jedidiah Mills and Benjamin Lord, and such former Old Lights as Ebenezer Devotion, Ezra Stiles, Chauncey Whittelsey, and James Dana. On the Old Calvinists see Gerald J. Goodwin, "The Myth of 'Arminian-Calvinism' in Eighteenth-Century New England," *New England Quarterly* 41 (1968), 214–16; Morgan, *Gentle Puritan*, 172–76; George Leon Walker, *Some Aspects of the Religious Life of New England with Special Reference to Congregationalists* (Boston, 1897), 128; Williston Walker, *Ten New England Leaders* (New York, 1901), 230–31; George Nye Boardman, *A History of New England Theology* (New York, 1899), 30–31; and Leonard Woods, *History of the Andover Theological Seminary* (Boston, 1885), 27–28.

44. For evidence of the evangelical success of New Divinity preaching, see the accounts of revivals in the first seven volumes of the *Connecticut Evangelical Magazine* (1800–1807) and the discussion in Joseph A. Conforti, *Samuel Hopkins and the New Divinity Movement: Calvinism, the Congregational Ministry, and Reform in New England between the Great Awakenings* (Grand Rapids, Mich., 1981), 175–190.

12

Calvinism and Consciousness from Edwards to Beecher

JAMES HOOPES

One Sabbath morning in the winter of 1738 when young David Brainerd was walking alone in the woods, God gave the Yale undergraduate such a sense of the danger of Almighty wrath "and hell, as it were, under my feet" that he "begrudged the birds and beasts their happiness because they were not exposed to eternal misery." For more than a year afterward he harbored secret hopes of pleasing God by works and, alternately, resentment that faith alone was the basis of salvation, till at last he was exhausted and truly humbled. Then, on a Sabbath evening in July, "walking again in the same solitary place . . . in a dark thick grove, unspeakable glory seemed to open to the view and apprehension of my soul." With conversion came enthusiasm and arrogance. He was over-heard to say that Tutor Whittelsey "has no more grace than this chair." Refusing to repent publicly, Brainerd was expelled for subverting the peace of the college. Having thus recovered his humility, he carried the faith to Indians at Stockbridge and then in New Jersey, which obliged him to ride horseback four thousand miles a year "and oftentimes over hideous rocks, mountains and swamps—frequently to lie out in the open woods" or gasp for breath in a smoky wigwam.[1] Subsisting on bread or meal baked in ashes, and sometimes not even that, he longed for nothing but God, even when, as happened more than once in winter, he fell into a river and continued his journey wet and cold and "without much sense of divine and heavenly things."[2]

Hardships endured in his mission soon increased the fatigue, weakness, and protracted fits of coughing and spitting up blood from which he had suffered since his undergraduate days. Jonathan Edwards, to whose home Brainerd had come to die, found no affectation of holiness in him, but rather, he seemed "to nauseate all such things." Indeed, his principal complaint was insufficient spirituality and the corruption he saw in even his best acts. Although God eased his doubt by showing him that he had sometimes "acted above the utmost influence of mere self-love. . . ," his humility was to be tested one last time by swollen limbs and diarrhea, by breaking of ulcers in his lungs and coughing up mouthfuls of pus, by alternately clear and distempered mind. Learning that it was "another thing to die than people imagined," he struggled not to dishonor God with impatience for an end to his suffering, till finally he expired on October 9, 1747, in his thirtieth year.[3]

That Jonathan Edwards edited and commended Brainerd's *Diary* as an example of piety and later sent his ten-year-old son, Jonathan Jr., to live among the Oneidas more than a hundred miles from the nearest English settlement in preparation for a career as a missionary, ought to shock us out of the commonly held idea that the great theologian somehow expressed the mood of our time better than his own. To what is sometimes called the modern, secular sensibility Brainerd's piety seems a horrifying, medieval fanaticism. Brainerd and Edwards were puritanical in the extreme. They longed for a death of the self, which Brainerd pursued literally and Edwards described almost poetically in his "Personal Narrative": "The person of Christ appeared ineffably excellent, with an excellency great enough to swallow up all thought and conception. . . . I felt withal, an ardency of soul to be what I know not otherwise how to express, than to be emptied and annihilated; to lie in the dust, and to be full of Christ alone . . ."[4]

Edwards seems not to have had much aptitude for personal, pastoral relations, but he was an effective preacher and revivalist who understood from experiences like Brainerd's and his own that for doubting sinners in search of Christ, "nothing is more necessary . . . than thorough conviction and humiliation; than that their consciences should be convinced of their real guilt and sinfulness." He devoted his greatest gift, his formidable intelligence, to defending humiliation and saving grace as necessary and authentic experiences in Christian life. Yet even on this level of theological and psychological theory, Edwards seems naive as to the conflicting impulses and tangled motivations of human beings, especially in his insistence that the cause of every human action is a conscious idea describable in a single phrase—the greatest apparent good. Paul Ramsey, in his introduction to the Yale edition of *Freedom of Will*, notes that John Locke's *Essay on Human Understanding* was not as monolithic, and asks whether Edwards does not adopt "a too extreme conception of the unity of human powers." Measured against the standards of both earlier and later eras, Edwards seems simplistic. There is little in his writings comparable to either the seventeenth century fondness for quoting Medea's lament—"I see and approve the better course; I follow the worse"—or the widely shared twentieth century view that the human self contains and is moved by unconscious as well as conscious mental processes.[5]

According to the once standard but now increasingly discredited story, Edwards followed Locke in rebelling against the convolutions of scholastic faculty psychology, and argued instead for a unitary view of the mind so modern that "it would have taken him about an hour's reading in William James, and two hours in Freud, to catch up completely." But as Daniel Walker Howe, for one, has pointed out in his writings on Whigs and Unitarians, faculty psychology was propounded well into the nineteenth century, and by many thinkers more secular and "modern" than Edwards. Moreover, as Norman Fiering has shown in his books on Edwards and on Harvard moral philosophy, Edwards, like Locke, was not in rebellion against faculty psychology, but only against hypostatization of faculties, the assumption that faculties were distinct entities rather than different abilities or functions of a unitary mind.[6] Neither he nor Locke was breaking new ground here; some medieval thinkers had argued the same thing. Nevertheless it is true, as Professor Ramsey says, that as compared with earlier writers, Edwards was singularly monolithic in his interpretation of human motivation, and what I have to add to the revision of the conventional account is that it was the hypostatizers of faculties, not Edwards, who would have been able easily to catch up with Freud.

The singularly little recognized fact in discussions of Edwards's religious psychology is that he was as far removed from the psychology of our time as from that of the Middle Ages. For in the last hundred years the sciences of the mind have taken a view of the psyche that is anything but unitary. Moderen linguistics, artificial intelligence theory, and experimental psychology all divide rather than unify the mind by exploiting the overarching psychological orthodoxy of the twentieth century, the view that the mind is capable of unconscious as well as conscious thought. The fundamental basis of this view is the same as the basis of the medieval hypostatization of faculties; it is the fact that human beings experience psychological conflict which they would not experience if the conscious mind alone or, as the schoolmen put it in a not quite parallel word, the understanding alone were in control of our thoughts and feelings. Our modern scientific and secularized discipline of psychology had taken incipient shape by 1896, when Charles Sanders Peirce, New England's acutest intellect in the nineteenth century just as Edwards had been in the eighteenth, pronounced that a unitary view of the person was a mere *a priori* "dictum of the old psychology which identified the soul with the ego, declared its absolute simplicity, and held that the faculties were mere names for logical divisions of human activity. This was all unadulterated fancy. The observation of facts has now taught us that the ego is a mere wave in the soul, a superficial and small feature, that the soul may contain several personalities and is as complex as the brain itself, and that the faculties, while not exactly definable and not absolutely fixed, are as real as the different convolutions of the cortex."[7]

Edwards, however, maintained a unitary view of the mind that not only dissented from the view that faculties were real entities but implicitly agreed with John Locke's rejection of the Cartesian notion of unconscious mental activity, the notion that "Man thinks always, but is not always conscious of it."[8] Edwards's idealist metaphysics constituted the entire universe in consciousness, which left no possibility of unconscious mental phenomena. Edwards's narrow, monolithic view of human motivation was therefore due at least in part to his idealist metaphysics, which he had adopted for the purpose of defending traditional religion against Locke's psychological empiricism. The successors of Edwards treated in this essay were unaware of his idealist metaphysics, and they consequently accepted both hypostatized faculties and psychological empiricism. Just as Edwards had foreseen, these theories proved incompatible with Calvinist fundamentalism. The unsuccessful attempt to make them compatible with Calvinism carried Edwards's successors instead toward the modern view of the mind as divided between conscious and unconscious phenomena.

Edwards was a fundamentalist in the sense that he believed in the literal truth of the Puritan teaching that genuine religious experience was due to an influx of the Holy Spirit into the human soul. In Edwards's time this doctrine was implicitly challenged by "the way of ideas," the seventeenth century view that though the universe is composed of two basic substances—matter and mind (or spirit)—we do not perceive those substances themselves but only the ideas they produce in us, either by bodily sensation or mental reflection. Locke, for instance, believed that the way of ideas invalidated Antinomian claims of direct intercourse with the Almighty—a divinely inspired vision or message, say, that Christ died for our sins. Even if the message was true, that did not prove that its appearance in the enthusiast's mind was owing to divine inspiration, for the enthusiast had empirical knowledge only of the idea or message, not of the substance that caused it: "These men have, they say, clear light, and they see; they have an awaken'd sense, and they feel: This cannot, they are sure, be disputed them. For when a man says he sees or he feels, no body can deny it him, that he does so. But here let me ask: This seeing is it the perception of the truth of the proposition, or of this, that it is a revelation from God? . . . These are two very different perceptions. . . ."[9] Orthodox Puritans were not enthusiasts and did not usually claim to have received explicit messages from God, but they did believe that they had direct experience in their souls of the saving presence of the Holy Ghost. This belief, as well as Antinomianism, was put on trial by Locke's implication that we have no empirically verifiable knowledge of anything divine.

Thanks to recent scholarship, especially that of Norman Fiering and the late Wallace Anderson, the myth that Edwards was a more or less unquestioning disciple of Locke has been discredited. It is now possible to see that Edwards was an opponent of Lockean empiricism, which he believed to be a threat to traditional religion at many points. For instance, Locke's notion that a person is constituted by continuity of consciousness, by remembered ideas of past experience, was a profound threat to the doctrine of original sin, for it implied that Adam's descendants, having no memory of his iniquity, bore no personal responsibility for it. Similarly, Locke's belief that all knowledge originates in simple ideas resulting from the experience of the five external senses threatened orthodox doctrines of predestination, efficacious grace, and the need of a "physical operation of the Spirit of God on the will, to change and determine that to a good choice." For if all mental activity originates with the external senses, then the difference between virtue and sin does not lie in any predetermined quality of soul but only in the degree of attendance to one's ideas, which if sufficiently assiduous ought "infallibly to attain the end." The belief that men could freely choose to be or not to be sufficiently assiduous was the basis of the notion that human willing is self-determined. Edwards maintained that belief in self-determination both characterized Arminianism and obstructed the work of the Calvinist ministry in bringing sinners to Christ. As Edwards knew from his own experience of self-abnegation and had tried to teach in his editing of Brainerd's *Diary*, "Nothing is more necessary for men, in such circumstances, than thorough conviction and humiliation," a sense of guilt and inability to redeem oneself, so that the sinner will turn to God. But in the Arminian scheme, "truly, man is not dependent on God."[10]

Edwards's strategy in attacking Arminianism was to try to locate the moral evil of human beings not merely in the quality of their actions but also "in that great and important truth, that *a bad will, or an evil disposition of heart, itself, is wickedness.*"[11] But a convincing demonstration that *all* men were sinful in "nature and essence" could hardly rest on the belief that the human mind begins as a blank slate whose subsequent knowledge is determined by the mere happenstance of whatever ideas it encounters in the natural world. The orthodox doctrine of a merciful, saving change of human nature requires some supernatural influx, rather than a chance encounter between the right ideas and a man willing to attend to them. Edwards meant to establish God's arbitrary control of, sovereignty over, and predestined determination of human affairs by a metaphysical system showing that human knowledge need not be based only on ideas acquired through the five external senses.

Edwards's metaphysics, like the Lockean empiricism he attacked, depended on the way of ideas. The universe must have come from something rather than nothing, he said, for the human mind cannot possibly possess an idea of nothing. An idea was, in Locke's phrase, "an object of the understanding," and an object must be something rather than nothing. "Nothing" is a concept of which we possess only what Edwards elsewhere called "speculative knowledge"—knowledge which is merely represented in the mind by a word or symbol but which does not itself exist in the mind as an "idea," an image or object of consciousness. A chair, for instance, can be represented in our minds by either an idea (image) of a chair or the mere verbal symbol "chair." The latter is mere speculative knowledge. So is the concept of "nothing," and unlike "chair" it can never be anything but speculative knowledge, for an experience must be an experience of something rather than nothing. Hence, if we base our opinions on ideas (images) we can actually experience in our minds, we must believe that something has always existed. Moreover, it is impossible for us to imagine that anything could exist without there being an idea of it in some consciousness somewhere. For when we try to imagine that unidealized something there is inevitably an idea of it in *our* minds. Again then, if we base our opinions on imaginable ideas, we must believe every object to be continually present as an idea in some consciousness. And since objects, say a table and chairs "in a room shut up," are not always present in human consciousness they must depend on idealization by the eternal being, who therefore obviously has a mind, obviously is a spiritual being. If the existence of any object depends on its being present in the consciousness of God, then there is no need for concepts of substance, either material or spiritual, to uphold the properties of either bodies or minds. Rather, the entire universe, including human beings, is constituted of ideas in the mind of God.[12]

Described thus crudely, Edwards's idealist metaphysics is easily recognized and well known, but it has not, I think, been well enough understood how basic it was to his defense of Calvinist piety. To reject any concept of either material or spiritual substance and then to constitute the universe of nothing but the consciousness of God was to leave no room for doubt of His absolute sovereignty and the utter dependence of human beings upon Him. A peculiar phrase in Edwards's "Personal Narrative" suggests that he viewed his idealist metaphysics as the essential expression of his personal piety. He does not merely say that during his mystical experience the person of Christ appeared "ineffably excellent," but adds that His was "an excellency great enough to swallow up all thought and conception, all ideas." Indeed, it is possible that Edwards was stating, however obliquely, that his 1737 spiritual paroxysm, when he was thirty-four years old, was touched off by his idealist philosophizing, touched off by, for him, an unprecedented "ideal apprehension" of the way in which his metaphysics established the absolute sovereignty of God. Wallace Anderson, reporting the findings of Thomas Schaefer, has told us that, contrary to the popular myth established by Sereno Dwight, Edwards's metaphysical speculation was not reserved to his teenage years but continued down to his last decade, the 1750s.[13]

While conjectures alone are possible about the relation between Edwards's philosophizing and personal piety, a much stronger case can be made for a relation between his metaphysical speculation and his defenses of specific orthodox doctrines. The fact that Edwards worked on his metaphysics in the 1740s and 50s supports the possibility of this connection between his philosophy and his theology, for that was the period when he produced the works on which his reputation as a major theologian principally rests—*Religious Affections*, Brainerd's *Diary*, *Freedom of Will*, *The Nature of True Virtue*, *The End for which God Created the World*, and *Original Sin*. Wallace Anderson has suggested that Edwards's defense of the doctrine of original sin depended to a significant degree on his metaphysics, and I have tried to show elsewhere that idealism was also the basis of "the new spiritual sense" of which Edwards wrote in *Religious Affections*. His insistence that the universe is composed of ideas meant that the seeming order of the natural world, including the apparent relation of sensory organs and simple ideas, did not depend on material substance but was only God's "stated order" for immediately raising ideas in our minds. Therefore the spiritual experience of a saint was connected to his mind in exactly the same way as was the experience of the five bodily senses—by divine constitution.[14]

Similarly, Edwards's treatise on the will, which attacked the Arminianism he viewed as the largest threat to the practical work of the Calvinist ministry in bringing sinners to God, rested to a large extent on his idealist metaphysics. It is well known that the principal device by which Edwards refuted the concept of the self-determining will was the infinite regression: "If there be an act of the will in determining all its own free acts, then one free act of the will is determined by another; and so we have the absurdity of every free act, even the very first, determined by a foregoing free act."[15] This and a great many other reductions to the absurd in *Freedom of Will* are simply extended elaborations of the principle of cause and effect, supported by Edwards's distinction between "ideal apprehension," or an image, on the one hand and "speculative knowledge" on the other. That is, we can always form an idea or image of one event, a "cause," and then an image of a subsequent event, an "effect." But to achieve ideal apprehension of the notion that an effect can be uncaused, we would have to imagine an idea of an event preceded by an idea of nothing, and Edwards had shown that the mind cannot possess an image of nothing. Hence he stated in "The Mind" that the notion that every event has a cause is an "innate principle" of human thought and in *Freedom of Will* called it a "grand principle of common sense." The distinction between ideal apprehension and speculative knowledge also underlay his appeals to "intuitive evidence" and the "natural sense of our minds," as well as his insistence that the Arminian notion of action could not "be conceived of" and "is something of which there is no idea." Of course the Arminians did have, in the speculative sense, a concept of action, but the concept could not be apprehended ideally, could not be made an image in the mind. For the *first* act of the will to be determined by a previous act of will was self-contradictory, and "No such notions as imply self-contradiction . . . can exist in the mind."[16] We cannot both have an idea or image of a thing and not have an image of it; we either do or do not.

Edwards's literary strategy in *Freedom of Will* drew on and supported his insistence that the test of the truth and existence of any notion is our ability to image it in our minds. Although the even now fairly awesome power of abstract reasoning displayed in Edwards's tract has been the subject of most commentary, he also supported his argument with numerous and vivid images. Thus he defended the distinction between natural and moral necessity—between physical coercion and psychological determinism— by citing the case of two traitors promised forgiveness by their prince if only they would come kneel to him. Was there not a great difference between on the one hand a subject eager to do so but prevented by natural necessity, "by strong walls, with gates of brass, and bars of iron," and on the other hand an unshackled man prevented from kneeling to his sovereign only by moral inability, by being "stout and stomachful, and full of haughty malignity?" Of the supposed indignity of psychological determinism, which Arminians said made human beings mere machines, Edwards replied that in the world of blind contingence implied by Arminian theory men would be "as the smoke that is driven by the wind!" Balance scales, drunkards, and drowning men are a few of the other images Edwards used to make his ideas clear, but his deservedly best-known figure is the one by which he showed that the contradictions in the notion of a self-determining will actually do prevent "ideal apprehension" of it. This was the hypothetical report by a "learned philosopher" of a beast in Tierra del Fuego, "that begat and brought forth itself, and yet had a sire and a dam distinct from itself; . . . that when he moved, he always took a step before the first step; that he went with his head first, and yet always went tail foremost; and this, though he had neither head nor tail." Even if the philosopher called the beast "by a certain name," that fact would indicate only speculative knowledge rather than ideal apprehension, so "it would be no impudence at all, to tell such a traveler, though a learned man, that he himself had no notion or idea of such an animal as he gave an account of, and never had, nor ever would have."[17]

Commentators seem generally to agree that Edwards's treatise *Original Sin* was not up to the level of *Freedom of Will*, and it is true that Edwards was not able to defend the doctrine of original sin with the same apparent ease as he did moral determinism. Part of the problem was that the distinction between speculative knowledge and ideal apprehension could not be invoked in defense of original sin as easily as in the case of divine determinism. The mind may not be able to possess an image of "nothing" as the cause of an effect, but it can conceive of a soul innately good just as easily as of a soul innately evil, for any concept of soul, Edwards held, is nothing but speculative knowledge; we expeience the soul's ideas, not the soul itself. An additional problem was that both Edwards's unpublished metaphysics and the published logic of determinism by which he hemmed in human action in *Freedom of Will* led straight back to God as the author of sin. He tried unsuccessfully to wriggle out of the consequences of his absolute determinism with a privative theory of sin, namely that God's only act in the chain of events leading inevitably to the Fall was to deprive Adam of the principle of virtue, so that he, not God, took the positive action whereby sin came into the world. Even so,

God initiated this series of events while foreseeing it would result in human iniquity, and liberals would therefore respond by asking, as James Dana did in 1770, if Edwards's doctrine did not contain the monstrously "plain consequence" that "God stands chargeable with doing wickedly?"[18] If Edwards had been alive to answer Dana he could have effectively used the same *tut quoque* with which he had answered earlier liberals: since the Arminians claimed to believe that God was, if not all determining, at least omnipotent, it was as wrong of Him in their scheme to *permit* men to sin as it was in the Calvinist scheme to *determine* it.[19] But Edwards might have done still better with a straightforward admission that God was the creator of sin. It would not have been popular, but it would have drawn the line between a Calvinism that faced up to all the consquences of its doctrines and an Arminianism that did not. And it would have been consistent with his metaphysical idealism, which constituted the entire universe, including sin, in the mind of God.

He made more effective use of his metaphysics in defending the justice of God's imputing Adam's guilt to his offspring. In the privacy of his notes on "The Mind," Edwards had rejected Locke's view that personal identity rests on continuity of ideas, for God might annihilate me, subsequently creating a new being with the same ideas as mine, "and yet I be in no way concerned in it, having no reason to fear what that being shall suffer, or to hope for what he shall enjoy." Edwards therefore asserted in *Original Sin* what must have seemed a mere *ex cathedra* statement to friend and foe alike, but in fact rested on his metaphysics: identity depends on nothing but *"God's sovereign constitution."* The identity of a human being as a person or individual was therefore not necessarily exclusive of other identities: "There are various kinds of identity."[20] Despite men's subjective experience of personal identity they may also share an unperceived moral identity with Adam, for no other reason than that God, whose mind constitutes the universe, so perceives the matter. Since in Edwards's metaphysics people did not have a substantial personal identity but were constituted in the mind of God, the question of justice did not apply to relations between God and man any more than to relations between men and their thoughts, fantasies, and dreams. But Edwards's successors, knowing nothing of his idealist metaphysics, assumed that each human being is constituted of some substance that gives him or her an identity distinct from that of other men and also of God. Therefore they believed the question of justice applied to the God-man relationship.

Calvinist piety suffered greatly by Edwards's early death and consequent failure to write his planned treatise on the mind, which would have made clear that his defense of orthodox doctrines depended largely on his idealist metaphysics.[21] Prominent heirs of Edwards in the late eighteenth and nineteenth centuries, such as Samuel Hopkins, Nathaniel Emmons, Asa Burton, Timothy Dwight, Nathaniel William Taylor, and Lyman Beecher, unwittingly played into enemy hands by accepting the Lockean notion of the soul as a substance formed by experience. These men represent only one strand (or a few strands) of post-Edwardsian thought, and one can find numerous more rigidly orthodox figures. However, the ones I treat briefly below conceived of themselves as, and were admitted by many others to be, the mainstream defenders of New England Calvinism in the century after Edwards, perhaps mainly because like him they tried to reconcile Calvinism to modern thought in general and psychological theory in particular. But since "The Mind" was not published until 1829, they knew nothing of Edwards's idealist metaphysics, at least during their most creative years. They were perforce driven by their belief that the soul was a substance to contradict almost all the major doctrines Edwards had defended.

Samuel Hopkins (1721–1803), pastor at worldly Newport and Edwards's theological heir apparent, was a gentle man of good causes who did not deserve his reputation as a harsh proponent of Calvinist dogma, for he attempted to make palatable to the post-Revolutionary generation men's infinite dependence on God by distinguishing between "regeneration" and "conversion." Regeneration was the silent unconscious transformation of the soul by the Holy Spirit, while conversion was the regenerate soul's subsequent effort to grow in grace. Anyone might be regenerate without knowing it, and therefore ought willingly to seek conversion. This was a clever—and among the theologians treated here, the last—attempt to encourage human activity while at the same time maintaining the position that men cannot help themselves. But Hopkins's position was tenable only if the soul could exist in a state of which it was not conscious, which in turn required that the soul be composed of something more than consciousness, be composed of some substance. That not even Hopkins knew of Edwards's disavowal of substance, either material or spiritual, indicates the extraordinary privacy in which Edwards had conducted his metaphysical speculation. As a young man Hopkins had studied for months with Edwards in Northampton, then was ordained in the rude Berkshire village of Housatonic, whose proximity to the Stockbridge mission where Edwards spent most of his last ten years gave Hopkins opportunity for frequent meetings with his mentor. Yet in 1770, long after Edwards first denied spiritual substance, Hopkins was nonplussed by "the *new* notion of no spiritual substance" (Hopkins's italics).[22] Hopkins could not refute the notion of no spiritual substance, since he agreed with Edwards that the saint has no direct knowledge of the soul; the ideas a saint has of holiness—such as new affections of the heart upon reading Scripture—are the consequence of a regenerate soul rather than the thing itself.

Hopkins's fundamentally Lockean position—namely that the mind is a substance but that men can have no direct knowledge of that substance—would result in the once famous, now largely forgotten, controversy between the "exercisers" and the "tasters." The exercisers would hold that in the absence of any empirical knowledge of human soul substance it was reasonable to hold God's immediate agency responsible for all of the soul's acts or "exercises," as they were called at the time, including sin. This was a strong view of the Creator, but it was also rigorously Calvinist. The tasters, on the other hand, would attempt to use a substantial view of the soul to create a human identity distinct from the immediate agency of God and thus relieve Him of responsibility for sin. Human behavior, they would assert, is based on a substantial bias, "disposition," or "taste of the heart" existing in the soul prior to even its first actions in infancy. Regeneration is then the acquisition of a new, holy taste resulting from a substantial or, as they often unphilosophically put it, a "physical" change in the soul. The controversy was only incipient in Hopkins's time, and properly fearful lest "the few Edwardsians should get into divisions among themselves," he attempted to straddle the fence. Basing human activity on a "taste," he also verged on Edwards's metaphysics by saying that "taste" might possibly "be resolved into divine [rather than substantial] constitution."[23] Nevertheless, the Edwardsians eventually became divided between "exercisers," who denied that regeneration was a substantial change of the soul, and "tasters," who affirmed it.

Foremost among the exercisers was the long-lived Nathanael Emmons (1745–1840), a country parson at Franklin, Massachusetts, renowned for his supposedly close reasoning and harsh doctrines. Among the few scholars now interested in Emmons it is customary to assert that his metaphysics resembled Edwards's. But the statement cannot stand; Emmons's *Works* contain almost no metaphysics, and he was an empiricist in the Lockean tradition. Emmons never offered any speculative system, substantial or ideal, remotely comparable in scope and sophistication to Edwards's articulation of the view that the universe is ideal and is constituted in the consciousness of God. Instead, Emmons found the question of "how God upholds us every moment" an ontological mystery which "we are utterly unable to explain." We are similarly ignorant of the constitution of the soul, for while consciousness tells us that the soul can perceive, reason, remember, and desire, "we can form no conception of the soul as distinct from these properties or as the foundation of them." Emmons therefore insisted that there was no empirical basis for the notion that the unregenerate soul is dominated from birth by a substantial taste for evil. Contrary to Edwards, he believed Calvinists ought to abandon the "absurd idea of imputed or derived depravity."[24]

Emmons's rejection of the doctrine of imputation amounted to an espousal of moral freedom, a position based also on his being one of the first of the many New England Calvinists who made an accommodation with what became known in the nineteenth century as "the evidence . . . of our consciousness" for moral freedom. The reasoning went that since introspection offers us our only truly empirical data on the mind, we must be as free as we feel, and since we feel free in our willing choices, we must indeed be morally free, despite Edwards's ingenious reasonings to the contrary. (This argument was answered satisfactorily but with little influence, first by Stephen West, Edwards's successor at the Stockbridge mission, and then by Jonathan Edwards, Jr., both of whom pointed out that we can be conscious of feeling free, but not of being free. Since by Locke's definition consciousness is constituted of ideas which are positive existents in the mind, said Edwards junior, "It is impossible for a man to be conscious of a negative, "impossible to be conscious" that our volitions are not the effect of an extrinsic cause.") Emmons unsuccessfully attempted to reconcile his belief in moral freedom with a properly Calvinistic insistence on predetermination by asserting that men can be morally free at the same time they are morally determined. In support of this preposterous notion he cited "distinct faculties of the mind." One faculty—"reason"—teaches us, as Edwards had done with powerful ratiocination in *Freedom of Will*, of the moral necessity under which our every thought and motion occurs. But the faculty of "common sense," or consciousness, intuits our moral freedom. By consulting these two different faculties we "discover the consistency between activity and dependence."[25]

The tasters, too, tendentiously adjusted faculty psychology to support the argument for human moral freedom. But they saw the logical impossibility of Emmons's attempt to reconcile human moral freedom with a universe where everything is determined by God's immediate agency. The tasters held instead that while man's faculties of understanding and willing give him moral freedom, he is simultaneously and inevitably depraved owing to the domination of the will by evil desires originating in a third faculty of "taste," or "heart." The best known proponent of this third faculty was a Vermont preacher named Asa Burton (1752–1836), whose *Essay on Some of the First Principles of Metaphysicks, Ethicks, and Theology* (1824), now forgotten by all save a handful of scholars, was considered by many divines, down to the end of the nineteenth century, to be "one of the great influential philosophical books of the world." The grandeur of Burton's system lay, as he succinctly stated in his autobiography, in the empirical observation that the "first principles" known to consciousness are pleasure and pain, from which he concluded that there "is a feeling faculty in the mind, and we can trace actions back no further." The reason these rather ordinary observations seemed profound to many New England divines was that by rooting willing in a still deeper aspect of human nature, the heart or taste or feeling faculty, Burton, more explicitly than any New Englander before him, offered a way to avoid the exercisers' implication that sinful volitions result from "the immediate agency of God."[26] And the orthodoxy of this solution to the question of divine justice seemed validated by the fact that Edwards himself often used the words "taste" and "heart" as names for the underlying disposition that determines the soul's action in willing. But in Edwards's system such terms as "taste," "heart," and "disposition" described the regular pattern of God's immediate operations in the human soul, rather than a substantial bias of it. And in any case Burton had hardly solved the problem of divine justice; it was as malicious of God to punish men for sin determined by His creating them with a blighted taste as to punish them for sin determined by his creating them with a blighted will.

Some tasters, among them Timothy Dwight (1758–1817), grandson of Edwards and president of Yale, saw that Burton's predetermined taste could not satisfy those who objected to a necessitated will. Like Burton, Dwight knew nothing of Edwards's idealist metaphysics and was committed to a substantial bias or taste of the soul as the basis of willful action. And like Hopkins and Emmons, Dwight believed that a consciousness consisting of Lockean ideas could possess no knowledge of soul substance. But in the absence of any experiential knowledge of spiritual substance, it was only fair, Dwight said, to presume God innocent of any responsibility for human sin. The fact of the existence of sinful ideas gave no clue as to the nature of the substance that produced them enabled Dwight to leave open the possibility that men form their own tastes or hearts, while refusing as a scrupulous "Calvinist" to affirm that they do. A "new heart" is only a name for an unknown cause of the habit of virtue, and Dwight was happy to be "ignorant" of the "metaphysical nature of this cause." Who is to say that the Holy Spirit does not regenerate the heart through second causes, including perhaps even—

contrary to Edwards and Hopkins—the sinner's self-interested efforts? Moreover, it may once have worked the other way round, with Adam's originally holy heart degenerating by second causes within the soul. In Adam's case, his "holy heart" was an unknown cause of hitherto virtuous volitions, with no guarantee that it would be equal to every future temptation, no matter how strong. Unequal to the apple, Adam fell from grace of his own Accord, not God's, and launched himself on a course of action that ruined his heart.[27] What Dwight had not done, however, was to relieve God of responsibility for giving Adam a heart insufficiently holy to resist all temptation.

Heir to this difficult problem was Nathanael W. Taylor (1786–1858), a student of Dwight's who became Yale's most prominent theologian in the 1820s. Taylor rejected the distinction between natural and moral necessity, telling his Yale students that "Edwards's mind was all confusion on the subject."[28] Edwards had written that the mind could not respond any differently than it actually did to the influences at work on it. But Taylor believed that men "have power of choice . . . [despite] every possible influence to prevent such choice." Wishing like Dwight and the others to remain in the Reformed tradition, Taylor tried to reconcile this assertion of moral freedom with divine determinism in his famous formulation that human action is characterized by "certainty," with "power to the contrary." When more orthodox Calvinists like Bennett Tyler objected sensibly enough that God could not possibly possess certain foreknowledge if men have genuine power to the contrary, Taylor humbly relied on men's lack of empirical knowledge as regards God's operations: "what if we cannot see *how* . . . ? Does this *prove* that he cannot do it?[29] Taylor's system implied an answer to the question that Dwight had left unanswered—why had God not given Adam a heart sufficiently holy to resist all temptation? God *had* given Adam a heart that could have avoided sin, for like all men Adam had power to the contrary. This amounted to the assertion that, at least as regards depravity, men form their own hearts, and are therefore self-determining.

Attempting to deal with Edwards's argument against self-determination—the impossibility of the soul's *first* choice being determined by a prior choice of the soul, Taylor resorted to circular reasoning but also arrived at a more complex view of the mind than Edwards's. Sin results from an original, amoral principle of self-love in the soul that "prompts to the choice [of sin] (not determines it)." That is, self-love moves the soul to action, but the soul then willfully chooses sin without reference to any heart bias. From then on, however, the heart has a sinful bias or taste, a "selfish principle" which determines subsequent willing choices, always sinful unless the selfish principle somehow loses control of the soul. Of this there is hope, for the same process of free choice which resulted in the soul's evil taste may "lead to a *change* of this preference." Since the formation of a holy taste, like the initial adoption of a sinful one, results from an act of choice, a soul in the process of regeneration must again compare God and mammon as potential sources of happiness. Despite his evil taste, the sinner may truly consider God as a possible source of happiness, because self-love, or the heart's original, amoral desire for happiness has not been totally extinguished. A candle which will "thrill in the secret chambers of the soul" of the worst sinner, self-love may awaken and suspend the evil taste or disposition. This is possible because "the mind is capable of opposite *tendencies* at the same time" [Taylor's italics].[30]

Taylor's argument was inelegant, but it was also a considerably more complex view of human motivation than Edwards's. The possibility of two conflicting tendencies or dispositions existing simultaneously in the soul was the advantage of a soul constituted of spiritual substance, rather than mere consciousness. A soul consisting, like Edwards's, of nothing but consciousness could not possess two tendencies or dispositions, for the conscious activity of an evil taste in us would preclude the existence of any other principle, either moral or holy. But a soul constituted substantially could contain a struggle between conscious and unconscious principles, since their existence would depend on an unperceived substance, rather than consciousness. Responsibility for sin then rested with man, who freely created his sinful disposition or taste, and whose free choice of holiness was necessary before the Holy Ghost would ensure its triumph in the soul. Taylor's assertion of the soul's moral self-sufficiency depended on his abandoning Edwards's monolithic view of the mind and fracturing the human self into two tendencies.

The impact of these theological developments on the practical work of the ministry is well illustrated by the great evangelist Lyman Beecher, Taylor's close friend. Beecher was a practical worker, a harvester of souls in the fields of the Lord, and his infrequent attempts at critical thought reveal a narrow, poorly trained mind. Missing, for example, the whole point of the revolt by Edwards, Locke, and others against treating psychological faculties as more or less independent entities, he argued that "If language has any meaning, a free will is a will which is free." Incapable of genuinely participating in theological developments, Beecher nevertheless kept superficially abreast of them and was in the mainstream of New England "Calvinism" when he repudiated Edwards's teachings, not only on free will but also on original sin and the moral accountability of infants. A man of action rather than a speculative thinker, Beecher conducted from 1826 to 1832 the largest revival in Boston since the Great Awakening. That he did not urge on his converts a traditional humbling of the soul is suggested by his belief that such teachings had not only hindered his own conversion but in other cases caused mental illness: "For cases like mine, Brainerd's Life is a most undesirable thing. It gave me a tinge for years. So Edwards on the Affections—a most overwhelming thing, and to common minds the most entangling. The impressions left by such books were not spiritual, but a state of permanent hypochondria—the horrors of a mind without guidance, motive, or ability to do any thing. They are a bad generation of books on the whole." Practicing a "clinical theology" based on insistence on a mild degree of moral ability in the sinner and a refusal to push troubled souls into total abjection, Beecher insisted that religious experience ought not to be confused with nervous depressions. For the unduly distressed he prescribed, according to his daughter Harriet Beecher Stowe, a week or two "of almost entire cessation from all religious offices, with a course of gentle muscular exercise and diversion." All this was combined with a shrewd debating talent that enabled him to take advantage of Taylor's division of the substantial soul into conscious and unconscious elements. When his unregenerate daughter, Catharine, conscious of no willful aversion to God, protested the injustice of her supposed depravity, Lyman nevertheless found her culpable, for "It is a common thing for men to be actuated [activated] by motives . . . of whose existence they are unconscious."[31]

Beecher and Taylor, at the height of their careers in 1829, took no notice, at least in print, of the posthumous publication that year of Edwards's notes on "The Mind." Indeed, I have been unable to find even one contemporary suggestion of the way in which Edwards's theology was founded on his idealist metaphysics. Apparently Sereno Dwight's mistaken dating of "The Mind" prevented his contemporaries as well as later scholars from connecting Edwards's idealism to the great theological writings of his maturity. And Edwards's putative successors as defenders of Calvinism may simply not have been up to following the rigors of his thought. The most likely reason of all, however, for their failure to follow his idealism is that by 1829 they believed that reconciliation of divine sovereignty and human moral autonomy depended on viewing the mind as a substance divisible into conscious and unconscious elements. To say this, however, is to say they had lost the battle the moment it began, more than half a century earlier, when Calvinists engaged Arminians on enemy terrain, on the question of divine justice toward human beings whose identity was constituted of a distinct spiritual substance, rather than in the consciousness of God. It is an unanswerable, counterfactual question, whether Edwards's idealism, had it become known to his followers in his lifetime, could have proven as effective a defense of Calvinism as it was reasonable. But in the absence of a metaphysical defense of Calvinism of the kind that Edwards alone could have written, by the 1830s public opinion would not support punishment of the morally unable, as is suggested by changing views of criminal law.[32] If it was becoming debatable whether courts could justly punish people conscious of doing wrong but compelled to do so by mental derangement, then God surely could not justly punish violations of His law if He created men morally deranged. For Calvinists striving to maintain a popular following, the only possible response to this situation was acceptance of the notion of human moral freedom, with whatever gymnastics and legerdemain were needed to maintain that they were also defenders of the Calvinist doctrine of God's absolute sovereignty.

It is not clear how large or small an influence these successors of Edwards exerted, in their turn, on the development of modern psychology. New England was only one of a number of centers, including Paris and Vienna, where the modern science of the mind took shape by the end of the nineteenth century. Obviously, these latter places were not much affected by halfhearted attempts to maintain Calvinist dogma. But however distinct its culture, nineteenth century New England was a center of psychological exploration, and peculiar local circumstances inevitably contributed to the science of the mind as it developed there.

Seen in the long view, Edwards failed in his largest intellectual objective, his defense of fundamentalism, which was meant to place religious experience on the same metaphysical level as natural experience. Instead, he was known principally even to many Calvinists as a powerful and skillful debater who somehow bested the Arminians but whose complicated arguments for moral inability were controverted by the sheer empirical evidence of consciousness in favor of freedom. Flailing and groping rather blindly after Edwards, his successors attempted to defend traditional religion through a commitment to the time honored distinction he rejected, the distinction between soul and body, between mental and material substance. Beecher and Taylor hoped that the possibility of unconscious motivation by a substantial soul would offer a way to reconcile conscious feelings of freedom with orthodox statements of determinism. Their notion of unconscious motivation did indeed have determinist implications. But in the absence of any immediate dependence on God's agency it has become synonymous with the secular modernism Edwards would have abhorred.

Notes

1. Jonathan Edwards, *The Life of David Brainerd*, ed. Norman Pettit (New Haven, 1985), 105, 106, 138, 155; Brainerd, *Mirabilia Dei inter Indicos* (Philadelphia, 1746), 237.

2. Edwards, *Life of Brainerd*, 231.

3. Ibid., 445, 450, 476.

4. Samuel Hopkins, *Life of Edwards* (Northampton, 1804), 38. Patricia J. Tracy, *Jonathan Edwards, Pastor: Religion and Society in Eighteenth-Century Northampton* (New York, 1979), 59–60 questions the accuracy of Edwards's recollection of this religious experience, since his diary shows him subsequently struggling for spiritual comfort; but inner turmoil after conversion was a common occurrence and not grounds to question the genuineness of former religious experiences. Charles E. Hambrick-Stowe, *The Practice of Piety: Puritan Devotional Disciplines in Seventeenth-Century New England* (Chapel Hill, N.C. 1982), passim, and Patricia J. Caldwell, *The Puritan Conversion Narrative: The Beginnings of American Expression* (Cambridge, 1983), 163–66 have recently reminded us that the order of redemption, in which the soul's humiliation for sin preceded its salvation from sin, characterized spiritual life after conversion as well as before (cf. Michael McGiffert, "Introduction," Thomas Shepard, *God's Plot* [Amherst, 1972], 16–24). Whatever initial experiences regenerate Christians had of the saving work of the Spirit, they marked not the end but the beginning of a rigorous spiritual life, replete with defeats as well as victories.

5. Edwards, *Freedom of Will*, ed. Paul Ramsey (New Haven, 1957), 466, 52; on Medea's lament, see Norman Fiering, *Moral Philosophy at Seventeenth-Century Harvard: A Discipline in Transition* (Chapel Hill, N.C. 1981), 115.

6. Perry Miller, *Jonathan Edwards* (New York, 1949), 183; Howe, *The Political Culture of the American Whigs* (Chicago, 1979), passim; Howe, *The Unitarian Conscience: Harvard Moral Philosophy, 1805–1861* (Cambridge, 1970), passim; Fiering, *Moral Philosophy at Seventeenth-Century Harvard*, 106; *Jonathan Edwards's Moral Thought and Its British Context* (Chapel Hill, N.C. 1981), 262–71.

7. Charles Sanders Peirce, *Collected Papers*, ed. Charles Hartshorne and Paul Weiss (Cambridge, 1934), I, 46.

8. Locke, *An Essay Concerning Human Understanding*, ed. Peter H. Nidditch (Oxford, 1975), 115.

9. Ibid., 700–701.

10. Edwards, *Freedom of Will*, 220, 466, 469.

11. Ibid., 467.

12. Locke, *Essay*, 47; Edwards, "782. Ideas, Sense of the Heart, Spiritual

Knowledge or Conviction. Faith," ed. Perry Miller, *Harvard Theological Review*, 41 (April 1948) 129–45; Edwards, "Of Being," in his *Scientific and Philosophical Writings*, ed. Wallace E. Anderson (New Haven, 1980), 202–4. For a more detailed version of the argument of this paragraph, see my article, "Jonathan Edwards's Religious Psychology," *Journal of American History* 69 (March 1983), 852–54.

13. Anderson, "Introduction" to Edwards's *Scientific and Philosophical Writings*, 326–29.

14. Anderson, "Introduction," 87; Hoopes, "Jonathan Edwards's Religious Psychology," 859–60.

15. Edwards, *Freedom of Will*, 176.

16. Edwards, "The Mind," in his *Scientific and Philosophical Writings*, ed. Wallace E. Anderson, 370; *Freedom of Will*, 182, 169, 345, 429; cf. Edwards's appeals to "intuitive evidence" (182) and the "natural sense of our minds." (427)

The effective use Edwards was able to make of the "way of ideas" against the concept of a self-determining will may account for his somewhat disingenuous characterization of Arminianism as based on the concept of self-determination. As Conrad Wright, *The Beginnings of Unitarianism in America* (Boston: Starr King, 1955), 100–104 has shown, Arminians such as Daniel Whitby and Samuel Clarke admitted Edwards's distinction between natural freedom and moral determinism—that is, that free will consists in being free to *act* as one wills, but not in being free to will in any other way that one actually does. Their heterodoxy consisted of a rejection of innate depravity, rather than of moral determinism. Still, with a little more elaboration Edwards could have used his determinist argument against Whitby and Clarke, for it does not follow that "Moral necessity without total depravity loses all its sting" (Wright, 104). Or rather, the two cannot be so easily separated. In view of the fact that sin does exist, the doctrine of moral necessity supports the conclusion that depravity is the proximate cause of sin.

17. Edwards, *Freedom of Will*, 362, 273, 345–46.

18. Edwards, *Original Sin*, 381–84; Dana, *The "Examination of the Late Rev'd President Edwards' Enquiry on Freedom of Will" Continued* (Boston, 1770), 50.

19. Edwards, *Original Sin*, 384–87.

20. Edwards, "The Mind," 386; cf. Anderson, "Introduction," 87; Edwards, *Original Sin*, 404.

21. I refer here to Edwards's list of "Subjects to Be Handled in the Treatise on the Mind," which was bound with "The Mind" in his private notes. Norman Fiering, *Jonathan Edwards's Moral Thought*, 363, calls attention to this neglected document but states there "is no direct evidence for assuming that this book project was still an important part of Edwards's writing plans when he was stricken at the height of his powers at age fifty-four." Fiering, however, did not have available Schaefer's new information for dating Edwards's manuscripts, which shows Edwards to have worked on "The Mind" into the 1750s. (Anderson, 323–24) Since the list of topics for the proposed treatise seems to have been

developed as a result of Edwards's work on "The Mind," it is quite possible that the treatise was part of his writing plans in the 1750s and that had his life not been cut abruptly short by smallpox he would have written the book.

Had Edwards written the book it would have revealed to his followers that while the overriding purpose of his work in moral psychology was to defend traditional religion, his idealist metaphysics was the basis of that defense. In particular, in item 8 Edwards enjoined himself, when "treating of human nature," to "treat first of being in general, and show what is in human nature necessarily existing from the nature of entity." Item 14 promises a discussion of "speculative understanding and sense of heart"; item 15, an examination of the nature of reflexive ideas; and items 30 and 31, a discussion of the way in which sensation only seems to depend on the body.

22. Hopkins, *Works* (Boston, 1852), III, 545–46; I, 200.

23. Ibid., I, 200; III, 553.

24. Emmons, *Works*, ed. Jacob Ide (Boston, 1860), II, 411; I, 412; III, 123.

25. Thomas Upham, *Elements of Moral Philosophy* (Boston 1831), I, 43; Jonathan Edwards, *Works* (Andover, 1842), 423; Emmons, *Works*, II, 415.

26. Frank Hugh Foster, *A Genetic History of the New England Theology* (Chicago, 1907), 243; *The Life of Asa Burton Written by Himself* (Thetford, Vt.: First Congregational Church, 1973), 63; Burton, *Essay on Some of the First Principles of Metaphysicks, Ethicks, and Theology* (Portland, Me., 1824), 53–61.

27. Dwight, *Theology; Explained and Defended in a Series of Sermons* (Middletown, Conn.: 1818–19), III, 63; I, 546–47.

28. Quoted in Sidney Earl Mead, *Nathaniel William Taylor, 1786–1858: A Connecticut Liberal* (Chicago, 1942), 28.

29. Edwards, *Freedom of Will*, 188; Taylor, *Lectures on the Moral Government of God* (New York, 1859), I, 195, 307.

30. Taylor, "On the Means of Regeneration," *Quarterly Christian Spectator*, I (1829), 22, 21, 227.

31. Lyman Beecher, *Autobiography* (New York, 1864), I, 386, 47, 74, 75, 514.

32. Isaac Ray, *A Treatise on the Medical Jurisprudence of Insanity* (Boston, 1838), passim.

13

Jonathan Edwards as
a Figure in Literary History

DAVID LAURENCE

For students interested in the question of Jonathan Edwards and American literature, the effect of the papers collected in this volume may be to intensify a certain conscientious hesitancy. It would be a hard enough task to relate *one* Edwards to the American literary tradition, assuming for the moment what can by no means be regarded complacently as assured starting points, that American literature does in fact form a relatively unified tradition, and that we have sufficiently developed ideas about its order to know that Edwards belongs to it or has some importance for it. As these essays make abundantly evident, however, we have multiple Edwardses to contend with, along with their several scholarly audiences. Which Edwards are we to select? Is it the Christian rationalist who is to stand as a figure in American literature, or the thoroughly precritical biblical scholar? The evangelical preacher of the sermons, or the religious psychologist of the *Faithful Narrative* and the *Religious Affections*? The printed Edwards, or the manuscript Edwards? The Edwards who is wholly representative of Puritanism in New England, or Edwards the unique original? The proper name designates not a unified oeuvre but a heterogeneous collection of jottings, notebooks, sermons, and treatises—a tangled diversity about which we come to feel less than confident that it all springs from a single, self-identical center. Faced with this multiplicity of disparate Edwardses and the many difficulties surrounding the term "American literature," especially as it has been applied to the literature of Britain's North American colonies, a literary critic might be justified in feeling the subject has become unmanageable. Wittgenstein's severe monition comes disquietingly to mind: "Whereof one cannot speak, thereof one should be silent." The remarks offered here are, by necessity as by choice, playful and speculative. It will be possible to do little more than offer a preliminary examination of the problems that make a satisfactory assessment of Edwards's place in American literature so difficult to achieve.

Since I am entering a discussion where analogical thinking has had so prominent, indeed so notorious, a place, it will be not quite improper, if not quite proper either, to begin with a brief analogy. Even the most shrewdly observant of travelers might probe and poke about Seattle, Washington, for days or even weeks without suspecting the import Mt. Ranier has for the inhabitants of that city. Life in Seattle follows patterns that prevail in any contemporary American city, for reasons that a good empirical sociologist could tell us, I am sure. On certain clear days, however, especially after a lengthy stretch of lowering weather, Seattleites engage in an odd local ritual. The clouds lift; the great, snow-capped cone of the ancient volcano hovers above the city; and it becomes the custom of the day for people to say to one another, "The mountain's out." It is as if they were giving honorific acknowledgment to the bearing this massive and archaic feature of the terrain has upon them all, by whatever disguised means and secret or even occult influences.

The place of Jonathan Edwards in our histories of American literature is a little like that: he endures as a massive feature in the intellectual and cultural terrain, yet one that has long since ceased to be active or have any obvious role in the literary culture that flourishes after him in his vicinity. Edwards's image in literary history is ambivalent and even contradictory. He assumes the giant proportions of an archetype, only to be reduced to the large irrelevance of an archaism. Like Seattleites speaking of their mountain, critics are accustomed to speak honorifically of Edwards's importance in American literature—meaning, for all practical purposes, his importance in the largely New England portion of American literature canonized as the American Renaissance. In the words of Thomas H. Johnson, writing in the official academic guide to the subject, Edwards "remains an initial force in one cultural tradition [in American letters], through Emerson to the present."[1] Yet only infrequently do these New England writers—Harriet Beecher Stowe, for instance—invoke Edwards or his theological followers by name. Even in the case of Stowe it turns out to be far from easy to establish just how Edwards or the Edwardsian theology is of paramount importance for understanding what makes her work special from a literary point of view—the "New Englandness," say, or even the "Stoweness," of her way with the novel, insofar as these may be distinguishable from her subject matter or her ideas. Description of Edwards's bearing on this classic portion of American literature has very often the air of description of an occult influence. Invoking him seems a local ritual of literary inquiry in our vicinity, our way of saying, "The mountain's out."

The final sentences of Johnson's chapter on Edwards in *Literary History of the United States* may stand here as a fair example of the many discussions in which the canonical figures of nineteenth century American literature are called as witnesses for Edwards's continuing presence as a presiding force in the American literary universe. "The voice, through these many American years, is the voice of Hawthorne, and Melville, and Emerson, and Whitman, and Adams. But the hand is the hand of Jonathan Edwards."[2] These sentences, with their evocative image of the voice and the hand, imply a large, indeed an audacious claim—and one that has always baffled me. If I understand the image, it means that Edwards gives us access to the tacitly directing norm that governs this tradition of American literary imagination. It is as if the separate voices of these several nineteenth century American writers represented so many acts of ventriloquism and Jonathan Edwards stood as the Grand Ventriloquist. In coming to know his thought, we come to know also the secret principle according to which the diverse writers fall into line as individuals in an evolving native literary tradition.

It could be shown that discussion of Edwards's relation to American literature has almost without exception been conducted according to one or another version of the approach I have just sketched. And it could be shown also that efforts to understand Edwards's relation to American literature using this general approach have been uniformly unhappy. But I do not wish to engage here in a discussion of particular critical arguments. Rather I want to see if the roots of the unhappiness that has characterized the literary discussion of Edwards can be brought to light.

The relative barrenness of the literary discussion of Edwards is at bottom a theoretical matter. It is not the unclear ideas or muddled arguments of individuals that are ultimately at fault; it is, rather, the unclarified status of the concepts through which the problem is to be attacked. Chief among these concepts is the concept "literature" itself. Then there is the concept "American literature," whose status is, if anything, even more dubious. Reflection on Edwards as a figure in American literature lands us in the middle of some very perplexing general problems. What is "literature"? And what, within the domain of the term "literature" is the logical and historical extent of the term "American literature"? What, that is to say, are the rules for declaring a piece of writing "American literature," and over what chronology, what territory, and what types of writings are these rules understood to have pertinence? Is Edwards inside American literature or outside of it? Inside or outside "the literary" in general? These are questions that literary inquiry into Edwards continually raises but has yet to reflect on with sufficient thoroughness.

It is well to recall that the discussion of Edwards in relation to American literature may be said to have effectively begun with readers who were curious to explain how it was that not just Edwards but the whole of what they understood to comprise American literature lay outside of what could, for them, properly stand as literature. Nor perhaps to this day has study of American writing entirely shaken off the burden of this original judgment and the understanding that determined it. It is no very large exaggeration to say that the entire body of contemporary criticism of American literature has been an elaboration of and dispute with a paragraph of Van Wyck Brooks's in his seminal *America's Coming-of-Age* (1915):

> Something, in American literature, has always been wanting—everyone, I think, feels that. Aside from the question of talent, there is not, excepting Walt Whitman, one American writer who comes home to a modern American with that deep, moving, shaking impact of personality for which one turns to the abiding poets and writers of the world. A certain density, weight and richness, a certain poignancy, a "something far more deeply interfused," simply is not there.[3]

The critical problem, as Brooks understood it, was how to explain this all but universal failure. His judgment of the aberrancy or oddness of the literature, a judgment never itself subjected to a thoroughgoing critical examination, led him, as it has led numerous commentators since, out of the literature to observations about the problematic character of American culture and the American mind. In the face of what at least appeared to be a marked form, a special case, investigation undertook the classical project of determining the extrinsic ground, whether in society or in ideas or in the American situation, on the basis of which the peculiarities of the texts in question could be explained. There were the literature and its causes; the peculiarities internal to the literary artifacts were presumably results of historical actualities resident in an outside, a context. "I have been trying to show," Brooks remarked, "in what way a survey of American literature would inevitably lead to certain general facts about American life."[4] The fact behind all particular facts was what he called "the peculiar dualism that lies at the root of our national point of view," and this affliction of mind and mores, the underlying cause of the aesthetic blight, was directly a consequence of the curious development of Puritan intellectual and religious culture in the context of American experience. In Brooks's words:

> The experience of New England was an experience of two extremes—bare facts and metaphysics: the machinery of self-preservation and the mystery of life. Experience of the world, of society, of art, the genial middle ground of human tradition existed only as an appetite. Painting, sculpture, architecture were represented by engravings; history, travel, world-politics, great affairs in general were represented by books. The habit of looking at things in the abstract, native to the old Calvinist temper, was extended over the range of social and intellectual interests, partly as a result of isolation, partly because of the highly tenuous connection between these interests and the primitive actualities of life as New Englanders knew it.[5]

As a philosophy for the conditions of early American experience, Puritanism had been effective for survival; but the cost, humanly and aesthetically, had been the elevation of deprivation from a temporary evil into a permanent and intricately buttressed ethos. *America's Coming-of-Age* sustains its statement at the level of an extremely fruitful impressionism. Though Brooks does not descend to particulars, it is unmistakable that, as the most thoroughly developed expression of American Puritanism, Edwards's writings must have a key role in any more detailed tracing of this unhappy genetic chain. As Brooks saw it, the emergence of Puritanism as an entrenched indigenous mentality was largely responsible for making American literature what it was; and what it was—this is the point that especially needs reiteration—was only marginally Literature in the major, upper-case sense.

Of course, in the years since Brooks published *America's Coming-of-Age* in 1915, a revision amounting almost to a revolution in taste has occurred. No one now questions the profundity and imaginative vitality of the much-studied classic works and authors of the American Renaissance, and students of at least these American writings are no longer obliged to struggle against others' overt condescension or their own secret suspicions that the objects of their attention do not bear prolonged consideration as works of art. I look again to *Literary History of the United States* for an exemplary statement. This encyclopedic volume, first published in 1946 and reissued thrice since, sums up what surely stands as the mid-twentieth century critical consensus.

In quality of style, and particularly in depth of philosophic insight, American literature has not yet surpassed the collective achievement of Emerson, Thoreau, Hawthorne, Melville, and Whitman. Having freed itself in these writers from its earlier tendencies either blindly to imitate or blindly to reject European models, American literature here for the first time sloughed off provincialism, and, by being itself—by saying only what it wanted to say and as it wanted to say it—attained, paradoxically, the rank and quality of world literature, a literature authentic not only in America but everywhere the English tongue is understood.[6]

Literary understanding quite naturally gravitates toward this high tableland of universally acknowledged artistic accomplishment. One might expect that this critical consensus, having established a canon of American writing on high aesthetic ground, would have insisted also on establishing the discontinuities by which, as *Literary History of the United States* puts it in phrases we shall presently examine more closely, American literature "freed itself . . . from its earlier tendencies." The period, however, witnessed the most concerted attempts to understand the essential continuity of American literature from its colonial, and especially its Puritan, beginnings to this great artistic flowering in the middle of the nineteenth century. The genetic model Brooks had promulgated to account for the failure of American writing to attain "the rank and quality of world literature" is not dislodged but remains firmly in place as a framework controlling historical understanding. It becomes all but irresistible to conceive of the literary history as a gradual evolution directed toward this literary fulfillment. What Brooks had thought of as an unhappy genetic chain and narrative sequence by which like produces like, metamorphoses into an inverse image of itself and becomes a happy genetic chain and narrative sequence by which like produces unlike.

In the absence of any rigorous examination and clarification of the relevant concepts, a gratifying but fallacious historical model confines research to results attainable within its doctrine. According to this model, American literature forms a continuous series in which Puritanism and Edwards have importance by dint of their precedence in the genetic chain; yet American writing only becomes Literature with the nineteenth century flowers atop the long, prickly, and rarely blossoming stalk that stretches back through the colonial past.[7] Within the limits of this teleological ordering, Edwards must be situated outside the literary. He must belong more to the prehistory than to the history of American literature. It is important to see, however, that, as in Plato, to belong to the prehistory of something may be to assume a position of privilege and priority over it. (We shall return to this point later.)

But there was one further twist given to the image of the genetic chain and narrative sequence in which Edwards was to be situated. The meritorious splendor of the aesthetic end is said to overflow with such excess as to be accounted to the credit of its faltering beginnings. Edwards is swept into the palace of Literature on the coattails of his literary offspring. The way from the Puritans to American literature, from Edwards to the great figures of the American Renaissance, is once again a lineage within which like produces like.

In each of these, or at least the last two, alternative genetic schemes for understanding Edwards's place in American literature, there is a confused alternation between a historical and a more purely formal and linguistic conception of literature. The literary critic, who begins work by observing the linguistic medium, suddenly, and without anything like an adequate recognition of the shift that has occurred, renounces such observation. The critic turns away from language and begins to speak as if effects produced by and in language depended wholly on an ideal content (a truth descended from the native sky) or a truthfulness to common experience (a truth sprung out of the native earth). The strain this shift produces is evident in the sentence from *Literary History of the United States* quoted above. Aesthetic judgment feels that in the work of its great mid-nineteenth century writers American literature for the first time attains the universality of Literature. This achievement is understood to have come about by dint of a sudden accession of freedom from a blind concern with literary models, whether in an active (rejecting) or passive (imitating) form. A blinding concern with language is cast aside in favor of a commitment to a wholly indigenous message or idea. In the nineteenth century literary flowering, this idea receives full expression for the first time because it finally refuses to subordinate itself to literary models. The entire textual sequence had been moving grudgingly toward expressing this idea, but until now it had never been self-trusting enough to do so. It is as if in the writings of the American Renaissance a slowly gathering indigenous content suddenly became manly enough or mature enough to stand up for itself unabashedly. The imagery of growth to maturation is subtle but unmistakable. To repeat the key sentence: "Having freed itself in these writers from its earlier tendencies either blindly to imitate or blindly to reject European models, American literature here for the first time sloughed off provincialism, and, by being itself—by saying only what it wanted to say and as it wanted to say it—attained, paradoxically, the rank and quality of world literature, a literature authentic not only in America but everywhere the English tongue is understood." The necessity of paradoxical formulation should alert us that an effort is being made to harmonize antagonistic perspectives. It is not just that the nineteenth century writings are more literary, within the limits of a certain aesthetic judgment. They are also and simultaneously more American because they, and they alone, succeed in saying what American literature must say in order to be itself; in doing so these writings complete a developmental progression for which they are understood to be the destined end.[8]

Consideration of the problem of Edwards and American literature turns out to be especially pertinent now because of the way it highlights gestures that commentary has been accustomed to make in defining what American literature is and how its development ought to be understood. These gestures, in turn, exemplify general and very difficult problems of literary history—that is, the problems that arise for any attempt at understanding literary artifacts, or the developmental order of a lineage of such artifacts, in terms of broad collective causes like society or culture or a national mind. There is a tension or ambivalence in the very idea of literary history that appears incurable. Literary history is a project divided between an aesthetic and a historical perception of its subject matter, and its effort to amalgamate these two perspectives shows all the strain of an effort to harmonize a profound antagonism. On the one hand we have a sense of works of art as possessing the strange power to speak with a deep immediacy, to make us feel that what really matters about them is exactly their startling, unexpected contemporaneousness. Works of literary genius are rare and have special value precisely in the way they take hold of us quite apart from any thought for the low considerations of historical circumstance. Considered aesthetically, all literature can seem to exist as a simultaneous order, irrespective of time or place or person. To put it in Kantian terms, in literature, as in all works of artistic genius, the profound commonality of human nature discovers itself and speaks to human feeling.

There is something anomalous about this power: it taxes thought as an enigma *that should not be*. Genius exceeds credulity, a view ironically seconded by all skeptical accounts as it is cheerily proclaimed by all idealizing ones. "Of the best books," Emerson observes, "it is hardest to write the history. Those books which are for all time are written indifferently at any time. . . . And yet," Emerson continues, picking up the other end of the stick, "is literature in some sort a creature of time."[9] We are subject not only to aesthetic attractions but to a lively sense of the literary record as a temporal display that prompts awareness of far-reaching transformations of culture, revolutionary changes in sensibility, important alterations in moral life and in society. To the collection of concepts that have reference primarily to linguistic structures such as comedy, tragedy, satire, and the various poetic kinds (epic, lyric, and so forth)—we would add the temporal divisions of periodization.

Something in the very idea of periodization invites and even compels arrangement into narrative and genetic sequences that satisfy our sense of historical and also moral order. To return to the problem of Edwards, any judgment about Edwards's position in American literature will almost certainly reflect a prior and essentially moral decision about the relation between Christianity and culture. Edwards is bound to become a case study in the long-standing and continuing debate about the historical and moral relation of romantic and modern literature to the literature of the periods which preceded it. Is romanticism an aesthetic disaster or an aesthetic triumph? A deplorable falling away from or within literature, or a renewal of literature? A decisive breakthrough or a point of maximum delusion for Western culture? And do we think of Edwards as a powerful antidote to romanticism's moral decadence? As an early phase of its malady? As a first faint stirring of its salutary vitality? Or as an obstruction to its historical destiny?

Whichever alternative corresponds to one's predilection, aesthetic judgment is amalgamated to larger patterns of history and belief that are understood to govern the literary works in question and to explain the literary record as it presents itself to us or as we represent it to ourselves. Reflection is drawn away from the power of art and the enigmas understanding confronts in considering the force of writing. Interest now attaches to the texts in relation to the climates of opinion they introduce, the social or political attitudes they betray, the moral awareness or moral decadence they can be seen to embody and out of which they are presumed to spring. Literary history becomes hardly distinguishable from intellectual history or the history of society, of culture, or of belief. Instead of investigating the rhetorical constructions that underlie the force of any particular piece of writing, one turns to writing the intellectual and moral history of the society of which literature is the reflection—a procedure explicit in *The Cambridge History of American Literature* and in Vernon Parrington's *Main Currents of American Thought*. For the reconstruction of the conditions of thought, morals, and society necessary to uncovering the proper cultural sequences, no part of the textual field can fairly be excluded from a due consideration. The unnaturally restrictive definition of literature imposed by "the narrow field of *belles lettres*,"[10] as it is frequently, and disparagingly, referred to, is effectively circumvented. Circumvented also are the complex problems of the linguistic medium, especially the problem of art and what the enigma of feats of genius within the medium of language forces into view that might otherwise remain hidden.

The contest and confusion of these two antagonistic impulses in literary study (roughly, the formalistic and the historical) has marked the investigation of American literature from the start, at the very least from the representative, opposing studies of Moses Coit Tyler and Charles Richardson.[11] Indeed, the historical and genetic model for American literature has the authority of an imposing literary lineage of its own. *America's Coming-of-Age* almost certainly represents Brooks's interpretation of the famous paper his teacher George Santayana delivered at Berkeley in 1911, "The Genteel Tradition in American Philosophy."[12] In that paper Santayana had formulated in terms cognate to Brooks's an indigenous evolution from Calvinism to Transcendentalism to Pragmatism. Behind Brooks and Santayana was Henry James's important study of Hawthorne. And behind all of these were remarks of Hawthorne himself in *The Scarlet Letter*—in the opening scene, for example, where the narrator meditates rather gloomily on the contrast between the robust vigor of the lately transplanted "wives and maidens of old English birth and breeding" who populate his tale and the pale delicacy of "their fair descendants, separated from them by a series of six or seven generations." "Throughout that chain of ancestry every successive mother has transmitted to her child a fainter bloom, a more delicate and briefer beauty, and a slighter physical frame. . . ." A little further on he concludes: "The morning sun, therefore, shone on broad shoulders and well-developed busts and on round and ruddy cheeks that had ripened in the far-off island, and had hardly yet grown paler and thinner in the atmosphere of New England." In this ominous genetics Hawthorne conveyed the essentials of the genetic model of New England's cultural history that informs so many of our standard accounts.

The embarrassments endemic to this general model for American literature are not primarily a matter of better or worse readings of the texts in question. Brooks performed almost no textual analysis in *America's Coming-of-Age*, yet his slender book, almost a pamphlet, has had an immense importance. It had a great part in establishing the essential framework in which we still see American literature, a framework in which a preliminary characterization of the field as the late and largely New England result of a continuous and essentially indigenous development dominates research. Within this framework, the trajectory of literary-historical argument falls sooner or later into a circle: textual analysis yields a certain historical reference; this reference is then made to serve as the ground from which the literary work springs. A brilliant, highly compressed example occurs in James's remark about Hawthorne: "The cold, bright air of New England seems to blow through his pages, and these, in the opinion of many people, are the medium in which it is most agreeable to make the acquaintance of that tonic atmosphere."[13] The axiological shift codified in *Literary History of the United States* turns out to be superficial and unimportant in comparison with the persistence of a genetic model which conceives of American literature in terms of the purported influence (whether salutary or the reverse) of a rather meager set of supposedly endogenous factors, like Puritanism or the wilderness—that is, which conceives American literature as a unified, even monolithic entity, whose character, order, and import are to be comprehended not in linguistic terms but in terms of conditions subsumed under the category of reference, naively and uncritically understood.

If any complacency must be unsettled preliminary to an effective reconsideration Edwards's place in American literature, or indeed to a reconsideration of the history of American literature generally, it must surely be the one surrounding the seductive notion that the literary achievement of our mid-nineteenth century writers is a matter of the triumph of an indigenous content over language. It may be urged with at least equal justice that insofar as these writings speak to us with the deep immediacy and power or literary genius, this achievement occurs by dint of the authors' intense engagement with language and literature, and the extraordinary level of their commitment to the text *as text*. That Melville's *Moby Dick* affects literary sensibility as a work of greater aesthetic power than Edwards's *Freedom of the Will* is no sign that Melville gave fuller expression than Edwards did to what makes American literature American. *In principle*, there is no reason to think that Edwards's text might not be quite as revealing about the fate of writing in America as Melville's, however aesthetic sensibility feels about it. The aesthetic judgment that produces literary ranking and sets literature off as a distinct segment of the textual archive must not be permitted to slide into a judgment that imposes one privileged text or set of texts as somehow expressing the meaning of American experience more fully, or as texts in which American literature becomes more fully itself, that is, more fully American. The situation is one in which a rich diversity of phenomena must be encountered in all their diversity, without yielding to the ever-powerful attraction of premature, reductive generalization.

By the same token, a judgment that Edwards represents the high-water mark and fullest expression of philosophical and theological truth in American letters must not be permitted to develop in the direction of a historical ordering in which those who come after are like creatures in a subordinate realm. Here I return to Thomas H. Johnson's evocative image of the hand and the voice with which I began. Somehow as if under the direction of Edwards's influence or "hand," the pantheon of American writers strives to equal his genius. All, however, produce mere copies or literary expressions of Edwards's difficult Truth—or perhaps (what is only to be expected within the limits of their fallen and confused condition) sad confusions of it.

In each of these versions of literary history Edwards's historical and textual reality has to be circumvented in order to make him fit smoothly into a continuous literary genealogy. One posits a teleological relation of source and end in images of propagation, derivation, and linear development or decline. Edwards becomes a figure in a wholly rhetorical sense, a synecdoche through which the relation of part to whole can be amalgamated to the demands, and the illusions, of the genetic idea. But it may be asked whether the ever-elusive distinctiveness of (some sample of) American writing, or literary force in general, are qualities subject to historical ordering according to a model of growth and gradual evolution. There is poetic justice, and in an uncommonly proper sense, when a strategy that placidly understands itself to be following the plain path joining what lies outside the text to the text's interior inscribes its injudiciousness by exemplifying unconsciously the very possibility it leaves most out of account—that the reference laid claim to as prior exterior source is an image engendered by rhetoric. Edwards is not outside and *below* American literature, if in some obscure way helping to produce that which will later be important to the mature distinctiveness of its aesthetic genius. Nor is he outside and *above* American literature, the shining example of American philosophic and religious genius, to whose encompassing truth and depth of insight all who come after must be as if under its command. He is simply one American writer—maybe even simply one writer, period.

It may seem that I have conducted a merry chase through the thickets of some rather complicated theoretical reflection to arrive at so modest a conclusion. The results for our assessment of Edwards from a literary point of view, and for a historical understanding of American literature, are more substantial than this at first sight less than promising reduction might lead one to expect. A first lesson of the foregoing discussion is that confusion follows where the aesthetic dimension of literary experience is either ignored or privileged. Literary history must be engaged with literature in a literary way, and to be engaged with literature in a literary way is to be engaged thoughtfully with its aesthetic dimension and satisfactions. Yet critical rigor requires a will not to deceive oneself about what follows from the feeling that some writings speak with greater immediacy and powers than others, seem more telling or "greater" than others. Works of literary genius confront us—dazzlingly, blindingly—with the enigmatic powers of language. We inevitably, and legitimately, consider language as a medium for the expression of a truth external to itself; and we likewise consider it as denoting a historical reference. But literary genius displays something in addition to these considerations, something that unsettles the assurance sheltering the constative and denotative purposes of language use and that we are therefore only too inclined to overlook: language as a force of enchantment in its own right, *not* language as it is invested with power borrowed from truth or experience or the self.

This understanding—the essence of what I understand to be the literary point of view—is difficult and uncomfortable. Paul de Man observes that literary study itself frequently takes refuge from it in methodologies that attempt to explain how it is that a text seems full of meaning in terms of reference to philosophic truth or truthfulness to experience.[14] Without a willingness to observe language as an active power in its own right, I do not believe it possible to conceive a literary history distinct from intellectual and social history. Edwards's entry into literary history becomes possible only if the force of language that works of literary genius display so conspicuously turns out to be pertinent not only in those works but in his text too.

The literary historian approaches the textual field looking to observe the working of language and its enchantments across the entire length and breadth of that field. Literary sensibility apprehends—or, it may be, is apprehended by—the charms of aesthetic power; theoretical understanding exposes the speciousness of methodologies that, in the thrall of these charms, proceed to divide the textual field too rigidly into "literary" and "nonliterary" segments. It is a simplification to suppose that only aesthetically satisfying works are "literary," while all other texts can be reassuringly established outside the literary, outside the realm of semblance, illusion, and troping. Aesthetically potent texts force into prominence the intervention of figures of speech, and all the aberrations that attend them, in the production of meaning, an intervention that may be impossible to keep safely confined. Figuration may prove a productive element in all texts, and one that neither reference nor intention can control. The literary historian's first premise in approaching Edwards's writings must be that they are texts and that texts are first of all constructed out of language. That we need continually to remind ourselves of so obvious and trivial-seeming a point offers some indication of the strength of the habits that keep language transparent and out of observation's way.

If Edwards counts in American literature, it cannot be that he counts solely in a retrospective way, insofar as we can convince ourselves that he anticipates, however weakly, aspects deemed significant in writers who come after him. Inquiry becomes fraudulent when it comes to little more than trying to preserve a place of honor in the canon for an Edwards whom no one wants to read or knows how to read seriously, by finding or inventing his pertinence to later writers whom everyone who reads at all seems ready to read with a will. Nothing then has any reality or worthwhileness of its own—except of course the favored texts of the mid-nineteenth century. Ritually preserved as a transitional point in a gradual progressive development from the Puritans to the American literature of the mid-nineteenth century United States, Edwards becomes unreadable except as an object of special pleading. What Edwards says, and the possible significances of both what he says and the force of the way he says it, remain inaccessible topics as long as students of literature are unable to think Edwards honestly worth reading for his own sake.

Does it then follow that the effort to read Edwards in terms of the purported distinctive "Americanness" of American writing has been entirely deluded? Certainly, there has been a notable tendency, especially among intellectual historians, to develop what wishes to be seen as a hard-headed cross-examination that would dispense with the question of the Americanness of things American as a question *mal posé*, the consequence of what revisionist understanding accounts an essentially puerile obsession of a previous generation. This cross-examination has a certain pertinence. It calls attention to the anomalies and paralogisms prominent in the older treatments—the homogenization of heterogeneous phenomena (like Edwards, Emerson, James), the parallel restriction of scope to New England and even to Harvard, the repeated failure to establish the developmental continuities on which the premises and arguments are predicated and toward which they aim. "The 'Americanness' of philosophy in America," Bruce Kucklick notes pointedly in Chapter 14 of this volume, "disturbs commentators in a way that the 'Englishness' of English philosophy, or the 'Finnishness' of Finnish philosophy, for example, does not." This remark is unexceptionable. It is worth observing, however, that it is not *quite* evident on the face of Kucklick's formulation under which premise commentators proceed the more blindly. Perhaps an assurance that the English are "doing philosophy" and not just "English philosophy" calls for cross-examining quite as much as the shibboleth that the Americans don't just "do philosophy" but "American philosophy." If commentators are disturbed by the "Americanness" of philosophy in America, is it quite certain that there is no disturbance in the texts determining this reading, however confused and unsatisfactory the commentators' accounts of it have been? This question remains even after taking into account the quite delusive pretensions of Americans to write not "philosophy" but "American philosophy," or to view what has been produced as not "philosophy" but "American philosophy," a form supposed to be exterior, and superior, to the old forms of European blundering.

From the first, American literature confronts us with "the enigma of place." Approaching these texts, lending an ear to them, we find ourselves asking what is taking place and where it is taking place—in the texts, in America, in American texts, or in European memory referred to a place not properly its own place. The question of the history of European memory in its second landmass, its second continent, its second container, raises all the grammatical complications Kenneth Burke summarizes as the relations of the container to the thing contained.[15] A tangle of affiliations entwines the geophysical sense of "place" with the rhetorical and grammatical sense, topography with topos.[16] The word "America," it is necessary to remind ourselves, can never be more than a word. It is a figure of speech whose reference must always be secondary to and dependent on its character as a figure of speech. In its most extensive meaning, "America" refers only indirectly to a geographical space and directly to acts of inscription by which the space became a container for European memory. On the question of the genesis of American literature, you could call me a catastrophist rather than a uniformitarian. As a distinct literary-historical region, America did not develop; it did not evolve; it did not grow to become itself. The writing contained within this region simply was of this region, immediately, and from the beginning. If writing in America, in all its irreducible variousness, clusters together as a collection of recognizable American variants, this clustering is not an occult, lately occurring effect of an archaic Puritan heritage or the archetypal philosophic power of an Edwards. Only in a limited sense may it be said that American literature, or some portions of it, derive from Puritanism or Edwards. Rather, we ought to consider how the Puritans and Edwards are already writers within a certain literary-historical region, and how this region is also the literary-historical region within which (to confine myself to classical instances) Emerson, Thoreau, Hawthorne and Melville wrote.

This way of considering the matter, it should be emphasized, cuts two ways. It looks in the direction of a surmise that the nineteenth century writers are, in their concern with "literary models," quite as "European" as any Americans before them; at the same time it moves toward a conjecture that earlier American writing may be, in its referral of European memory to a locality not Europe, quite as "American" as any later texts customarily accorded the honor of that designation. This point of view is also prepared to regard writings produced in what became the United States as partial examples in the much broader inscription of European memory in and on the New World landmass. The political and territorial formation designated "the United States" may be, in this perspective, itself an example of this broader phenomenon of inscription. The period of American literature in which literary history ought to situate Edwards is most properly pictured as a series of discontinuous literary and intellectual episodes contained within a historical ground whose salient characteristic, so far as writing is concerned, resides in its alterity, in its being not-Europe. As this strange region receives European memory into itself, deflections or inflections occur in individual textual embodiments given to a variety of attitudes and literary forms. These effects may be myriad, not homogeneous. They may be rare and not pandemic. There is need for caution and restraint in generalization, and we should be prepared for surprise and multiplicity in taking up each individual writer, almost each separate text.

But it may be that to say all this is to have predicted a change in what we conceive the Americanness of writing in America to be. It is to conjecture that Americanness is not exactly Americanness—that is, that it is not in the first place a positive, monolithic product of the air or ground but a multiplicity of miscellaneous, fragmentary events of which we should expect to see the like, even within Europe itself, where and when Europe confronts its own edge, enters the space of its margin. America is, where it passes under that designation, already a European entity; its literatures are European literatures. European literature's differing from itself is the condition for the possibility of American literature differing from European. American literature can differ from European only insofar as it is already the case that European literature produces and reproduces itself in a play of metaphor or whirl of terms which precludes the production and reproduction of meaning as the sameness, invariance, and unity of universal truth, an invariance and unity this very play nonetheless posits as the goal, ideal, and destiny of writing. This is almost to say something that may be imaginatively true even if logically absurd, that American literature both is and is not

American, that it carries, but in a way peculiar to itself, the burden of all writing, the burden of being "the same yet different."

I realize these are large claims. Unfortunately—or perhaps fortunately—I can only present, here, the broad outlines of the general approach I advocate. That mother of geniuses Mary James wrote in a letter to her daughter Alice:

> My daughter a child of France! What has become of high moral nature, on which I have always based such hopes for her for this world and the next? That you should so soon have succumbed to this assault upon your senses, so easily have been carried captive by the mere delights of eating and drinking and dressing, I should not have believed. . . . Indeed I see it all now, to be merely the effect of a little cerebral derangement produced by the supernatural effort you made in crossing the Channel.[17]

Disburdened of the moralizing, it is in some such manner as this that we ought to think about America as a literary region. From the start and across a not yet precisely determined unit of chronology, American writing displays—fragmentarily and variously, in patches here and there that resist assimilation to a single overarching general scheme—little textual derangements produced by the supernatural effort of crossing the Atlantic—that is, the effort of physically, bodily, reaching the border of Christendom and philosophy and making Christianity and philosophy live. Santayana was right: philosophy could not spread into this marginal region without thinning out, without holes and tatters becoming apparent. America is so physical, so embodied a criticism of European usages, especially its philosophical and literary usages, that an intellectual criticism was, not unnecessary exactly, but unbearable. Christianity at the physical edge of Christendom confronts and passes beyond the end of Christendom differently than a Christian culture that reaches the end of Christendom intellectually, without ever, in this particular, physical way, knowing it to have always had an edge, a margin, a limit in space as well as in time.

The American writers whose resemblance we are concerned to define know this edge, this margin, this limit in their bodies and their bones. Is it possible that an awareness may take hold of someone's body and yet be unable to find cognitive representation, for lack of a vocabulary or set of concepts within which this particular sort of awareness can be acknowledged, or by force of the domination of a set of concepts within which such awareness can never be acknowledged? This is of course something like a description of neurosis. And, as in neurosis, one wonders whether the knowledge held, stored, and confined in the body may nonetheless, by various subterfuges, slips, and eccentric mannerisms, betray itself even in such higher cognitive performances as writing.

It is some such conjecture I want to advance about American litera-ture. We might explain this further by making use of a famous maxim of Kant's: "*Thoughts without contents are empty, intuitions without con-cepts are blind.*"[18] Knowledge stored in the body would be something like a content without a thought and even without an intuition—an excess, not an emptiness. There would be a confused feeling of being *overfilled*, which might, in whatever formal and linguistic resources happen to lie at hand, emerge as a kind of haunting; or as an unexpected and baffling buzzing in the ear, a kind of textual static; or as a defensive, compensa-tory excessiveness in the pretense that nothing has changed. What is the New World, we might wonder, but the Old World exposed, unmasked, put in jeopardy?

Frank Hugh Foster expressed from the point of view of the history of theology the puzzle and paradox of Edwards about which the literary historian too will frame his own speculation. Edwards's theology, Foster wrote, is "the old system reproduced . . . and yet it is a new system."[19] Admittedly, it can hardly be taken as given that anything in Edwards's system is new. Nor may every newness we might be prepared to accredit in Edwards's system divulge his character as an American writer. But there is one feature in Edwards's text—I would by no means suggest it as the only one—that I would like to conclude by asking whether it may not place him in the tradition in American literature which criticism has ever felt him joined to. In "The Dialectic of Romantic Poetry in America," Harold Bloom describes how American poets in the romantic or Emer-sonian tradition seek a humanizing and essentially Wordsworthian stance toward Nature, only to find that they must abandon this in obedience to a more extreme and troubling demand imagination makes of them. These poets realize themselves poetically, not in an identifica-tion with the incarnation of the human that they are, but in identifying themselves with inhuman and impersonal Force, dreaded and sovereign Necessity. "The great among our poets seek to become each a process rather than a person, Nemesis rather than accident. . . ."[20] Is there not in Edwards, too, a constant raising and transformation of the possibility that the life of the spirit will degenerate into a dreadful worship of impersonal force? Edwards's theology begins and, in the case of the damned, ends with the perception of naked, impersonal power. His main effort as a writer is to represent force and worship of force as turning back on itself and overcoming itself, so that force and worship of force transform themselves into love and worship of love. Edwards's main literary task was to construct a figurative scheme in which a God whose natural form is naturalistic force is transformed into a God whose spiritual and human form is love, a system of metaphor in which a creature whose natural bent is to love power and who wants to be Fate comes to love love and learns to be human. From the literary point of view, Edwards's is a text in which the critic observes the rhetorical devices, the tropings, by which this transport of force into love attempts to effect itself. This figurative scheme or system represents Edwards's inflection of a traditional religious theme. It shows us his embodiment of a received theology. It carries the singular force of his writing—what makes Edwards Edwards. In concluding, I submit it to be the future of literary study of Edwards to investigate the place of metaphor in his text and to determine whether the historical, biographical, and regional scene of Edwards's writing—a scene intensified and condensed in the last years of his career, when he became a Christian missionary to the Housatunnuck at the rim of Christendom and at the front of the imperial wars of conquest—is wholly indifferent to the place and functioning of metaphor in his text.

Notes

1. Robert E. Spiller, Willard Thorp, Thomas H. Johnson, Henry Seidel Canby, Richard M. Ludwig, eds., *Literary History of the United States: History*, 3d. Ed. Revised (New York, 1963), p. 79. (Hereafter, LHUS.)

2. LHUS, p. 81.

3. Van Wyck Brooks, "Our Poets," *America's Coming-of-Age* (Garden City, N.Y., 1958), p. 20.

4. Brooks, "The Precipitant," *America's Coming-of-Age*, p. 57.

5. Brooks, "Our Poets," pp. 38–39.

6. LHUS, p. 345.

7. See the opening paragraph of Brooks, "The Sargasso Sea," *America's Coming-of-Age*, p. 76: "A fresh and more sensitive emotion seems to be running up and down the old Yankee backbone, that rarely blossoming stalk."

8. Nina Baym offers a shrewd account of the follies that ensue when theorizing decays into tautology and criticism models its understanding of what is American about American literature on a narrow selection of great writings that conform to a monolithic idea of Americanness the critic holds beforehand. "Before he is through, the critic has had to insist that some works in America are much more American than others, and he is as busy excluding certain writers as 'un-American' as he is including others. . . . [The] final result goes far beyond the conclu-

sion that only a handful of American works are very good. *That* statement is one we could agree with, since very good work is rare in any field. But it is odd indeed to argue that only a handful of American works are really American" (p. 127). "Melodramas of Beset Manhood: How Theories of American Fiction Exclude Women Authors," *American Quarterly* 33 (1981), pp. 124–39.

9. Ralph Waldo Emerson, "Thoughts on Modern Literature," *The Dial*, vol. 1, no. 2 (October, 1840), in *The Dial: A Magazine for Literature, Philosophy, Religion*, 2 vols. (New York, 1961), I, p. 137.

10. Vernon Louis Parrington, *Main Currents in American Thought*, Vol. 2, *The Romantic Revolution in America: 1800–1860* (New York, 1927), p. xiii.

11. Moses Coit Tyler, *A History of American Literature, 1607–1765* (1878; rpt. Ithaca, N.Y., 1949) and Charles Francis Richardson, *American Literature, 1607–1885* (New York, 1887–89).

12. Douglas L. Wilson, ed., *The Genteel Tradition: Nine Essays by George Santayana* (Cambridge, Mass., 1967), pp. 19–23.

13. Henry James, *Hawthorne* (1879; rpt. Ithaca, New York, 1956), p. 3.

14. Paul de Man, *Allegories of Reading: Figural Language in Rousseau, Nietzsche, Rilke, and Proust* (New Haven, 1979), p. 79.

15. Kenneth Burke, *A Grammar of Motives* (1945; rpt. Berkeley, 1969).

16. See "Deconstruction in America: An Interview With Jacques Derrida," *Critical Exchange* 17 (Winter 1985), p. 4.

17. Mary James to Alice James, quoted by Rosemary Dinnage in *The New York Review of Books*, May 31, 1984, p. 4.

18. Immanuel Kant, *Critique of Pure Reason*, tr. F. Max Muller, (Garden City, N.Y., 1966), p. 45.

19. Frank Bloom Foster, *A Genetic History of New England Theology* (1907); rpt. (New York) p. 163.

20. Harold Bloom, "Bacchus and Merlin: The Dialectic of Romantic Poetry in America," *The Ringers in the Tower* (Chicago, 1971), p. 301.

14

Jonathan Edwards and American Philosophy

BRUCE KUKLICK

By "American philosophy" I do not mean the practice of philosophizing in America from the Puritans to the present. I rather refer to a certain area of inquiry—its organization, conceptualization, conventions, and standard arguments and works of scholarship. The area has vague boundaries, and is considered to extend temporally from the time of Jonathan Edwards to that of John Dewey. The field is sometimes alternatively called American thought, even American intellectual history. American philosophy is a field that has been defined by philosophers *and* by people in American studies. The work in the field is usually carried out by philosophers. They have, from an analytic perspective, provided the philosophical component. The general shape of the field, however, was produced by the writings of American historians and literary critics during the early days of American studies, the 1940s and 1950s. These scholars gave to the field its *American* quality.

The foundation stone in the history of American philosophy is Jonathan Edwards, and this essay describes how Edwards secures this interdisciplinary study. I shall also, however, attempt to address wider issues than those of interest to scholars of Edwards without losing sight of the rock on which American philosophy has been built.

The essay has two parts. In the first part I sketch the conventional view of American philosophy and suggest the substantive weaknesses of this view. The second part is more theoretical. I diagnose the weaknesses of the conventional view as philosophical history. The problem here is the same problem that plagues most work in the history of philosophy;

American philosophy is merely a special case. Moreover, this second part examines the troubles of the conventional view when it links thought to culture. These troubles also illustrate issues that arise when intellectual historians (and historians of philosophy) join texts and contexts. But American philosophy is a peculiarly good example, for the "Americanness" of philosophy in America disturbs commentators in a way that the "Englishness" of English philosophy, or the "Finnishness" of Finnish philosophy, for example, do not.[1] Thus, I dissect two theoretical problems in this discipline, one contributed by philosophers, one contributed by people in American studies.

Surveys of American philosophy treat the same canonical figures. Although scholars dispute how these figures are to be interpreted, they agree on who is to be interpreted.[2] Canonical histories begin with the undeniably gifted and influential work of Edwards and its Puritan background and then move to the Massachusetts religious liberals who attacked Calvinism and to the Founding Fathers, represented by Franklin, Hamilton, Jefferson, and Madison. Thus, the first step in these histories is tracing the movement from evangelical religion to liberalism in both politics and religion. Thereafter politics vanishes as the evolution of religious liberalism continues from Boston Unitarianism through Concord Transcendentalism; then to the writers of the American Renaissance—Hawthorne and Melville—where the literary concerns of the Transcendentalists are translated into fiction. William James is next seen as the heir to Emerson's views and the foreshadower of those of John Dewey, the quintessential twentieth century liberal.

The canon stresses thought that is seen to anticipate the secular values of contemporary intellectuals. Present liberal scientific ideals are traced through a triumphal succession of eighteenth and nineteenth century figures. Ironically the Calvinist Edwards is seen to have given birth to progeny who bring about the denouement of his cherished ideas. At the same time, while America rejects Edwards's substantive ideas, the American mind is often interpreted as having embraced his spirit. For example, Perry Miller wrote that Edwards was two hundred years ahead of his time, a modern; and Alan Heimert has argued that the triumphal American ideas have also typified the democratic revival spirit.[3]

Knowledgeable readers will note that my canonical history is an ideal type and eliminates idiosyncrasies in individual scholarship. The history is best reflected in reading lists and syllabi for undergraduate courses, where the demands of simplicity are often overriding. For more sophisticated audiences, for example, the novelists ("easy" reading) may go by the boards, as Charles Peirce, the founder of pragmatism, is inserted.

The canonical history has serious problems. The first is the problem of consistency. Edwards and Dewey were formal system builders, but in the time between them radically different sorts of minds are studied. Franklin and the Transcendentalists, self-conscious popularizers, disdained systematic rumination. The men of the American Renaissance wrote fiction. The Founding Fathers were interested not so much in the metaphysics of the social order as in the application of political ideas. In short, conventional histories lack the consistency of studies of German idealism, British empiricism, Greek naturalism, or other accounts of philosophical traditions.

This problem is implicitly recognized in two divergent justifications given for the existence of American philosophy. Europeans often comment that it results from the requirements of undergraduate education and the inevitable popularity of American studies in the United States. A ragtag and ill-assorted group of "thinkers" is created and some "thought" teased out of them. American historians often accept part of this critique but assert that in a democratic and pluralistic society, formal thought— perhaps barren in any case—is not all important. Gifted "representative men" who, like Franklin, Emerson, or James, express the deepest concerns of an entire culture may also be significant.

A second problem with the canon is its continuity. The standard history fails to link its parts. It does not clarify the ambiguous and complicated relation between religion and politics in the late eighteenth century. Moreover, the novelists have only a slight connection to other areas of intellectual inquiry. Emerson, as we know, did not give birth to James; if anyone did it was the French philosopher Charles Renouvier, or the Cambridge Unitarian Francis Bowen. And as I hope it can be shown, James did not give birth to Dewey.

Finally, there is the problem of Boston. The critical aspects of canonical history focus on southeastern Massachusetts: the rise of Boston's religious liberals and Unitarians after the Great Awakening, the elaboration of the thought of the Concord Transcendentalists and of the Cambridge pragmatists. Southeastern Massachusetts may have been the center of philosophical life in the eighteenth and nineteenth centuries, but we must recall that many of the most influential expositors of standard views have had Harvard connections. Harvard professors Barret Wendell and Josiah Royce gave early expression to the canonical history. Their successors, Perry Miller, F. O. Matthiessen, and Morton White also taught there. Wendell, Matthiessen, Vernon Louis Parrington, Van Wyck Brooks, and Murray Murphey were all undergraduates at Harvard.[4]

I suspect that the canon reflects more Harvard's dominance of the academic world in the late nineteenth and twentieth centuries, when the canon was established, than the truth about the eighteenth and nineteenth centuries. Indeed, the non-Boston elements of the canonical narrative appear to be accretions designed to give greater significance to what is essentially a tale of local religious change. During this long period Cambridge was idiosyncratic, more religiously liberal than other intellectual centers. Thinkers in Boston were not interested in systematic thought. From Samuel Willard's *Compleat Body of Divinity*, posthumously published in 1726, to John Fiske's *Cosmic Philosophy*, of 1874, Cambridge did not produce a single systematic effort.

Students of American philosophy have found in it a usable past: a heroic tale of liberation from religious superstition and the growth of spiritual autonomy. But if this is the chronicle of Harvard, it should not be mistaken for the chronicle of America. Neither should the gaps in the narrative go unnoticed, nor should we accept the doubtful wisdom of calling "philosophy" a collection of activities that consist of systematic theology, popular religious thought, cultural and speculative musings, politics, and fiction.

Let me sketch one different story. The work of Jonathan Edwards immediately inspired the ruminations of two generations of gifted Calvinist thinkers in the colonies and the new nation. The theologians involved included Joseph Bellamy, Jonathan Edwards, Jr., Stephen West, John Smalley, Asa Burton, Nathan Strong, and Moses Hemmenway. The two most important of these men—Samuel Hopkins and Nathanael Emmons—were the leaders of what was known as the New Divinity movement, the first and most provocative stage of a 125-year-long religious tradition in Trinitarian Congregationalism called the New England Theology. In the late eighteenth and early nineteenth centuries, the New Divinity, under the leadership of Hopkins and Emmons, curbed the power of the liberals. Centered in the Connecticut Valley, and with its institutional locus at Yale, where almost all of its worthies had been educated, the New Divinity made religious liberalism a local, Boston phenomenon. Although the establishment of the Harvard Divinity School about 1815 insured the survival of Unitarianism as a denomination, the liberals were isolated and soon ringed by a formidable array of Calvinist institutions of advanced learning. Andover Seminary had been founded in 1808 because of Harvard's inclinations, the Princeton Theological Seminary in 1812, Yale Divinity School in 1822, Hartford Theological Seminary in 1832, and Union Theological Seminary in 1837, as well as many others.

The focus was still at Yale, however, and in the 1830s the Congregational Yale Divinity School produced a creative successor to Hopkins and Emmons, Nathaniel William Taylor. While the appraisal of intellect may not be the first task of the historian of ideas, Taylor is the most talented systematic thinker in America between Edwards and Dewey. His ruminations gave birth to what was sometimes castigated as the New Haven Theology. Taylorism, as it was also called, was the next major phase of the New England Theology, after the New Divinity.

In the forties and fifties, it is true, further elaborations of the New England Theology displayed a falling away in sustained achievement. Even the sympathetic observer, I think, cannot help but appraise the developments as more akin to the growth of astrology than astronomy. The lack of vitality suggests that professionalism—here exhibited by American divinity—need not be progressive. The divines were insular and ignored European currents of thought. They were inbred and hired only within the narrowest of circles. Most important, they dismissed the challenges science posed to their enterprise and, consequently, also the possible answers to these challenges.

In the middle third of the century, reigning ideas were modified by a heterogeneous collection of preachers, gentlemen of leisure, and people on the periphery of the academic system. These thinkers were innovative, as the divinity school ministers were not, but they were not positioned to formulate, and were usually not interested in formulating, systematic thought. Emerson is to us the most famous of these men, but the group included people like James Marsh of the University of Vermont in Burlington, John Williamson Nevin and Philip Schaff of the Mercersburg Seminary in western Pennsylvania, and William Torrey Harris, leader of the St. Louis Hegelians. From the perspective of the Trinitarian Congregational philosophy of religion we have been examining, the most influential was the Hartford minister, Horace Bushnell.

Unlike his professional peers, Bushnell interested himself in German thought, and used it to reconstruct an orthodoxy threatened by perplexing problems. A student of Taylor's, Bushnell defended the Calvinist essentials of depravity and grace, the Fall, the natural sinfulness of man, and the need for redemption. Yet Bushnell made Christological concerns central in his Calvinism; he brought God and man together, unlike the followers of Edwards. He also gave a role to history, in dramatic contrast to the ahistorical individualism of New England religion.

Within Congregational circles there were two successive responses to Bushnell, the first conservative, the second more radical. The first, in the fifties and sixties, inspired a modest renaissance in Calvinist thought; the second, in the seventies and eighties, was part of a dramatic shift.

The first response was that of Henry Boynton Smith of Union Theological Seminary, the leading New School Presbyterian, heavily influenced by Congregational theology, and Edwards Amasa Park of Andover, the leading Congregational theologian of his era. Both Smith and Park were interested in German ideas, and soberly took up Bushnell's ideas in an academic setting. They emphasized his historic Calvinist affirmation and not his dismissal of some of the conundrums central to Trinitarianism. Like their predecessors, Smith and Park worked on variations of Edwardsian ideas.

Both of these men were swept aside by the "New Theology" movement of the 1880s and 1890s. Led by a group of Park's students at Andover, the new theologians used Bushnell to undercut Calvinist ideas. They downplayed Bushnell's traditionalism and stressed his iconoclasm. At Andover the new theologians, known as the Andover Liberals, drove Park's journal, *Bibliotheca Sacra*, to Oberlin, and founded their own magazine, *The Andover Review*. The young turks also saw to it that Park's successor there was not Park's hand-picked choice but one of their own. Well past seventy and in retirement, Park fought his ungrateful students tooth and nail, but by the late 1880s Andover Calvinism in the tradition of Edwards had been replaced by the distinctive doctrines of the New Theology known as "progressive orthodoxy," the precursor of genuine liberal theology in Congregationalism.

Look at this tradition: Jonathan Edwards, Samuel Hopkins, Nathaniel Emmons, Nathaniel William Taylor, Horace Bushnell, Henry Boynton Smith, Edwards Amasa Park, and the Andover Liberals, a tradition that takes us from Calvinism to liberalism in Trinitarianism.

The last part of the story does contain a revolution. But the overthrow of Park by the Andover Liberals turned out to be a palace coup, for at the same time theology of whatever description was giving way to philosophy as the speculative science sanctioned by crucial legitimating communities on the east coast. The end of the nineteenth century was the period of the rise of the modern university system in the United States, the growth of disciplinary scholarship other than divinity, and the emergence of a host of secular, scientifically oriented creeds that came into existence in response to Charles Darwin's *Origin of Species*. In this intellectual environment theology was unable to prosper, and it lost its hold on the literate, upper-middle-class public. Philosophy came to command the respect of this public at the expense of theology. Philosophy departments attracted the money, talent, and social support that had previously been devoted to theology. At Harvard President Charles Eliot built "the great department" that a European of the stature of Bertrand Russell recognized as "the best in the world."[5] In the nineties—the same time—Andover seminary went into radical decline, and shortly thereafter merged with Harvard. At Princeton James McCosh asserted the primacy of philosophy over theology after the dominance of the Princeton Seminary over the college for well over fifty years. At new universities like that of Chicago, philosophy became preeminent while divinity was relegated to a secondary status.

This context is appropriate to account for the career of John Dewey. Dewey was born into a staunch Congregational Calvinist family in Burlington, Vermont. The most formidable influence on his life was his mother, who often made old-fashioned fear and degradation the core of religious life. Dewey's personal religion was also shaped by the work of the Congregational minister in Burlington. Lewis O. Brastow, who later taught at the Yale Divinity School, enunciated in Vermont a popular blend of evangelical beliefs similar to what was being propagated by the Andover liberals. Dewey underwent a conversion experience when he was in his early twenties, taught Congregational Sunday school, and was a loyal church member until he went to teach at the University of Chicago in his mid-thirties.

Dewey had two academic mentors: H. A. P. Torrey, the professor of philosophy at the University of Vermont, and George Sylvester Morris, of Johns Hopkins, where Dewey took an early doctorate in philosophy. Both Torrey and Morris had been Congregational students of Henry Boynton Smith at the Union Seminary. But both had given up the ministry—Torrey actually left a pulpit—for careers in philosophy. Both were philosophic defenders of a Protestant Christianity based on German thought, and Dewey their student took up their concerns.

As a philosopher of religion, Dewey believed that the New Theology of the Andover liberals had an inadequate philosophical base. In its attachment to Bushnell, Andover had not fully escaped the careful logical categories of Edwardsian Calvinism. In particular, progressive orthodoxy had no compelling way of disputing the older Calvinist dualisms between God and man, the natural and the supernatural, although the progressives did denigrate these dualisms. The German thought on which Andover had fallen back, thought Dewey, was still too dualistic. Hegel relied on a dichotomy between absolute and individual spirit—between God and man—and Kant distinguished between the phenomenal and noumenal worlds—nature and the supernatural. Dewey wanted to reconstruct German thought on antidualistic lines and thus provide a solid philosophic base for progressive orthodoxy. Indeed, much of his early writing appears in the *Andover Review*, the journal that had replaced Park's *Bibliotheca Sacra* at Andover, although he also wrote an essay for Park's magazine, and later turned to *Mind* and *Philosophical Review*.

Commentators have regularly noted that the young Dewey was a Hegelian, and although this is a bit of a distortion it is near enough to the mark. What they have neglected to note is that Dewey's "Hegelianism" promoted a philosophy of religion designed to fortify the latest developments in Trinitarian Congregationalism. What Dewey was doing had little to do with the pragmatism of Charles Peirce and William James. Though Dewey became a disciple of Morris at Hopkins, he avoided Peirce, believing that Peirce's "formal" logic typified just the sort of dualism that had to be avoided. Though Dewey found much of value in James's *Principles of Psychology* (1890), the book appeared after Dewey's own position had been formulated, while James had previously poked fun at Dewey's characteristic ideas.

In the 1880s Dewey argued that we could not separate God and man, absolute and finite spirit. God *was* only as individual selves realized him; the dynamic evolution of self-consciousness in human beings in history was God. Dewey also denied a cleavage between the natural and the supernatural, phenomenal and noumenal. The two worlds were one; spirit was in nature; nature was a symbol of spirit. The physical world evolved into the spiritual; it had spiritual potential in it. Nature *became* moral and religious.

In both of these attacks on philosophic dualisms, Dewey developed his own philosophical dialect, a German teleological vision of Darwinian science. But in the late eighties and early nineties he abandoned the language of German idealism for a more scientific vocabulary. Instead of speaking of the union of man and God, Dewey spoke of the intrinsic meaningfulness of experience and the ability of men, using the scientific method, to uncover greater and greater syntheses of meaning. Rather than writing of the human realization of God, Dewey wrote of science progressively increasing human harmony and tranquility through the growth of meaning.

Dewey also ceased to write of the connection between the natural and the supernatural worlds. He wrote that the scientific method had previously been applied to nature and could now be applied to the social world. The spheres of nature and morality were of a piece, and the method perfected in physics could be used in the arena of culture. Thus, questions about nature and supernature were transformed.

By the early 1890s Dewey's concerns are the recognizable ones of "our" Dewey. One way to construe these changes is cosmetic, as changes in rhetorical strategy. The issues for Dewey in the late seventies and early nineties are the same; the mode of expressing them alters. Why did Dewey alter his linguistic strategy? In part, like most other American intellectuals, he was captivated by the ideal of applied science. He was only the most prominent among American thinkers who read Darwin in a benign way that promoted a new way of thinking about man and the world. In part Dewey was also a man on the rise. He knew that systematic theology was no longer a sure route to success. He wanted to be a respectable theoretician in his culture, and this meant coming to terms with science. Whatever we make of this mix of motives, it is well to remember that Dewey did not *merely* change his language. He was also a creative genius. In casting the problems of the philosophy of religion in a new set of formulas, he shifted the axis in which intellectual problems were conceived. He had begun his career by intending to shore up Andover liberalism. The changing milieu in which he wrote meant that he came to maturity as the founder of modern secular thought.

Commentators argue that Dewey naturalized German thought by a stress on the concrete growth of cultures and the interaction of organisms in their environment. Dewey's "instrumentalism" was a hard-headed, tough-minded creed that grounded the hope for scientific politics; it was the mature philosophy of social science. What is more important, however, is that Dewey began his professional life as a certain sort of philosopher of religion. Although he shifted the contours of thought in the United States, his instrumentalism bore the telltale marks of his older interests. The locus of the divine shifted from the supernatural to the natural, and science could be applied to what was formerly supernatural. But there was still a godly residue in things. Edwards believed that man was redeemed only through grace. For Dewey man was still redeemed, but the instrumentality was the ostensibly secular technique of science.

In the twentieth century, science serves what in the nineteenth century was clearly the purpose of religion. In effect the theoreticians of social science function as the theologians of old had done. Dewey provided the grammar for a common faith in an era when traditional religion was no longer compelling for intellectuals. To say that Dewey was the chief exponent of secular liberalism is unnuanced; he rather transformed religious concerns in a new language acceptable to his contemporaries partly because it allowed them to avoid old problems and look at new, but also because it gave them a creed to live by.

"American philosophy" is a confused discipline, because the story it narrates is not a genuine history—the figures brought together are part of a dialogue only in the minds of recent philosophers. The discipline is not about "America" but about Boston; the material the field covers is not "philosophy," either in our present or any past definition. The other account I have given of the links between Edwards and Dewey is not, however, meant to be the basis of a new "American philosophy." It is a history of some connected aspects of Congregational theology and an account of how it lost its intellectual dominance in New England. That is, I do not think there is any way we can rescue "American philosophy" as a field.

I do not mean to deny that certain activities that can be labeled "philosophy" took place in the colonies and the United States between 1740 and 1930. Nor am I concerned with the quality of these activities. Rather, it is not sensible to tie together these activities with theology, politics, literature, and speculation on culture. Moreover, it is mistaken to argue that these activities embody a quintessential American quality. The field of American philosophy may try to refer to some patterns in the past that do not exist. It is at least unclear how the field could be redefined in order to carve out a more coherent area of study. One could examine, for example, various leisured "natural philosophers" in the colonies, nineteenth century collegiate philosophers, and professional philosophy in the late nineteenth and early twentieth century. But I do not know if these activities could be usefully connected, or if they could be constructively construed as American. Certainly scholars have displayed little attention to such endeavors.

We must examine theoretical issues to explain the indefensible nature of the enterprise. The first issue concerns the nature of philosophical history as scholars, usually philosophers, conceive it. The second concerns the nature of the history of American philosophy as scholars, usually nonphilosophers, have conceived it.

Philosophers customarily display an interest in their past, but their motives are rarely pure. The works of illustrious predecessors are often simply pillaged to find argumentation that supports some contemporary idea, allowing the pillager to use not only the argumentation but also the prestige of the predecessor. On the other side, if arguments can be attached to certain currently despised thinkers, more recent exponents of the same sorts of doctrines can be dismissed by a procedure of philosophical guilt by association. These uses of the past are nonetheless honorable. Philosophers are trained to find out which speculative positions are true, which notions sound. When they study their history, they relentlessly approach it with a view to learning which ideas are justifiable over the long haul, which beliefs stand up to present scrutiny, which texts are now worth reading. The focus is the cogency and relevance of a past practioner's argument. We learn that a now-deceased speculator has something to say about a problem that is of interest today, or that his writing can be reconstructed to cast light on a problem of current importance.

Philosophers' predilections in thinking about the past often result in misconstruing the intentions of the men they write about. Philosopher-historians are less interested in their subjects than in their present concerns, and so are more prone to get their subjects wrong. But my chief complaint now is not this sort of "presentism," but the presentism involved in simply deciding who is to be studied.

Philosophers usually write histories of "American philosophy" about characters whom they or other scholars think are great. R. G. Collingwod taught us long ago that historical narratives are answers to questions. Initially, in the United States, scholars asked: What past American thinkers are great? and: How are they connected to what interests us now? More recent scholars, confronted with an acceptable canon, have even further reduced interrogative complexity. They ask only: How are the conventionally great thinkers related to what interests us now? Why do *I* think that Edwards or Dewey is great?

This imaginative poverty has made the field lackluster and has led many to go so far as to reject intellectual history. Yet the problem is not the life of the mind in America, but the questions we ask about it. These questions avoid all variety of exploration of past ideas in exchange for learning what a subgroup of historical practioners thinks is "worthy" in past thinking. The questions are not wrong; they just display a feeble inquisitiveness. Instead of asking: What are Franklin's politics? why not ask: Why does Franklin exercise such a hold on twentieth century American literary critics? Instead of asking: What did Emerson think? why not ask: Why did Nathaniel William Taylor drop completely out of sight less than thirty years after he was the most influential thinker in the United States? Instead of asking: Why is Edwards important for American philosophy? why not ask: How did various groups of intellectuals use Edwards in the late eighteenth and nineteenth centuries?

Part of the problem with American philosophy is that scholars, often but not always philosophers, are flat-footed in the questions they ask. The other problem is that scholars, often but not always historians, are overeager to link ideas to society. The philosophers are usually enamored with the history of *philosophy*, and again and again raise "personal" exegetical questions. The historians generally ponder the *history* of philosophy, and have sought relevance for their work by trying to show how ideas are tied to culture.

For a long time, during the earlier period of the American studies movement, it was popular to speak of the American mind, and clichés about the practicality of American ideas, the quest for community, the self-conscious concern for national identity, and similar ideas would come tripping to the tongues of scholars. Scholars of American studies have become wary of the attempt to use national character as a way of linking ideas to society. But the notion is embedded in American philosophy that thinkers are included for study because of their peculiar or distinctive or characteristic Americanness.

There is little need here to explore the deficiencies of this approach. But following it has entailed that, in addition to the sorts of questions I have suggested are implicit to the field, others are asked, like: What is American about Edwards? How does Emerson incarnate the American spirit? How are Franklin and James similar?[6]

The problem with American philosophy is certainly not Jonathan Edwards, who gave rise to the most sustained, systematic, and creative intellectual tradition produced in this country—the New England Theology; and whose work created the context out of which Dewey's instrumentalism came. Nonetheless, the conception of "American philosophy" for which Edwards is made the first spokesman, if not mistaken, is at least the product of some unfortunate queries. I believe there are no past activities to be fruitfully connected and studied under the rubric "American philosophy." But let us put aside the issue of what "really" occurred in the past, and think of historical inquiry only as the formulation of questions and answers. If "American philosophy" does not refer to the nonexistent, it in any event asks unhelpful questions.

It is not *improper* to ask the questions that have generated "American philosophy." It may not a conceptual failing to ask: Who are the great thinkers in America? Or the followup sort of question: What makes these great thinkers American? It is rather that these questions are at best not very interesting, at worst silly. When we begin to ask better questions,

American philosophy will vanish like the wonderful one-horse shay. Edwards's achievement, unlike that of the contemporary scholarship I've been criticizing, should survive. A brick can serve as a cornerstone in any number of buildings.

Notes

1. The substantive issues raised in this essay are treated at length in *Churchmen and Philosophers: From Jonathan Edwards to John Dewey* (New Haven, 1985), where extensive citations can be found. P. 301 of that work cites the series of methodological articles in which I have raised issues similar to the ones raised in this essay. In "Does American Philosophy Rest on a Mistake?" in Marcus Singer, ed., *American Philosophy* (Cambridge, 1986), pp. 177–89 I examine these issues from a more strictly philosophical perspective.

2. See, for example, Paul Conkin, *Puritans and Pragmatists* (New York, 1968); Morton White, *Science and Sentiment in America* (New York, 1972); Elizabeth Flower and Murray G. Murphey, *A History of Philosophy in America*, 2 volumes (New York, 1977); and finally Murphey's explicit criticism of his own work, "Toward an Historicist History of American Philosophy," *Transactions of the Charles S. Peirce Society* 15 (1979), pp. 3–18.

3. Perry Miller, *Jonathan Edwards* (New York, 1949); Alan Heimert, *Religion and the American Mind from the Great Awakening to the Revolution* (Cambridge, Mass., 1966).

4. For Wendell, see *A Literary History of America* (New York, 1900); and for Royce, "William James and the Philosophy of Life," in *William James and Other Essays in the Philosophy of Life* (New York, 1911). Miller's most important works in this connection are his *The Life of the Mind in America from the Revolution to the Civil War* (New York, 1965), and his anthology *American Thought: Civil War to World War I* (New York, 1956). Matthiessen's fame rests on *American Renaissance* (New York, 1941). White's and Murphey's synthetic works are cited above. Parrington wrote *Main Currents in American Thought* (New York, 1927–30); Van Wyck Brooks, most prominently, *The Flowering of New England 1915–1865* (New York, 1936); Curti, *The Growth of American Thought* (New York, 1943).

5. Bertrand Russell, *Autobiography*, volume 1 (Boston, 1967), p. 326.

6. Many American historians have long since given up the quest for national character as a way of linking ideas to society. But old ways die hard, and from the ashes of national character has risen the phoenix of the social history of ideas. There is indeed now a sophisticated theoretical literature to warrant the concerns of historians who want to situate ideas in a culture: the work of Thomas Kuhn, Clifford Geertz, and Quentin Skinner. The trouble is that although this literature has given us a new way of talking, it has dubiously advanced the history of ideas.

So far as the history of ideas is concerned, the alliance with social history that paradigms, thick descriptions, and context have brought about is like the Munich Pact.

The instrusion of social history into intellectual history may have given us fine historical works, but the history of ideas has vanished in them. The "new" intellectual history is unconcerned with the elaboration of ideas at all; the nuances of ideas, the concern for elaborate traditions of discourse, disappear. On the other hand, if we examine the best examples of the history of ideas that we have, they are substantively uninfluenced by the social history of ideas. The *experimentum crucis* here is the work of Quentin Skinner, famous for his view that text and context must be jointly explored. Yet while Skinner's *Foundations of Modern Political Thought* (New York, 1978) is rich in elaborating the *intellectual* context of ideas, it relies on the standard "background" of social context that has been conventional for intellectual historians for years; and does not overcome the dualism between ideas and the social world.

The problem is that we have been guided overmuch by a belief that intellectual history has to be made important by being linked to culture. Thus, the bloated claims of intellectual historians of the last generation. More recently, intellectual historians have adopted for their own use a series of theories that claim to link thought and life. The same underlying motive is at work: a desire to make ideas more respectable by showing their relevance to what is somehow thought to be more important—the social order, the culture. The more recent development is unfortunate for the history of ideas because it has allowed other people's theories to guide our practice. Why should theoretical work in symbolic anthropology, the philosophy of language, or even the history of the hard sciences generate models for what to do in the history of ideas? In the first instance our best practice ought to be a guide for our theoretical musings, if we must have them; to make other people's theoretical musing the guide to our practice seems to me to be wrong.

15

Jonathan Edwards and Nineteenth-Century Theology

MARK A. NOLL

Jonathan Edwards appeared in several guises during the nineteenth century. For vast segments of the English-speaking world, and beyond, he was an honored figure from the annals of piety. To a sizable number of educated Americans, Edwards was not so much an inspiration to piety as an irreplacable cultural artifact, viewed either as a Founding Father worthy of high honor or as an incubus to be shaken off. To a small number of post-Christian British intellectuals, Edwards was an intriguing philosophical curiosity. But for many Americans and Scots, as well as a curious few from England and Holland, Edwards still counted most as a theologian, as the author of doctrinal sermons, of treatises on *True Virtue, Original Sin, The History of Redemption*, and above all *The Freedom of the Will*.[1]

An examination of Edwards's place in nineteenth-century theology must deal with two issues. The simpler, if more cumbersome, task is to chronicle the way in which Edwards commanded allegiance, provoked opposition, and precipitated controversy. The more complex is to assess the way in which Edwards's theology comported with the larger commitments of those who took notice of him.

If we define the nineteenth century, from an American perspective, as stretching from the Revolution to the First World War, we can trace three interrelated stories concerning Edwards during the period up to 1870.[2] The first concerns theologians who worked to dignify their own efforts by associating them with Edwards's name. This is often the story of conflict which arose when appropriators of Edwards encountered others who, with sometimes antithetical convictions, did the same. The second concerns those who found Edwards an impediment rather than an inspiration. It is the tale of efforts to rebut his arguments and overthrow his conclusions. The third concerns those who were not so much disputants about Edwards as developers of his insights.

During the last third of the century, Edwards became more clearly an anachronism. The reasons for this are found in the larger changes taking place in western intellectual culture at that time. After describing Edwards's growing irrelevance as a theological force, the paper concludes with general comments about the fate of Edwards's theology in the nineteenth century.

One final introductory word is required. This paper would have been impossible without the superb Edwards reference guide by M. X. Lesser, a work which, while ably assisted by other recent retrospectives, is now the *sine qua non* for serious reflection on Edwards in the nineteenth century. It is a model of industry for bibliographers, and a beacon for historians.[3]

The Struggle for Edwards's Mantle: Revival

Shortly after Charles Finney (1792–1875) began his famous evangelistic itinerations in 1824, he encountered the writings of Jonathan Edwards. And at least early in his career, Finney "often spoke of them with rapture."[4] Finney was especially encouraged that Edwards had defended evangelistic innovations. By the time Finney published his *Lectures on Revivals of Religion* in 1835, he had received stout blows from leaders of the older Calvinistic churches, who regarded his novel methods with a jaundiced eye. Against such critics, Finney paraded a long list of Christian worthies who had also forsaken traditions. Prominent in this list was "President Edwards," a "great man [who] was famous in his day for new measures." Specifically it was Edwards's refusal to baptize the children of unregenerate parents and his willingness to tolerate lay preachers that appealed to Finney as an anticipation of his own "new measures," like protracted meetings and the anxious bench. Each of these tactics broke convention to reach spirituality. But just as an "Old School" had opposed the colonial "New Light," so now other petty-minded naysayers obstructed means of "seeking out ways to do good and save souls."[5] With Edwards on his side, Finney possessed an unassailable precedent.

Almost as soon as Finney announced that he had discovered a new champion, however, his opponents rushed to retrieve Edwards for themselves. In the late 1820s and 1830s the conservative Congregational revivalist, Asahel Nettleton, his activistic colleague, Lyman Beecher, and Presbyterians Samuel Miller and Albert Dod led efforts to strip Finney of his Edwardsian pretensions.[6] Dod's criticism was the most sweeping. Finney's "use of the name of this great man" to defend his new measures was "to slander the dead." Finney might claim that Edwards sanctioned the widespread use of "lay exhortation," but this merely illustrated his "ignorance of Edwards's opinions and writings." To prove that point, Dod quoted directly from the very works on revivals that Finney himself had cited, where "Edwards makes known, with all plainness his opposition to lay exhortation." Finney's "bold misrepresentation" of Edwards was merely one further "illustration of that unscrupulousness in the use of means for the attainment of his ends, which he too often manifests."[7]

It is significant that the first nineteenth century struggle to claim Edwards's mantle took place in connection with revival, for Edwards's relationship to the Awakening was a key to much of the controversy that followed. Finney and other Jacksonian evangelists valued Edwards for his place in the history of revival, even though they felt it necessary to set aside the specific convictions of his theology. New England Congregationalists, on the other hand, valued Edwards as a revivalist and preceived precisely in the exposition of revival his central theological contribution. By contrast, the more conservative, or Old School, Presbyterians valued Edwards's specifically theological pronouncements, but worried that these had been compromised by his revivalistic experiences. The Scots and the more romantic, or New School, Presbyterians had yet another perspective. To them it was important that Edwards combined the strictness of Old Calvinism with the experimental piety of revival.

The Struggle for Edwards's Mantle: "New" Theology versus "Old"

The dispute over Charles Finney's methods was only a curtain raiser to the main theological contention for Edwards, which pitted Old School Presbyterians against New England Congregationalists. This debate involved the three leading seminaries in the country—Andover, Yale, and Princeton—and many of the nation's finest intellects, including Yale's Nathaniel William Taylor, Andover's Edwards Amasa Park, and Princeton's Charles Hodge.[8] It was part of perhaps the most comprehensive American discussion at mid-century of the Great Questions concerning God, human nature, and the fate of civilization. To sum up a complicated picture, Princeton held sternly, if with some confusion, to traditional conceptions of human dependence and divine sovereignty. New England, while no less fervent in its faith, had begun to place greater confidence in human nature as defined by modern opinion. Because both parties felt that Jonathan Edwards had played a determinative role in defining Calvinism, the Enlightenment, and the American character, their contention for his mantle was a significant part of their more general controversy.

By mid-century the conservative Presbyterians and the mainstream New England Congregationalists had clearly diverged.[9] The Plan of Union, which had joined Presbyterians and Congregationalists in 1801 for the Christianizing of the frontier, came apart in 1837. The institutions of New England Congregationalism, like Andover and Yale, reflected an eclectic intellectual heritage made up of the mingled Puritan-Enlightenment assumptions of eighteenth-century Harvard and Yale, the more recent assumptions of philosophical Common Sense, a smattering of the nineteenth-century's new thought (at least as filtered through Coleridge), and the ideals of political freedom and ecclesiastical Independency. The institutions of the Old School Presbyterians, like Princeton Seminary and the College of New Jersey, defined their allegiances more simply as Scripture, the Reformed confessions, and Common Sense moral intuitions.

Attitudes toward Edwards were well in place before the polemics began. To New England, Jonathan Edwards was a treasured possession. Uniformly the Congregationalists held that he had established the course which they followed. Timothy Dwight, Edwards's grandson, a revered president of Edwards's alma mater (1795–1817), and the beloved mentor of Congregationalism's two great leaders in the first half of the century, the activist Beecher and the theologian N. W. Taylor, well illustrates this feeling of propriety. In a poetic flight of youthful fancy Dwight had called Edwards "that moral Newton, and that second Paul" who "in one little life, the gospel more/Disclos'd, than all earth's myriads kenn'd before."[10] Frank Hugh Foster, who composed the last full history of the New England theology, summed up nicely the Congregationalist attitude in the first half of the nineteenth century: "To agree with Edwards was still the high ambition of them all; and when they consciously disagreed, as did Taylor, they thought they were only expressing better Edwards's true meaning."[11]

Old School Presbyterians did not possess this same intimacy with Edwards, though they eventually came to make much of the fact that Edwards once expressed a preference for presbyterian polity over congregational.[12] Only Charles Hodge among leading Presbyterians expressed serious reservations about Edwards, and these were more than balanced by Hodge's general approval.

Although New England's bond to Edwards was closer than that of Princeton, it was nonetheless the Presbyterians who made the first contentious claims for Edwards's mantle. Presbyterian attention to Edwards arose within the context of church politics, especially the Presbyterian division into Old and New School denominations in 1837 and the reunion in the North of New and Old School in 1868. At issue was the extent to which New England's theological orientation and the specific ideas of Yale's N. W. Taylor had infected Presbyterians. In a word, Princeton abominated Taylor's theology and any other system in which they spied the barest trace of New Haven's errors. To Princeton it seemed especially galling that the New Haven and other faulty New England systems would continue to call themselves the descendents of Edwards who, the Old Schoolers felt, had taught pretty much what they did.

From the time of the Presbyterian division in 1837, Princeton authors wrote steadily about Edwards.[13] As they saw it, Edwards had too easily tolerated enthusiasm in the colonial Awakening, he had promoted eccentric views of a common humanity in his work on *Original Sin*, he had fostered unsound habits of metaphysical speculation, and his *Dissertation on the Nature of True Virtue* had been misguided in itself and a bad influence on later New England theology. Yet these were all relatively minor matters. In general, Edwards was a sterling example of an orthodox theologian who had distinguished himself in the "full and zealous maintenance of the old Calvinistic doctrines." By contrast, later theologians in New England had abandoned Edwards's dearest convictions and, drawing unwarranted conclusions from his foibles, promoted serious error. New England protestations about following Edwards were a sham. As one Princeton author asked pointedly in 1840, "Shall we not heed his counsels as well as revere his name?"[14]

These jabs had the inevitable consequence. New England responded to assert its claim to Edwards, and for twenty years the battle was joined. In the course of the exchange Princeton usually got the better of debate on the question of the will. Try as they might, New Englanders could not convincingly link their belief in the will's "power to the contrary" with the arguments for moral necessity in Edwards's *Freedom of the Will*.[15] New England, on the other hand, showed that Princeton did not understand Edwards's ethical principles. Its theologians mounted a convincing case to demonstrate the continuity from Edwards's *True Virtue* to their more modern theories of benevolence.[16]

In the course of the debate three authors offered comprehensive interpretations of the Edwardsian heritage. The first of these was Andover's
Edwards Amasa Park (1808–1900) who was goaded into action in 1851
after Charles Hodge had claimed that Park and his Congregationalist
contemporaries taught an "anti-Augustinian system" which contradicted
the major positions of Edwards.[17]

Park responded with a prodigy of exegesis, tracing the continuities of
theology in New England from Edwards to Park's own generation. In a
very abridged summary, Park contended that New Englanders from
Edwards onward believed: (1) that there is, strictly speaking, no sinful
nature lying behind individual acts of sin—all sinfulness arises from the
acts of evil themselves; (2) that, as a consequence, no guilt, or absolutely
foreordained certainty to sin, passes down from Adam throughout the
whole human race—guilt before God is not imputed from Adam but is
each person's own responsibility; and (3) that by nature people have the
power to do what God's law demands—there is no bondage of the will to
the sinful inclinations of a sinful nature.[18]

Even in his own day, Park's effort to make Edwards conform with later
New England views on free will, the voluntary character of sinfulness,
and the rejection of imputation was not persuasive.[19] Edwards, in fact,
did believe in the bondage of the will, he did believe in a sinful nature
underlying sinful deeds, and he did hold to something like traditional
views on the imputation of Adam's sin. In these regards, Hodge the
interloper saw Edwards more clearly than Park the heir.

Park himself provided a clue as to why Princeton could regard his
views as diverging so far from those of Edwards. Park's "scheme," as he
put it, benefited from "the philosophy of Reid, Oswald, Campbell,
Beattie, Stewart . . . *the philosophy of common sense.*" The great
strength of this Scottish contribution was "to develop 'the fundamental
laws of human belief.'" Moreover, it "has aided our writers in shaping
their faith according to those ethical axioms, which so many fathers in
the church have undervalued." The result was that "the metaphysics of
New England Theology . . . is the metaphysics of common sense."[20] So
great was Edwards that Park could not give him up, even if Edwards had
denied Park's understanding of the natural and universal moral sense.
Yet so powerful had modern moral philosophy become that Park's only
course was to read Edwards through the lenses which it provided.

In addition, however, Park's account of New England theology did
properly spotlight a major Princeton misreading of Edwards. It had
become standard for Old School Presbyterians to treat Edwards's
Dissertation on the Nature of True Virtue as a badly flawed effort. On

several occasions Princeton had described this essay as a late and ill-conceived product of Edwards's pen which encouraged Antinomianism, egotistic utilitarianism, revivalistic excess, and theological absurdities (e.g., Samuel Hopkins's "willingness to be damned for the glory of God"). Park showed, by contrast, that *True Virtue* was a mature product of Edwards's thought and that it lay at the heart of his general theological concerns.[21] Park's efforts to translate this victory into a defense of his substantive theological affirmations were not convincing, but he did expose a persistent Princeton inability to grasp an important element in Edwards's thought.

Park was fooling himself if he felt that his counterattack would silence the Old School. In 1858, Princeton's Lyman Hotchkiss Atwater (1813–83) offered the definitive Old School interpretation. Atwater was a Connecticut Congregationalist who had been both a parishioner and student of N. W. Taylor, but this early training had not taken, and he stood foursquare with the Old School Presbyterians. From 1840 to 1868 Atwater was the major voice in the *Princeton Review* defending Edwards and attacking the later New England theologians. His review of theological history spared no tender feelings in New England:

> Edwards held and devoted his labours to prove the doctrines commonly known as Old Calvinism, with the single exception theologically, that he taught Stapfer's scheme of the mediate imputation of Adam's sin; and with the further qualification, that he held an eccentric philosophical theory of the nature of virtue, as consisting wholly in love to being in general. . . . Neither of these peculiarities, however, was allowed to act upon or modify other parts of his theology. . . . We think it easy to show . . . that the distinctive features of this New Divinity, in all its successive forms, are utterly abhorrent to his entire system.[22]

Atwater surmised that New Englanders perceived such a connection only because Jonathan Edwards, Jr., bore his father's name as he led succeeding generations away from the elder Edwards's views.[23] In the course of his account, Atwater paused to make explicit what had been implicit in Princeton's earlier attacks on New England. If the Congregationalists succeeded in disposing of original sin and the imputation of Adam's guilt, the heart of Christianity was imperiled—"the whole doctrine of atonement and justification is implicated with that of imputation."[24] The battle for Edwards was part of a much larger struggle for the faith itself.

In response to Atwater's Old School reading, Noah Porter (1811–92), professor of moral philosophy and metaphysics at Yale, a student of

Taylor and also his son-in-law, shifted the grounds of debate. In 1861 Porter set out to vindicate N. W. Taylor as Edwards's legitimate heir and to disabuse Princeton of its errors concerning Congregationalist thought.[25] Unlike Park, however, Porter did not attempt to show that the *substance* of New England Theology had been carefully preserved from generation to generation. Rather he intended to show that Edwards's *spirit* had been the motivating force among the theologians who gathered under his name.

Porter first pointed out that, like Edwards, Taylor's "first so-called discoveries in theology were reached in the revivals of religion in which he was so earnest and fervent a laborer." He went on to suggest what the dogmaticians at Princeton had overlooked: that the "leading peculiarity which distinguished Edwards as a theologian, was, that he was a philosopher as well as a divine." Edwards was not content with "servilely copying the compromising philosophy" of the Westminster divines, but rather aspired to show the "unphilosophical" errors of his contemporaries. "The secret of Edwards's influence" was his willingness to contradict inherited authority, to strike out boldly for the truth. To Porter, the enduring Edwards was an Edwards of innovation: "He asserted principles in respect to philosophical theology, which excited and directed the minds of his so-called successors, and which, by right, entitle them to the appellation of Edwardsean—which made them what they were, bold, enterprising, logical, consistent thinkers."[26]

Porter was not concerned if bits and pieces of Edwards's inheritance had been rearranged as time went by. He conceded that contemporary New England theologians held to propositions that differed from Edwards's—that people possess a moral freedom to choose good or evil, that morality is a quality of action rather than enduring character, that neither guilt nor righteousness can fairly be imputed from one person to another, and the Jesus's death was a demonstration of God's moral government rather than a placation of divine wrath.[27] But these were trifles. Taylor's predilection for bold and independent inquiry, for refined philosophical reflection, was the key which marked him as Edwards's true successor.

According to Porter, Taylor's great accomplishment was to build a system logically from first principles of reason—"no teacher could possibly be more alive to the absolute necessity of intuitions, or more enforce the obligation to believe in and ascertain them as the necessary precondition of all logical deductions and all philosophy." This insignia routed Princeton and proved Taylor's right to speak as an Edwardsian. Taylor displayed his superiority especially in the clarity with which he perceived "first moral truths that are self-evident." Unlike the Old School Presbyterian, "who by shuffling statements and self-contradictory propositions and scholastic refinements and questionable interpretations, patches up a vindication of what he calls Orthodoxy," Taylor "used conscience and common sense to assail traditionary and fantastic speculations."[28] The final result was an advance for the Christian cause which paralleled the advance under Edwards.

The clash between Princeton and New England over Edwards continued until the late 1860s.[29] But the basic positions remained constant. Princeton held up Edwards as a great exponent of orthodox Calvinism, in spite of his lack of caution concerning revivals and religious experience and in spite of his foibles on virtue and unity with Adam.[30] By contrast, New Englanders held from first to last that Edwards belonged to them. To E. A. Park, the continuity resided in the dogmas, to Porter in the method.[31]

Several features of this struggle deserve special notice. First and most obvious was its testimony to the enduring theological stature of Edwards. Second, the nature of the struggle over Edwards testified to the presence of a philosophical revolution in America. Princeton, Yale, and Andover had become centers of Common Sense philosophy.[32] As such they accepted assumptions that were not only foreign to Edwards, but which he had largely opposed. To be sure, it made considerable difference which aspect of Common Sense prevailed at the various theological institutions in the nineteenth century. Princeton showed greatest fondness for the methodological aspects of Common Sense, Andover and Yale for the moral. And both Andover and Yale tinctured their Common Sense commitments with at least a modest infusion of Coleridgean romanticism, something which Princeton did not do until the arrival of James McCosh at the College of New Jersey in 1868.[33]

For Princeton, the Common Sense commitments altered the framework rather more than the substance of theology. In New England the deliverances of the moral sense became crucial principles of theology. In this regard, the investment in Common Sense moved New England further from Edwards's theology than it did Princeton.

Third, however, New England clearly perceived the intellectual spirit of Edwards more accurately than did Princeton. Edwards had indeed been an independent inquirer. As Samuel Hopkins put it in the first biography: Edwards "took his religious principles from the Bible, and not from any human system or body of divinity. Though his principles were *Calvinistic*, yet he called no man father. He thought and judged for himself, and was truly very much an original."[34] The New Englanders, especially Hopkins, Nathaniel Emmons, and Taylor, were also bold and original thinkers who likewise wished to be known as Calvinists while calling no man father. The Princeton Theology, on the other hand, defined itself as a conserving effort. It was willing to say "father" to a whole host of orthodox divines. The protests of Yale and Andover against Princeton's reactionary intellect were valid. And in this *they* stood closer to Edwards.

The Rejection of Edwards

While Princeton struggled with Andover and Yale to lay claim to Edwards, a more diverse group of theologians attended to Edwards for different purposes. Charles Hodge, E. A Park, and Noah Porter took Edwards's positive contribution for granted. These others called that assumption into question. During the nineteenth century at least forty-one substantial refutations of Edwards's major books appeared, ranging from Charles Chauncy's offended rejection of Edwards's *Original Sin* in 1785 to Lewis French Stearn's attack on the determinism of *Free Will* in 1890.[35] In between came a number of extended refutations (one reaching nearly a thousand pages), some carefully reasoned rebuttals, and a host of works marked more by wounded indignation than cautious reasoning. While most of Edwards's principal treatises came under attack, the *Freedom of the Will*—"the work," in Perry Miller's phrase, "through which his fame has been most widely spread abroad"—bore the brunt.[36]

The story of those who ventured into print against Edwards is an involved one, taking in Christians and skeptics; theologians from Scotland, England, and America; some who tried to separate the wheat from the chaff and some who consigned Edwards *en bloc* to oblivion. Yet the criticism, for all its variety, can be reduced to a very few themes.

The central objection was that Edwards's "iron network of philosophical necessity," though reflecting an intelligence of "gigantic power," led to conclusions which violated the commonly perceived morality of the universe.[37] To this central objection commentators added manifold protests concerning Edwards's use of logic, a number of complaints about the imprecision of his language, and a few counterarguments from the Bible. But the central point was the way in which Edwards's conclusions violated the moral conscience.

This theme dominated the attacks on Edwards's convictions about eternal damnation and the Adamic source of original sin. The same note predominated in protests against Edwards's beliefs about original sin, including his unusual assertion that all humanity participated in Adam's first sin. Such contentions, according to his critics, undercut the human sense of equity and cast aspersions on God's righteousness.

During the nineteenth century, however, Edwards's theological reputation did not rest primarily on his tracts concerning hell or original sin, but with his treatise on *The Freedom of the Will*. Of Edwards's works, only the life of Brainerd appeared more often. At no time for a century and a half from its first publication in 1754 did more than fifteen years elapse between separate editions.[38] It was largely through this book that, in spite of Kantian philosophy, utopian republicanism, and the blooming of romanticism, Americans still took the first part of Samuel Johnson's famous epigram so seriously: "All theory is against the freedom of the will; all experience for it."[39] Henry Philip Tappan, sometime president of the University of Michigan, and author of the most extensive attack on Edwards's view of the will during the century, testified to the stature of this book in the introduction to his refutation:

> There is no work of higher authority among those who deny the self-determining power of the will; and none which on this subject has called forth more general admiration or acuteness of thought and logical subtlety. I believe there is a prevailing impression that Edwards must be fairly met in order to make any advance in an opposite argument.[40]

Arrayed against the *Freedom of the Will* were at least twenty-nine serious nineteenth-century refutations.[41]

Tappan's effort was atypical in its judicious tone and its length, but not in its argument. In the first of three volumes Tappan exposed Edwards's logical fallacies, especially confusion over the nature of causation. He also demonstrated the inevitable drift of Edwards's theory to pantheism or atheism. The second volume undertook an elaborate discussion of consciousness, which provided the same kind of "knowledge of the phenomena of mind" as "of the phenomena of body." The deliverances of consciousness, so defined, demonstrated for Tappan the self-determining power of the will.[42] His third volume concluded the refutation by arguing for a tripartite division of the inner self into Will, Intellect, and Sensitivity. Tappan's faculty psychology was a typical device in the nineteenth century for attaching Edwards, for it allowed a separation of volitions from other actions and states. Needless to say, it was consciousness that revealed the presence of the faculties.

Nineteenth-century attacks on the *Freedom of the Will* occasionally showed flashes of psychological wisdom. Rarely, however, did they penetrate to the levels of human insight or to the careful sifting of ordinary language which marked Edwards's treatise.[43] This is a judgment as applicable to Horace Bushnell, who opposed Edwards's "tricks of argument" with "the truth" of "consciousness," as to Charles Finney and Asa Mahan, whose works on the will carefully described the moral character of action but dismissed Edwards out of hand.[44]

The persistence of Edwards's nineteenth-century opponents in responding to his major works testified once again to his prominence in the theological arena. A consensus seemed to be growing, however, that reason, Scripture, and consciousness had finally dealt with Edwards, especially his arguments in *Freedom of the Will.* Yet whether because of doubts about these modern certainties, uneasiness about the security of their refutations, or respect for Edwards himself, theologians until the last third of the century could not leave him alone.

The Fruitful Use of Edwards

Despite the chorus of dissent from his views, Edwards did not lack for defenders, proponents, and admirers thoughout the nineteenth century. Besides those in the larger Calvinist family who contended with each other for the Edwardsian bequest, a number of others expressed admiration for his work. And Edwards still enjoyed a number of capable advocates. Jeremiah Day, president of Yale College during N. W. Taylor's tenure as professor of theology, authored two of the century's most perceptive defenses of Edwards on the will. Yet the comment of a favorable reviewer speaks as well for almost all of these productions. Day's work was a worthy effort, but it was "indispensible" only to those who did not have the patience to work through Edwards themselves.[45]

During the nineteenth century there were fewer successors to Edwards than admirers or proponents. If this is a tenable distinction, the category "successor" would include those who knew Edwards's work, respected it, and drew some inspiration from it. It would exclude those who used Edwards primarily for polemical purposes. And it would feature those who attempted to do theologically in their century what Edwards had done in his—that is, to exploit contemporary philosophy and sensibility on behalf of the traditional faith. Guardians of Edwards usually preserved either his creed, his piety, or his intellectual creativity. Successors attempted to preserve creed, piety, and creativity together.

In the United States, the New School Presbyterian Henry Boynton Smith (1815-77), longtime professor at Union Seminary in New York, came closest to being a successor of Edwards.[46] A mediator by temperament and conviction, Smith did not fear to draw resources from the Edwardsian tradition, from Old School Calvinism, and from nineteenth-century Europe. Yet his theology was consistently conservative. Smith had almost as much difficulty with N. W. Taylor's New Haven views as did Princeton. Theologically he differed from his American contemporaries by placing unusual stress on the person and work of Christ as the heart of the theology. Princeton, by contrast, regularly moved from authority—whether creedal or scriptural—and New England from consciousness, to Christ.

It would take us too far afield to examine the results of Smith's efforts to construct a theology with both Edwards's commitment to modern learning and his fidelity to historic Calvinism. But it is significant that in the programmatic exposition of his method, "The Relations of Faith and Philosophy," Smith singled out Edwards as one who saw "the necessity of bringing the subtlest researches of human reason into harmony with the truths which lie at the basis of all piety. . . . Intellect and faith acted together in him, distinct, yet as consentaneous as are the principle of life and the organic structure of our animal economy."[47] In his theology, Smith followed where Edwards had led. Neither philosophy without faith (which was Smith's harsh assessment of New Haven) nor faith without philosophy (his milder criticism of Princeton) provided for the nineteenth century what Edwards had offered to his.[48]

In only one other venue did a significant number of nineteenth-century theologians appropriate Edwards as Henry B. Smith did. This was in Scotland, where Edwards had been famous before his death and where he continued to be widely read into the twentieth century. Scottish interest in Edwards was no mystery. Scotland shared a common Calvinistic heritage rooted in the English Reformation. Both New England and Scotland were cultural provinces of London, yet both resisted British alterantives to the older Calvinism, whether Latitudinarian Anglicanism or Arminian Methodism, well into the nineteenth century. Scotland was the home of that variety of the Enlightenment which Americans domesticated for themselves, and regular cultural interchange went on throughout the eighteenth and nineteenth centuries.[49]

Edwards's own history was interwoven with Scotland as well. He appears to have given serious, if not prolonged, consideration to Scottish offers for clerical employment after his dismissal from Northampton. Edwards also enjoyed the epistolary friendship of several Scottish clergymen. And many Scots remembered that Edwards's *Humble Attempt to Promote Explicit Agreement and Visible Union of God's People, in Extraordinary Prayer, for the Revival of Religion and the Advancement of Christ's Kingdom on Earth* (1747) was a response to a memorial with the same goal from Scotland.[50]

To be sure, Edwards had his Scottish detractors as well, but these only echoed the negations to be heard in North America. Much more interesting were those who made use of Edwards for positive purposes. The two most conspicuous of these were Thomas Chalmers (1780–1847), Scotland's greatest divine during the first half of the nineteenth century, and John McLeod Campbell (1800–1872), its most creative nineteenth-century theologian. They were thinkers who shared a common respect for Edwards, made a common criticism of his works, and yet developed his insights in very different ways.

Edwards's impact on Thomas Chalmers was especially profound. Chalmers had been a young ministerial student, with a predilection for "Moderate" spirituality and a fondness for William Godwin, when he encountered Edwards's *Freedom of the Will* in 1796. The result was electric. As an elderly man Chalmers recalled that there was "no book of human composition which I more strenuously recommend than his Treatise on the Will,—read by me forty-seven years ago, with a conviction that has never since faltered, and which has helped me more than any other uninspired book, to find my way through all that might otherwise have proved baffling and transcendental and mysterious in the peculiarities of Calvinism."[51] Edwards's lasting bequest to Chalmers was twofold: he gave Chalmers a sense of how God's omnipotence was manifest in every aspect of creation, and he greatly impressed Chalmers by embodying both intellectual acuity and spiritual fervor. Chalmers eagerly took up the phraseology of an American correspondent when he wrote in 1821 that Edwards was "perhaps, the most wondrous example, in modern times, of one who stood richly gifted both in natural and spiritual discernment."[52]

For all their respect, the Scottish theologians had a common criticism of Edwards. Chalmers expressed it indirectly when writing about his adolescent encounter with *Freedom of the Will*:

> I remember when a student of Divinity, and long ere I could relish evangelical sentiment, I spent nearly a twelve-month in a sort of mental elysium, and the one idea which ministered to my soul all its rapture was the magnificence of the Godhead, and the universal subordination of all things to the one great purpose for which He evolved and was supporting crea-

tion. I should like to be so inspired over again, but with such a view of the
Deity as coalesced and was in harmony with the doctrine of the New
Testament.[53]

This indirect criticism became more pointed in John McLeod Campbell. Campbell remains an important figure in the history of the Kirk
because of a spectacular theological trial in 1831, which led to his being
dismissed from the ministry, and because of the creativity of *The Nature
of the Atonement* (1856), the book which summed up his heterodox
views. A good part of Campbell's *Atonement* carries on a dialogue with
Edwards, particularly in an effort to render Edwards's conception of
Christ's redeeming work more human.[54] Built into Campbell's construc-
tive theology, therefore, is an answer to the criticisms raised by Chalmers.

These two Scottish theologians were not descendents of Edwards, like
the New Englanders, nor were they his advocates, like the Princetonians.
They were rather those who attempted more generally for theology in
their age what Edwards had desired in his. They esteemed the Calvinist
heritage and wished to preserve it as more than a merely spiritual legacy.
Yet they wanted also to respond to the world in which they lived with
proper appreciation of the insights which could improve their Calvinism.

For Chalmers this meant adjusting the Scotish Realism of the eighteenth century to the demands of religious experience, leavening his
natural theology with a sense of the limitis of apologetics, and urging the
Kirk to respond to the altered social conditions of early industrial Scotland. Chalmers, himself an able mathematician, was the leader in his day
of practical godliness. He sought a faith which could be at home in the
furthest reaches of comtemporary science. He sought a theology with
room for careful reason and unbounded response to grace. And he
looked for a church which could use its resources to relieve practical
suffering. When these aspirations failed in the established church,
Chalmers became the leader of the famous Disruption of 1837 which
created the Free Church of Scotland.[55]

For Campbell, following Edwards's course meant exchanging the older
views of a legal, penal atonement for an ethical, subjective one. Campbell's theology arose from a practical need. Several of his most faithful
parishioners felt trapped by the fear that they were not of the elect, and
others seemed to pursue good works only in order to win safety for
themselves. In response, Campbell began to reassess the nature of Jesus's
death for sinners. Was it true, as the Kirk held, that Christ died only for
the elect? Did his death not rather suggest the possible reconciliation
between God and all humanity? Was it not possible to think of Christ's

sacrifice as a kind of supererogation of suffering which opened the way to God? In working out his positive answer to these questions, Campbell made specific use of a suggestion Edwards had raised in a treatise on *The Necessity and Reasonableness of the Christian Doctrine of Satisfaction for Sin* (published with the collected works in the nineteenth century). There Edwards suggested that for the greatness of evil "either an equivalent punishment or an equivalent sorrow and repentance" must exist. Although Edwards had not considered the second possibility, Campbell took it seriously and argued that the atonement is best explained by the infinite nature of Jesus's sorrow for sin. This solution pushed Edwards's Calvinism out of its own orbit, away from an objective to a subjective view of the atonement. And it certainly took the enormity of sin less seriously than had Edwards. Yet Campbell still manifested a remarkably fruitful effort to put Edwards to use in a situation where the problem was not, as for Edwards, waking the unconcerned to their spiritual need, but assuring the faithful of the certainty of God's love.[56]

Whether Chalmers and Campbell were as successful as Edwards in their theological efforts is not at issue here. What is clear is that these Scottish theologians had read Edwards with profit. They, along with H. B. Smith, did not try to duplicate his work or to dignify their innovations by associating them with his name. They rather drew together piety, learning, and doctrine to make the effort Edwards had made, which was to give each of these elements its proper attention in an integrated exposition of theology. They were, in this sense, Edwards's most faithful disciples in the nineteenth century.

The Irrelevance of Edwards as Theologian

While published commentary on Edwards continued to build thoughout the nineteenth century, specifically theological interaction declined dramatically after the Civil War. Publication of Edwards's works also faltered at mid-century before falling off rapidly toward the end of the period. In the first quarter of the twentieth century, fewer editions of his works combined were published than the number of editions of *Freedom of the Will* alone which had appeared in New York by itself during the third quarter of the nineteenth century. Theological commentary followed a similar curve. Fewer theologians felt it necessary to refute Edwards; the last major effort of this sort was published in 1890. No serious defense of Edwards appeared after 1865. Periodicals and books teemed with genealogical, filiopietistic, antiquarian, historical, and even literary and philo-

sophical assessments. But as a theologian, Edwards was becoming irrelevant.[57]

The reasons for Edwards's theological eclipse at the end of the nineteenth century are patent. Edwards lived in a world which assumed the
existence of God pretty much as defined by the Protestant reformers,
which assumed that the Bible could provide authoritative teaching for all,
which assumed that theological discussion deserved a prominent place in
the culture, and which assumed that sophisticated intellectual labors were
compatible with piety. Some of these assumptions weakened in the
hundred years after Edwards's death. But they still were close to the center
of American civilization. None of them, however, survived in intellectual
circles at the end of the nineteenth century. In spite of Edwards's efforts,
which had helped keep alive the agenda of that earlier world, his questions
were no longer those of America's dominant intellectuals.

This did not mean that the cultural arbiters had lost their respect for
Edwards. Some very learned people even held to a Calvinism similar to
his. Yet even for these ones Edwards had become a fossil.

A trio of works published in 1908 encapsulates the situation. The
Congregational church historian, Williston Walker, lauded Edwards in
his volume *Great Men of the Christian Church* as "the ablest theologian
and most powerful thinker that colonial New England ever produced."
To Walker, however, Edwards's significance lay mostly in his inspiration
for the modern missionary movement.[58] The country's first historian of
American philosophy, I. Woodbridge Riley, claimed to find "the real
Jonathan Edwards" not in the "sulphurous" Calvinist, but in a "philosopher of feelings, a fervent exponent of the dialect of the heart." By
making this distinction Riley continued a tradition that extended back at
least thirty years to the time when Moses Coit Tyler, in his *History of
American Literature*, had distinguished between the enduring Edwards
of artistic imagery, who missed his true calling by becoming a minister,
and the constricted Puritan thinker.[59] The third assessment came from
the modernist theologian, George A. Gordon, who defined Edwards's
place in "The Collapse of the New England Theology." Gordon was full
of praise for Edwards's intellect, "a mind of singular openness and of
unceasing movement." Yet in very short compass he wrote off the lasting
significance of the New England Theology—Hopkins, Dwight, Taylor,
and Park, as well as Edwards—because of its immature views on Scripture, human freedom, divine morality, world religions, and proper humanism.[60] The one thing which bound these disparate assessments together was the absence of serious theological interaction. All treated
Edwards as a major figure. None paid attention to his theology.

This disposition prevailed widely at the turn of the century. A conservative like Princeton Seminary's B. B. Warfield could still praise Edwards for his unremitting labors in defense of a system that was "simply Calvinism." He could speak much as Hodge and Atwater had a generation before of Edwards's substantial identity with "the doctrines of the Calvinistic schoolmen" and use that judgment to trace the defalcations which followed in New England.[61] But Warfield, who was busy defending conservative theology against modern enemies, appears to have made no use of Edwards's ideas as such. Edwards was an honored figure in Calvinist history, but no longer a resource.

By the end of the century Edwards had become the subject of doctoral dissertations and articles in professional journals. The bicentennial of his birth in 1903 was the occasion of a raft of publications. Historians, like Frank Hugh Foster in his still useful *Genetic History of the New England Theology*, were able to put Edwards into a chronological framework. But the vast majority of those who paid attention to Edwards treated him as a person without a word for the present, or translated his contribution into terms which Edwards would not have understood. One of the best late-century studies of Edwards, the life by the romantic Episcopalian A. V. G. Allen, exemplified and furthered this trend. To Allen, Edwards was important precisely in spite of his theology:

> The divine revelation, as it came through him as its vehicle, was associated with much that was untrue. If we can make allowance for the human equation in his teaching, for the reasoning which however solid or true was based upon false premises, if we can look at the negative side of his theology as the local and transitory element of his time, there will then remain an imperishable element which points to the reality of the divine existence, and of the revelation of God to the world, as no external evidence can do. Indeed, it is only by exposing what was false or distorted in his theology that the real man stands forth in the grandeur of his proportions.[62]

By the end of the century, critics in a salvage operation had begun to track the path from Edwards to Emerson.[63] On this journey there was no room for his theology.

Edwards and Nineteenth-Century Theology

"The marvel," as Henry May once put it, "is that [Edwards] affected American culture as deeply as he did."[64] There are no immediately obvious reasons why Edwards's theology should survive through the nineteenth century. Thomas Chalmers and Henry B. Smith may have moved in directions similar to Edwards's. Theologians like the Princetonians may have preserved the letter of his major convictions. And the more adventuresome New Englanders certainly aspired to Edwards's metaphysical accomplishments. Yet the tide everywhere in the century was running the other way. Where Edwards preserved intellectual unity, the nineteenth century mind was falling in two. Where Edwards distrusted the self, the self became the originator of truth in the century after his death. And where Edwards tightly circumscribed the deliverances of the unregenerate consciousness, the nineteenth century made universal consciousness the one unquestioned oracle.

Edwards's thought was always in pursuit of unity. In the most famous instances, as H. B. Smith saw clearly, Edwards gave himself to "the reconciliation of divine sovereignty with the consciousness of freedom [*Freedom of the Will*] . . . [and] the radical identity of virtue and religion [*The Nature of True Virtue*]."[65] Already in Edwards's own day, however, American thought was dividing against itself. On the one hand, Americans became the champions of freedom and self-determination. On the other, they pursued the certainties of law, whether Baconian and positivistic or organic and romantic. Henry Philip Tappan, Edwards's most persistent nineteenth-century opponent, illustrates this later bifurcation. Although Tappen devoted three volumes to disposing of *Freedom of the Will*, yet when he became president of the University of Michigan in 1852, he imported a Prussian model of education which aimed at the discovery of predictable necessities for the moral and physical worlds alike.[66] At the end of the century, precisely when American intellectuals were swarming to discover the necessary regularities of the new social sciences, A. V. G. Allen interpreted Edwards's "denial of the freedom of the human will" as an "awful conception of humanity and its destiny."[67] The difference was that Edwards's determinism and his freedom were unified as functions of his theism, while the determinism of the nineteenth century was a function of nature and its freedom a function of the transcendental self. Edwards may not have succeeded in his effort to gather the entire universe under God's majesty. But his consistent efforts in that direction set him apart from the intellectual polarities which followed.

Again, Edwards lived before it grew fashionable to bestow great trust upon the self, yet in the nineteenth century no principle was more firmly in place. The myths of the American Revolution pointed in this direction, the deliverances of Scottish moral philosophy took it for granted, the newer Kantianism agreed, and prominent varieties of piety—whether Schleiermacher's reliance upon a sense of dependence or Wesley's upon experience—began at the same place. The Great Awakening had taught Edwards to distrust the self's deliverances, to beware the great capacity for self-delusion.[68] In the nineteenth century this caution was overridden. In its place came the conviction that the self was where the journey to knowledge and spiritual fulfillment began.

This attitude toward the self underlay the overwhelming confidence in the revelatory character of consciousness. Over and over in the nineteenth century, the attack on Edwards returned to his inadequacy with respect to modern sensitivities. His system, to cite just one of the many expressions of this complaint, was simply "contrary to the common consciousness and experiences of mankind."[69] No one expressed this opinion with greater force than Oliver Wendell Holmes, a Unitarian who also spoke for those more theologically conservative than himself. In an essay from 1880, Holmes praised Edwards's character and logical abilities. But he had no sympathy for Edwards's ideas. Edwards did not really belong to the civilized history of New England. "His whole system," rather, "had too much of the character of the savage people by whom the wilderness had recently been tenanted." It belonged more to Scotland or New Jersey, "where the Scotch theological thistle has always flourished." The reasons for his disapproval had everything to do with consciousness, with genteel perceptions of the world:

> Edwards's system seems, in the light of to-day, to the last degree barbaric, mechanical, materialist, pessimistic. If he had lived a hundred years later, and breathed the air of freedom, he could not have written with such old-world barbarism. . . . The truth is that [his] whole system of beliefs . . . is gently fading out of enlightened human intelligence.[70]

Edward's assessment of consciousness had been much more complicated. He learned a great deal from Locke, Hutcheson, and other theoreticians of the mind. But his fundamental difference from those who followed was that he restricted himself, in D. H. Meyer's phrase, to using "the language of morality . . . the language of Lockean psychology" in order "to reestablish the truths of faith."[71] In the nineteenth century it became much more common to use the substance of moral sentiment to recast the truths of faith. In whatever form it took—simplistic Baconianism, sophisticated Scottish ethics, or the new romantic idealism—the nineteenth-century appeal to consciousness left Edwards far behind. The difference between Edwards and the nineteenth century on this score fully justifies the recent arguments of Norman Fiering, David Laurence, and Harold Simonson concerning the immense distance which separated Edwards's perceptions from the common sensical, the Emersonian, and the romantic conceptions that followed.[72]

All this having been said, the question does not go away. How was it that Edwards remained so important throughout the nineteenth century? How did it come about that he continued as a full partner in the theological enterprise for more than a century after his death?

To these questions there are historical answers. In spite of their uneasiness about his ethics and his metaphysics, the handful of Americans predisposed toward Calvinism found Edwards's majestic vision of divine sovereignty irreplacable. In spite of his determinism, the much larger number of American Protestants recognized that his theology reflected a depth of piety which demanded attention. And in spite of the whole overlay of theology, numerous intellectuals still realized that Edwards's profundity of thought required at least some account.

Yet it may not be inappropriate, in conclusion, to suggest the sort of theological reasons with which Edwards himself may have felt more at home. In this view, Edwards survived not because he anticipated the norms of nineteenth century intellectual discourse, but because he was their foil.

Perry Miller once again provides a key. His essay, "From Edwards to Emerson," with its unbalanced, if evocative account of intellectual descent from the Northampton minister to the Concord sage, may have put later scholars off the track of Edwards's fundamental significance. His book on Edwards may be full of mistaken philosophical judgments. But Miller still could put his finger on reasons for Edwards's survival by recognizing that "there come periods, either through diaster or self-knowledge, when applied science and Benjamin Franklin's *The Way to Wealth*" are not enough.[73] Since Edwards wrote for such situations, and since they have been, in fact, the general fate of humanity through the ages, and the special lot of even intellectuals in the twentieth century, our culture could not be rid of him.

Edwards greatly influenced the first part of the nineteenth century, in spite of the axioms which governed theological discourse in that period. He possessed enough staying power to survive the last part of the century, when theologians were convinced that the world really had become a better place. And so in the twentieth century he could be resurrected when holocausts and meaninglessness once more intruded into the common consciousness. The final reason may well be that while others preached self-reliance or sang the song of the self, Edwards drove nearer the truth—that nothing can be saved without confronting its own damnation, that freedom is found within necessity, that the way to gain one's life is to lose it.

Notes

1. For an excellent overview of reactions to Edwards during the nineteenth century, see M. X. Lesser, *Jonathan Edwards: A Reference Guide* (Boston, 1981). Further references to this work are noted by year and enumerated title for that year, e.g., Lesser 1845.1. All information concerning the publication of Edwards's works is from Thomas H. Johnson, *The Printed Writings of Jonathan Edwards, 1703–1758: A Bibliography* (Princeton, 1940).

2. Henry May, *The Enlightenment in America* (New York, 1976), and *The End of American Innocence: A Study of the First Years of Our Own Time, 1912–1917* (New York, 1959), nicely define the beginning and end of this cultural entity.

3. The value of Lesser's guide (full citation in note 1) is enhanced by a fine introductory essay tracing reactions to Edwards since the publication of his first works. Other valuable introductions include Daniel B. Shea, "Jonathan Edwards: The First Two Hundred Years," *Journal of American Studies* 14 (1980), 181–97; Nancy Manspeaker, *Jonathan Edwards: Bibliographical Synopses* (New York, 1981); and Donald Louis Weber, "The Image of Jonathan Edwards in American Culture" (Ph.D. dissertation, Columbia University, 1978).

4. S. C. Aiken to Lyman Beecher, Apr. 20, 1827, in *The Autobiography of Lyman Beecher*, ed. Barbara M. Cross (Cambridge, Mass. 1961), II, 67.

5. Charles, G. Finney, *Lectures on Revivals of Religion*, 2nd ed. (New York, 1835), 241–42.

6. *Letters of the Rev. Dr. Beecher and Rev. Mr. Nettleton, on the "New Measures" in Conducting Revivals of Religion* (New York, 1828), 14, 20, 29. Samuel Miller to W. B. Sprague, Mar. 8, 1832, in Sprague, *Lectures on Revivals of Religion* (London, 1959; orig. 1832), 24–25, 28–30, 41–42 of separately numbered Appendix. Similar comments from Miller are also found in his biography, *Life of Jonathan Edwards*, in *The Library of American Biography*, ed. Jared Sparks (New York, 1849; orig. 1837), 193.

7. Albert Dod, "Finney's Lectures," *Princeton Review* 7 (Oct. 1835), 657–58.

8. In 1840, Andover had 153 students and 5 faculty, Yale 72 students and 4 faculty, Princeton 110 students and 4 faculty. The only other seminaries of comparable size were the New School Presbyterian Seminary in New York (90 students, 5 faculty) and the General Theological Seminary of the Episcopal Church, also in New York (74 students, 5 faculty); figures from Robert Baird, *Religion in the United States of America* (New York, 1969; orig. 1844), 368–69.

Bruce Kuklick's *Churchmen and Philosophers: From Jonathan Edwards to John Dewey* (New Haven, 1985), redresses neglect by treating the theological discussions at mid-century as serious intellectual endeavors. Basic information on these figures may be found in Sidney Earl Mead, *Nathaniel William Taylor 1786–1858: A Connecticut Liberal* (Chicago, 1942); Anthony C. Cecil, Jr., *The Theological Development of Edwards Amasa Park: Last of the "Consistent Calvinists"* (Missoula, Mont., 1974); and Archibald A. Hodge, *The Life of Charles Hodge* (New York, 1969; orig. 1881).

9. Various aspects of this disengagement are treated in George M. Marsden, *The Evangelical Mind and the New School Presbyterian Experience: A Case Study of Thought and Theology in Nineteenth-Century America* (New Haven, 1970), 7–87; Sydney E. Ahlstrom, *A Religious History of the American People* (New Haven, 1972), 456–69; and Fred J. Hood, *Reformed America: The Middle and Southern States, 1783–1837* (University, Ala., 1980), 178–85.

10. Timothy Dwight, "The Triumph of Infidelity" (1788), in *The Connecticut Wits*, ed. Vernon Louis Parrington (New York, 1969), 260.

11. Frank Hugh Foster, *A Genetic History of the New England Theology* (New York, 1962; orig. 1907), 369.

12. See, for example, Miller, *Life of Edwards*, 118–19.

13. Miller, *Life of Edwards* (1837); J. W. Alexander and A. B. Dod, "Transcendentalism," *Princeton Review* 11 (Jan. 1839), 38–43; Charles Hodge, *The Constitutional History of the Presbyterian Church in the United States of America* (Philadelphia, 1851; orig. 1840), II, 39–101; Anonymous, "The Law of Human Progress," *Princeton Review* 18 (Jan. 1846), 26; Anonymous, "Short Notices," *Princeton Review*, 27 (Oct. 1855), 701–2.

14. Miller, *Life of Edwards*, 245; Lyman Atwater, "The Power of Contrary Choice," *Princeton Review* 12 (Oct. 1840), 549.

15. For debate over free will, see Atwater, "The Power of Contrary Choice," *Princeton Review* 12 (Oct. 1840), 532–49; Atwater, "Dr. Edwards's Works," *Princeton Review* 15 (Jan. 1843), 57, 64; Atwater, "Modern Explanations of the Doctrine of Inability," *Princeton Review* 26 (Apr. 1854), 236–46; and Atwater, "Whedon and Hazard on the Will," *Princeton Review* 36 (Oct. 1864), 679–703. Congregationalist responses are found in Edward Beecher, "The Works of Samuel Hopkins," *Bibliotheca Sacra* 10 (Jan. 1853), 76–80; and Edwards Amasa Park, "New England Theology," *Bibliotheca Sacra* 9 (Jan. 1852), 170–220.

16. Princeton misreadings of *The Nature of True Virtue* are found in Miller, *Life of Edwards*, 241–44; Archibald Alexander, *Outlines of Moral Science* (New York, 1852); Atwater, "Outlines of Moral Science by Archibald Alexander," *Princeton Review* 25 (Jan. 1853), 19–23; and Hodge, *Systematic Theology* (Grand Rapids, Mich., 1979; orig. 1872–73), I, 432–34. Convincing replies came from Beecher, "The Works of Samuel Hopkins," *Bibliotheca Sacra* 10 (Jan. 1853), 77–78; Anonymous, "Dr. Alexander's Moral Science," *Bibliotheca Sacra* 10 (Apr. 1853), 390–414; and Anonymous, "President Edwards's Dissertation on the Nature of True Virtue," *Bibliotheca Sacra* 10 (Oct. 1853), 705–38.

17. Hodge, "Professor Park and the Princeton Review," *Princeton Review* 23 (Oct. 1851), as reprinted in *Essays and Reviews* (New York, 1857), 631–32.

18. Park, "New England Theology," *Bibliotheca Sacra* 9 (Jan. 1852), 174–75.

19. One Episcopalian reviewer, for example, passed off Park's entire effort as simply a modern manifestation of Pelagianism. Anonymous, "New England Theology," *Church Review* 5 (Oct. 1852), 352. A Congregationalist, Parsons Cooke, had this conclusion about Park's reading of theological history: "We have rarely met with an instance, in which so distinguished an author as Edwards has met with so much injustice at the hand of a commentator." Cooke, "Edwards on the Atonement," *American Theological Review* 11 (Feb. 1860), 118. A review more favorable to Park is R. P. S., "The Andover and Princeton Theologies," *Christian Examiner and Religious Miscellany* 52 (May 1852), 309–35.

20. Park, "New England Theology," 191–92. Foster, *Genetic History*, 472–76, puts Park's reliance upon Common Sense moral philosophy into broader context.

21. A representative statement of Park's argument is in "New England Theology," 196–97.

22. Atwater, "Jonathan Edwards and the Successive Forms of New Divinity," *Princeton Review* 30 (Oct. 1858), 589. "Stapfer's scheme" refers to Edwards's belief that all humanity sinned in Adam at the Fall; see *The Works of Jonathan Edwards: Original Sin*, ed. Clyde A. Holbrook (New Haven, 1970), 392n.

23. Atwater, "Jonathan Edwards," 602, 613. On the emergence of a more utilitarian ethic and a governmental theory of the atonement in Jonathan Edwards's son, see Robert L. Ferm, *Jonathan Edwards the Younger 1745–1801* (Grand Rapids, Mich., 1976), 114–33.

24. Atwater, "Jonathan Edwards," 617.

25. Noah Porter, "The Princeton Review on Dr. Taylor and the Edwardean Theology," *New Englander* 18 (Aug. 1860), 726–73.

26. Ibid., 731–32, 737, 739.

27. Ibid., 744.

28. Ibid., 770–71, 743, 744, 772.

29. The last exchange again involved strife over N. W. Taylor. See Charles Hodge, "Presbyterian Reunion," *Princeton Review* 40 (Jan. 1868), 52–83; George Park Fisher, "The Princeton Review on the Theology of Dr. N. W. Taylor," *New Englander* 27 (Apr. 1868), 284–348; Fisher, "The Augustinian and the Federal Theories of Original Sin Compared," *New Englander* 27 (June 1868), 468–516, with reference to Edwards on 507; Timothy Dwight, "Princeton Exegesis: A Review of Dr. Hodge's Commentary on Romans V. 12–19," *New Englander* 27 (July 1868), 551–603; Lyman Atwater, "Professor Fisher on the Princeton Review and Dr. Taylor's Theology," *Princeton Review* 40 (July 1868), 368–97; and Fisher, "Dr. N. W. Taylor's Theology: A Rejoinder to the Princeton Review," *New Englander* 27 (Oct. 1868), 740–63.

30. A late statement of this position is Atwater, "The Great Awakening of 1740," *Presbyterian Quarterly and Princeton Review* 5 (Oct. 1876), 685–89.

31. For late statements, see Park, "Jonathan Edwards," in *Cyclopdeia of Biblical, Theological, and Ecclesiastical Literature,* ed. John McClintock and James Strong (New York, 1882; orig. 1870), III, 63–67; and Noah Porter, "Philosophy in Great Britain and America," Appendix I in *History of Philosophy from Thales to the Present Time,* by Friedrich Ueberweg (New York, 1874), II, 443–48, Lesser 1874.3.

32. I have developed at greater length the discussion in this paragraph and reviewed some of the important literature on this subject in "Common Sense Traditions and American Evangelical Thought," *American Quarterly* 37 (Summer 1985), 216–38.

33. On McCosh's fondness for Edwards, which did not, however, make him a complete disciple, see J. David Hoeveler, Jr., *James McCosh and the Scottish Intellectual Tradition: From Glasgow to Princeton* (Princeton, 1981), 53–54.

34. Samuel Hopkins, "The Life and Character of the late Reverend Mr. Jonathan Edwards," in *Jonathan Edwards: A Profile,* ed. David Levin (New York, 1969), 41.

35. Charles Chauncy, *Five Dissertations on the Scripture Account of the Fall; and its Consequences* (London, 1785), 191–99, 260–64, Lesser 1785.1. Lewis French Stearns, *The Evidence of Christian Experience* (New York, 1890), 84–87 and passim, Lesser 1890.10.

36. Perry Miller, "General Editor's Note," *The Works of Jonathan Edwards: Freedom of the Will,* ed. Paul Ramsey (New Haven, 1957), vii.

37. Fisher, "The Philosophy of Jonathan Edwards," *North American Review,* 128 (1879), 300; Albert Taylor Bledsoe, *An Examination of President Edwards's Inquiry into the Freedom of the Will* (Philadelphia, 1845), Lesser 1845.2.

38. Publication data are from Johnson, *Printed Works of Edwards.*

39. James Boswell, *The Life of Samuel Johnson,* Library of English Classics (London, 1922), II, 464.

40. Henry Philip Tappan, *A Review of Edwards's "Inquiry into the Freedom of the Will"* (New York, 1839), xi.

41. See Lesser, *Jonathan Edwards.*

42. Tappan, *The Doctrine of the Will, Determined by An Appeal to Consciousness* (New York, 1840), 8. The third book was *The Doctrine of the Will, Applied to Moral Agency and Responsibility* (New York, 1841).

43. This judgement is based on a rapid perusal of a handful of nineteenth century works and on the extracts in Lesser, *Jonathan Edwards,* and Manspeaker, *Jonathan Edwards.* See Paul Ramsey, "Introduction," in *Freedom of Will,* 10 n. 3, for a better-informed judgment which comes to roughly the same conclusion.

44. Horace Bushnell, *Nature and the Supernatural . . .* (New York, 1858), 48, 49; Charles Grandison Finney, *Lectures on Systematic Theology,* ed. J. H. Fairchild (New York, n.d.; orig. 1878), 323; Asa Mahan, *Doctrine of the Will* (New York, 1845), 10.

45. Anonymous, "A Review of *An Examination of President Edwards's In-*

quiry on the Freedom of Will, by Jeremiah Day," *American Biblical Repository*, 2nd ser., 5 (Apr. 1841), 500–504, Lesser 1841.1. The two works by Day are described in Lesser under 1838.1 and 1841.3.

46. On Smith, see Marsden, *Evangelical Mind and New School Presbyterian Experience*, 157–81; and Richard A. Muller, "Henry Boynton Smith: Christocentric Theologian," *Journal of Presbyterian History*, 61 (Winter 1983), 429–44.

47. Smith, *Faith and Philosophy: Discourses and Essays* (Edinburgh, 1878), 59–61, 90.

48. This formulation of Smith's concerns is from Marsden, *Evangelical Mind and New School Presbyterian Experience*, 163.

49. On the status of America and Scotland in relation to London, see John Clive and Bernard Bailyn, "England's Cultural Provinces: Scotland and America," *William and Mary Quarterly*, 3rd ser., 11 (1954), 200–213. The nature of cultural exchange is nicely illustrated by L. H. Butterfield, *John Witherspoon Comes to America* (Princeton, 1953).

50. On Edwards's extensive correspondence with one notable Scotish divine, see Henry Moncrieff Wellwood, *Account of the Life and Writings of John Erskine* (Edinburgh, 1818), 196–225; and on Edwards's brief contemplation of a Scottish pastorate, ibid., 514–15.

51. Chalmers to William B. Sprague, *Annals of the American Pulpit* (New York, 1854), I, 334.

52. Chalmers, *The Christian and Civic Economy of Large Towns* (Glasgow, 1821), I, 318. Chalmers here paraphrases what an American correspondent had written concerning Edwards only shortly before: Henry Hollock (from Savannah) to Chalmers, Sept. 11, 1818, in Thomas Chalmers Papers, New College, University of Edinburgh. (This reference is courtesy of Professor Robert Calhoon of the University of North Carolina at Greensboro.) For a full account of Chalmer's intellectual and social efforts, see Stewart J. Brown, *Thomas Chalmers and the Godly Commonwealth in Scotland* (London, 1982), with specific reference to the influence of Edwards, 14–15.

53. Quoted in William Hanna, *Memoirs of the Life and Writings of Thomas Chalmers* (Edinburgh, 1851), I, 17.

54. John McLeod Campbell, *The Nature of the Atonement and its Relation to Remission of sins and Eternal Life* (London, 1959; orig. 1856), 51–75. A helpful recent treatment of this work is Brian Gerrish, in *Tradition and the Modern World: Reformed Theology in the Nineteenth Century* (Chicago, 1978), 71–97. For general context, see J. H. S. Burleigh, *A Church History of Scotland* (London, 1960), 331–32.

55. See Burleigh, *Church History of Scotland*, 313ff.; Brown, *Thomas Chalmers and the Godly Commonwealth*; and for theological assessment, two essays by Daniel F. Rice, "Natural Theology and the Scottish Philosophy in the Thought of Thomas Chalmers," *Scottish Journal of Theology* 24 (Feb. 1971), 23–46, and "An Attempt at Systematic Reconstruction in the Theology of Thomas Chalmers," *Church History* 48 (June 1979), 174–88.

56. Campbell, *The Nature of the Atonement*, 137. I am indebted to Professor David Wells of Gordon-Conwell Theological Seminary for helpful explanation of Campbell's theology.

57. See Lesser, *Jonathan Edwards*, and Johnson, *Printed Works of Edwards*; there were only 18 reprintings of Edwards's major works in the period 1876–1925 (compare 76 for 1826–1875), while the number of secondary works on Edwards totaled 372 in the period 1876–1925 (compare 232 for 1826–1875).

58. Williston Walker, *Great Men of the Christian Church* (Chicago, 1908), 339–53, Lesser 1908.3.

59. I. Woodbridge Riley, "The Real Jonathan Edwards," *Open Court* 22 (Dec. 1908), 705–15, Lesser 1908.2; and Moses Coit Tyler, *A History of American Literature* (New York, 1878), II, 177–92, Lesser 1878.7.

60. George A. Gordon, *Humanism in New England Theology* (Boston, 1920), 12; this is an expanded version of "The Collapse of the New England Theology," *Harvard Theological Review*, 1 (Apr. 1908), 127–68, Lesser 1908.1.

61. Warfield, "Edwards and the New England Theology," *Encyclopedia of Religion and Ethics*, ed. James Hastings (New York, 1912), V, 221–27; reprinted in *The Works of Benjamin B. Warfield* (Grand Rapids, Mich., 1981; orig. 1932), IX, 528, 531–38.

62. Alexander V. G. Allen, *Jonathan Edwards* (New York, 1975; orig. 1889), 386–87.

63. Allen, *Jonathan Edwards*, 68, where Allen cites Edwards's sermon *Divine and Supernatural Light* as proto-Emersonian. The first effort Lesser records to identify a link between Edwards and Emerson came in 1880 (Mrs. John T. Sargent, ed., *Sketches and Reminiscences of the Radical Club of Chestnut Street*, Boston [Boston, 1880], 362–75, Lesser 1880.9), sixty years before Perry Miller's famous essay, "From Edwards to Emerson," *New England Quarterly* 13 (Dec. 1940), 589–617.

64. May, *The Enlightenment in America*, 50.

65. Henry B. Smith, *Faith and Philosophy*, 16.

66. See Charles M. Perry, *Henry Phillip Tappan: Philosopher and University President* (Ann Arbor, Mich., 1933), 212–48; and Alan Creutz, "The Prussian System and Practical Training: The Educational Philosophies of the University of Michigan's First Two Presidents," *Michigan History* 65 (Jan./Feb. 1981), 32–39.

67. Allen, *Jonathan Edwards*, 73.

68. See Norman Fiering, *Jonathan Edwards's Moral Thought and Its British Context* (Chapel Hill, N.C., 1981), 174: "The deepest lesson he took from the Great Awakening may have been a renewed appreciation of the labyrinth of the human heart."

69. George B. Cheever, "Review of Professor Tappan's Works on the Will," *American Biblical Repository*, 2nd ser., 7 (Apr. 1842), 422.

70. Oliver Wendell Holmes, "Jonathan Edwards," in *Papers from an Old Volume of Life*, in *The Works of Oliver Wendell Holmes* (Boston, 1892; orig.

1880), VIII, 392, 394, 395, 398. Although he was a champion of free will, Holmes could not resist ascribing Edwards's theological views to his "ill-health," ibid., 396–98.

71. Donald H. Meyer, *The Democratic Enlightenment* (New York, 1976), 28.

72. Fiering, *Jonathan Edwards's Moral Thought*; David Laurence, "Moral Philosophy and New England Literary History: Reflections on Norman Fiering," *Early American Literature* 18 (Fall 1983), 187–214; and Harold P. Simonson, "Typology, Imagination, and Jonathan Edwards," in *Radical Discontinuities: American Romanticism and Christian Consciousness* (Rutherford, N.J., 1983), 19–43.

73. Perry Miller, *Jonathan Edwards* (New York, 1949), xiii.

Index